# Career Education in the High School

KENNETH HOYT
RUPERT EVANS
GARTH MANGUM
ELLA BOWEN
DONALD GALE

Olympus Publishing Company  Salt Lake City, Utah

*Copyright © 1977 by Olympus Publishing Company*
*Two Olympus Plaza, 1670 East Thirteenth South*
*Salt Lake City, Utah 84105*

**Library of Congress Cataloging in Publication Data**

Main entry under title:

Career education in the high school.

    Includes bibliographies and index.
    1.  Personnel service in secondary education.
2.  Vocational education.  I.  Hoyt, Kenneth B.

LB2343.C3275          370.11'3          76-51319

ISBN 0-913420-56-5

# Contents

Preface     *page* 5

1     Career Education     15

2     Career Development     51

3     Value Formation     81

4     Role Stereotyping     111

5     Transition to Work     135

6     Decision Making     173

7     Academic Foundations     201

8     Vocational Education     241

9     Practical Applications     281

10     Work Experience     315

11     School Counselor     351

12     Community Resources     391

13     The Ideal Approach     425

Index     *page* 449

# Figures

1    Educational Attainment of Various Types
of Workers    108

2    Combining Skill Lists into Occupational
Areas for Selection of Job Search
Objectives    160

3    Summary Sheet for Data from Personal
Analysis Inventory    190

4    Sample Lesson Plan Outline Which Includes
"Career Implications" as a Subtopic    209

5    Career Education's Place in Education
393

# Preface

This volume is a continuance of our career education series which began with *Career Education: What It Is and How To Do It* (First Edition 1972, Second Edition 1974) and continued through *Career Education and the Elementary School Teacher* (1973) and *Career Education in the Middle/Junior High School* (1973).

Of course, we have not been idle in the career education field during the intervening years. With others, we have produced *Career Education for Gifted and Talented Students* (1974), *Career Education for the Academic Classroom* (1975), and *Career Education: Contributions to an Evolving Concept* (1975). Kenneth Hoyt, has published a flood of speeches, monographs, and papers in his official capacity as Director of the Office of Career Education in the U.S. Office of Education. In addition, Olympus Publishing Company has published other contributions to career education in which the authors of this volume had no hand.

But throughout we have had every intention of continuing the series with a treatment of career education for the senior high school. We now know why career education has emerged more rapidly in the elementary schools and junior highs than

5

in the high schools. It is simply easier to start from scratch to design a career education system for a situation where one teacher has major responsibility for each student than it is to weld together an array of related, but independent, activities packaged in 45- or 50-minute time sequences. High school is the time for decisions which can no longer be delayed: drop out of school, graduate and then end schooling, or go on to post-secondary education. These exhaust the alternatives. There is already vocational education, cooperative education, work-study, and so forth. Few students are without some work experience at this age. There is a great deal of existing occupational preparation to be shaped and molded into a coherent program. We trust the two years' effort will be a worthwhile contribution. Thus, we submit this book and move on to our next effort — home-based career education — to aid parents in providing a sound basis for career success where it can be most effective — in the home.

This book, *Career Education for the Senior High School*, emphasizes career decision making and career preparation; yet it does not neglect career awareness and career exploration.

Chapter 1 relates the concepts of career education to the goals of the high school. Chapter 2 discusses career development and the significant role of the high school in that process. Chapter 3 deals with the subject of work values, with particular emphasis on the concern for values characteristic of high school students. The chapter provides several exercises for clarification of values. Chapter 4 provides cautions and guidelines concerning career opportunities to help the reader avoid stereotyping the kinds of work that society has traditionally assigned to women and members of minority groups (with women *from* minority groups at the lowest end of the scale). Chapter 5 treats the vital transition from high school to "work" or additional preparation for work. The chapter indicates how career education can help ease the transition, and it includes a section on job placement activities in the high school.

Chapter 6 is a basic introduction to decision making as it relates to career choice. It will be useful to help students both understand and employ the decision-making process. In chapter 7, we move into the classroom itself and show how career education can be incorporated into the academic subject matter in such a way that it will motivate students and help them along in the process of career development without in any way diluting the course content. Chapter 8 analyzes the place of vocational education in the career education spectrum and indicates some of the changes which might add to its value.

Chapter 9 gives examples of career education applications to vocational education programs currently operating in high schools around the country. Chapter 10 concerns the benefits of work experience, with particular emphasis upon cooperative education programs. It is significant to note that we had to select the examples we use in these chapters from among literally hundreds of successful programs which have come to our attention. We make no pretense that these are the "best" programs, only that they are representative. Chapter 11 suggests how the high school counselor fits into career education and indicates the special role which she or he plays in the student's career development process.

Chapter 12 tells how the community can become involved in the career education program in the local high schools. Business and industry and their relationship to high school students are discussed.

Finally, chapter 13 is an attempt to outline the "ideal" high school career education program. While some may consider the effort a "blue sky" proposal, it should be remembered that every component of the "ideal" program is taken from some "real" operation currently being practiced in one or more high schools or districts.

This brings us full circle to the reasons why a community might adopt career education into its high schools as well as its elementary and junior high schools. Our experience to date has identified and given substance to at least ten positive strengths of the career education movement:

☐ The educational and societal needs to which career education seeks to respond have been well documented. These needs are real. They can no longer be ignored. Career education represents one clear response to the call for change reflected in these needs.

The needs are dealt with specifically in chapters 1 and 3, but it is worthwhile to state them in oversimplified fashion here. The needs are apparent in the after-the-fact analysis of statistics, in the before-the-fact analysis of sociology, and in the day-to-day experience of education. Statistically, we have an unnecessarily high rate of dropouts at the high school level, we have a high degree of dissatisfaction with the education experience, and we have a disturbing level of unemployment. Sociologically, we have dissipated the value-forming function of the home without providing adequate substitutes, we have created a complexity of career opportunities without providing adequate means for understanding that complexity, and we have forced our citizens to make career decisions earlier and more frequently without providing adequate guidelines. Educationally, we have continued valued traditions without providing them current relevance, we have assumed the existence of value structures which may or may not have been formed, and we have attempted to meet the complex career needs of today with the simple career tools of the past. Our students and our society *must* find answers to these problems and needs. Career education offers a means by which the education system can perform a function in meeting those needs.

☐ Basic elements in the career education concept have been identified. The degree of consensus among leading career education practitioners, administrators, and conceptualizers is extremely high. The term "career education" carries a clear conceptual meaning.

This may seem an unimportant consideration until one examines the value of consensus in the process of communication. In a system as complex as our education system, it is absolutely vital that we establish common understandings about the programs we consider. The proponents of career education have worked hard to develop a conceptual base and to broadcast those concepts to all parts of the land. This process has required many years and much effort, but it is now an accomplished fact, for the most part, and it is indeed a strength of the movement. This is not to say that differences of understanding do not exist, but we find fewer and fewer individuals who confuse career education with vocational education or who consider career education as a curriculum unit as opposed to its proper position as a component of all curriculums.

☐ The conceptual base of career education, using the word "work" as its core, is one that can be made applicable to all persons, of all ages, in all educational settings, and in all communities. This, of course, is not to say that it will appeal to all, but only that it is a concept that can be logically considered and discussed by all.

"Work" seems to be a word with almost universal understanding among English-speaking peoples. It has a variety of applications — from the short-term description of energy expended to the longer term designation of job or career — but each variation is understood reasonably well by persons of every age, sex, or ethnic background. The use of the word "work" provides that base concept so necessary to adequate communication.

☐ The career education concept has been endorsed by a greater variety and a greater number of leading national organizations — both within and outside formal education — than any other call for educational reform now in existence.

Organizations at all levels of education, from preschool through adult education, have accepted the goals of career education as being vital components of the educational process. In addition, organizations outside education — in government, business, and labor — have formally supported career education in one way or another. A partial list of such organizations was recently published by the Chamber of Commerce of the United States. In many instances, these organizations have created internal committees or other entities specifically to deal with and promote career education. Such support provides a solid foundation for improving relations between the schools and other community organizations, and it underscores the importance of career education to interests which encompass a large segment of society.

☐ Career education became a part of the law of the land with the passage of P.L. 93-380 in 1974. In addi-

tion to this federal legislation, ten state legislatures
have enacted career education legislation. Also, more
than thirty state boards of education have adopted
official career education policy positions, and more
than forty state departments of education have
appointed one or more persons as state coordinators
of career education.

This high level of support is indicative of the validity of
career education's concepts and the esteem in which they are
held. But just as importantly, it is a testimonial to the great
energies and efforts which have already been expended to build
the career education movement and to the many dedicated
individuals who continue to develop new vehicles and new
models to express the values of career education. A movement
which has already established this solid foundation of support
is in a strong position to build a lasting and beneficial structure.

☐ Career education has emerged primarily as a local,
rather than a state or federal, initiative.

Here again is evidence of the strength which comes from
broad-based support. Although only eighty career education
programs are currently federally funded, one-third of the nation's seventeen thousand school districts had formal career
education policies, and nearly every district reported some
career education activity during the 1975–76 school year. However, there is still a long way to go, since only 3 percent of the
nation's students were in districts with truly comprehensive
programs.

☐ How-to-do-it examples abound for those interested
in initiating career efforts at the kindergarten through
twelfth grade level. Examples are readily available.
And where career education efforts have been evaluated, results have been generally positive. More than
three score studies have demonstrated higher motivation and performance from students engaged in
career education than from control groups in standard
curriculums.

The number of high school-level operating programs which
we uncovered in preparation for this book was astounding.
Thousands of different programs exist at the various levels of

education, and we have finally reached a point where it is almost never necessary to start a program "from scratch." In almost every case, a similar program can be located as an aid in avoiding the inevitable pitfalls encountered by new efforts in education. Finding ways to share these many examples is an important challenge facing career education proponents over the next few years. In this regard, the U.S. Office of Education recently conducted a series of mini-conferences at which teachers and administrators from various parts of the nation came together to "share" their experiences with career education — both positive and negative. Additional conferences are planned, and other means of communication will doubtless be employed to facilitate the sharing process.

☐ Career education demonstration efforts are currently aimed at demonstrating the most effective career education methods and procedures at the K–12 levels, as well as proving the viability of career education at both the secondary level and for special segments of the population.

The development of career education is so far advanced, and its proponents are so confident of its viability and effectiveness, that programs based on career education are being "plugged in" to virtually every level and type of education. Moreover, results continue to be positive in almost every case where the basic elements of career education serve as guidelines for program development. The obvious positioning of career education programs is in grades kindergarten through twelve, and success in those grades has been clearly demonstrated. However, projects are currently being planned or are under way in such diverse fields as preschool education, business-labor-industry training, handicapped education, community colleges, armed forces training, adult education, and liberal arts colleges. These efforts will doubtless continue as new applications are identified.

☐ The Education and Work Task Force at the National Institute of Education is continuing its strong efforts to support a program of basic research required for the long-run effectiveness of career education.

As we mentioned, the reactions of those teachers and administrators who have worked with career education have been overwhelmingly positive, but we still need the kind of evidentiary and statistical data which can be provided only by a long-range research effort. Teachers continue to report that career education provides benefits for both teachers and students. (As one teacher put it, career education "takes the blahs out of teaching.") But we need to determine both the type and degree of benefits in short- and long-range contexts. The fact that this type of data is being accumulated through an organized research program is another strength of the career education movement, and it is also another demonstration of the validity of the extended time and concept base already established by career education proponents.

☐ Where career education efforts have been initiated, they rarely have been dropped because they were unsuccessful or disliked. The pattern has been one of growth, not abandonment.

It is no longer possible to consider career education as just "another education fad." It has resisted the cyclical pattern of faddishness by not only retaining but expanding its support in almost every instance where it has been tried.

The ten strengths of career education outlined above provide a solid rationale to justify an expression of interest in career education on the part of any education system, any school, and any community. But naturally not all observers are converts to career education concepts. Those who disagree with the principles or practices of career education should be provided access to the same forum occupied by proponents of the movement so that the dialog can move forward. We can all learn from each other, and career education can be strengthened further if we listen carefully to its detractors. At one of the recent career education mini-conferences, a teacher from the Midwest eloquently and persuasively challenged career education. His basic stance can be summed up in one thought-provoking statement: Career education promises too much!

Those of us who believe in career education must constantly remind ourselves not to overpromise. In our zeal to promote career education as a significant movement in American education, we must remember that it is *a* movement and not *the* movement. American education is in need of change in order to meet the ever-changing challenges it faces. Career education is one possible type of change designed to help solve a specific range of problems. Proponents of career education have never claimed or pretended that it is the *only* goal of American education; nor have they maintained that it is necessarily the most important goal. However, career education is and should be *one* of the fundamental goals of American education.

This book provides a basic foundation for helping to achieve that goal at the high school level. It promises a great deal but not, we hope, more than it can reasonably deliver. This book should not be considered in isolation but as part of a growing body of career education literature. Career education is a process, not an event. It begins at birth and extends through adulthood. This book examines a short, but highly important, segment of that process.

Kenneth Hoyt's participation in the preparation of this book does not reflect endorsement by the U.S. Office of Education. Rupert Evans participated from his post as professor of vocational-technical education at the University of Illinois where Ella Bowen, now at the University of Michigan, was Dr. Evans' graduate assistant at that time. Garth Mangum and Donald Gale are at the University of Utah, where Gale's participation was supported from a manpower institutional grant from the Office of Research and Development, U.S. Department of Labor, to the Human Resources Institute where Mangum is director. None of these institutions has any responsibility for the conclusions of the authors.

# 1

# Career
# Education

The daughter of a successful businessman announced one evening that she and her boyfriend were dropping out of school. They had decided that school was "meaningless," she told her father, and so they were moving in with a group of people their own age who had rejected the "materialistic values of society" and were devoted to "mind-expanding" experiences free of the restrictions imposed by outsiders. The girl said that she was not interested in money, but from her comments it was obvious to the father that she assumed if money should ever become a problem for her, the father would provide it.

A COLLEGE SENIOR asked his professor what he had to do to obtain a teaching certificate in biology.

"Why do you want a teaching certificate?" the professor asked.

"Well," answered the student, "I'm graduating with a degree in biology this spring. What else is there to do with a degree in biology except to go into teaching?"

A YOUNG MAN, recently graduated from high school, walked out of yet another personnel director's office feeling rejected and looking dejected. There seemed to be no jobs available for which he was qualified. He had applied for work at service stations, restaurants, department stores, manufacturing companies, and now a service business. But, he thought, I've got to keep looking until I find *something*; I need a job.

This young man was determined to keep looking for a job until he found one, whatever it might be. It is likely that he would eventually find something, but his lifetime career would be determined by accident, not by planning. In twelve years of formal education he had learned to read, to write, and to compute, but he had never learned how to make plans for using those skills in the world outside the classroom. In twelve years he had learned to work math problems from a book, to read stories which he found interesting but seldom relevant to his own needs, and to write a passing theme — complete with footnotes. But he had never learned how to compile a résumé for himself — or even that such an instrument might be useful in helping him acquire work.

THESE ARE BUT three examples of the kinds of problems which students face when leaving the school system, at whatever level. Too often the education experience seems meaningless to them, senseless, as if it is "going nowhere." Too often it has included a series of failures which have destroyed that vital feeling of self-worth. Too often college was not a step along the path toward a goal but merely an extension of an experience which had the attractiveness of familiarity or was a means of delaying for four years the career decision which every individual — male and female alike — must make eventually.

Whether they drop out of school or whether they finish high school (or even college), few students will have been explicitly taught work values, attitudes, and habits. Few will have been led to explore the world of work and their own relationship to it. Few will have examined themselves and their preferred life-styles as a function of career choices.

It is true, of course, that most students do find jobs, and most of them do learn the requirements of the workplace. Fortunately, some of the same attitudes of diligence and some of the same interpersonal skills which make for success in the classroom are also attitudes and skills which contribute to labor market success. Fortunately, in many instances parents, friends, teachers, and television give students a little occupational direction, even though the exposure is usually narrow. Also fortunately, many students acquire work-related skills through summer jobs or part-time jobs during the school years. And, again, fortunately, employers who need employees will actually search them out and train them in the prerequisite fields.

But unfortunately, few students achieve to the utmost of their potential, and too many lose out or are left out.

One must ask some key questions about education. How many students leave American high schools with a negative attitude toward work? How many teachers instill such negative attitudes in their students, not by the things they teach, but by the failure to include career education concepts in their courses? Should high school teachers teach their students work values, career choices, self-exploration, skills development, and preparation for the world of work? Does the study of work have a place in each of the classes taught by every American high school teacher? What responsibilities do high school teachers have in preparing students for careers, for getting jobs, and for participating in the world of work?

Work is not everything, but most of us must work, and in many cases those who are most successful at work seem also to be most successful in other aspects of their lives. It is relevant, then, to ask the twofold question: What are the goals and objectives of the high school, and where does career education fit among them?

## The Goals of High School Education

Elementary education, consistent with the needs of childhood, is concerned primarily with the provision of basic skills. Middle and junior high schools overlap later childhood and early adolescence and stress exploration and self-discovery. High school is a time of transition into decision-making preparations for adult responsibility in employment, additional schooling, marriage, and so forth.

Historically, teaching about work has always been part of the assignment of American high schools. The issue was not whether work values should be taught but for whom the school should be designed, and for what occupations students should be prepared. Benjamin Franklin proposed that Americans develop an academy which would provide occupational preparation as well as academic competence for students from many walks of life. He viewed the academy as a place where youth would be treated with affection and assisted in occupational preparation and placement in a wide variety of practical occupations. However, the academies established in America during the nineteenth century did not follow the model proposed by Franklin; instead, they adopted the European model which taught Latin and Greek in order to prepare young men for a narrow range of occupations, the clergy, the law, and college teaching — professions taught in the colleges. Thus we derived the term "prep school" from the function of "preparation" for college.

Since most young men did not enroll in college, the need for occupational education beyond grammar school persisted. This need resulted in the creation of the first public high school in Boston in 1820. Because this institution taught English rather than Latin and Greek, it was called an "English high school," but the major purpose was to prepare youth for the world of work. English high schools were established in many cities before the Civil War, but they created much public controversy, not because of the curriculum but because some Americans opposed paying taxes to support high schools.

The controversy continued for many years, but its resolution was assisted by the passage of the Morrill Act in 1862. This act appropriated money to support preparation for practically oriented agricultural and engineering professions requiring higher education. The land-grant universities which were assisted by the Morrill Act found it necessary to establish their own preparatory high schools so that students would be ready for college-level practical education. Then, in 1870, the U.S. Supreme Court issued its decision in the KALAMAZOO case which declared the constitutionality of tax support for high schools. Thus the English high schools won their battle for existence. But another conflict soon challenged the occupationally oriented high school curriculum.

In 1870 many of the private academies, or prep schools, in the nation were encountering financial difficulties. By 1890 these difficulties had become so severe that the academy movement in the United States was near collapse. One plan advanced to save the academy was to combine it with the tax-supported English high school and form a "comprehensive high school." It was argued that such a high school would meet the needs of all adolescents in the community, whether they were preparing for college, business, agriculture, labor, or homemaking. This new comprehensive high school was to be a unique American educational institution which nations throughout the world would appreciate and emulate.

The new high school saved the tradition of the academy in America, but the original curriculum of the English high school, which was to prepare *all* youth for the world of work, was co-opted by the curriculum of the academy. With that development, the struggle to provide education for all youth to participate in the world of work began a new split into two factions. Those educators who were concerned primarily with "manual training" in various occupations found focus after 1906 in a National Society for the Promotion of Industrial Education. They joined with agricultural educators, representatives of business and industry, and advocates of wider opportunities for women to promote legislation which culminated in the Smith-Hughes Vocational Education Act in 1917. Other educators gave periodic recognition to the need for a broader approach to preparation of all students for the world of work, but without the continuing efforts of vocational educators, little realistic implementation of the concept would have occurred.

In 1913 the Commission on the Reorganization of Secondary Education — with Charles Eliot, President of Harvard University, as chairman — established goals for secondary education. Most of the committee members were products of the academy, and their report emphasized the goals of the academy more than the goals of the English high school. Nevertheless, they saw preparation for work as a major goal among their seven *Cardinal Principles of Secondary Education:* (1) health, (2) command of fundamental processes, (3) worthy home membership, (4) vocation, (5) civic education, (6) worthy use of leisure time, and (7) ethical character. The statement accompanying goal 4 said (Alexander *et al.*, p. 131):

Vocational education should equip the individual to secure a livelihood for himself and those dependent on him, to serve society well through his vocation, to maintain the right relationships toward his fellow workers and society, and, as far as possible, to find in that vocation his best development.

To this day these seven cardinal principles remain the most widely accepted statements of the goals of the high school, but most high schools emphasize goals 2 and 5 much more than the other five.

In 1918 the Educational Policies Commission developed a list of ten "needs" which were recommended for attention to high school curriculum specialists (Alexander *et al.*, p. 134):

(1) All youth need to develop salable skills and those understandings and attitudes that make the worker an intelligent and productive participant in economic life. To this end, most youth need supervised work experience as well as education in the skills and knowledge of their occupations.

(2) All youth need to develop and maintain physical fitness.

(3) All youth need to understand the rights and duties of the citizen of a democratic society and to be diligent and competent in the performance of their obligations as members of the community and citizens of the state and nation.

(4) All youth need to understand the significance of the family for the individual and society and the conditions conducive to successful family life.

(5) All youth need to know how to purchase and use goods and services intelligently, understanding both the values received by the consumer and the economic consequences of their acts.

(6) All youth need to understand the methods of science, the influence of science on human life, and the main scientific facts concerning the nature of the world and man.

(7) All youth need opportunities to develop their capacities to appreciate beauty in literature, art, music, and nature.

(8) All youth need to be able to use their leisure time well and to budget it wisely, balancing activities that yield satisfactions to the individual with those that are socially useful.

(9) All youth need to develop respect for other persons, to grow in their insight into ethical values and principles, and to be able to live and work cooperatively with others.

(10) All youth need to grow in ability to think rationally, to express their thoughts clearly, and to read and listen with understanding.

Even though the development of salable skills and work activities was listed first on the Educational Policies Commission list, implementation of that concept never became even number ten in most high school curriculums. Perhaps it was because vocational educators emphasized skills rather than attitudes. Perhaps it was because educators themselves were college graduates and had a natural leaning toward high school curriculums designed for students who intended to go to college. Perhaps it was because vocational education was limited by federal legislation to occupations *not* requiring a baccalaureate degree. Whatever the reason, career preparation was relegated to vocational training for a limited number of occupations in the high school and to a somewhat larger group of occupations in post-secondary institutions. Since the most influential elements in American society wanted their children to be prepared for college and the professions, vocational education was always for "someone else's" children, and it was therefore given low priority.

Thus there emerged essentially three high school curriculums: (1) the highly academic college preparatory, (2) the vocational, and (3) the general, with few objectives other than basic education. The smaller the high school, the fewer the occupations it presented in its vocational curriculum. But even in large high schools students could choose only one of a very

limited number of occupations. Most students had no opportunity to prepare for work or even to explore the world of work,
even though all would someday enter the work force. And even
the colleges and universities did not attempt to prepare students
for work; those institutions assumed that college graduates
would somehow "find their way."

In 1959 Conant, in *The American High School Today*,
argued that the goals of the American comprehensive high
school had not been achieved. He identified three basic goals
for high school education: (1) to provide general education for
all future citizens, (2) to provide good elective programs for
students who wish to use their acquired skills upon graduation,
and (3) to provide satisfactory programs for those whose vocations depend upon college education. In 1964 Conant again
reported on the comprehensive high school and noted the
difficulties in providing adequate vocational programs in many
high schools. He reiterated his belief that vocational studies
should be part of the regular comprehensive high school rather
than confined to a separate school and program.

In 1971 the Commission on the Reforming of Secondary
Education proposed reforms to enable secondary education
to cope with the changing needs of society and the changing
high school population. The Commission claimed that the
"larger problems of American society are reflected in the high
schools," and that "education is warped by the tension between
a rapidly changing society and a slowly changing school." It
claimed that the problems of American high schools arose from
"society's insistence on sudden and traumatic changes in their
mission." In the 1950s and early '60s, the report said, national
education efforts had focused upon advancements in science
and mathematics because of the cold war and national security
needs. Schools concentrated upon math and science. Then the
focus shifted to compensatory education for the culturally
disadvantaged. By 1970 society was demanding that basic skills
be taught to everyone and that high schools provide for the
well-being of all students.

The Commission on the Reforming of Secondary Education
also presented thirteen goals for secondary education. The
goals were divided into "content goals" and "process goals":

*Content Goals*

*Achievement of communication skills.* The secondary school must ensure that every student masters the basic skills of reading, writing, speaking, listening, and viewing. Mastery should be acquired through a wide variety of appropriate experiences and activities in each of the skills areas. The high school has an obligation to certify that every graduate has mastered the skills of reading and writing to a level of functional literacy.

*Achievement of computation skills.* The secondary school is obliged to ensure that all students master those computational and analytical skills necessary for the understanding of everyday problems. The high school has an obligation to certify that every graduate has mastered the skills of computation to a level sufficient for the management of household responsibilities.

*Attainment of proficiency in critical and objective thinking.* The secondary school is obliged to ensure that all learners develop, to the extent of their abilities, the skills of critical and objective thinking through research, analysis, and evaluation.

*Acquisition of occupational competence.* The secondary school must seek to prepare students for a successful life of work through increasing their occupational options. It must ensure that those students who wish to do so acquire job-entry skills before leaving high school. This effort must be coupled with employment opportunities, which are the responsibility of the society as a whole.

*Clear perception of nature and environment.* The secondary school must equip all students with an understanding of the wonders of nature, of the effects of man upon his environment, and of man's obligations to the viability of the planet.

*Development of economic understanding.* The secondary school is obliged to help students understand the American economy, its relationship to individual rights and freedoms. Each learner should understand his role in the economy as both producer and consumer of goods and services.

*Acceptance of responsibility for citizenship.* The secondary school must help students understand the American system of government, and equip them with the knowledge and experiences necessary for dealing purposefully with the political process. Citizenship responsibilities include respect for the opinions of others, the ability to conduct rational and informed discussions of controversial issues, respect for public and private property, and the acceptance of social duties.

### Process Goals

*Knowledge of self.* The secondary school is obliged to assist every learner in assessing [his or her] own mental, physical, and emotional capacities to the end that [he or she] has a positive self-image and can cope with problems of personal and family management. Schools also have an obligation to help learners understand their own physical nature and the extent to which their subsequent potential may be affected by their habits in eating and drinking and use of leisure time.

*Appreciation of others.* The secondary school must help each student develop an understanding of the differences and similarities and of the common humanity of members of different ethnic and religious groups.

*Ability to adjust to change.* The secondary school must endow students with the knowledge and attitudes necessary for survival in the twenty-first century and for coping with the unprecedented expansion of knowledge.

*Respect for law and authority.* The secondary school is obliged to seek to develop within each student a respect for duly constituted authority and public laws as well as a knowledge of the strategy for changing both through the democratic process.

*Clarification of values.* The secondary school must assist each learner in developing increased awareness of himself and of his relations to others and to the universe as he seeks to discover values and ethical standards which can promote growth toward his highest potential.

*Appreciation of the achievements of man.* The secondary school is obliged to help students understand and appreciate man's historical achievements in art, music, drama, literature, and the sciences so that they may acquire reverence for the heritage of mankind.

After developing this list of goals, the Commission conducted a survey of superintendents, principals, teachers, parents, and students in which it asked each group to rate the thirteen goals according to their essentiality in the high school curriculum. Interestingly, 69.3 percent of the parents and 68.1 percent of the students felt occupational competency was essential, but only 48.6 percent of the teachers felt occupational competency was an essential part of the high school curriculum. Students ranked critical thinking first, communications skills second, and occupational competency third. Parents ranked occupational competency as the sixth most important goal. The three groups of educators ranked occupational competency as the ninth most essential function of secondary education.

The fact that both parents and students give higher priority to the development of occupational competency than do educators seems to shatter the frequently expressed notion that schools give low priority to occupational competency because society demands high priority for "academic" pursuits. It seems more likely that educators who make such a statement are merely expressing a preference for continuing to do what they know how to do.

The National Commission on the Reforming of Secondary Education was not content with listing goals. It also made 32 specific recommendations for the improvement of secondary education. Four of those recommendations dealt with career-related goals:

### Recommendation No. 8: Expanding Career Opportunities

Secondary schools must realign their curricula to provide students with a range of experience and activities broad enough to permit them to take full advantage of career opportunities in their communities. To meet this objective, basic components of the school program will have to be offered in the late afternoon or in the evening for some students.

### Recommendation No. 9: Career Education

Career education advisory councils, including representatives of labor, business, community, students, and former students, should be established to assist in planning and implementing career education programs in comprehensive high schools....Career awareness programs should be initiated as an integral part of the curriculum to assure an appreciation of the dignity of work....In grades 11 and 12, students should have opportunities to acquire hard skills in a career area of their choice. This training should equip the student with job-entry skills.

## Recommendation No. 10: Job Placement

Suitable job placement must be an integral part of the career education program for students planning to enter the labor force upon leaving school. Secondary schools should establish an employment office staffed by career counselors and clerical assistants. The office should work in close cooperation with the state employment service. Agencies certifying counselors for secondary schools should require such counselors to show experience in job placement as a condition for granting initial certification.

## Recommendation No. 14: Credit for Experience

Secondary schools should establish extensive programs to award academic credit for accomplishment outside the building, and for learning what occurs on the job, whether the job be undertaken for pay, for love, or for its own sake. Community involvement will, of course, be required in such a program and should be as encompassing as possible.

The report concluded with the statement: "Educators must come to terms with the fact that sooner or later every student must work."

Another study of education, this one funded by the Ford Foundation (1968), concluded that high schools need to provide more education for work in academic areas. In a technological society, liberal arts education and education for work "need each other, and no education can be regarded as comprehensive unless it finds ways of fitting them together." This study explained that high schools cannot solve the problem of unemployment in our economy, but they can do a great deal about underemployment and employability by improving their efforts in teaching about career education. The approach that high schools take toward career education now will have a profound influence on the attitudes people have toward work in the future.

While all of these commissions were recommending policy for the "someday" school, Congress was reflecting national concern for the allocation of education resources. The Vocational Education Act of 1963 and its 1968 amendments overturned the occupational emphasis of the Smith-Hughes Act of 1917. No longer was the emphasis to be the skill needs of the labor market but the employment needs of the people. Any recognized new or emerging occupation which required less than a four-year college education and all persons who might desire work in such occupations were to become the province of vocational education. Consequently, enrollment in vocational education increased from one million in 1931 to over eight million in 1970, but still less than a third of high school students were affected.

Even with the increased enrollment of students in vocational education, a large majority of youth continues to leave school with no specific preparation for gainful employment. Few schools give serious attention to successful transition of youth into the world of work. Writes Tanner (1972, p. 402):

> It is paradoxical that vocational education has gained a recognized place in our colleges and universities at the same time that the overwhelming majority of our youth who do not continue their education beyond high school are denied the opportunity for vocational education. Thus while the college student is preparing for an occupation, whether it be that of an accountant, historian, or zoologist, the youngster who ends his education with high school typically is lacking the preparation necessary for skilled, gainful employment.

In fact, many high schools do not offer any programs in vocational education, and most offer very limited programs. In these schools, noncollege-bound students are placed in general programs where they find little or no connection between school and their future life. College-bound students pursue studies that prepare them for college, where they can embark on career goals, but noncollege-bound students are denied the opportunity for career preparation. Not only is this an injustice to the individual, but it leads to social problems that are not easily solved once they are created. Youth unemployment is only the tip of the iceberg of such social problems. It reflects the difficulties of absorbing into the labor market the inexperienced and underprepared, but it does not identify the disillusionment of those who find jobs but not meaningful and satisfying careers. Tanner writes: "Only recently has our society come to realize that its future well-being rests just as much with those who enter the world of work from high school as with those who go on to college."

This recognition that secondary education has an obligation to provide occupational competency is widespread. John W. Gardner explains that the high school is

> ...responsible for educating the boy who will be an atomic scientist and the girl who will marry at eighteen; the prospective captain of a ship and the future captain of industry. It is responsible for educating the bright and the not so bright with different vocational and professional ambitions and with various motivations. It is responsible, in sum, for providing good and appropriate education, both academic and vocational, for all young people within a democratic environment which the American people believe serves the principles they cherish (Conant, 1969, p. ix).

Alexander *et al.* (1971, p. 79) list twelve hallmarks of secondary schooling for democratic living; among them is the goal to provide the basis for achieving competency in an occupation. High schools can build the foundation for successful careers by the kinds and quality of programs offered to students. Emphasis upon this hallmark alone is undesirable, but omission of this hallmark from high school curriculums is unforgivable.

Gorman (1971) claims that the high school stands as a reminder of the American belief that there are no unimportant people. Among his proposed changes for high schools, Gorman includes the need to extend the general education of all students, which includes "equipping citizens who earn their own livelihood to read, write, calculate, and reason well enough to take and follow some kind of technical directions" (p. 45). He emphasizes the importance of developing individual responsibility but laments that this goal is a neglected aim of modern secondary education. The way to learn responsibility is to exercise it in the world of work. Gorman points out an education paradox of modern times: "The tendency to overprotect children and youth from the world of real work has come in the same two generations that have seen the domestic chores formerly assigned to them rapidly reduced to nearly zero" (p. 48). After explaining how work responsibilities of youth in the home have been almost eliminated by changes from rural to urban society and by increased dependence on technology, Gorman states: "These changes have been harder on youth than is commonly supposed. Never before have so many of them had so much cause for feeling useless" (pp. 45–50).

Alexander *et al.* (1971) advocate that high schools provide students with learning opportunities and experiences that hold the promise of providing maximum values to adolescents and young adults (p. 119). Objectives and learning activities associated with occupations and careers are most easily recognized by youth as having those values.

Erik Erikson, in *Identity: Youth in Crisis* (1968, p. 185), finds that self-doubt and self-destructiveness result when individuals are denied a sense of "apprenticeship" or "work identity" for participating in societal progress. Havighurst explained in *Developmental Tasks and Education* that if adolescents are denied the opportunity of preparing for an occupation, they are hindered in such normal tasks of development as desiring and achieving socially responsible behavior, achieving emotional independence from parents and other adults, achieving masculine or feminine social roles, achieving new and more mature relations with peers, achieving assurance of economic independence, developing skills and understandings necessary for civic competence, acquiring a set of values and an ethical system as a guide to behavior, and building a future basis for marriage and family life. Such claims imply that occupational preparation is essential for the development of good citizens. Good citizenship is indeed a goal of high schools, and thus occupational preparation must become a part of all high school curriculums.

Tanner (1972) concluded: "Ordinary work is the most essential kind of work in society because it is tied to the most elemental functions of society. When such work in a democratic society comes to be regarded as inferior and odious, it is unlikely that the society can continue to function as a democracy."

The National Advisory Commission on Civil Disorders recommended that vocational programs be greatly expanded and strengthened (Tanner, 1972, p. 407), and an editorial in *Science* stated: "One of our greatest mistakes has been to accord special prestige to a college degree while displaying indifference toward quality craftsmanship. We reward verbal skill and abstract reasoning and deny dignity to manual workers."

In an article, "The Children Have Outgrown the Schools," Coleman (1972, pp. 16–21) proposed the thesis that schools, as they presently exist, are obsolete because they still perform an information-giving function in a society rich in availble information sources such as television and other media. Schools therefore should provide students with the types of experience and responsibilities offered by home and community a hundred years ago — those that made them productive and valued members of the family, community, and economy. He further suggests that "schooling is not all of education, and the other parts of education require just as much explicit planning and organization as does schooling."

Harold Howe, former U.S. Commissioner of Education, agrees that education is not something that takes place only inside a schoolbuilding. He recommends that schools need to do more to help young people find paid and volunteer work opportunities with real meaning and value to them. He further recommends that mastery of basic skills and important fundamental subjects such as science, mathematics, foreign languages, and history should be set in a context that highlights the importance of these fields in today's world, rather than trying to motivate students by vague generalizations about future utility or college requirements (Weinstock, 1973, p. 16).

Despite the consistency of this historical and contemporary educational philosophy, no satisfactory vehicle emerged to fill the frequently stated need until the career education movement of the 1970s. The high school served only one youth in ten in 1901, compared to eight or nine out of ten by 1970. The curriculum which was dominated by academic and classical studies at the turn of the century had added vocational education by 1920, but it was limited to the job skills of a relatively narrow range of occupations. Most occupations were virtually untouched. Few high schools had developed ways of preparing students for unskilled, semiskilled, professional, or managerial jobs. Within vocational education, stress was placed almost exclusively on becoming a good employee, with little mention made of entrepreneurship. Preparation for the first job was emphasized, rather than preparation for a career.

Left out were the values, attitudes, habits, and interpersonal skills which are vital components of all occupational competencies. The school seldom was involved in placing its students in employment; nor was information from placement and follow-up fed back as a contribution to curriculum revision. Employer and employee advising committees existed more on paper than in practice.

Given that the high school's goals and objectives were to provide the competencies necessary for the next phases of life — marriage, parenthood, citizenship, employment, higher education, cultural activities, meaningful leisure — some reform was necessary. Career education is only part, but a vital part, of that needed reform in secondary education. It has already made substantial inroads in elementary education and at the middle/junior high school level. It has equal post-secondary applications, but the high school is the appropriate current emphasis.

## Concepts and Content of Career Education*

This book's ambition is to portray the advantages of career education and to guide its applications at the high school level. To do so, we must first make certain that the reader understands what career education is all about before we plunge into its secondary school versions. Now that career education has an official definition (after three years of undefined life), this introductory task becomes simpler.

Career is the totality of work one does in his or her lifetime. Work is conscious effort aimed at producing benefits for oneself or for others. Education is the totality of experiences through which one learns. Therefore, career education is the totality of experiences through which one learns about and prepares to engage in work as part of one's life-style. Work refers to all such productive effort, paid or unpaid, including the productive uses of leisure time. It cannot be easily contrasted

---

*Many readers will be familiar with the concepts of career education and can skip to the final section of this chapter. The career education buff will recognize in it selections and paraphrase from *An Introduction to Career Education,* a November 1974 policy paper of the U.S. Office of Education written by Kenneth Hoyt in February 1974.

with play, because the issue is "did it produce goods or services for someone's benefit?" not "was it enjoyable?" "Career," in this sense, is a developmental concept, beginning in the very early years of childhood and extending well beyond retirement. "Education," defined here, includes more than the formal school system. It involves all of those ways in which one can learn about work, in and out of school, through experience as well as instruction. But career education does not desire or claim to supersede all of education's many worthwhile objectives. Career education asks only that it be given equal emphasis with citizenship, culture, family life, general knowledge, and other objectives of the education process.

We can simplify our discussion of the nature of career education by summarizing in outline form the various assumptions, criteria, experiences, and goals of career education as they have thus far developed.

## The Basis for Career Education

Career education is based on the assumption of the validity of certain concepts related to careers and to education:

(1) Since both one's career and one's education extend from the preschool through the retirement years, career education must also span almost the entire life-cycle.

(2) The concept of productivity is central to the definition of work and thus to the entire concept of career education.

(3) Since "work" includes unpaid activities as well as paid employment, career education's concern, in addition to its prime emphasis on paid employment, extends to the work of the student as a learner, to the growing numbers of volunteer workers in our society, to the work of the full-time homemaker, and to work activities in which one engages as part of leisure (free) time.

(4) The cosmopolitan nature of today's society demands that career education embrace a multiplicity of work values, rather than a single work ethic, as a means of

helping each individual answer the question: Why should I work?

(5) Both one's career and one's education are best viewed in a developmental rather than in a fragmented or piecemeal sense.

(6) Career education is for all persons – including the young and the old, the mentally handicapped and the intellectually gifted, the poor and the wealthy, males and females, students in elementary schools and in graduate schools.

(7) The individualistic goals of career education are to make work (a) possible, (b) meaningful, and (c) satisfying for each individual throughout his or her lifetime.

(8) The societal goals of career education are to help all individuals to: (a) want to work, (b) acquire the skills necessary for work, and (c) engage in work that is satisfying to the individual and beneficial to society.

(9) Protection of the individual's freedom to choose – and assistance in making and implementing career decisions – are of central concern to career education.

(10) The expertise required for implementing career education exists in many parts of society and is not limited to persons employed in formal education.

## Program Considerations

In developing a career education program of any type, certain assumptions condition the ways in which the goals of career education might be incorporated into the education system:

(1) If students can see relationships between what they are being asked to learn in school and what exists in the world of work, they will be motivated to learn more in school.

(2) No single learning strategy exists that is best for all students. For example, some students will learn best

by reading books, and others will learn best by combining reading with other kinds of learning activities. A comprehensive educational program should provide a series of alternative learning strategies and learning environments for students.

(3) Basic academic skills, a personally meaningful set of work values, and good work habits represent adaptability tools needed by all persons who choose to work in today's rapidly changing occupational society.

(4) Increasingly, entry into today's occupational society demands that those who seek employment possess both a specific set of vocational skills and personal attributes attractive to employers. Unskilled labor is less and less in demand.

(5) Career development, as part of human development, begins in the preschool years and continues into the retirement years. Its maturational patterns differ in tempo from individual to individual.

(6) Work values, a part of one's personal value system, are developed to a significant degree during the elementary school years and are most readily modifiable during those years.

(7) Specific occupational choices represent only one of a number of kinds of choices involved in career development. They can be expected to increase in realism as one moves from childhood into adulthood, and to some degree, to be modifiable during most of one's adult years.

(8) Occupational decision making is accomplished through the dynamic interaction of limiting and enhancing factors, both within the individual and in his or her present and proposed environment. It is not, in any sense, an elemental matching of individuals with jobs.

(9) Occupational stereotyping hinders full freedom of occupational choice, especially for females and for minority persons. These restrictions can be reduced, to some extent, through programmatic intervention strategies begun in the early childhood years.

(10) Parent socioeconomic status acts as a limitation on occupational choices considered by children. This limitation can be reduced, to a degree, by program intervention strategies begun in the early years.

(11) A positive relationship exists between education and occupational competency, but the optimum amount and kind of education required as preparation for work varies greatly from occupation to occupation.

(12) The same general strategies used in reducing worker alienation in industry can be used to reduce "worker" alienation among pupils and teachers in the classroom.

(13) While some persons will find themselves able to meet their human needs for accomplishment through work in their places of paid employment, others will find it necessary to meet this need through work in which they engaged during their leisure time.

(14) Career decision-making skills, job-hunting skills, and job-getting skills can be taught to and learned by almost everyone. Individuals can effectively use such skills, once they are learned, to enhance their career development.

(15) Excessive deprivation in any aspect of human growth and development can retard career development. For persons suffering such deprivation, special variations in career development programs will be required.

(16) An effective means of helping individuals discover both who they are (in a self-concept sense) and why they are (in a personal awareness sense) is through helping them discover what they can accomplish in the work they do.

(17) The attitudes of parents toward work and toward education act as powerful influences on the career development of their children. Such parental attitudes are modifiable through education.

(18) The processes of occupational decision making and occupational preparation will be repeated more than once for most adults in today's society.

(19) One's style of living is significantly influenced by the occupations he or she engages in at various times in life.

(20) Relationships between education and work can be made more meaningful if infused into subject matter than if taught as a separate body of knowledge.

(21) Increasingly, education and work will be interwoven at various times in the lives of most individuals rather than occur in a single sequential pattern.

(22) Decisions that individuals make about the work they do are considerably broader and more encompassing in nature than are decisions made regarding the occupations in which they are employed.

(23) Good work habits and positive attitudes toward work can be taught effectively to most individuals. Assimilation of such knowledge is most effective if it is begun in the early childhood years.

(24) The basis on which work can become a personally meaningful part of one's life will vary greatly from individual to individual. No single approach can be expected to meet with universal success.

(25) While economic return can almost always be expected to be a significant factor in decisions which individuals make about unemployment, and even in decisions about occupations, it may not be a significant factor in many decisions that individuals make about their total pattern of work.

### Requisites of Program Implementation

Career education now has behind it several years of experience in many types of pioneering schools. Where it has been successfully implemented, many segments of the community participated in significant role functions. Those segments included a wide range of school personnel, parents, employers, and community leaders. Therefore, it can be assumed from experience that the requisites for the successful implementation of a career education program include:

(1) *All* classroom teachers must —

    (a) Devise and locate methods and materials designed to help students understand and appreciate the career implications of the subject matter being taught

    (b) Use career-oriented methods and materials in the instructional program, where appropriate, as one means of educational motivation

    (c) Help students acquire and use good work habits

    (d) Help students develop, clarify, and assimilate a personally meaningful set of work values

    (e) Integrate, to the fullest extent possible, the programmatic assumptions of career education into their instructional activities and teacher-student relationships

(2) Some, but not all, teachers must —

    (a) Provide students with specific vocational competencies at a level that will enable them to gain entry into the occupational society

    (b) Help students to acquire job-seeking and job-getting skills

    (c) Participate in the job-placement process

    (d) Help students acquire decision-making skills

(3) The business-labor-industrial community must —

    (a) Provide observational, work experience, and work-study opportunities for students and for those who educate students (teachers, counselors, and school administrators)

    (b) Serve as career development resource personnel for teachers, counselors, and students

    (c) Participate in job placement programs for persons interested in part-time and full-time work

(d) Participate actively and positively in programs designed to reduce worker alienation

(4) Counseling and guidance personnel must —

(a) Help classroom teachers implement career education in the classroom

(b) Serve, usually with other educational personnel, as liaison between the school and the business-labor-industry community

(c) Serve, usually with other educational personnel, in implementing career education concepts within the home and family structure

(d) Help students in the total career development process, including the making and implementing of career decisions

(e) Participate in part-time and full-time job placement programs and in follow-up studies of former students

(5) Home and family members must —

(a) Help students acquire and practice good work habits

(b) Emphasize development of positive work values and attitudes toward work

(c) Maximize, to the fullest extent possible, career development options and opportunities for themselves and for their children

(6) Educational administrators and school boards must —

(a) Emphasize career education as a priority goal

(b) Provide leadership and direction to the career education program

(c) Secure the widest possible community participation in career education policy decision making

(d) Provide the time, materials, finances, and staff development required for implementing the career education program

(e) Initiate curriculum revision designed to integrate academic, general, and vocational education into an expanded set of educational opportunities available to all students

### Goals for the Individual Student

Once a career education program has been implemented and students have had an opportunity to obtain the benefits of the program, proponents of career education anticipate that when students leave the formal school system *at any age or level*, they will be:

(1) Competent in the basic academic skills required for adaptability in our rapidly changing society

(2) Equipped with good work habits

(3) Capable of choosing and having chosen a personally meaningful set of work values that foster a desire to work

(4) Equipped with career decision-making skills, job-hunting skills, job-getting skills, and job-keeping skills

(5) Equipped with personal vocational skills at a level that will allow them to gain entry into and attain a degree of success in the occupational society

(6) Equipped with career decisions based on the widest possible set of data concerning themselves and their educational-vocational opportunities

(7) Aware of opportunities available to them for continuing and recurrent education once they have left the formal system of schooling

(8) Successful in being placed in a paid occupation, in further education, or in unpaid work consistent with their current career preferences and objectives

(9) Successful in incorporating work values into their total personal value structures in such a way that they are able to choose what, for them, is a desirable life-style

### *Other Educational Reform Supported by Career Education Proponents*

In addition to career education and the concepts outlined above, many of those who consider themselves "career educators" also support a variety of basic educational reforms which have been advocated by others. These individuals feel that many different types of reform movements are harmonious with the goals of career education. Among them are:

(1) The quantity, quality, and variety of vocational and occupational education offerings at the secondary school level and at the post-secondary school level should be substantially increased.

(2) The number and variety of educational course options available to students should be increased, with a de-emphasis on the presence of clearly differentiated college preparatory, general, and vocational education curriculums at the secondary school level. This includes provision for individual students to change career goals without delaying their high school graduation.

(3) Performance evaluation should be installed as an alternative to the strict time requirements imposed by the traditional Carnegie unit for the purpose of assessing and certifying educational accomplishment.

(4) Systems should be provided for granting educational credit for learning that takes place outside the walls of the school.

(5) Noncertified personnel from the business-industry-labor community should be used more extensively as educational resource persons in the education system's total instructional program.

(6) An open entry, open exit education system should be created to allow students to combine schooling with work in ways that fit their needs and educational motivations.

(7) Programs in adults and recurrent education should

be increased and should be a responsibility of the public school education system.

(8) A year-round public school system should be created which provides multiple points during any twelve-month period in which a student may leave the education system.

(9) Teacher education programs and graduate programs in education should receive major overhauls, including the incorporation of career education concepts, skills, and methodologies.

(10) Career guidance, counseling, placement, and follow-up functions should be substantially increased and should become integral parts of all American education.

(11) Substantial increases are needed in program and schedule flexibility to allow classroom teachers, at all levels, greater autonomy and freedom to choose educational strategies and devise methods and materials they determine to be effective in increasing student achievement.

(12) Improvement should be sought in the use of educational technology for gathering, processing, and disseminating knowledge required in the teaching-learning process.

(13) Expansion should be sought in the participation of students, teachers, parents, and members of the business-industry-labor community in educational policy making.

(14) Educational institutions should increase their own participation in comprehensive community educational and human services efforts.

## Responding to the Critics of American Education

The suggestions listed above are but a few of the proposals which have been advanced to help the education system. The proposals would not have been advanced if the system were not under severe criticism from a variety of sources. As we have emphasized frequently in these pages, career education is not the *only* program which shows promise of solving some of the problems pointed out by the critics, but the evidence is rapidly accumulating that career education *can* significantly help to overcome some of the problems. Among those criticisms which career education can alleviate if it is widely adopted are the following:

(1) Too many persons leaving our education system are deficient in the basic academic skills required for adaptability in today's rapidly changing society.

(2) Too many students fail to see meaningful relationships between what they are being asked to learn in school and what they will do when they leave the education system. This is true of both those who remain to graduate and those who drop out of the education system.

(3) American education, as currently structured, best meets the educational needs of that minority of persons who will someday become college graduates. It fails to place equal emphasis on meeting the educational needs of that vast majority of students who will never be college graduates.

(4) American education has not kept pace with the rapidity of change in the American occupational society. As a result, when worker qualifications are compared with job requirements, we find overeducated and undereducated workers are present in large numbers. Both the boredom of the overeducated worker and the frustration of the undereducated worker have contributed to growing worker alienation in the total occupational society.

(5) Too many persons leave our education system at both the secondary and collegiate levels who are not equipped with the vocational skills, the self-understanding and career decision-making skills, or the work attitudes that are essential for making a successful transition from school to work.

(6) The growing need for and presence of women in the work force has not been reflected adequately in either

the educational or the career options typically pictured for girls enrolled in our education system.

(7) The growing needs for continuing and recurrent education of adults are not being met adequately by our current systems of public education.

(8) Insufficient attention has been given to learning opportunities which exist outside the structure of formal education and are increasingly needed by both youth and adults in our society.

(9) The general public, including parents and the business-industry-labor community, has not been given an adequate role in formulation of educational policy.

(10) American education, as currently structured, does not adequately meet the needs of handicapped, minority, or economically disadvantaged persons in our society.

(11) Post-high school education has given insufficient emphasis to educational programs at the sub-baccalaureate degree level.

### What Does Career Education Offer the High School?

The definitions, concepts, and goals we have discussed sweep across the entire formal schooling process. Within this structure, the high school is expected to manifest a special decision-facilitating emphasis because it is the end of a structured, formal education sequence for most students, and because it plays a key role in determining the types of further education all students will need and desire in universities or in continuing education.

Career education is a continuing process. Beginning no later than the start of elementary school, youth will become aware of work as an individual and societal function and as a source of materials goods, services, and personal satisfactions. During the early school years and continuing through the middle school, they will be assisted and guided in the development of their own value structures, including work values within those human value systems. They will begin to develop good work habits in their schoolwork, they will acquire basic cognitive and motor skills, and they will view academic subjects from the vantage point of career applicability. At various points in the process they will acquire a vision of the broad sweep of occupational alternatives and the life-styles which accompany them, and they will understand the education and training implications of those alternatives.

When youth reach the high school level, all of these developments will still be incomplete and must be continued. However, in the high school years emphasis will shift to decision making and to occupational preparation. Neither of these considerations will be new to the youth who have reached high school, but at that stage the considerations become more immediate and crucial. The availability of data for decisions and the acquisition of skills necessary for the decision-making process are an immediate necessity in high school, because the youth face vital decisions about education, marriage, occupation, earning and spending, character development, and many other things.

Therefore, high school is a time to go beyond hearing and studying about work and begin experiencing it in realistic settings. It is a time to learn what work means and how it feels. It is a time to improve the potential for wise decision making by bridging some of the remaining gaps between education and experience. It is a time to encourage students to ask and seek answers for the "hard" questions which will determine much about the course of their lives: Should I pursue post-secondary education? What course of study would be best for me? Why? Where? What consequences can I expect from the available alternatives? What kinds of temporary work can I obtain? Will they help me in my career goals? How? Why should I make a choice now? Will I be able to change my mind at a later time? How will my current decisions affect any subsequent decisions I may want to make? How do I get a job? What kind of training do I need?

Many other questions are vital to young persons of high school age. These are but a few considerations. But they are the questions with which career education deals, not in *one* classroom or a specific course, but in *all* disciplines. Furthermore, students must be assisted in finding answers to these questions without diminishing the attainment of the other valued objectives of education.

How can such comprehensive goals be achieved? In the education amendments of 1974, Congress endorsed career education as a national priority. By that time, ten states had legislated, and had appropriated money to support, development of career education programs, and more than five thousand of the seventeen thousand school districts in the nation had instituted some sort of career education effort. Most of that early action took place in elementary and junior high schools. High schools lagged behind in career education, perhaps because many people confused career education with vocational education, and there were already vocational education options for many of their students.

Whatever the reason, administrators and faculty of the high schools have not been convinced that they should move into career education, or, if they were convinced, they have not known how to implement programs at the high school level. Unfortunately, this situation has kept many of them from bringing the benefits of career education to their students.

Let us examine once again some of the promises and results of career education. One must bear in mind that the following are not mere conjecture or assumptions; these are benefits suggested by consensus of teachers who have actually had experience working with career education programs:

(1) Career education provides a new source of motivation to study subject matter.

(2) Career education relates the knowledge of the various disciplines to societal goals and individual needs.

(3) Career education helps students learn basic skills required for success in the world and life — decision-making skills, skills in analyzing life-styles and work styles, and skills in clarifying values and recognizing problems of human relations.

(4) Career education is a vehicle whereby teachers can use community and parental resources to enrich and improve the teaching processes.

(5) Career education is a vehicle through which parents

and interested members of the community can become involved in the educational processes.

(6) Career education can develop a sense of dignity toward work and for people employed in all occupations.

(7) Career education can help end racial and sex stereotyping in occupations.

However, for career education to succeed in high schools, staff competencies need developing, teamwork must occur, and there must be a collective commitment to career education. For a complete career education program to be developed, the entire staff of a high-school — administrators, counselors, teachers, and other staff members — must develop a philosophy toward career education. How does the world of work relate to the values and philosophy of the high school? Are we committed to work values? Which ones? What values relate to different subjects? What values do the students and community possess? Should high school staff teach values related to certain occupational clusters and not to others?

High schools must establish career education objectives that are compatible with the objectives of the high school. To do so they must define the high school's broader educational goals as well as those of career education. Which career education objectives relate to objectives of different departments, teachers, and students?

Once objectives are formulated, coordinated programs need to be developed. How does career education affect instruction in the various disciplines and in interdisciplinary areas? How can community resources be used by different disciplines? What responsibility for placement exists in career education programs of different disciplines? How can career education be infused into the entire range of subjects? What collaboration must occur between teachers of different disciplines? Between teachers and counselors? Between the staff and the community? Between teachers and students?

The organization of the school will need analysis. What role should the principal perform in developing and implementing career education programs? Counselors? Teachers? Students? Secretarial staff? Custodial staff? District personnel?

The Board of Education? Parents? Lay persons in the community? Elementary and junior high teachers? Instructors in area vocational schools, community colleges, and universities? How should the staff be organized to facilitate working with each other and with persons outside the high school?

High school administrators need to analyze their personnel, physical facilities, and resources. What in-service training will be required? Which teachers and counselors can provide in-service training? What competencies are essential? What community resources are available?

Finally, finances must be considered. Is extra money needed? Is the school adopting career education for the chance to get government funding or because its leaders truly believe in career education? Does the product justify the costs? The answers to these questions will reflect the philosophy and commitment of the school.

Career education in high school means that every teacher of every subject accepts responsibility for teaching career education. No longer can work values, work skills, and career decision-making exercises be the exclusive domain of the vocational, industrial arts, business, and home economics educators. Teachers of academic subjects must analyze their own feelings toward work. They must analyze the subject they teach to determine how and where career education concepts and skills can be taught in connection with their subject. These teachers must learn about sources of career information, about the availability and job requirements of alternative occupations, about the workings of the labor market and the existence of labor market intermediaries, about job hunting skills, and about ways to involve persons and places in the community.

Career education at the high school level means greater flexibility of schedules and greater involvement of students and teachers with the community. Teachers will have to work with different lay persons in the community for orientation activities and preparation opportunities. Teachers of academic subjects will plan learning activities with vocational teachers for students enrolled in cooperative, distributive, work-study, work-experience, and other work-based programs. This will require more flexible scheduling, preparation periods, and creative planning.

Rather than high schools spending large amounts of money to build and equip additional training centers in the school, educators may identify persons and businesses in the community where students can learn different occupational skills on the job. In such cases students may be taught by nonprofessional educators in conjunction with high school teachers. But where these opportunities do not exist in the community, the school has the responsibility to provide substitute activities to the maximum extent possible.

Counselors must change their emphasis from administrative and disciplinary roles to more counseling for career choice and self-understanding. Counselors will collaborate more with teachers, the community, and all students, perhaps in the key role of liaison between the school and community. Counselors will also be involved in group counseling and spend more time working with teachers in classrooms. Teachers will assume additional responsibility for providing some counseling for some students.

Administrators must get more involved in the execution of career education programs. Greater involvement of parents and the community means that the principal must provide leadership, arrange for programs, and oversee public relations. High schools will lose their provincialism and become a more integral part of the community.

What happens to career education in a particular high school will depend largely on the school's commitment to and interpretation of career education. Some staff members will hope others will do it, but a majority will see opportunities for career education to enrich their teaching experiences and student learning. Most will see their subject area as an appropriate vehicle to include career education. They will use career education to improve the teaching of subject matter, to provide an exciting educational stream and a curriculum option. But career education is not a responsibility assigned solely to selected members of the faculty. It is a commitment to a theme infecting and transcending the entire education system at all grade levels and in all content areas.

The high school is a pivot point in the lives of all students. It is a place where students not only acquire knowledge and skills but learn how to use those things in the pursuit of satisfying, meaningful lives, lives which will inevitably revolve round work. Career education provides a dimension of understanding which can add satisfaction and meaning to both the high school experience and to the work experience it precedes.

## References

Alexander, William M.; Saylor, J. Galen; and Williams, Emmett L. *The High School: Today and Tomorrow.* New York: Holt, Reinhart, and Winston. 1971.

Coleman, James. "The Children Have Outgrown the Schools." *The National Elementary Principal* (Oct. 1972), vol. 52.

Conant, James B. *The American High School Today.* New York: McGraw-Hill Co. 1959.

Educational Policies Commission, Secondary Education Association. *Education for All American Youth.* Washington, D.C.: Secondary Education Association. 1944.

Ford Foundation. *Designing Education for the Future.* Denver, Colo.: Ford Foundation. 1968.

Erickson, Erik. *Identity: Youth in Crisis.* New York: W. W. Norton and Co. 1968.

Gorman, Burton W. *Secondary Education: The High School America Needs.* New York: Random House. 1971.

Havighurst, Robert J. *Developmental Tasks and Education.* New York: Longman, Green and Co. 1952.

National Commission on the Reforming of Secondary Education. *The Reforming of Secondary Education: A Report to the Public and the Profession.* New York: McGraw-Hill Co. 1971.

Tanner, David. *Secondary Education: Perspective and Prospects.* New York: Macmillan Co. 1972.

Weinstock, Ruth. *The Greening of the High School.* New York: New York Educational Facilities Laboratory. 1973.

# 2

# Career
# Development

Career education can be successful only insofar as it is consistent with and contributes to the process of career development which is going on in the life of every individual. Therefore, those interested in applying career education at the high school level must understand the process of career development as it occurs in the life of the student of high school age.

The original U.S. Office of Education (USOE) model for career education viewed the senior high school years as a period of career preparation and career decision making. According to this model, elementary school students would be made *aware* of the general nature of the world of paid employment through exposure to fifteen broad occupational clusters. These fifteen clusters represented a classification scheme for the more than twenty thousand occupations in the world of work. During the junior high school years, each student would select three of the fifteen clusters for more in-depth exploration. At the senior high school level, each student would select one cluster only and would pursue combination career decision-making and career preparation activities within that cluster. By the time the student left the senior high school, she or he would be

51

equipped with sufficient knowledge and marketable job skills so that each would be able either to enter the world of paid employment or to continue occupational preparation at the post-secondary level.

That model, while still widely quoted, is no longer being championed in specific fashion by career education personnel in USOE. Increasingly, both within USOE and in operating career education programs across the land, career education leaders are refining their procedures and recommendations in light of what is known about the psychology of career development, the current structure of American education, and the current nature of the occupational society. When these three major areas are each taken into account, it becomes obvious that both the problems and the promises of career development at the senior high school level are much more complex than originally envisioned.

For example, we know now that we must consider the topic of career development in the senior high school from at least three perspectives: (1) personal and environmental restraints, (2) career development practices, and (3) dilemmas of career decision making which face today's youth.

## *Personal and Environmental Restraints*

The first step in understanding the career development process as it impacts upon the fifteen- to eighteen-year-old individual is to explore what is known about personal maturation and the environmental restrictions which may surround the individual youth.

### *Career Maturation*

In most states, the twelfth grade still represents the last year of so-called "free" public education. Thus when a young person leaves the senior high school, he or she is expected to have made some personal decisions with respect to future plans. Some solve this problem by announcing that their plans are to "go to college." This may be a means to avoid the topic of career decision making altogether. Others, having made some tentative career choices, implement such choices by attending a post-secondary occupational education institution, thus avoiding the necessity of seeking any kind of specific employment. Still others make career choices which they pursue appropriately through post-secondary education designed to help them reach the first stages of their career goals. However, large numbers of youth see no kind of post-secondary education as being available to them or desirable for them. Most of these, recognizing that work is an accepted and expected form of post-high school activity, are faced with making rather specific commitments with regard to both occupational and job choices. Some enter employment in an occupation of their choice, but the majority simply accepts what becomes available or remains without employment.

Career education seeks to meet the needs of each of these types of students by emphasizing that education in preparation for work should be a major goal of all who teach and all who learn. In this connection, career education experts have urged that high school seniors contemplating college attendance do so only after taking into account their career aspirations and plans. If this can be done, going to college will not be a way of avoiding work, but rather a way of readying oneself for a particular kind of work that the student has chosen. The decision not to attend college will be an equally conscious choice, with other career alternatives in mind. How realistic is this part of the career education effort for senior high students?

If one studies the literature on the theory of career development, one typically finds a developmental scheme that begins with some kind of "fantasy" stage, and moves in a developmental fashion through a series of stages until a point is reached which can be characterized as having some degree of stability of occupational choice and progression. While the names used by various theorists to describe these stages may differ, most are recognizable under a classification that ranges from "fantasy" to "realistic" or, if viewed differently, from "awareness" through "maintenance and progression."

One issue most all career development theorists seem to agree upon is that the senior high school years do *not* include the period in the life of an individual when final and firm occupational decisions are expected to occur. Each of these theorists pictures the late adolescent years as a period of "tentative" occupational choice. In most theories, establishment of firm career patterns seems to be reserved until at least the age range of the mid-twenties. Several of these theories are accompanied by a considerable body of research evidence confirming the fact that most adolescents do not make firm and final occupational choices during the senior high school years. Of course, this is not to say they wouldn't like to do so, or that they could not do so if their environments were more conducive to decision making. It says only that the making of firm occupational decisions does not now seem to be an expected part of normal career maturation for persons between fifteen and eighteen years of age.

Career education programs should be deeply involved in assisting youth in the career development process. However, it would be both unrealistic and unproductive were career education programs to be aimed at speeding that process by ignoring both the research and the theory which now exist in the realm of career maturation.

Unfortunately, too many persons still seem to be interpreting the expression "career maturity" as representing a condition that leads to a firm and final occupational decision. That is not at all what the term means. In fact, many people, particularly the most successful, seem prepared to make a change in career directions any time alternatives become more attractive than the current commitment. The term "career maturity," as defined by those whose professional lives are devoted to the study of this area, refers primarily to the individual's readiness to make reasoned career decision. In turn, this readiness is described typically in terms of some combination of the individual's understanding of self and of environmental opportunities available for choice. The criterion appropriate for use is the degree to which the individual's career decisions are "reasoned," not the degree to which they are "final."

In this sense, the expected "tentative" stage of career development during the adolescent years should in no way be used as either a rationale or as a justification for failure to raise questions of career choices with senior high school students. Increasingly, career decisions of *both* youth and adults have become "tentative" in that they can be expected to change, in degree if not in kind, at later times in life. There is much evidence to indicate that senior high school students are thinking and worrying about their career decisions. They are not helped greatly if we tell them they are too young or too immature to worry about such things now. Problems are seldom solved by refusing to recognize their existence.

Career development is most properly viewed as part of human growth and development. Just as physical development can be enhanced through a combination of information, environmental manipulation, and direct assistance to youth, so too can career development. In both cases, we approach the task, not with a view toward speeding it up but rather with a goal of enhancing its completeness so that the individual will be able to function more fully and more effectively as an adult. We do not stop teaching physical skills to adolescents because they are awkward and poorly coordinated in their physical development. We should not avoid assisting them in career development simply because many of them will not become fully "career mature" during their senior high school years.

## The Certainty of Occupational Change

The certainty of uncertainty facing today's youth is a challenge to all. Not only does the occupational structure change rapidly, but the job content within occupations changes and so do the interests and desires of workers who are less likely to put up with the working conditions they have accepted in the past. The national occupational structure can be reasonably predicted several years ahead, but those projections do not necessarily hold for any particular locality. Individual preferences are changed rapidly by the emergence of popular heroes or heroines, and slowly, but surely, by changes in the economic ranking of occupations. Change in the nature of occupations, in the geographic location of occupational opportunities, in the complexity of occupations, and in individual career preferences are realities to be dealt with.

Today's senior high school students — more than ever before — cannot afford to think of occupational choice as a single and final event, or even as a single process. The process of occupational choice will be experienced several times in their working lives. The day of planning a lifelong occupational choice and then preparing for and persisting in it is past, if in fact it ever existed. Instead, students must increasingly come to accept as their lifetime careers a series of occupational segments, each of which calls for a process involving occupational choice, preparation, placement, and adjustment.

As each of these segments occur, these youth will have to reexamine themselves in terms of their backgrounds, abilities, skills, interests, motivations, and values. The high school will represent only one of the environments in which this process must be experienced. While physical adolescence occurs only once, occupational adolescence — and even occupational "childhood" — can be expected to occur more than once after the period of physical adolescence is completed.

A major problem facing youth — and all of the rest of us — is to retain individuality in a society which is becoming both more complex and more demanding. The heart of this problem is to be found in society itself — a society which, as it becomes more complex, more automated, and more technology oriented, tends to restrict the range of choice available to some of its members while opening the decision field for others. Society's efforts to attack ignorance, poverty, and disease can expand the range of occupational choice, but the size and complexity of the bureaucratic organizations created to pursue those goals may have a countereffect. In its very concern for people, society tends to make more and more provisions for doing things *about* people, *to* people, and *for* people, each of which serves essentially to keep people from doing things for themselves. As a result, we are seeing thousands of today's high school students growing up with such attitudes as: "What's the use?" "So what?" "It doesn't make any difference what I do," "I don't care," and "Somebody else will take care of me." They avoid their own problems of career development by assuming that such problems cannot be solved or that they will be solved by chance or by some outside agent not yet identified.

Because life is becoming more complex does not mean that it must become more chaotic. If in senior high school career education programs we spend part of our time impressing students with the inevitability of change, we must be prepared to spend much more time helping them plan some constructive steps for coping with change. Because things will change does not mean that they do not exist already in some form today. Our best weapons for dealing with the uncertainties of the future are those that equip us to deal with the realities of today. We must spend at least as much time with the microscope of current opportunities as we do with the telescope of long-range social and occupational change. If we can help our students plan ahead from five to eight years beyond the high school, we will have done very well indeed.

Thus the rapidity of occupational and personal change is a factor that must be taken into account in planning and operating career development programs.

## Problems in Informing Students of the World of Paid Employment

The *Dictionary of Occupational Titles* (DOT) contains some 22,000 separate occupations described by more than thirty thousand titles. Study of each of these occupations would be impractical, so the occupational structure must be organized and classified in order to acquaint students with its scope and basic nature. There is no uniform agreement regarding how this should be done. For example, the DOT classification scheme places occupations together basically in terms of similarity of job skills and job duties. Each occupation is assigned a DOT occupational code number, and jobs with similar skills and duties have similar code numbers. In addition, the last three digits of each number add information about the extent to which the occupation is related to people, data, and things. In contrast, Holland's occupational classification scheme (1973, pp. 2-5) is based on a theory of personality types of individuals and an assumption that individuals will tend to choose occupations consonant with their personality types. This helps explain the title of Holland's instrument, *The Self-Directed Search*.

Considerable differences exist between the way occupations are grouped in the DOT and the way they are grouped in

Holland's six-category system. If one studies the "Occupations Finder" published for use with Holland's instrument, it can be seen that for any one of Holland's six categories there exists considerable variation in the first digit of the DOT code for occupations included in that category. There also seem to be considerable differences in the last three DOT digits corresponding to people, data, and things.

The problem is greatly compounded when one considers other occupational classification schemes now in common use. For example, the census system has essentially a sociological basis, differentiating people by the color of their collars as well as by type of industry or employment setting. Roe's classification scheme (1956), with Super's additions (1969), is three dimensional, involving eight fields, six levels, and nine types of enterprise. Here again are two quite different ways of classifying occupations, with great variations in implications for action, depending upon which system is in use.

The USOE system of classifying employment into fifteen occupational clusters appears basically to represent an industrial mode. Thus in any given USOE cluster — e.g., "transportation" — one finds a large number of occupations related to one another by type and level of job skills required, but at the same time the total field of "transportation" includes some persons working in a variety of other occupations, such as typing and computer programming, that one would not think of as belonging exclusively in "transportation." Those responsible for devising USOE's fifteen occupational clusters were apparently intent on presenting a classification scheme that would allow for occupational decisions to be made within any given cluster by persons at any level of ability or educational background.

Each of the common systems for classifying occupations seems particularly valuable from at least one standpoint and relatively lacking in value from other standpoints. The question of which has the most worth must depend largely on the individual whose career development is under consideration and on the particular stage of career development she or he appears to have reached. It would seem unwise to build an entire career development program for a single school or school system based exclusively on any one of these systems. True, one system must be chosen operationally, for purposes of storing and classifying occupational information, but this should not deter the consideration and use of other systems in building other parts of the career education program or in dealing with particular students.

For career development purposes, the critical question regarding the nature of occupations is: What should youth learn about them? Each of the various systems now in use for classifying occupations seems to have arrived at a somewhat different answer. The outline accepted by most persons in the field of career development begins with the name and classification identification of the occupation and includes some information regarding: (a) nature of the work performed, (b) job skills required for performance, (c) entry requirements and the methods for entry, (d) training or educational requirements, (e) working conditions, (f) pay and benefits, (g) prospects for employment opportunity, and (h) opportunities for advancement.

On the surface, such topics present an appropriate and logical basis for occupational decision making. The question to be considered in career development programs is whether these topics are actually the criteria on which today's students make occupational decisions. Do these represent the questions students themselves most want answered? No one would pretend that students know all of the questions they should ask about career decisions. At the same time, most will agree that real questions asked by students of differing ages from differing subcultures should not be ignored.

In any case, it is a mistake to concern ourselves with providing youth with information about occupations until we have first provided them with information about work and with the means to help each one make personal decisions regarding the meaning and meaningfulness of work in his or her life-style.


## Informing Students about Work

Concepts regarding the nature of work must be made clear to youth from economic, sociological, and psychological viewpoints. These perceptions of work as a generic concept can and should be considered independent of perceptions of occupations or jobs which in reality represent vehicles for the accomplishment of work as part of one's total life-style.

From an economic standpoint, work must be pictured as an essential ingredient in any self-sufficient society. That is, the necessity of work for societal survival can be pictured independently of the desirability of work for individuals in that society. The ways in which the economic rewards, benefits, and handicaps associated with specific occupations relate to and influence the total economy should be made clear to all youth. Therefore, economic education is an essential ingredient in a comprehensive career education program. The substantive content of economic education can provide a valuable and positive part of the total array of information given to youth as part of a career development effort.

Work, as a generic concept, must also be understood from a sociological point of view in a total program of career development. It is both unfair and unrealistic to teach youth about the "worth and dignity of all honest work" unless simultaneous attention is given to the varying degrees of worth our society has accorded various occupations and the dynamics by which such differential worth is assigned. It is equally dishonest to talk about the concept of "equality of occupational opportunity" unless simultaneous serious attention is devoted to problems of race and sex stereotyping that are currently acting to prevent full career development for minorities and for girls and women.

The interdependence of various forms of work in terms of the total societal good is a second important sociological concept to be included in a generic view of work. Work as a service to society is an essential part of this concept. An equally important part is the notion that work begets work — that work on the part of one individual helps make work possible for other individuals. A third significant part of this concept is the considerable degree to which the individual worker must depend on others to produce work useful to himself or herself in order that each might in turn produce work useful to others. This aspect can be thought of in terms of the total society, in terms of the microsociety represented by the community in which the person resides, and in terms of the still smaller portion of society represented by the work setting in which the individual currently works. While the principle is the same, it takes on different meanings when viewed from these three perspectives.

From a psychological point of view, the meaning of work to the individual can be considered quite independently of the psychological dynamics involved in the making of specific occupational choices. That is, the way the individual answers the question "Why should I work?" may be quite different from the answer to "What is likely to happen to *me* if I choose to enter *that* occupation?" Both are highly personal questions, and both *must* be answered in the career development component of career education. Many earlier career development programs made basic mistakes by ignoring the first of these two questions and giving only scant attention to the second. The first question is one of work values, while the second is one of occupational values. Both are part of the individual's total personal value system, and thus they are related to each other. This does not mean that they are the same thing.

Work values are in the process of societal change just as the nature of work itself is in flux (see chapter 3). A realistic career development component of career education must recognize and act upon this fact. The work values of many youth differ considerably from those of the current adult society. If we are to be successful in helping youth understand and consider incorporating into their personal value structures some of the work values of the current society, we cannot do so by ignoring or undermining those of the youth culture itself. We must face the fact that some occupations are regarded as dirty, smelly, uncomfortable, lacking in challenge, boring, uninteresting, noncreative, low-paying, hazardous, and supervised by uncompromising, unsympathetic, nonhumanistically oriented individuals. Yet such jobs exist because society needs their products, be they goods or services. Who will choose to do such jobs? Why will they make such choices? Youth are not as unaware of such conditions as many adults seem to assume. They need to consider, however, why a job that is boring to one individual may be challenging to another, why dirt does not disturb one worker as much as it does another, and why some people place much less value on high pay than do others.

The concept of work, as we view it in career education, revolves round the need of all human beings to do, to accomplish, to achieve something. It is the clearest possible way for the individual to discover both *who* he or she is and *why*. A career development program that fails to center its efforts round a humanistic view of work, viewed from the perspective of individual work values, misses both the point and the promise of career education.

## Career Development Practices in Senior High Schools

By the time most students reach the senior high school, they have been well saturated with concepts regarding the complexity of the occupational structure and the rapidity of change now being experienced within that structure. This is not to say that such an emphasis should be abandoned in teaching high school students about the world of work. Rather, it is only to emphasize that relatively more attention should be devoted to the "here and now" aspects of career development.

The senior high school student, as a normal adolescent, can be expected to be suffering both the joy and the pain of what has been referred to as the "wonderful age of absolutism" — the age where one is convinced that somewhere there is one and only one "best" answer to every problem. This is simply a reflection of the natural kind of insecurity adolescents experience as they become more and more aware of the fact that eventually they are going to have to take care of themselves and assume responsibility for their own lives. The school career development program that continues to focus primary emphasis on the "broad picture" and the "inevitability of change" will find many senior high school students "turned off." If students are to graduate in June, each needs to have some plans with respect to what he or she might do in July. This kind of normal adolescent need should be recognized and taken advantage of in the senior high school's career development program. Three major kinds of activities aimed at meeting these here and now needs are discussed in this section.

### Emphasis on General Career Skills

Considerable confusion and controversy have been evident regarding the career education concept that by the time they

leave the secondary school, individual students should be
equipped with either a marketable job skill or the ability to
continue on to post-secondary education. Taken at face value,
at least two things are seriously wrong with this concept. First,
it assumes that a skill which is "normally" salable will in fact
be salable at the time an individual leaves the senior high
school. Second, it assumes that those who plan to continue on
to some form of post-secondary education will actually do so,
and that those who plan not to go on to school will not change
their minds. Both of these assumptions are questionable.

However, if one considers the domain of general career
skills, one could easily contend that every student should be
equipped with such skills prior to leaving the secondary school.
This would include those who plan to continue into some form
of post-secondary education as well as those who do not. The
term "general career skills" means those kinds of skills that
are useful for entry into a wide range of occupations, not those
skills which are job specific to a single occupation or a very
limited set of occupations. Such skills are less subject to sudden
changes in employment opportunities than are job-specific
skills. In addition to career decision-making skills these general
skills include: (a) the basic academic skills, (b) general vocational skills, (c) good work habits, and (d) job-seeking, job-
getting, and job-holding skills.

Above all else, it seems to us that the senior high school
should do all in its power to ensure that each student will be
equipped with the basic academic skills of mathematics, oral
and written communication, and human relations which are
prerequisite to success in most occupations. For those students
who find it difficult or distasteful to acquire such skills in the
regular academic classroom, a variety of other means should
be used, including vocational education classes, work experience, and concurrent work-education programs. These are
among the most basic of adaptability skills expected by nearly
every employer; development of such skills should be given
first priority.

Second, the schools are increasingly expected to take some
responsibility for providing all students with general career
skills applicable across a wide range of occupations. These include such capabilities as reasoning from cause to effect, per-

ceptual skills, tool-handling skills, and typing. Whereas such skills were once considered largely a matter of innate aptitude, they are increasingly being considered as teachable skills that should be provided to all students. This is a second type of adaptability skills for those whose choices are tentative.

Third, beginning in the elementary school and continuing through the senior high school, considerable attention should be devoted to helping students acquire and use good work habits, including good study habits. This requires conscious effort to instill in students such qualities as: (a) coming to work (to school) on time, (b) doing one's best, (c) finishing a task that was begun, (d) cooperating with fellow workers, (e) following directions, and (f) budgeting one's time. Again, we see a format for giving students adaptability skills that will be useful to them no matter what occupations they eventually enter.

Finally, there is an obvious need to teach all students basic skills related to seeking, finding, and holding a job. This includes such things as filling out application forms, searching for job leads, identifying employer expectations, and interviewing for positions. It often also includes such matters as union membership, basic laws and regulations governing work, and some general principles regarding pay, fringe benefits, and social insurance.

These four basic kinds of general career skills will be important to every secondary school student, those contemplating college attendance as well as those who are not. To provide all students with such skills is consistent with all that we know about the expected tentativeness of occupational choice for the high school–age student and the expected number of occupational changes the student will probably experience during adult working life.

In addition to the general career skills needed by all, career skills which are salable in only one or two occupational clusters are sought by a portion of the high school student body. These skills are provided in vocational education programs and work experience. They are discussed further in chapters 8, 9, and 10.

### Accomplishment as a Basis for Understanding

The central importance of the concept of work in the conceptualization of career education holds many implications for career development practices in the senior high school. Perhaps the most obvious is the degree to which the concept of work focuses on accomplishment, on performance. The research literature of guidance has clearly demonstrated that the best prediction of future performance is past performance. Yet in typical student appraisal programs, we often seem to have overlooked the operational significance of this common research finding. For example, we know that the best single predictor of future grades is past grades. Yet many counselors continue to value various so-called scholastic aptitude tests more than they value previous grades as predictive devices. John Holland (1973) has demonstrated that the best predictor of future vocational activities is to *ask* students about their vocational interests, not measure them with interest inventories. This, too, has had little apparent effect on practices.

One of career education's tenets is that to a large degree a person is a product of his or her past accomplishments and experiences. When we ask "Who are you?" the individual tells us primarily about his or her past accomplishments. True, they often begin answering the question by describing their own characteristics — name, age, physical characteristics, interests, and values — and such descriptions help us differentiate one person from another. they serve as "identifiers." But they do not help us greatly in our attempts to understand the person. To only a limited degree do we predict a person's behavior by the way in which we combine data concerning the person's characteristics. We understand another person primarily through his or her behavior. In the past, senior high school career development programs have put an undue emphasis on describing students by their characteristics and too little emphasis on understanding students through their behavioral accomplishments.

In addition, a positive emphasis on accomplishment holds great potential for increasing meaningful student self-understanding. In the past, we have spent too much time *telling* students they are worthwhile and too little time letting students *discover* their own worth through successful accomplishments. Of course, the key word here is "success." The guidance literature is heavily burdened with normative approaches to increasing student self-understanding — with attempting to help students understand themselves through letting them know how they compare with others on some set of norms. The prime approach to self-understanding used in career education is one of helping the student see what he or she has accomplished, not in seeing what each has failed to accomplish. Career education emphasizes success, not failure.

Also, the emphasis on "work" found in career education holds great potential for helping individuals discover a personal meaning and meaningfulness of work in their total life-style. Too often in the past counselors have spoken to students about work only in terms of the world of paid employment. Discussions of the broader life-style implications of occupational decisions have too often failed to consider either the desirability or the necessity many individuals have for work during part of their leisure time. This is particularly tragic for those individuals (and there are many) who find their roles in the world of paid employment so dehumanizing that those activities could not possibly be called something as attractive as "work." Instead, they might more accurately be regarded as "labor," as primarily an involuntary set of activities individuals endure in order to gain enough economic benefits so that they can find some happiness when away from their place of paid jobs.

Those who find themselves in such dehumanizing roles in the world of paid employment have no less human need for accomplishment through work than do other human beings. A discussion of occupational goals devoid of discussion of the meaning and meaningfulness of work in the total life-style of the individual results in many individuals finding both their paid jobs and their total life-style largely lacking in significant personal meaning. In the past, career development programs have put an undue emphasis on work in the world of paid employment, and a relative lack of emphasis on work as a positive part of an individual's leisure time. This is an imbalance that must be corrected if career development is to become an integral component of a comprehensive career education effort.

### An Emphasis on Career Decision Making

The goals of career choice lie in its process, not in its end results. It is not *what* individuals choose that concerns us; rather, the important consideration is that each *chooses*. It is the *reality* of choice rather than the *realism* of choice that is our primary concern. The wisdom of the basis on which individual choices are made is much more germane than any judgments regarding the supposed wisdom of the choices that are made.

This is not merely a play on words. The importance of the concept and the meaning of individual freedom cannot be overemphasized; such freedom is measured by the range of choice available to the individual. Ideally, freedom of choice should be without limitations; however, some personal and institutional restrictions are inevitable. Lowering these barriers and broadening the range of choice have been the long-term goal of American public policy. This goal is as appropriate for the occupational arena as it is for society and for the economy at large. Freedom of occupational choice encompasses not only the freedom of individual students to choose things which are different from those we would choose for them but also the freedom to refuse to choose whatsoever. To insist that the individual make a choice is to deny real freedom. Thus we resist as inappropriate any attempt to force every student to make a career choice before leaving the secondary school. It is even possible that "successful" career guidance may have occurred with the student who makes no career choice.

This is not to argue that anyone — the student, the counselor, the parents, or the school staff — will be pleased with such a result, but only that the studens' freedom is more important than the wishes of those around them. Candor demands that the student be aware of the potential costs as well as the rewards of delayed choice or no choice, but once the consequences are clear, freedom of choice still must include the freedom to choose not to choose. Given bona fide choices and adequate assistance in the decision-making process, we have no doubt that most individuals will choose in ways beneficial both to themselves and to society in general. This belief, like our belief in individual freedom, is philosophically absolute.

Freedom to choose demands, as a prerequisite, that real choices be available. The term "choice," when applied to various alternatives, implies that there is no automatic or universal social ordering of such alternatives from "best" to "worst." Rather, it implies that the ordering of alternatives will be an individual matter — that the best choice for one individual may be the worst choice for another. Further, this view holds that simply to increase the number of choices without simultaneously providing assistance in decision making is to create confusion among those being asked to choose. To provide information regarding choices is not equivalent to providing opportunity for choice itself. Information, properly assimilated, leads to knowledge, and it is the internalization of knowledge in the personal value system of the individual that leads to the wisdom required for good decision making.

Finally, among the considerations of career choice must remain the right to change, for the right to change is held to be as fundamental as the right to choose itself. The concept of irreversibility of career choice applies only to the obvious fact that once a choice is made, certain consequences flow from it. Once an action has occurred, it cannot be wiped from the slate of historical actuality. But this does not preclude change of course or even backtracking. The irreversibility concept speaks not at all of the right of the individual to change choices whenever and wherever it seems appropriate to do so. Unlike good wine, a choice does not necessarily get better with age. In these times of rapid social and occupational change, the concept of a stable and unchanging career choice has an increasingly hollow ring. The best career choices are those which, from their inception, hold the possibility of change as a concomitant to changing times, changing opportunities, changing experience, changing preferences, and changing knowledge.

Career decision making is a process, not an event. For most individuals, the process of career choice begins early in life and may continue with varying degrees of intensity through much of their lifetime. It includes decisions made with respect to both paid and unpaid work. And it must be remembered that the wisdom of any particular decision is related to the temporal necessity for implementing it.

Three important questions must be resolved by the individual in making a career decision. The first of these is: What is important to me? Of course, this is a question of personal work values. The concept of personal work values extends far beyond vocational interest. In addition to interest in a vocation, it includes such variables as the importance of income, security, variety, leisure time, and prestige; the willingness to make educational and other long-term investments; and many other personal reasons why a person might choose one kind of work over another. This is the central beginning point in the making of wise career decisions. It represents a question that can truly be answered only by the individual who asks it.

A second essential question to be answered is: What is possible for me? The question of possibilities is quite different from the question of probabilities, and it should be considered separately in the career decision-making process. The question seeks to establish the boundaries of the alternatives among which the individual is free to choose. The nature of all such alternatives, both educational and vocational, should be considered in light of answers the individual has discovered and is discovering from introspection of a personal work value system. Those attempting to assist individuals in career decision making are charged with responsibility for maximizing the number of such alternatives and clearly specifying differences among them in ways that leave the individual free to decide which alternative to consider further.

The third, and final, question in the career decision-making process is: What is probable for me? This is the traditional "trait and factor prediction" question which was of prime importance under the "matching men and jobs" approach to vocational guidance. While we have now gone far beyond any such oversimplified view of career guidance, the question of probable outcomes for various possible decisions remains an important part of the career decision-making process. As is also true for the other two questions, the prediction question will provide differing meanings for different individuals, even though the data may be the same. Again, we are dealing with value systems. Some persons place a high value on "playing it safe" while others are high risk individuals who may find the risk itself a powerful source of motivation.

The wisdom of career choice decisions is to be found in ways in which the individual is able to gather accurate data pertinent to each of these three questions, ways in which the individual combines such data with his or her own personal value system, and ways in which the individual is able to construct meaningful relationships among answers given to all three questions. When this has been done, we contend that the individual has a basis for making a *reasoned* career decision — and that is the goal.

## Dilemmas of Career Decision Making
## Which Face Youth

All youth are faced with problems of career decision making. While these have been discussed in general terms throughout this chapter, problems facing certain segments of our youth population are unique and sufficiently serious as to deserve special consideration.

### Gifted and Talented Youth

Much of the trouble with the concept "talent" arises from the way we talk about it. Our prime task in considering career guidance for "gifted and talented" youth must be ridding ourselves of certain basic misconceptions regarding talent which have found their way into the general folklore of America.

For example, a misconception exists that somewhere and somehow we should find a simple, standardized paper and pencil test of talent which counselors could add to the other kinds of tests they administer to students. Three things are wrong with that notion. First, the variety of talents is so vast that generalized talent tests are unfeasible as a part of a career guidance program. Second, the proper method of talent determination is behavioral demonstration, not results from a paper and pencil test. Third, the assessment of talent is operationally more a matter of judgment than of measurement; that is, it involves viewing a pattern of things which should be measured for an individual in a clinical, rather than in a statistical, fashion.

Another misconception exists that "talent" and "aptitude" are synonymous terms. The word "talent" refers to the ability to accomplish a given task. It does not mean the potential for learning how to accomplish the task, which we call "aptitude." Nor is it an observation of actual accomplishment of a set of minor tasks, which is "achievement"; and it is not a desire to accomplish a particular task, which may be termed an "interest" or "motivation." Rather, an operational definition of talent must encompass all of these things — aptitude, achievement, interest, plus personality — as they combine to predict the probability that an individual will in fact be able to perform a complex set of tasks at a given level of proficiency. Talent is what employers hope to purchase when they hire an employee — the expectation that this individual will be able to do what the employer needs to have done better than any other person available to fill the vacancy which the employer has. Similarly, talent is what a customer often seeks from an entrepreneur. In short, talent always carries an external referent. It is not something which can be defined simply in terms of qualities that exist within the individual.

A third misconception regarding talent is that each of us has some necessary societal responsibility for using the talents we have — that each should do all she or he is capable of doing. To penalize a student by requiring him or her to use talents in this way is to punish the student for having them, and in a democratic society this is something which surely must be regarded as wrong. In career guidance we are charged with responsibility for helping students discover their talents, helping them decide which ones they will choose to develop further and use, and helping them plan courses of action which would allow them to implement decisions they have made. That is all, and it is quite enough.

A fourth misconception regarding talents is that individuals should necessarily use them in the world of paid employment. While it seems likely that most gifted and talented individuals will probably choose to use such gifts and talents in formulating a more meaningful life-style, there should be no assumption that they will necessarily use them in the course of a job. Individuals may well use such gifts and talents in work performed during their leisure time and may regard the world of paid employment as merely an inconvenience to be endured for purposes of gaining enough money so that they can enjoy the work they do during their leisure time. We see nothing necessarily wrong with persons who make this kind of life-style decision. They have a right to do so if they choose. Indeed, the realities of the employment market may make it impossible for all of the persons who are talented in a particular sphere (e.g., the performing arts) to obtain even part-time employment which uses this talent. In such cases, volunteer or other unpaid work outside paid work hours may provide the only feasible outlet for talent over a period of months or years.

### The Physically and Mentally Handicapped

Approximately 2.5 million handicapped youth will leave our school systems between 1976 and 1980. Of them:

(1) Around 21 percent (525,000) will be either fully employed or enrolled in college.

(2) A million (40 percent) will be underemployed and at the poverty level.

(3) Some 8 percent (two hundred thousand) will be in their home community and idle much of the time.

(4) At least 26 percent (650,000) will be unemployed and on welfare.

(5) At the bottom end of the scale, 3 percent (75,000) will be totally dependent and institutionalized.

These predictions raise grave concerns for career education and for career guidance. To have a million handicapped youth *underemployed* would be a serious matter indeed. The concept of underemployment is one that pictures a person as possessing a greater degree of productive capability than is required by the tasks he or she is routinely asked to perform. Underemployment leads to boredom on the job and is seen by many as a major contributor to the worker alienation said to be prevalent in our society at the present time. To predict that this will be the fate of two out of every five handicapped youth leaving our school system in the next four years can only be regarded as a serious indictment of our education system and of the larger society.

For far too long, we have acted as if the handicapped should be both pleased with and grateful for any kind of work society might provide them. We seem to assume that if someone is handicapped, boredom on a job is impossible. Worse, much of society seems to assume that while most should seek work compatible with their interests and aptitudes, such considerations are less necessary for the handicapped who seek to find employment. If *any* job in the world of paid employment can be found for the handicapped person, society is too often indignant when the handicapped individual is anything less than effusively grateful.

Similarly, we seem to assume that those handicapped people who are not employed in the world of paid employment are not and cannot be working. In the philosophy of career education, this is both false and wrong. We know, for example, the fact that an individual is unemployed and on welfare does not necessarily mean that he or she does not work. Considerable work is being carried out in many welfare homes, the results of which are readily apparent to any who visit such homes. Equally apparent are the consequences when this work is not done. But because those on welfare are not engaged in the world of paid employment, society seems to assume that they are not working. Even more tragic, some seem to assume that people on welfare do not want to work. If the career education concept that humans need to work has validity, it applies to those on welfare as well as to all others.

Each year approximately fifty thousand youth join those who are idle much of the time in their home communities. Indeed, they cannot be written off as not being interested in work or as having no personal need to work. Something should be provided for such persons, whether it be paid or unpaid work. For years, those who work with the handicapped have been promoting the concept of the sheltered workshop for individuals who are unable to compete effectively in the world of paid employment. The prime rationale for the sheltered workshop must surely lie in recognition of the human need for work and accomplishment. If this concept is valid for those in sheltered workshops, it is also valid for those who are not.

Career education seeks to make work possible, meaningful, and satisfying for *all* individuals. To do so for the handicapped demands, first of all, that we regard their right to choose from among the widest possible set of opportunities equally as important as it is for any other individual. Too often, we seem to be satisfied when we have found *something* that a handicapped man or woman can do. We should be dissatisfied until and unless we have explored to the fullest possible extent the total array of work that might be possible for each handicapped person. To stop prior to reaching this point is being less than fair to those who are handicapped and to the larger society.

One further basic principle of the career education movement would seem to have some relevance for the handicapped. This principle holds that we should seek to emphasize the individual's successes, not the failures. In career education, a conscientious attempt is made to emphasize accomplishments — attainments, achievements, *doing*. This can best be carried out by our refusing to emphasize failures and shortcomings. It would seem that this principle holds some positive potential for working with handicapped people who far too often are made well aware of their limitations, and in the process effectively limited in discovering their aptitudes. Sometimes we have been too much concerned about helping the handicapped realize and appreciate how much society is doing *for* them. In so doing, we run the risk of deemphasizing how much they can do for themselves.

### Minority and Low-Income Youth

Special problems exist for minority and low-income persons at every stage in the process of career development. Only brief mention of such problems can be made here.

Career awareness aims at acquainting the individual with a broad view of the nature of the world of work, including both unpaid work and the world of paid employment. For two groups of youths in particular — those from the inner city and those in isolated rural areas — that world cannot be seen in its entirety in their immediate neighborhood or locality. Moreover, that world is not known clearly by many of their teachers and counselors or by their parents. This problem is pervasive in most inner-city and rural elementary schools, but it extends into the high schools which have a low retention rate for these youth.

Career exploration seeks to help individuals consider possible occupational choices based on their interests and aptitudes, and coupled with an understanding of the basic nature of various occupations and their requirements for entry. To be effective, career exploration must be more than a vicarious experience. Reading about work is like reading about sex — it may be stimulating, but it is seldom satisfying! If inner-city minority and low-income youth are to leave their neighborhoods to explore the world of work firsthand, it is vital that they see some men and women in that world who are products of low-income inner-city neighborhoods. If youth cannot visualize occupational opportunities as realistically possible for them, career exploration may be more self-defeating than productive for them. The "role model" is less a problem for rural youth, but the logistics of exploring a broader work world are likely to be more difficult.

Career motivation concerns itself with work values, and centers round helping the individual answer the question: Why should *I* work? If persons from an extremely low-income family are asked whether they place more value on "making money" or on "helping people," it should not be surprising if they choose economic over altruistic values. The danger, of course, is in assuming that the individual has no altruistic work values. If money is the sole motivational base, one has difficulty developing long-term self-sustaining motivational patterns. Unless minority and low-income young people can be given access to a broader motivational base, they cannot be expected to persevere toward full career development.

Career decision making for minority and low-income youth cannot be based simply on increasing self-understanding and understandings of occupational opportunitites. Unless the process is accompanied by understandings of how to take advantage of such opportunities, it is likely to be more frustrating than helpful in its results. Decision making is preceded by indecision. It isn't inordinately serious to remain occupationally undecided if one's father owns a factory or a large successful farm. However, for the minority and low-income youth who have immediate economic needs, occupational indecision is a serious matter indeed. Unless high-quality career decision-making assistance is available, pressures of time will continue to force many such youth to settle for lower levels of occupational aspiration than they should.

Part of career decision making leads to occupational preparation programs. Problems of minority and low-income youth are particularly serious in this area of career development. It is obvious that solutions to long-run problems of minorities are dependent in part on more minority persons assuming community leadership roles. Currently, such roles are being taken largely by college graduates. Thus there is an unqualified necessity for encouraging more minority and low-income youngsters to attend college. If career education goals are to be met, college attendance will be seen as preparation for work, not just to gain a degree. Too many such young men and women seem to be regarding the college degree as an end in itself, rather than as a means to an end.

While we recognize and emphasize the great need for more minority persons to become college graduates, it would be both tragic and unfair to fail to emphasize post-high school occupational preparation programs at less than the baccalaureate level. There can be no freedom if the full range of possible vocational preparation choices is not made available for selection. Career education cannot ignore or play down opportunities in vocational education for minority and low-income people simply because more of them should be going to college. Instead, the widest possible range of educational opportunities must be made freely available for choice on the part of all minority and low-income youth, along with the financial aid necessary for implementing whatever choices they make.

Finally, the continuing problems that minority and low-income youth face in career entry and progression must be recognized. In recent years an increasing amount of attention has been focused on helping these youth solve problems of career entry. Solving problems of career progression and advancement are equally imperative. For those who are likely to be victims of discrimination in hiring and advancement, teaching them that legal advice and assistance are available through antidiscrimination legislation and enforcement is as much a part of career education as any other aspect of labor market realities. If career education does not assume an active role in working with others to solve such problems, it will not have been as beneficial as it has promised to be for minority and low-income youth.

### Career Development Problems for Girls and Women

There is little that has been said above, with respect to minority and low-income persons, that could not be considered applicable to females as they face problems of career development and career decision making in these times. (Chapter 4 addresses this problem in greater detail.)

Occupational sex stereotyping is fully as serious and pervasive a problem in our society today as is racism. The freedom of choice so vital to both career development and career education should obviously apply as much to girls as it does to boys. Unfortunately, this premise to which most would agree in principle is largely overlooked in practice. Occupational sex stereotyping problems will not be solved in our society unless males, as well as females, are brought into the discussion, and unless the problems faced by both groups are recognized. It is significant that one of the leading feminist groups in the country is called the National Organization *for* Women, not the National Organization *of* Women. That organization opposes sex stereotyping for men as well as for women.

Women have been and are being discriminated against at every stage of career development — in career awareness, career exploration, career preparation, career decision making, career entry, and career progression. Career development personnel in the senior high school have an inescapable responsibility for making sure that this problem is recognized and attacked at the earliest elementary school grade level. The problem cannot be solved if it receives its first formal recognition in the senior high school career development program. This involves conscious efforts to examine elementary school textbooks and to campaign vigorously for removal of those having occupational sex bias. It also involves discussion of problems of sex stereotyping with parents of elementary school children.

Perhaps most important, it involves a personal assessment and determination of commitment on the part of every educator at every level of American education. While occupational sex stereotyping cannot be eliminated easily or quickly, it is essential that all educators recognize that we do not have another generation to wait. The role of women in U.S. labor markets has changed in one generation from a situation in which a third of the adult women were working or looking for work to the present situation where nearly half are so engaged. Women now comprise two-fifths of the labor force, and that figure is continuing to rise. Probably as many as 90 percent of women work in paid employment at some time during their lives. If one adds their parenting and homemaking roles and the numerous amount of voluntary activities in which they participate, women have a work role as vital to the society as the role of men, and work plays a part in the lives of women which is as critical as the part it plays for any man. There is no justification for the freedom of career choice to be constricted for women. And it is not enough merely to protest that this is a long-range problem which will require generations to solve.

## *Concluding Remarks*

This chapter has attempted to provide an overview of the career development process as it impinges upon the life of high school–age youth, and of career development programs in the senior high school as part of a comprehensive career education effort. It has intentionally avoided a discussion of the counselor as a key actor in this process; that is a subject for chapter 11. It is more essential here to stress the many kinds of persons who must be involved in this effort. Counselors are key people, but each is not the sole person with career development responsibilities.

We have tried to make clear the key and crucial significance of career development in a comprehensive career education effort. However, it will be vital to keep in mind in studying the remainder of this book that career development, as it is, represents only one of the essential components in career education.

## *References*

Holland, John L. *Making Vocational Choices: A Theory of Careers.* Englewood Cliffs, N.J.: Prentice-Hall, 1973.

Roe, Anne. *The Psychology of Occupations.* New York: John Wiley and Sons. 1956.

Super, Donald E. "Vocational Development Theory: Persons, Positions, and Processes." *The Counseling Psychologist* (1969), vol. 1.

# 3

# Value
# Formation

For the current generation, and perhaps for all generations to follow, career education must provide the answer to a question rarely asked by students in the past: Why work?

Traditionally, work has been both a necessity and a duty. In the past, productivity was of such a nature and at such a level that the full effort of an entire family was required just to maintain subsistence; therefore, anyone capable but who did not work was viewed as a parasite and a threat to others. Only a few individuals could enjoy material abundance without work, and in most cases this was possible only through the exploitation of others as subservient workers or slaves. But as people learned to augment their physical strength through mechanical means, the margin of abundance increased. Thus more and more individuals were freed from the necessity of producing material goods and were pressed into the "production" of various services for others. A higher and higher proportion of the goods and services produced was not essential to life, and a smaller proportion of the population was required to produce abundance. In this evolutionary fashion, the need for every member of society actually to produce — to work — has gradually been reduced. But this process took many years, and it is only in this generation and only in Western Europe, North America, Japan, and perhaps the Soviet Union that the margin of abundance has become sufficient so that the parasitic role of those who do not work is not immediately and painfully felt (although it is still demonstrably real).

During that period when the need for work by all was so imperative, only those whose moral code allowed them to ignore the welfare of their fellow human beings could enjoy the goods and services produced by others without contributing in return. Particularly confronted with a moral imperative to be productive were those whose Judeo-Christian ethic exalted the worth of every human being. Perhaps it was possible for those individuals to avoid the full implications of their philosophy of the infinite worth of the human soul, but some rationalization was required. Of course, as the direct connection between work and service to others became obscured by job specialization and by layers of mechanization, individuals have found it somewhat easier to accept the rewards of production without directly contributing to it.

However, if the meaning of work in the life of the individual has changed and is changing, the role of work still remains an important consideration in distributing status and rewards among the members of society. Indeed, much of that which divides men and nations has its origins in disagreements over the operation of that distributive role of work. Americans generally accept the premise that status and material rewards should accrue to those individuals whose productive contributions are valued most highly by the supply and demand relationships in the marketplace. We assume it to be basic human nature that people are motivated primarily by self-interest. Some, of course, conceive of a society in which the nonmaterial rewards of service are sufficient motivation for its members, and in which the guiding philosophy is "from each according to his ability, to each according to his need," the stated philosophy of many socialist societies.

In truth, we have modified our system considerably from that described by Adam Smith as being at the mercy of a divinely guided invisible hand or that system described by Herbert Spencer as characterized by the survival of the fittest through what he called "social Darwinism." Socialist societies also have found it necessary to modify their philosophic egalitarianism in order to "get the work done." Some of these societies have income inequalities which are as great as those of any private enterprise society. A few have managed to function with relatively small income differentials. In any case, one who would understand the society in which he or she lives must understand the social values underlying such fundamental relations as those between work and consumption.

In Western thought, the work ethic has emerged from a series of such relationships. It has evolved from the mutual obligation of the peasant to work the land while the feudal lord of the manor provided military protection, from the Catholic obligation to accept one's assigned role in society, and from the Protestant ethic of demonstrating by one's accumulation of wealth a position among the elect of God. In all of these traditions existed the conviction of "oughtness" — one *ought* to work as a religious duty.

Just as the specialization of modern industrial society has weakened the visible link between work and production, so too has the secularization of modern life weakened the strength of religious commitment as a factor in the work ethic. Relative abundance has made it less obvious that one who does not produce goods or services survives at the sufferance of those who do, and the movement away from religion has made it less likely that individuals will work from a sense of duty. Of course, these conditions may change, but they are currently operative and they must be dealt with, particularly at the high school level.

The teacher who would participate in career education must be able to participate in dialog with students concerning work values. Students are likely to ask such questions as: If not everyone, then who should work? Why? Why not escape the obligation to work if to do so is possible? What is work? Who are those people who are working now? Why do they work? Why are some paid high salaries for work which seems so pleasurable, while others are paid so little for work which seems like drudgery? How can a worker find satisfaction in work when its contribution is so obviously indirect and intangible?

While most of these questions must be answered by the individual and not by the teacher, we can provide in these pages some assistance to the teacher in helping students arrive at their own value system regarding work.

## *Toward a Work Ethic*

If work is not a religious obligation — and thus has departed from the arena of divine command — then work obligations are ordained of men and can be challenged by men. As is true with many of the moral values in our society, attitudes toward work constantly change. Work is no longer a moral imperative, and it is frequently a matter of individual choice. Each individual develops his or her own values toward work and acts accordingly. Furthermore, society is becoming less and less likely to challenge these individually derived values on ethical grounds. Those who can maintain a high standard of living without working may even tend to be admired. Those who are willing to subsist without requiring assistance from tax-supported programs are tolerated. Those whose age or handicaps require special considerations are generally provided societal support without rancor. However, this permissiveness toward diverse work values does have its limits. The nonhandicapped of working age, who rely upon public assistance, are widely resented as economic parasites, but at the same time, we are unwilling to let them starve. It appears that as a nation we are still somewhere between full adherence to the traditional work ethic and the total permissiveness of a value system which allows true independence.

This indefiniteness increases the obligation of the career educator to guide the student in pursuit of a set of work values which is not only individually derived but is also socially acceptable. Thus while the school may no longer feel comfortable teaching a prescribed set of values, there remains the obligation to assist the student in clarifying values already held, in examining alternative sets of values, in understanding the implications of such values, and in preparing to accept the personal costs which society's reaction to those values may impose.

High school students have a high propensity to differentiate strongly between the "right" values and the "wrong" values. Educators should help students understand that just as individuals differ, so do their value systems. Career education can help students search out and identify their own values with regard to work itself, to work habits, and to work goals. It can help them understand both long- and short-range implications of those values. And it can help them identify the types of career goals which are compatible with their individual value systems.

## Teaching Work Values in the High School

Should schools restrict themselves to teaching theory, fact, and skills, or should they also be concerned with the individual value structures within which students process and respond to information and use skills? The controversy characterized by this question is an old one in education. Typically, schools have tended to stay away from consideration of individual values, because values are personal, because they differ for each individual, and because they are likely to be controversial. Lately there has been growing concern that sets of values harmful to society's long-run interests may be emerging from the values vacuum in education.

For those in career education, the controversy is necessarily resolved in favor of including value development in the education process. The field of career education is *all* learning which contributes to career success, and perhaps even more important than job skills themselves are the values from which occupational and career choices are made, the attitudes with which a worker approaches a job, the compatibility which a worker is able to achieve with employers, customers, and other employees, and the adaptability of the worker toward new ways of doing things. If a student's values are dysfunctional by labor market standards, and if the student desires to enter the labor market, then career education is a waste unless it includes serious consideration of value structures. It must be remembered that even such universally accepted work values as responsibility and punctuality may appear less than self-evident to students. It is important to consider how those values may apply to the workplaces of both the school and employment.

Values do differ. Each person may be convinced that his or her own are "right." But one must differentiate between attempting to convince others of the rightness of one's own values and forcing those values on others. Everyone is entitled to his or her own set of values, so long as exercising those values does not infringe upon the rights of others. However, every student should be given the opportunity to learn how the values each has developed will affect the way in which others evaluate him or her. If the student's values conflict with the values of most employers or customers, then the student should understand that he or she must expect to "pay" for those values in terms of more unemployment or lower income. The career educator has an obligation to help students explore alternative work values and choose those for which they are willing to pay the price.

No student will enter high school without *some* values. Values will have been developed from observation of and inter-action with parents, siblings, other relatives, peer groups, and community institutions. But, fortunately, at the high school age the value system is still in flux, it is still being formed. The role of the high school is to aid students in assessing the values each has already adopted, in assessing whether each of the values held is consistent with the others, in determining their implications, in replacing potentially dysfunctional values with new ones, and in pushing value development to the extent needed for success in a job or in college or in other post-high school preparation for a career. The first step in that process is to aid the student in identifying the set of values with which he or she is currently operating. Those values must be clarified, and their implications must be recognized. In order to accom-plish this, the counselor, the teacher, and the administrator in the high school must understand the role of values in general — and work values in particular — as well as the process of values clarification.

### The Meaning and Clarification of Values

"Man is a creature who not only does things but thinks about what he does. Accordingly, we do things for reasons"

(Rescher, 1972). This statement does not mean that we deliberate over every act and judge it by its consistency with or potential contribution to the things we value. The process is much
more complex. Each of us has developed a certain set of values
out of whatever lifetime of experiences we have behind us. We
rarely make these values explicit, even to ourselves, but they
predetermine many of our actions and decisions. The most
important of our values we call "ideals." Those ideals include
our highest aspirations, and they determine who we are and
what we will become. Few persons ever fully achieve their
ideals, but reaching upward toward them stretches us farther
than we would have reached without the ideals. Thus ideals
act as goals.

On a less exalted level, the value system we adopt determines whether and to whom we are courteous or discourteous,
kind or cruel, unselfish or selfish, diligent or lazy. To some
extent these everyday values are reflections of our ideals, but
the everyday values guide our actions whether they reflect
goal-oriented ideals or short-term expediencies.

The term "values" encompasses that set of beliefs which
guides and justifies the actions of individuals. Our values,
whether explicit or implicit, predispose us to prefer one choice
over another, whether in moral judgments, personal relationships, occupations, consumption decisions, or any other area
of life. Values are not needs, but they predispose us to recognize
a certain hierarchy or priority of need. Values are not necessarily goals — except in the long-term sense — but they do
provide the criteria upon which goals are chosen. Values are
more than beliefs, because values involve a commitment to act,
whereas belief can remain passive. Similarly, values are not
attitudes, but they provide the predisposition toward attitudes.
Values are also not interests. Interests emerge from values and
relate to the ways values goals may be achieved.

Most of the time, we attempt to make our actions correspond to our values. If we don't succeed, we must then either
change our values or suffer from guilt feelings. Of course, the
person who consistently espouses one set of values but acts
according to another is regarded as a hypocrite. And unless
individuals have clarified their own values by explicating the
implicit, then hypocrisy may be an unintended result, and each

individual may find himself or herself confused or dissatisfied. We are well aware that we cannot understand others unless we know something about their values; it is just as true that we cannot understand ourselves unless we know enough about our own values to be able to talk about them. To "know thyself" has been an admonition of wise men throughout the ages; it should be no less an objective for all students in all schools.

The process of clarifying values begins by asking questions and seeking answers to them, answers based on experience as well as on desire. What do I want to achieve or become? What type of personality is best for me? Do I want people to respect me for kindness or toughness? What sort of world would I like to live in, and what am I prepared to do to make it that way?

The questions asked in the process of clarifying values are not questions which can be asked but once and then forgotten. They should be asked periodically as one goes through life. Students in high school should learn that values change as they go through life's experiences. If one is concerned with self-development, she or he should recognize those changing values, examine their implications, and be sure they lead in the direction the individual wants to go. This implies that there are values within values, and this too is an important concept that should be learned early. Values shift constantly within each person's highly complex value structure. They change in their order of priority, and they change in their relationships to one another. For example, marriage and family may not be high priority values for high school students. Those values may be subordinate to education or travel or just "having fun." However, as marriage and family increase in priority, the attendant responsibilities may necessarily reduce the priority of education, travel, and "fun." High school students have a difficult time understanding that their values may change over time, but if they begin to examine their own values early and continue to examine them periodically through the school years, they will be better prepared to accept the inevitability of change.

We are concerned here specifically with values related to work. Of course, some values affect us so strongly that they tend to predetermine our actions in all aspects of our lives, including work. But there is a particular subset of values within each individual's value system which we might classify as work values. They comprise only one subset of values, but they are an important subset.

Once again, students must ask themselves the questions which are most likely to reveal their own value systems: Given a choice, shall I work or be idle? Shall I seek a job now or be dependent upon my family during my school years? If I do not need money, shall I perform volunteer work of value to the community? What about my work at school? Shall I work diligently or just slip by with minimum effort? How will that affect future performance? What kind of work do I prefer? Do I prefer to work alone or with others? Do I prefer to work with people, with data, or with things? Do I prefer to lead or be led? Am I concerned with making money, with helping others, or both? Which is more important to me, independence or security? What kind of life-style do I prefer? Where do I want to spend my life?

These are but a few of the critical work value questions which are vital for the high school student as each considers key career decisions. The specific answers to the questions are not so important as the fact that the questions are fully considered and some answers are sought.

Research has shown that work values emerge early in life as the individual observes the actions and feels the attitudes of parents, relatives, and close acquaintances. These values will differ from individual to individual, depending upon socio-economic background, geographic location, and similar factors. For instance, children whose parents are employed in low-skill occupations may place a higher premium on job security than children whose parents are in professional or managerial occupations. The latter may be more concerned with intrinsic rewards from work. Children raised in rural areas will likely have a different attitude toward physical work from those raised in urban settings. Herr (1974) describes the importance of these early value images:

> When students use terms such as trying to find "meaning in life," "something worthwhile," or "their thing," they are essentially describing a search for a system of values that can be incorporated into their view of life or their self-concept. When students accept values, it is assumed

that they have developed a set of criteria by which to guide
behavior with purpose and consistency. This does not mean
that their values are frozen, without the possibility of
change. Obviously, values can change over time. After
coming to terms with a consistent value system, however,
the individual is likely to remain in equilibrium as experience and new value possibilities refine and reshape the
value system.

Parodoxically, the greater the agreement on values and
the fewer the value issues in the society, the easier it is for
schools to teach values — and the less that teaching is needed.
It is during times of change, when familiar values are being
challenged, that students have the greatest need to examine
and clarify their own values. That is exactly when value issues
become most troublesome in the schools. It is easy to teach
values when there is general consensus throughout society
about which values are most important; it is much more difficult to deal with a wide range of individual values, all of which
have some validity, even though they may be controversial in
some circles.

The present time appears to be one of those historical
periods when values which have been widely accepted in the
past are being challenged. Values formerly regarded as social
norms are being questioned. Indeed, few institutions and few
ethical values are not being subjected to question these days.
Usually such periods occur when the gap between the ideal
values of the culture and the actual values displayed in daily
behavior becomes too wide to accept. For example, the values
of equality and altruism are sure to be challenged when personal ambition and acquisitiveness appear to be the reality,
and when the ideal of the sanctity of human life is contradicted
by the continuing development of sophisticated weapons of
mass destruction. Also, when values are too shallowly based,
they are vulnerable. For instance, the arguments against pre-
marital sex based on threat of pregnancy or venereal disease
were not adequate for a time when it was thought medical
technology had substantially reduced both dangers. Other
values simply outlive their usefulness; frugality may not be a
meaningful value in an economy based on mass consumption,

and prohibitions of charging interest for money lent could not survive in an economy which required borrowing.

The relationship between society's values and the values of the individual is an interesting one. In a free society — and even in many restrictive societies — the values of society are the sum of individual values. But individual values are shaped by the values of the society within which they develop. It is a circular relationship (Herr, 1974):

> Personal values are not independent of the values of society at large. But neither is the individual an automation accepting all possible values unequivocably. Societal values represent familiar anchor points, benchmarks of stability, around which members of society can rally and from which they can draw personal perspectives. When societal value systems are in transition, or when they are unclear, it is likely that personal values will also lack definition.

At the same time, societal values which are challenged by or become unacceptable to too many individuals must give way or be modified to incorporate new or changing values.

Those whose values clash too seriously with society's norms, or who are repelled by the values generally held within the society, may attempt to rebel against the society and change it by violence. This may occur whether or not the rebellious group has explicit values of its own with which to replace the traditional values. Another alternative is for the dissident individuals to reject or "opt out" of the society. However, there is a limit to the amount of dissent any society, including our own, can tolerate. When that limit is reached, the society must either change its norms to accommodate the divergent values, or it must resort to totalitarian methods to force compliance. These complex relationships are the proper concern of sociological and psychological studies. They are mentioned here only as a caution against approaching the study of values in a simplistic fashion. Values are in constant flux, both within the individual and between the individual and society. Educators must always allow adequate room for the development of highly individualized value systems.

Nevertheless, the absence of explicit values in an individual's life leaves that person without criteria to choose among life's opportunities. Behavior becomes unpredictable because there is no pattern to impose order on experience. Excessive instability of this nature leads to alienation, because these individuals feel powerless before the unpredictable forces which surround them. Actually, it is the individual in these cases who is unpredictable, not the forces of society.

The educator's answer to this complex situation is not to advocate a particular set of values, but to design approaches which will assist the student to identify and understand each one's own values. This is usually called "values clarification," and it has assumed a position in the curriculums of many modern schools. It is designed to help students make explicit their own values and examine them, as well as the values of the society around them. It encourages students to visualize the implications of the values they hold, and to do the same with other alternatives. It allows each student the opportunity to select from among many values those which most nearly reflect the type of individual they might want to be, and to understand how the values of society might be changed.

This approach still provides considerable leeway for students to select values which may not be in accord with those of their teachers. It accepts the reality that young persons, like adults, will not always act consistently with their espoused values. It is aware that students may be no happier as a result of values clarification, and they may not be better citizens. But those educators who have worked with values-clarification programs are confident that students benefit from such programs, that they will be more likely to respond to decision situations in a more reasoned manner, and that they will better understand themselves and their relation to the society around them. In a broader sense, such educators are confident that this approach to values will ultimately infuse society with greater rationality and will lead in the direction of the general welfare.

## Building a Program for Values Clarification

The explicit self-identification and clarification of the value structure within which each individual operates is vital not only to the career educator but to every teacher and administrator who cares about the student's self-discovery and decision-making ability. But that which is everybody's business is, in reality, nobody's business. The creation of a high school course explicitly concerned with values clarification is unlikely. However, teachers are increasingly encouraged to explore values with all students as those values relate to the subject matter of the course. To do so requires not only an instrument or format for values clarification but also teachers who have explored and clarified their own values. Thus in-service and preservice teacher training efforts should include activities to aid teachers in clarifying their own values. Since the values of teachers, students, and the community may differ widely, teachers will want to construct their own values-clarification exercises or at least select those most appropriate for their setting.

In most instances, values-clarification programs have tended to neglect work values. This is a regrettable oversight, since one's career is so integrally involved in one's life-style. Career education should begin with the exploration of broader values and then narrow to the discovery of values which are more job related.

The goal of values clarification is just that — clarification. It is not to moralize over the values of others. Participants will not "open up" or explore their goals if they are subjected to censure for them. This does not imply that the clarification of values and their origins should not include following those values through to their logical implications for self and society, or that clarification should not lead to reexamination and sometimes rejection of those values which exhibit antisocial consequences.

The process of selecting values — valuing — has been described by one author as a seven-step process which can be divided into three stages: choosing, prizing, and acting (Simon et al., 1972):

*Choosing*

1. Choosing freely — Values must be *freely* selected if they are to be really valued by the individual.

2. Choosing from among alternatives — Only when a choice is possible, when there is more than one alternative from which to choose, can a value result.

3.  Choosing after thoughtful consideration of the con-
    sequences of each alternative — Impulsive or thought-
    less choices do not lead to values; only when the con-
    sequences of each of the alternatives are clearly under-
    stood can one make intelligent choices.

*Prizing*

4.  Prizing and cherishing — Values are prized, respected
    and held dear; they come from choices we are glad to
    make.

5.  Affirming — When we have chosen something freely
    after consideration of the alternatives, and when we
    are proud of our choice, we are likely to affirm that
    choice when asked about it.

*Acting*

6.  Acting upon choices — Where wè have a value, we are
    likely to budget time and energy in ways that nourish
    this value.

7.  Repeating — Values tend to have a persistency; they
    tend to make a pattern in life.

If values are developed in this way, then a similar pattern
should be useful for values clarification. Again, according to
Simon *et al.*:

> In general, the purposes of value clarification are
> to sensitize people to value issues, to give them experiences
> in thinking critically about such issues, to give them
> opportunities to share perceptions with others and learn
> cooperative problem-solving skills and to help them learn
> to apply the valuing processes in their own lives.

Those individuals who are able to clarify their values on
a continuing basis are not only likely to be more successful in
their working careers, they will be better citizens, those who
know what type of society they want and what they are for and
against. They are likely to be less susceptible to demagogy and
more responsible in social action. They are likely to be better
family members, recognizing not only their own values and
goals but those of their fellow family members.

A considerable body of literature has already accumulated regarding the values-clarification process and its position

in the school curriculum. The book by Simon *et al.* is particularly helpful. It supplies literally hundreds of values-clarification exercises for classroom use.

## Values-Clarification Exercises

We are concerned here with work-related values. The literature contains a few exercises which are related to work, but its most important application in this regard is to provide models for building additional values clarification exercises in the field of career education. We suggest only a few examples.

### Exercise 1 – Twenty Things You Love to Do

*Purpose:* This exercise helps the student answer the question: Am I really getting what I want out of life? At the same time, it also helps the individual recognize what meaning current choices of activities may have for long-range life goals and the costs involved in working for those goals.

*Procedure:* Have students list the numbers 1 through 20 down the center of a sheet of paper. (The teacher also follows the procedure.) Then ask students to list the twenty things they most enjoy doing to the right of the numbers. These may be big things (very important, time consuming, and so on) or small things (seemingly insignificant or unimportant). The teacher may mention some of his or her own items as illustrations. It should also be pointed out that it is acceptable to have more or less than twenty items.

When most students have finished their lists, the items can be coded to the left of the numbers according to the following code:

(1) Place the letters "LT" beside those activities which have *long-term* interest; i.e., those activities which the individual will want to continue doing well into adulthood.

(2) Rank the five most important items from 1 to 5, placing the figure "1" beside the most preferred activity, "2" beside the next most preferred activity, and so on through "5."

(3) Place either "PL" or "WK" beside each listed activity to indicate which items the individual thinks of as primarily *play* (PL) or recreation and which are primarily *work* (WK) activities.

(4) Place either "R" or "I" beside each item to indicate those

activities which are performed *regularly, routinely,* or *repetitively* (R) and those which occur *irregularly, infrequently,* or with considerable *variability* and change (I).

(5) Place "S" or "O" beside each item to indicate whether it is essentially directed, initiated, or controlled by *self* (S) or *others* (O).

After the coding has been done, patterns and their significance may be identified and discussed, particularly from a career-choice point of view. For example, if some students list as highly preferred activities those which are costly, play oriented, and marked by the absence of routine and regularity, the question might be asked as to how those individuals will support such activities over a long-range period of time.

Other issues which may emerge include:

☐ *Compartmentalization of work and leisure activities:* For the individual who consistently places a high value on self-directed activity which is essentially recreational in nature (i.e., non-income producing or not performed in a workplace or for an employer or customer under constraints of regularized time periods and repetitive, controlled behaviors), discussion might lead to consideration of how work can be used as a means to an end or as a concession toward providing the means of supporting the leisure activity. Perhaps it would be possible to keep one's investment in or submission to obligatory activity within such limits as would allow maximum opportunity for the most highly preferred recreational activities.

☐ *Integration of work and leisure activity:* An obvious alternative to compartmentalization as a way of managing conflicts between work and leisure values is to integrate what might normally be thought of as two distinct and competing types of activity. Thus those who place value on self-directed activity and limited routine may elect to be self-employed as entrepreneurs, provided they can tolerate the prospects of the risks involved. This in turn can lead to consideration of the extent to which an entrepreneur is free to direct his or her own activity and to avoid routine.

In such discussions, it might be discovered that many who reject the standard "work ethic" do so because of the highly stereotyped way in which they have learned to think of it. One of the benefits of values-clarification exercises might be the opening up of new ways of thinking about how one might use imagination and ingenuity to reconcile what otherwise may seem to be irreconcilable value conflicts within oneself or between the individual and the expectations of the social environment.

☐ *Prioritizing and sequencing:* Another way to handle conflicts between work and leisure values is to get some help in ordering them. In stable and relatively simple societies of the past, such values organization was implicit in the total social structure, and its occurrence in the individual could almost be taken for granted. In those days, the young submitted to the performance of routine, menial tasks which were relatively unrewarding. The prerogatives of increased leisure time in which to change direction and control one's own activities and income were assumed to be concomitants of increased age and status. While not everyone could be absolutely assured of such rewards, these were nevertheless potentially available through reasonable adherence to and conformity with "the system." Today, the situation is hardly so neat and clean. Some help is needed in the process of personal planning for the identification and realization of life goals. As part of this process, the ability to order one's values seems crucial, in terms of both time and instrumentality. That is, one can learn to defer the realization of some values or goals until a later time, while at the same time recognizing that some goals attained now in deference to others may be instrumental in the later achievement of those deferred goals. Such ordering of values is inherent in planning and decision making associated with most of the career development processes.

## Exercise 2 — Values Voting

*Purpose:* This exercise provides a "quick and dirty" method for introducing values issues into a classroom study unit or discussion and for eliciting individual and group responses. It also provides some indication of where everyone "stands," and it offers opportunities for the individual to practice making public declarations.

*Procedure:* The teacher or a class member announces the "issues" for voting from a prepared list. As each item is announced, the class votes, nonverbally, by raising hands to indicate agreement and by pointing thumbs down to indicate disagreement. Uncertainty or neutrality may be shown by folded arms. The strength of opinion can be indicated by vigorous waving of hands or by the pumping up and down of the "thumbs down" sign. The exercise can occur periodically, using different lists. The lists should not always be prepared by the teacher; student input should be encouraged.

The following suggested list covers some work and career attitudes. It is not exhaustive, by any means.

(1) Without a college degree you "just don't get no respect."

(2) Anyone with enough brains to do it should figure out some way to make a living that doesn't involve punching a time clock.

(3) Just about *anyone* can learn a craft or trade such as plumbing or carpet laying or cement finishing.

(4) I would be embarrassed ten to fifteen years from now to have to tell those who are currently my best friends that I still make a living with my hands.

(5) Workers and wage earners would be victimized by employers if it weren't for labor unions.

(6) Labor unions just encourage laziness, waste, and the attitude that you ought to get away with anything you can on the job.

(7) Life isn't worth living if the work you are doing is boring.

(8) Someone must do the hard, dirty, or boring work in our society, but it sure isn't going to be me!

(9) If a person thinks about it and really tries to do his or her best, that person can get satisfaction even from a job that nobody else wants.

(10) It doesn't really matter how hard you try. If the boss doesn't take a liking to you, you'll get stuck with the dirty work forever.

(11) Once you get in bad with someone on the job, there's nothing you can do to change that opinion of you, and you might as well leave.

(12) The only way you can be happy in your job is if you find one that fits your individual interests and abilities.

(13) If you try too hard to turn out good work rapidly, they'll just keep expecting more and more from you.

### Exercise 3 — Rank Order

*Purpose:* This exercise provides students an opportunity to choose from among alternative courses of action or conditions. It allows them to work out the value conflicts that may often be involved.

*Procedure:* The teacher presents a question to the class orally. Three or four alternative choices are written on the chalkboard, and students are asked to rank their first, second, third, and fourth choices. Discussion of the choices then follows, with the teacher asking five or six students to tell how they ranked the responses and why. Other comments or questions are encouraged. The procedure may be repeated as often as one deems necessary so that new insights can be revealed.

Following are a few sample questions and alternative choices:

(1) What kind of job would you rather have?

    (a) Where you know what's expected of you.

    (b) Where you have to figure out what to do or how to do it.

    (c) Where no one cares what you do.

    (d) Where only you are affected if you don't do well.

(2) If you could determine how much you got paid and there were no educational or training requirements involved, what would you rather be?

    (a) A bus or truck driver.

    (b) A medical doctor.

    (c) A gardener.

    (d) A ski instructor.

(3) Which would it be most important for you to be?

    (a) Rich.

    (b) Famous.

    (c) Powerful.

    (d) Helpful.

(4) If you had your choice of employers or supervisors in your first job, which type would you pick?

    (a) Someone who is considerate and easy-going.

    (b) Someone who won't tolerate any "goofing off."

    (c) Someone who shows you how to get the job done.

(5) What do you think would be the best reason for rewarding you with a promotion?

(a) Putting in more time than is required.

(b) Outproducing everyone in your group.

(c) Suggesting a highly successful innovation.

(d) Starting a highly successful employee morale program.

(6) What do you think would be the most justifiable reason for getting fired?

(a) Refusing to follow an order that you think is stupid.

(b) Refusing to follow an order that you think will result in harm to yourself or others.

(c) Leading a protest against unfair hiring and promotion practices.

(d) Being consistently late for work.

(7) What is the best way to get a job?

(a) Get your folks to call their friends for you.

(b) Answer the want ads.

(c) Go to the state employment service.

(d) Go to a private employment agency.

(8) When you get information about a job opportunity, what is best to do?

(a) Go to the firm immediately.

(b) Call on the telephone and make an appointment.

(c) Get one of your parents to call and make an appointment.

(d) Write a letter telling about your qualifications and asking for an appointment.

(9) If your foreman or supervisor gets "ticked off" at you for sloppy work, which should you do?

(a) Just be quiet and take it.

(b) Explain that you had something else on your mind.

(c) Promise not to let it happen again.

(d) Explain that you aren't really any worse than anyone else.

(10) In relationship to your father's or mother's career, which pattern should your own career follow?

(a) It ought to be at least as prestigious.

(b) It ought to be in an entirely different field.

(c) It shouldn't matter at all.


Exercises of this type are useful as an aid to students in clarifying and making explicit their internalized values. However, such exercises do not measure the intensity of those values; nor do they indicate ranking of those values under all possible conditions. Yet both intensity and ranking of values are important because most choices involve conflicts. We may desire many things, but eventually our desires involve conflicts; eventually these desires become excessive and we cannot have everything we want. We must make choices. And insofar as values predetermine our choices, it is the hierarchy and the intensity of these values that is important. For example, in occupational choice, salary may be the number-one consideration until a certain level is reached; then security or prestige or some other factor may slip into first place. Since these considerations are so significant, test instruments which examine either the strength of values or their relative intensity, or both, can be useful in values-clarification programs.

An example of one such test instrument is the Occupational Values Inventory developed by Impelletteri and Kapes (1971) at Pennsylvania State University. The test instrument is based upon empirical work which suggests the following as the most important values areas related to occupational choice:

(1) Interest and satisfaction

(2) Advancement

(3) Salary

(4) Prestige

(5) Personal goals

(6) Preparation and ability

(7) Security

The Occupational Values Inventory tests the relative importance of values by requiring participants to establish rank among groups of three values which are related both within and across their areas. The instrument may be deficient in that its authors chose to leave out "altruism" as an area of consideration, and there is reason to think that the desire to be of service is a value of rising interest among young persons in recent years. However, the Occupational Values Inventory is an example of a useful approach to values ranking. Participants are asked to examine 35 groups of three value statements each, and to indicate the value which they regard as "most important" and "least important." The following are samples from the inventory. The guiding statement concerns reasons for choosing a job.

(1) I can lose myself in this kind of work.
There is a good possibility of elevation to top jobs.
I can make a lot of money in this work.

(2) This work is what I've planned for.
I have the educational preparation for the job.
There is a labor shortage in this field.

(3) I like the possible earnings from the job.
People in this work are held in high regard.
It has been my lifelong intention to get into this field.

(5) There is an opportunity to do the things I've always wanted to do.
I like working in a job environment that is attractive.
The "size of the paycheck" interests me most.

(6) There is honor associated with the work.
I can be sure of a job even in hard times.
I like the opportunities for advancement.

(8) There is a lack of good people in this field.
I can move upward quickly in this job.
There is personal satisfaction for me in doing this work.

(10) The work is stimulating to me.
I can become financially well-off.
Workers are wanted for this job.

(11) There are higher positions which can be attained later.
The job gives me a chance to be somebody.
I am able to meet the requirements.

(16) People on this job are admired by others.
I am happy doing this work.
The job is within my reach.

(17) The job fits into my plan of life.
There is a short supply of workers for this job.
This career offers openings for better jobs in the future.

(25) It's what I'd like to do as my life's work.
This job can lead to better jobs.
The work gives me a feeling of importance.

(33) It's a job that I can give much attention to.
There is a good beginning salary offered.
I like the high regard which the job carries with it.

(34) There is a necessity for workers in this area.
The work brings with it a lot of prestige.
I enjoy doing this kind of work.

It should be apparent from the nature of the groupings in this interest inventory that the key to its use is in the scoring, since it involves such a complex series of relationships between statements within groups and between groups. Therefore, it requires professional scoring and analysis.


## The Future and Meaning of Work

It would not be proper to conclude a discussion of value formation — particularly as it relates to work values — without providing some background information about the place of work in our society and about the probable future of work. In recent years work itself has come under attack by sociologists, psychologists, and popular writers in a series of articles and books based largely upon supposition and highly selective interviews with workers.

As a result, one of the frequent challenges with which career educators are confronted is: Why emphasize preparation for work when work is becoming of lessened importance in the lives of us all? The motivations behind that question vary. Some foresee a day when machines will have become so productive that few people will need to work. They argue that people should be prepared for leisure rather than for careers. Others argue that the quality of work is deteriorating, that it is at best a necessary evil and not worthy of major emphasis among life's goals. Students should be allowed to make their own decisions regarding these arguments, but their decisions should be based on reality. Consequently, it is worthwhile here to examine briefly what is happening to work from a more scientific point of view.

### The Disappearance of Work?

Given the rhetoric, many persons are surprised to learn that the *proportion* of people who work for pay is rising rather than falling. In 1940, 54.8 percent of all persons in the United States over fourteen years of age were either working or looking for work. By 1947 this had risen to 58.9 percent, and by 1975 some 62 percent of all those over sixteen years of age were members of the labor force; that is, they were either employed or actively searching for a job. It is true that men are experiencing more leisure over a lifetime, but that does not mean fewer of them work. They enter the full-time work force later because, on the average, they remain in school longer. They also retire earlier. Nevertheless, about 95 percent of U.S. men between the ages of 25 and 54 are in the work force, a figure which has not changed appreciably for a generation.

Even the proportion of those in their late teens and early twenties who are either working or looking for work is on the rise in recent years, with many such persons working or seeking part-time work while continuing school. And because he is now healthier and lives longer, the U.S. male now spends an average of six more years in the labor force than he did at the turn of the century. However, because he stays in school longer, retires earlier, and lives longer, he also experiences nearly *twice* as many nonwork years (thirty rather than sixteen) than in 1900. Unfortunately, there is one male group whose labor force participation is falling during their middle years: nonwhite men suffer more than their share of discouragement because of inadequate preparations for work and unequal access to job opportunities.

The experience of women is even more opposite to the popularized view of work. Their labor force participation rate is rising at all ages, doubling since 1940. Before the Second World War, the pattern was for a minority of young women to enter the labor force, remain until marriage, and then, for most of them, to leave the labor force, never to return. After the war a new pattern emerged: women enter the labor force, remain until their first pregnancy, leave the labor force until the last child enters school, and then return to the labor force where they stay until retirement. More recently such women leave the labor force for shorter periods of time because they have fewer children and have more facilities available for child care. The nonwhite woman has a higher labor force participation rate than her white counterpart and is far more likely to be the primary wage earner of her family. Given this rising commitment to work, it seems apparent that, indeed, "work is here to stay, alas" (Levitan, 1974).

If we look at work from another point of view, any reduction in the length of worklife or any increase in the proportion of time spent in leisure has implications for the standard of living for us all. We share in some fashion in the total output of the economy, the gross national product, which can be computed by multiplying the total hours worked by the output per manhour. If leisure time is to be increased, either the average standard of living must fall or productivity — output per manhour — must rise. Over a long period of years, output per manhour in the American economy has risen an average of about 3 percent per year. This has meant either that leisure could increase or that standards of living could rise in some combination not exceeding that 3 percent per year.

In the years before the Second World War, productivity increased persistently, and the American worker chose to take two-thirds of that increased productivity in higher incomes and assigned one-third to a decrease in working hours, reducing the average workweek from sixty hours to forty hours. Since World War II, despite the rhetoric about a leisure society, we have chosen to add about nine-tenths of our rising productivity to our incomes and allocate only about a tenth to reducing working hours. After achieving the forty-hour week, there seemed to be little interest in further shortening of the workweek. The much-discussed four-day workweek is only a different ordering of the standard forty hours, and even that does not appear to be catching on. We seem to want work about as much as we want leisure.

But in keeping with our discussion of value formation, let us consider some alternatives. If the 3 percent average productivity increase continued to prevail, and if we were to choose to allocate it all to leisure, the impact would be spectacular. In twenty years we could all retire at age 38, *or* work a 22-hour workweek, *or* enjoy 25 weeks of vacation each year, *or* retrain 45 percent of the worker force each year, *or* add another 17.5 years to the 12.5 years of schooling the labor force already averages. Alternatively, we could nearly *double* in real terms our current average per capita income of about $5,000 and that would be in real dollars, not inflated ones (Kreps and Spengler, 1966), pp. 128–34. Which alternatives are we likely to select?

It all sounds good, but there is one catch. The issue may not be how to use our rising productivity but how to maintain it. Much of our earlier gains resulted from a shift of the labor force from relatively low-productivity subsistence farming to high-productivity manufacturing, agriculture, transportation, and communication. But recently, each year finds a higher proportion of the labor force engaged in service activities; e.g., teaching, consulting, writing, policing, and healing. Moving from highly mechanical activities to labor-intensive personal services may well reduce the accustomed rate of productivity growth, putting greater pressure on living standards, price levels, and our ability to compete with other nations which are still in a less advanced stage of industrialization. Simultaneous increases of abundance and leisure do not seem to be in the cards. The hard choices of relative scarcity will always have to be made, even in history's wealthiest society.

Another criticism of work has to do with its very nature. The critics say too much of it is demeaning, boring, and dangerous. This criticism may have more substance than other criticisms, but the rhetoric is probably misapplied. The nature of work is not deteriorating, as some charge; it is not improving rapidly enough to accord with some expectations. In the ancient and recent past, employment consisted either of subsistence agriculture or skilled craftsmanship. Either activity encompassed a completeness of the production cycle and considerable autonomy in the workplace. The outgrowth of the industrial revolution was specialization, epitomized at its ultimate in the 2 percent of the labor force who currently work on the assembly line. Through specialization, each individual worker could become more productive. Total output could increase, and the average standard of living could rise. But the worker would no longer have the satisfaction of seeing a total product emerge from individual effort, and the workplace would be governed by a web of rules and discipline. However, that specialization reached a peak for the average industrial worker a generation or two ago. (The white-collar worker, the technician, and the craftsman may have experienced some added specialization in recent years.) As the size of organizations has grown, the web-of-rules phenomenon has been experienced by many to whom it is new — schoolteachers, engineers, typists in clerical pools, and others.

Another, and perhaps more important, factor in worker unrest has been the disappointment in expectations. From at least the GI bill of World War II, there has been the implied promise: Get an education and be a professional; enjoy a high income, status, and independence. But educational attainment has risen more rapidly than skill requirements. Figure 1 shows an across-the-board rise in educational attainment by occupation. Some of these jobs have become more technical, but the Bureau of Labor Statistics estimates that only 15 percent of the rise in education by occupation can be accounted for in that way. When the average member of the labor force has 12.5 years of education (compared to 10.9 years in 1952), the average job must be held by a worker with some post-secondary education, and the large majority of jobs must be held by workers with high school diplomas, with or without change in job content. The immigrant worker, with a rudimentary education, welcomed the security and relatively high pay of the early automobile assembly line, despite its boredom. His grandson, with a high school or college education, may find nothing else that pays so well, yet he may be frustrated because he expected a more challenging career.

Confronted by worker frustration, many alert managements experiment with job enlargement and job enrichment. Rather than break jobs down into smaller and more specialized segments, industrial engineers strive to find ways in which productivity can be maintained while workers are engaging in the manufacture of an entire component, if not a total product. Rather than require the punching of a time clock at prescribed times for a prescribed number of hours, some workers are allowed some discretion in arrival and leaving times so long as they put in the prescribed hours or produce the prescribed output.

Doubtless, many things have been and will be done to improve the quality of work. Fortunately, it is often the dullest and most repetitive of jobs which are the most susceptible to mechanization and automation. More and more humans are

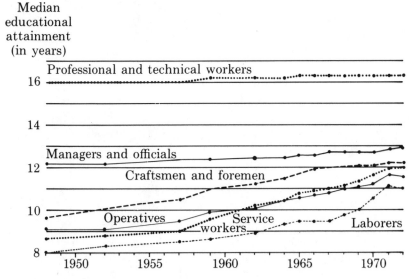

**Source:** U.S. Department of Labor, *Manpower Report to the President, 1973* (Washington, D.C.: U.S. Government Printing Office, 1973), Table B-12.

**Figure 1.** Educational Attainment of Various Types of Workers

released to do the unique and more varied things machines cannot easily be prepared to do. Humane use of human beings does creep closer.

Nevertheless, a large number of repetitive, dull, and unchallenging tasks remains to be done. There are narrow limits to the amount of job enrichment which can be achieved without losing the abundance offered by industrial processes. In guiding the career decision-making process, the career educator must assist the student in recognizing the realities of the workplace, to develop a set of work values consistent with the desired life-style, to choose and prepare for an occupation which meets, insofar as possible, those individual expectations, and to develop sufficient interests beyond the job to find satisfaction in the nonworking hours in order to offset some of the inevitable career frustrations.

## *Toward Meaningful Work*

Career education begins with the assumption that most individuals can find fulfillment through work. Work will not be their only fulfillment, but it can provide one of the sources of satisfaction and a growing sense of self-worth. Work is productive activity undertaken to produce goods and services for the benefit of oneself or others. A career is the total of all work done in a lifetime, and career education encompasses all learnings contributing to that career. Work's rewards include fulfillment of those intrinsic values derived from a sense of accomplishment, social relations with other workers, and other factors arising from the actual performance of the tasks. Those rewards also include extrinsic values emerging from the job but not directly associated with performing the tasks. Among such extrinsic values are pay, fringe benefits, and other such external rewards.

Industrial psychologists have recognized that seeking to satisfy workers with extrinsic rewards alone is impossible. Such rewards motivate and satisfy only temporarily. As soon as they are familiar and customary, they become the base for further demands and expectations. Few jobs are intrinsically so attractive that many workers would be prepared to perform them for the intrinsic rewards alone, even if they did not need money. Some combination of intrinsic and extrinsic rewards is a necessity for career satisfaction and peaceful industrial relations.

The wise career educator will help the student understand the nature and need for both types of rewards. The need to achieve and be recognized for achievement, the satisfaction of taking responsibility, of advancing and growing, the need to find a place in the complex network of status relationships and human interactions in the workplace...all these needs exist in most of us. They are expressed through our value systems. Career education can help students understand how these needs relate to the students' work values and how work itself might become a part of satisfying these needs.

### References

Hales, Loyde W.; and Fenner, Bradford. "Work Values of 5th, 8th, and 11th Grade Students." *Vocational Guidance Quarterly* (March 1972).

Herr, Edwin L. "The Counselor and Values Clarification." *SICA Newsletter* (November-December 1974).

Impelletteri, Joseph T.; and Kapes, Jerome T. *The Measurement of Occupational Values.* VDS Monograph No. 3. Philadelphia: Department of Vocational Education, Pennsylvania State Department of Education. September 1971.

Kreps, Juanita; and Spengler, Joseph. "The Leisure Component of Economic Growth." In *Automation and Economic Progress.* Edited by Howard R. Bowen and Garth L. Mangum. Englewood Cliffs, New Jersey: Prentice-Hall, Inc. 1966.

Levitan, Sar. *Work Is Here to Stay, Alas.* Salt Lake City: Olympus Publishing Company. 1974.

Rescher, Nicholas. "What Is Valuing?" *Spring Forum* (Spring-Summer 1972).

Simon, Sydney B.; *et al. Values Clarification: A Handbook of Practical Strategies for Teachers and Students.* New York: Hart Publishing Co. 1972.

# 4

# Role
# Stereotyping

Never in their history have Americans taken more seriously the basic notion that every human being should have not only an equal right but an equal opportunity to be and do whatever he or she would like. Some would insist on even more than equal opportunity; they demand equal results. The particular cry of youth is for freedom to "do my own thing," but many adults seek the same sort of opportunity. In this regard, we are encouraged by the realization that the reason we hear so many demands for "equal rights" is not because the supply of equal opportunity has diminished but because the demand for true equality has increased. Surely, education shares some of the credit for this increased movement toward the ideals of our society.

With laws against discrimination by race, sex, or age in employment, housing, and other social areas, and with greater public awareness, both *de jure* and *de facto* discrimination has been greatly reduced. But some institutionalized vestiges still remain. One of the most irritating and most effective obstacles to equality, particularly in employment, is the stereotyping which persists in the minds of most individuals. The main difficulty with stereotyping is that it impedes even the recognition that discriminatory obstacles exist. In fact, since many of the victims of stereotyping share the same stereotypes, they themselves do not always recognize that they are being discriminated against. They may blame themselves for the problems they encounter, when in fact they are victims of society's shortcomings. We have long recognized that such stereotyping existed with regard to minority racial groups, and we have made some progress in correcting that problem in most parts of the country. At present, however, it is sex stereotyping that is most pervasive and most under attack.

Since most stereotyping involves work roles, its eradication should be of primary concern to the career educator. The problem of stereotyping emerges in the home from birth and spreads to the neighborhood, the school, and the community as the child grows. The youth entering high school will have been the victim of stereotyping from infancy through the primary and intermediate schools. For most, the high school is the last organized chance to attack occupational stereotyping. This is the point at which crucial decisions are being made and preparations for particular occupations are beginning. Therefore, eradication of stereotyping should be of particular concern to the high school teacher and administrator and to those among them most dedicated to career education.

### The Nature of Stereotyping

Stereotyping involves assigning characteristics to individual persons because of their membership in a group. Some of the most common stereotypes are related to the ability of group members to perform well in an occupation. The origin of most stereotyping is myth. Examples of such myths are beliefs that women are better suited for secretarial duties because of their "natural attention to details," or are superior homemakers because of their "cleanliness," or that jobs requiring physical strength should be set aside for men because they are stronger. Another common stereotype based upon myth concerns blacks, who some consider to be natural athletes but deficient by nature in some other skills.

All educators should be aware of the key role of the school in either perpetuating or diminishing undeserved classifications and stereotyping. Many educators argue that the primary job of the schools is to teach the basic skills. However, educators cannot deny that while doing so, far more than facts are communicated to the students. In addition to the words and actions of the teacher, the curriculum and textbooks put forth specific images of competence and success and what is desirable or undesirable in many aspects of life.

Textbooks and other audiovisual aids begin presenting limited career options early in the student's school life. White men are shown in occupations that vary from the adventuresome animal trainer to the inspiring public official and run the gamut of virtually all conceivable careers. On the other hand, women — especially women of minority groups — are presented in few occupations. Professional women are rarely seen, and when they are pictured, they are usually in a position supportive to a male boss; e.g., woman nurse and man doctor, woman secretary and man executive, woman technician and man scientist. While the major sex stereotypes are more limiting to women than to men, these same stereotypes can harm males who desire occupations in which the majority of workers is female. For example, male nurses, interior decorators, and cosmetologists are often stereotyped as being effeminate.

Illustrations and photographs, particularly in textbooks, which fail to show both women and men, both whites and non-whites as present and past contributors to society, tend to limit the concepts of all students regarding the status of women and minorities. To name just a few examples we should all remember — but more accurately don't remember — from our own school texts, women lawyers, women mathematicians, black judges, female mail carriers, and minority politicians were not highly visible. Textbooks *are* changing, but we must continue to support these changes.

Career education proponents should consider the importance of the "role model" and make an honest attempt to alleviate not only sex discrimination in the curriculum but other forms of discrimination based upon such factors as job status, socioeconomic status, race, religion, and age. For instance, the "role model" of a father who is a laborer rather than a doctor is seldom seen. And our negative values about poor families or minority families are often reinforced by the absence of positive images in the literature or by the absence of any images whatsoever regarding these groups.

Curriculum content is not the only area of concern. Career educators should also give attention to sex-segregated courses and plans of study. The segregation of practical arts classes encourages a sex-based dichotomy in terms of both present and future roles for the students. Perhaps through career education, teachers can become convinced that all individuals need to learn how to function (work) in the home. Basic cooking, homemaking, and repair skills are necessary for both sexes. These tasks should not be assigned to persons of a specific sex, and yet many schools discourage nontraditional courses of study or offer only modified curriculums in homemaking for male students (hamburger frying) and in shop for female students (toy making). Such policies cause the students to view themselves and plan their future careers within an unnecessarily narrow scope.

Vocational training, or the lack of it, greatly affects the job opportunities of the graduates. Automatic tracking of girls into secretarial studies and boys into agricultural or industrial education is not only discriminatory, it also helps perpetuate discrimination in the job market.

Secondary education teachers must be concerned about those activities in school which inadvertently teach sex stereotyping; e.g., the practice of having girls line up on one side of the room and boys on the other, the inclination to designate books, toys, sports, and games as suitable for only males or only females, and the tendency to assign light cleanup tasks to girls and heavy cleanup tasks to boys. Minorities are also sometimes "kept in their place." For example, certain courses considered to be lower level courses are often suggested by teachers, counselors, or other school personnel for minorities, especially those from families with low socioeconomic status.

Reverse stereotyping may also be a problem in some vocational fields. For example, some of the more extreme proponents of women's rights would seem to demean the roles of mother and homemaker. They argue that the tasks involved in such roles are subservient and menial. To the extent that these proponents are successful, they diminish the self-image and limit the valid choices of those who would prefer these roles, with or without accompanying labor market participation. Parenting and homemaking are essentially partnership roles for both men and women. Either may choose them as primary roles, and they should be free to do so without criticism. The important things are to recognize the dignity of any worker who fills an honorable and productive role and to maintain free and unhampered individual choice.

The school cannot be charged with the sole responsibility for either instigating or correcting sexist or racist practices or other forms of discrimination, but there is little question that the school can greatly influence either perpetuation or elimination of these attitudes. The first step is to convince teachers of the necessity for eliminating sexism, racism, and other forms of stereotyping in the public schools at all levels. Each student should be able to draw from the schools in accord with her or his own individuality, irrespective of sex or race or socioeconomic status, the type of education which will fully prepare that person to participate in society and to use the best of each unique ability. The implementation of career education concepts can aid in solving this persistent problem.

## Sex and Race Stereotyping in Early Readers

High school educators must be aware that youth will come to them already damaged by experiences in earlier school levels as well as in the home and community. Research indicates that agents outside the home are important as differential socializers. For example, developmental theory points to the influence of the total environment on the rate and mode of a child's development. Stereotyping begins in the home, is reinforced in the neighborhood and the elementary school, and then must be confronted in secondary education.

Hidden curriculum aspects of classroom interactions contribute to the images children have of themselves and others. Sex, race, religious, and socioeconomic stereotyping pervades every aspect of education. The images presented in basic readers interfere with the development of positive self-concepts on the part of minority groups, women, the handicapped, and others. Such individuals are thus almost inevitably steered toward occupations which are "traditional" for their race or sex or condition, since even their own perceptions of possible goals and accomplishments are limited by what they see and hear in the classroom.

A child's first contact with school is likely to leave a lasting impact. Much of the content of the school day in the first few grades is focused on learning to read and write. whether the child is taught in an open classroom or in a traditional one, at some point the child encounters reading textbooks. The teacher who is aware of stereotyping and aware of career education can help the students overcome the limitations of the textbooks by making a concentrated effort to point out career options either pictured or discussed in the texts and by referring students to other books with more extensive career implications for all types of students. This is a process which should continue throughout the school years, so that when the student reaches high school, she or he is aware of a wide variety of available career options. Certainly, little freedom of choice is available when only one or two alternatives are offered.

When the available literature for children is researched, several striking differentiations of roles by sex and race have been found. Female characters more often show affiliation, nurturance, and harm-avoidance; they are the ones who are nurtured. Males more often provide information and show activity, aggression, achievement, construction, and behavior directed at gaining recognition. Equally as striking as the differences in behavior is the general absence of females in the readers studied. Representatives of racial minority groups are also often left out of the stories or are portrayed in less positive ways than white males. Of special interest to career educators, studies have found few stories for males or females which center round a child who has mastered a skill or a child involved in constructing a project.

A 1971 study recommended by the California State Board of Education (U'Ren, 1971) found 75 percent of the main characters in children's textbooks to be male; less than 20 percent of the story space was devoted to females. While many of the stories with male characters presented no females whatsoever, most of the female-centered stories also included male characters. The researcher did not comment on the variety, or lack of variety, of career options for males and females in the readers she researched. Nor did she report on the inclusion or exclusion of males and females of all races and nationalities in the stories.

In another recent study (Graebner, 1972), the researcher tried to determine whether the role of women in elementary school texts has changed over the last decade. She analyzed 554 stories, using textbooks from two leading publishers of elementary texts during the period from 1961 to 1971. She concluded that almost no change had occurred in the portrayal of the role of women, and that textbooks had not kept pace with a changing society.

In an analysis of a series of social studies books and readers produced by ten publishing houses (DeCrow, 1972), the researcher found no women portrayed as working outside the home except as teachers or nurses. Furthermore, the teachers and nurses were all addressed as "Miss," perhaps implying that no married women work for pay outside the home.

Another study conducted by a group called "Women on Words and Images" (1972) also revealed some startling statistics. This organization studied 134 elementary school readers from fourteen different publishers which were being used in three suburban New Jersey towns. Boys and men were present in the readers in far larger numbers than were girls and women. Only 26 occupations were shown for women, as opposed to 147 different occupations for men. Women were engaged only in the "womanly" occupations of teacher, dressmaker, nurse, governess, and telephone operator. There were no female lawyers, doctors, college professors, or other professionals.

It is worth mentioning once again that stereotyping by sex also has a reverse component in that it implies discrimination against the opposite sex in those occupations illustrated.

Teachers at the secondary level will find that students often enter the high school with stereotypes and biases well developed. A great many of these biases could have been formed as a result of messages received at the elementary school level. The kind of stereotyping we have discussed should be eliminated at the elementary school level as soon as possible, but where it persists, secondary school teachers will have to counteract it. However, they will also likely be confronted with similar stereotyping in their own textbooks.

## Occupational and Sex Stereotyping
## in Secondary Textbooks

Some educators would excuse elementary texts for stereotyping on the grounds that they are primarily fiction. We do not share this opinion. However, few observers can find any excuse for denying reality to the readers of secondary school textbooks. But just as the elementary readers deny the reality of working women, so do high school texts deny to women, minorities, and persons of different nationalities their full historical roles. In a report titled *Sex Bias in the Public Schools* (Trecker, 1971), the researcher notes that women in secondary texts are passive and incapable of sustained organization of work. In her study of such texts, the researcher found no discussion of the struggle by both women and men to gain entrance into higher education, of their efforts to organize or join labor unions, of other battles for working rights, or of the different aspects of the struggle that ended with the suffrage act of 1920.

Stereotypes are found in all kinds of secondary school textbooks: history, social studies, psychology, mathematics, literature, and English, to name a few. We can hope that publishers will eventually expunge stereotypes from most textbooks, and indeed they are attempting to do so. But it is difficult to eliminate such references in literature and English books, since female characters were frequently portrayed as weak and submissive in classic works of literature, and since the value of many of those works may be timeless. One solution to the problem in these cases is for the secondary education teacher to be able to point out stereotypes in both literature and other texts so that students may have a greater understanding of the way in which traditions are perpetuated. Of course, the goal is to portray all members of all groups as complete, mature, and intelligent human beings.

In addition to eliminating stereotype portrayals in books and media, more accurate information must be included in

textbooks — particularly history texts — regarding the contributions of both sexes and all races to society. For example,
too few students of history are aware that Sojourner Truth and
the Grimke sisters were as active in the Abolition Movement as
was William Frederick Douglas. There is also a need for a new
attitude, one that will alleviate some of the biases which now
exist. Carefully planned career education activities can provide
patterns for the treatment of all persons as equals in our society.

The language of textbooks, as well as our everyday language, should be revised to present a balanced view of both
sexes. In the past, words such as "man" and "men" have been
used to represent human achievement. As a result, students
may form mental pictures which exclude females. Several
reference works have been published to help eliminate sexist
language. One author lists the following as alternatives (Willard, 1972):

| *Sexist* | *Better or Nonsexist* |
| --- | --- |
| Man | People; person; human being |
| Manpower | Human energy; human resources; working men and women |
| Chairman | Chairperson |

Since we do not have a sex neutral third person pronoun in
the English language, and since the use of "he/she" is awkward,
we sometimes have difficulty substituting a nonsexist term for
the traditional sexist term. Nevertheless, every attempt should
be made to eliminate sexist terms from school textbooks and
school conversation. Teachers may look to newspapers, magazines, and the newer textbooks for guidance, because most
publishers are now becoming conscious of the problem and are
working to correct misusages within the pages of their
publications.

In the meantime, students and teachers must work with
textbooks and attitudes which still contain the stereotypes of
an unenlightened age. Barbara Sizemore, Superintendent of
Schools for the District of Columbia, noted the extent of the
problem in a workshop on racism and sexism in the schools
when she said: "You can count on one thing in public school
textbooks — they'll be racist, sexist, and elitist."

Pressure from teachers, students, parents, and other interested groups will eventually force a change in the situation. Career education will play a meaningful role in that process, because it can be a major force in eliminating pigeonholed concepts about conventional image participation of stereotyped individuals in occupational fields. It can be a force in helping both students and the society in which they will work understand that every person — regardless of sex, race, or handicap— has the right to freely consider any career without fear of exclusion based solely on some preconceived notion of group proclivity.

## *Curricular Requirements*

One consequence of sex stereotyping is the sex tracking of students in the public schools. It must be eliminated. We hope that this chapter will motivate secondary education teachers to alter their traditional courses and texts, and to grow more sensitive to the existence of stereotypic expectations and behavior in the high school. If the function of career education is to help individual students develop their highest potential, then the high school must cease being an accomplice in imposing predetermined roles upon students, thereby stunting their emotional, intellectual, and physical development.

Sex tracking is at least as engraved in the practices of most schools as sex stereotyping is in the pages of textbooks. Acceptable avenues for the expression of a variety of interests are prescribed differently for males from those of females. Girls are told at an early age that boys are mechanically and scientifically inclined, while girls excel at reading and language. This idea is reinforced by dividing males and females into shop and home economics classes at the junior high school level. Later, vocational education tracks usually vary by sex. Boys acquire a series of shop and mechanical skills, while girls prepare for a life as a mother and wife — sometimes with secretarial skills on the side in case there is a need to supplement a husband's income. Physical education classes are also segregated by sex, for the most part, and they establish different physical expectations for individual performance based on the sex of the individual.

Sex bias in vocational and physical education curriculums can be easily documented in the majority of secondary schools in the United States. Data available from the U.S. Office of Education's Bureau of Adult, Vocational and Technical Education substantially reflect this heavily skewed sorting of students into "sex-appropriate" vocational tracks. The data reveal that 95 percent of all students in vocational agriculture courses are male. (This represents the beginning of a new trend, for in 1970 *no* females were enrolled in agriculture.) The field of health has also recently experienced a shift of minimal magnitude. In 1965, males constituted 4.9 percent of those registered in health courses, as compared to 12.3 percent of the health student population in 1971. Male and female distribution in other categories for which the Bureau supplies data conforms to similar stereotypic patterns (U.S. Office of Education, 1972).

The National Education Association's Educational Research Service reports that no states patently discriminate by sex in the specifications of curricular items considered mandatory or those considered to be the option of local school boards and administrators. It should be noted also that decisions about curriculums and the sexual composition of classes at the secondary level usually become the prerogative of local authorities. Certain vocational programs, such as fashion design or drafting, are often labeled as being appropriate for one sex or the other (Educational Research Service, 1972). Where the courses are not specifically segregated by sex, some counselors may achieve the same result by the counsel they give. Where they do not, parental advice or student choice based on stereotypic reasons may have the same result. This kind of sex discrimination in vocational courses definitely limits potential occupational roles for men as well as for women.

As recognition of the problem increases, some school systems are beginning to design new programs which will no longer channel girls into a year of home economics or other "female-oriented" courses, such as typing and shorthand. These courses — as well as the traditional "male-oriented" courses, such as auto mechanics or carpentry — should be open to both sexes.

An article in *Social Education* (Farquhar and Mohlman, 1973) listed two major problems which have to be overcome in making the transition from girls or boys only courses to courses designed for all young people. First, the course content and teaching materials used in some courses have been oriented toward one sex or the other. Second, the teaching staff of former sex-segregated courses may tend to reinforce traditional sexist patterns by harboring different expectations for male and female students and by representing traditional sex distributions in teaching assignments.

The authors concluded that if the desegregation of practical skills courses is to be successful, the teaching of such skills must be conceived as entirely appropriate for members of either sex. A course specifically designed to touch on practical skills that are needed by everyone in our society, regardless of sex, was proposed by the authors. The course was titled "Life competence," and included six suggested units: (1) foods, (2) fabric shop, (3) basic repairs around the home, (4) money management, (5) personal relations, and (6) care of living things.

While this suggestion has merit, it may lead to another problem — stereotyping by socioeconomic status. If the units are electives, then it seems logical to suppose that students from a low socioeconomic background may select the units in foods and basic repairs around the house, while the children with high socioeconomic status may be expected to select units in money management and personal relations.

### Extracurricular Activities

Sex role and other kinds of stereotypes are also reinforced through the extracurricular activities offered to students in the high school. For example, girls who like sports are referred to as "tomboys." Also, there is a lack of facilities and funding for female-oriented physical education activities. This same kind of stereotyping can hinder the nonathletic boys and can put too much pressure on the black youngster who is assumed to be a natural athlete. There is a need for more intermural sports which will allow all students to participate without the pressures of having to become star athletes. Teachers sometimes expect student clubs and the student council to have male presidents and female secretaries. In most cases, the audiovisual aides are all boys, thus bringing about another "club" exclusively for males. Likewise, girls are usually expected to join the arts and crafts, sewing, cooking, drama, and secretarial clubs. Boys who indicate an interest in participating in such clubs are considered to be somewhat abnormal.

All teachers should check their schools for these and similar kinds of attitudes. There should be an honest effort on the part of all concerned persons to provide a full range of options in sports and other extracurricular activities for males, females, and minorities. Teachers have a responsibility to their students to stress the fact that shorthand and typing skills can be as useful to boys as can woodworking and drafting, and minority students can excel in academic classes and leadership as well as in basketball and football.

In addition to the activities already discussed, teachers can ask themselves some of the following questions:

(1) Are girls or whites expected to excel in verbal areas (i.e., drama and speech clubs), while boys are expected to do well in math and science clubs, and minorities expected to succeed in sports?

(2) Are girls expected to be interested in the family, home, and children, while boys enjoy games and cars?

(3) Does the school have physical education, home economics, and industrial arts clubs which are segregated by sex or race?

(4) Are boys encouraged to play certain instruments in the band or orchestra (e.g., drums or saxophone), while girls are expected to play other kinds of instruments (e.g., flute or violin)?

We hope this section will encourage secondary education teachers to look at their schools and work to eliminate some of the stereotypic attitudes present in the schools. Those teachers who are parents may also find it interesting to examine their expectations for their own children.

### Special Concerns of Minorities

Many minority parents and their organizations fear career education as but another device for stereotyping and tracking, rather than regarding it as a tool to reduce those practices. These parents feel that just as in the past certain students were discouraged by subtle and not so subtle means from preparing for certain professions, today the methods are less crude but the end result may still be the same. They see career educators are reacting against overemphasis on college, and they fear that it is another device to sidetrack their children from the sources of upward social and economic mobility at a time when such children are beginning to "catch up" in educational opportunity.

Obviously, career education *could* be used to supress some segments of the community and, given the diversity of our education system, it will be a wonder if this does not occur in some schools at some time. But the danger is no greater than with other programs, and the benefits of career education can and should be available to everyone.

Numerous programs have been introduced to provide compensatory education to the culturally disadvantaged, but in many cases parents have become suspicious because the programs appear to emphasize deficiencies within the child and the home. Many representatives of minorities and of low socio-economic groups feel that the school itself may be encouraging the deficiencies rather than correcting them. The attitudes and behavior of teachers can be contributing factors to student failure. Therefore, teacher reaction to children from lower socioeconomic backgrounds may well be intertwined with the lack of success by those children. Thus there is need to clarify the relationship between career education and compensatory programs.

Many previous attempts to provide education for children from minority groups were based on the idea of acculturation. The compensatory model rested on the fundamental assumption that minority children needed *more* of what had been provided to children who were already achieving. The model perceived the minority group child as deficient in comparison to the mythical norm. The most striking feature of the model was its failure to acknowledge the validity of any culture other than the dominant culture. The children involved in these compensatory programs were labeled "underprivileged," "culturally deprived," "culturally disadvantaged," or "culturally handicapped." During the middle 1960s, members of minority groups began to point out the message conveyed by such labels — that those who were different were inferior. They also sensed that the compensatory programs rested implicitly on the premise that the melting pot approach was the only approach.

This suspicion can be alleviated if career educators can assure parents that this is *not* just another compensatory program. Instead, it is designed to serve all students. Nor is it based on filling what is seen as a void in the lives of minority children. Instead, it recognizes a need in all students for better awareness of self and of the world of work. Career educators will have to demonstrate to minority communities that career education does not view as valueless any culture or life-style that differs from the norm. Career education can be effective only if the basic concepts and goals serve all of the schools' population and not just a select group.

Minority parents are all too familiar with having their children placed in various programs on the basis of race rather than achievement, and they tend to resent any form of tracking. No one knows better than America's minority groups the harmful effects of tracking in schools, and this is one reason minority group people have expressed fears that career education might become a device to limit, rather than to enhance, horizons by relegating their children to vocationally, rather than academically, oriented schooling.

Much of this concern can be eliminated if minority parents could be more informed and involved in developing and presenting the curriculum for career education. It is up to the career educator to convince these parents that the negative counseling which resulted in the tracking system can be alleviated by the career education movement. They will also have to be assured that career education has no intention of screening their children out of desirable programs by emphasizing only academic accomplishment in school.

Career educators do not intend to devalue a liberal arts education or to stress occupational preparation at the expense of personal and humanistic development. Career education is not an approach designed to track minority students into blue-collar jobs, to deny them the advantage of a college education, or to place undue emphasis on a particular type of work ethic.

Career education is a way of making sure that every student becomes aware of all sorts of career options.

It is essential that minority group parents be made aware of the fundamental concepts of career education — that some parts of all types of education experiences, curriculum instruction, and counseling will be geared to preparation for economic independence and appreciation for the dignity of work. The main thrust of career education is to prepare all students for a successful life of work by increasing their options for occupational choice. These options can be increased by eliminating barriers — real and imagined — to attaining job skills, and by enhancing learning achievement in all subject areas and at all levels of education. Minorities should be made aware of these critical factors and assured that the career education thrust is not designed especially for the socially and economically disadvantaged, but for *all* students.

Failure to recognize the validity of a variety of life-styles may result in increasing the gap between white and minority students. Minorities recognize the fact that their children are sometimes placed in school programs on the basis of race rather than achievement. Researchers have found that tracking programs hold people to the social class levels of their parents, even if ethnic background is held constant.

These difficulties for minority group students must be corrected, and career education can be a significant factor in bringing corrective action if it has the support and understanding of all groups in our society.

### Stereotyping of the Handicapped

Handicapped students suffer less from career stereotyping than from simply being ignored in almost all occupationally oriented treatments in texts, curriculum materials, and tracking.

A 1969 study (Kelly and Simon, pp. 58–64), involving companies which employ handicapped workers, revealed the following conclusions:

(1) When properly placed, the majority of mentally retarded employees performs tasks assigned to them as
efficiently and as rapidly as normal employees.

(2) The use of retarded individuals in repetitive kinds of
jobs will reduce labor costs caused by tardiness, absenteeism, and high turnover.

(3) The fact that mentally retarded workers have a high
degree of job satisfaction on routine jobs, do not actively seek promotions, and are motivated better than
their counterparts also tends to reduce turnover, so
that costs of training, retraining, and personnel procedures of the employment process are reduced.

In spite of these findings, a large percentage of the handicapped
students who somehow manage to enter into the labor force
is severely underemployed and subsists at the poverty level.

Of course, retardation is but one of many handicap conditions with which our school systems must deal. Specialists
in education for the handicapped and special education are
becoming more and more convinced that we must find ways
to place and keep handicapped students in the mainstream of
our educational programs, that we must reduce levels of segregation of those special students to an absolute minimum, and
that we must afford *all* students equal opportunity for
advancement.

These are also worthy — and attainable — goals for career
education. Career education programs should offer the handicapped student educational training that is relevant to the
job market and meaningful to each's career aspirations. Properly planned career education programs can help handicapped
persons reach their fullest potential. The Bureau of Education
for the Handicapped intends that by 1977 all handicapped
students leaving school will have experienced career education.
As a part of this goal, all teachers and all schools can help
individual handicapped students achieve a favorable self-image
and sufficient faith in their own future to motivate the pursuit
of opportunities.

### *What to Do about Stereotyping*
### *in the Classroom*

The existence of stereotyping is not to be blamed solely on the school system. It is a product of many social institutions. But to assume that the schools can do little to change the role stereotypes established by society as a whole is to assume that schools are always to be followers, never leaders, always re-actors, never creators.

Career education programs can and should bear some of the responsibility for: (1) removing barriers from the paths of secondary school students that could possibly limit their potential for learning, (2) improving textbooks that distort reality, (3) presenting role models to expand students' perceptions of their options in educational and occupational settings, (4) liberating the secondary school by eliminating stereotyping, and (5) providing support personnel for secondary education teachers, such as student personnel workers, consultants, and others.

Teachers are in a position to aid in implementing career education programs that could alleviate some of the stereotyping that currently takes place. Following are a few examples of the type of activities which could be planned for the high school.

### *Teacher and Student Activities*

Many opportunities are available in the classroom and in the community to pull down the barriers to opportunity which have been erected by the practice of stereotyping, such as:

(1) Use community resources to help students see men and women of all races, religions, and socioeconomic strata in nontraditional roles. Arrange for classroom visits by a woman attorney or judge or engineer, by a male in the arts, by parents with occupations not requiring college degrees, or by minorities in occupations traditionally considered to be for whites only. Students themselves may be able to make recommendations along these lines.

(2) Schedule field trips as part of the career education

program. It may take some searching, but places can be found where all races and both sexes work together on an equal basis.

(3) Try to develop school contacts with fathers as well as mothers, blacks as well as whites, and parents from all socioeconomic levels.

(4) Examine after-school programs and club activities. Try to include girls in some of the activities that have been considered to be only for boys, and include boys in some of the activities that have been reserved for girls. Consider new activities which could be offered to boys and girls together.

(5) Try to find stories, films, and other learning materials which depict girls operating machinery and constructing things, or featuring mothers employed outside the home as independent working women. Include stories with men participating in household chores and women in outdoor tasks. Also, try to find stories or other materials showing minorities involved in nonstereotypic occupations.

(6) Ask students what they want to do after graduation from high school. Discuss differences between male and female responses, between white and nonwhite responses, between responses of members from various socioeconomic levels, and between responses of students from different religious backgrounds.

(7) Make a bulletin board from magazine or newspaper pictures showing people in nontraditional roles, such as a woman doctor or scientist, a male nurse, a woman driving a tractor, a male airline steward, a female politician, a policewoman, a black judge, an Oriental architect, and so on.

(8) Have students examine the media, such as television, magazines, and newspapers, for stereotypes in articles and advertisements. Have them report on the examples, and encourage class discussion.

(9) With the aid of students and other staff members,

organize an "occupational fair" at which all races, sexes, and nationalities in nontraditional roles can inform students of opportunities in various careers. Discuss the fact that there is dignity in all work and that no presumptions need to be made about which jobs have prestige or which jobs do not, depending upon the amount of education needed.

(10) Develop a suggested outline that can be used by you and other secondary education teachers for evaluating material regarding stereotyping. Use the following questions as guidelines:

(a) What abilities, traits, interests, and activities were assigned on the basis of male or female stereotypes?

(b) What were the evidences of care taken to avoid sexist or racist assumptions and stereotypes in teachers' manuals and other teacher aids?

(c) How frequently do occupational terms ignore the existence of women workers (e.g., business*men*, repair*men*, mail*men*, congress*men*)?

(11) Discuss the topics of sex, race, socioeconomic level, or religious stereotyping in occupations with at least four people in your school. (The sample should include a range of sexes, ages, teachers at different grade levels, and teachers from different subject areas.) Write a summary of the different attitudes you encounter.

(12) Make a list of at least four projects you could introduce to your class which involve men and women, minorities, and other stereotyped groups in traditional as well as nontraditional occupations.

(13) Meet with a group of teachers or with the entire faculty to discuss the issues of sexism, racism, and other forms of stereotyping. Discuss direct actions or curriculum projects that already may have been tried in other schools.

(14) Examine classroom programs and curriculum materials currently used in your school to see if they reinforce sexism, racism, or other kinds of stereotypes.

(15) Consult with the administrators of your local school district concerning hiring and promotion practices for men and women and members of minority groups.

## Educational Proposals

The publication titled *Sexism in Education* (Willard, 1972) lists the following educational activities for various segments in the high school:

(1) History

    (a) Study women's suffrage as a legitimate reform movement, not as an appendage to male-dominated history.

    (b) Add women and members of all races to history texts, e.g., Sojourner Truth.

    (c) Place more emphasis on "domestic" or "cultural" history and less on military and political history.

    (d) Study practices, laws, and institutions that have kept women and minority group members in inferior positions.

(2) Literature

    (a) Investigate literature for evidence of a misogynistic tradition.

    (b) Discuss the characterization of women and men, whites and nonwhites, and persons from a number of religious backgrounds in literary works — do they seem real or stereotyped?

    (c) Add literature written by all races and sexes to reading lists.

    (d) Recommend books which portray all persons as complete, mature, intelligent human beings.

(3) Sex education

    (a) Discuss double-standard moralizing.

    (b) Discuss the present family roles and the division of labor.

(c) Discuss forms of family (or nonfamilial) organization other than the nuclear family.

(d) Discuss marriage, its role in our society, and the student's personal expectations.

(4) Current events

(a) Conduct rational, knowledgeable discussions of the women's movement and the fight for racial equality.

(b) Discuss legal changes that affect women and minority group members.

(c) Discuss how some recent changes can affect both men and women and all races and nationalities.

(5) Sociology

(a) Discuss racism and sexism and its effect on people.

(b) Study sex-role socialization processes.

(c) Discuss women's liberation and its opponents.

(d) Discuss student's own attitudes about "proper" behavior for males and females.

(6) Vocational guidance

(a) Discuss career goals in light of sex-role expectations.

(b) Discuss marriage as a career itself.

(c) Investigate the employment structure for obstacles that keep women and minority group members from functioning fully within it.

(d) Implement fair and impartial college and job counseling.

(e) Eliminate vocational interest and aptitude tests that use separate criteria for males and females or for minorities.

(f) Eliminate restrictions and inhibitions that keep members of one sex or race or religion from enrolling in a course.

(7) Physical education

    (a) Create athletic programs for girls equal to those for boys, plus mixed programs where feasible and desired.

    (b) Provide training in self-defense for women and men, with advice on what to do in case of attacks.

(8) Educational materials

    (a) Use textbooks and other materials that picture all persons in a variety of roles and life-styles.

(9) Educational personnel

    (a) Enroll in in-service courses for all educational personnel that examine sexist and racist attitudes and practices.

    (b) Work to eliminate sexist attitudes, materials, and practices in teacher and counselor training.

    (c) Enroll in human relations programs that are non-sexist and nonracist.

Career education programs, with their focus on the role of work and the workplace where most stereotyping occurs, can do much to alleviate the debilitating effects of stereotyping in our society. Teachers will know when they have succeeded when Richard can speak of his feelings of tenderness without embarrassment and when Lois can reveal her career ambitions without shame or guilt. However, it is important for all teachers to realize that human rights in the classroom must not be isolated to a two-week unit on "Women in History," or to a five-day "Black History Week." The problems of racism, sexism, and other forms of stereotyping must be tackled with changes in attitude and point of view that permeate the entire curriculum and all the extracurricular activities in the high school.

### References

Bureau of Adult, Vocational and Technical Education, U.S. Office of Education. *Trends in Vocational Education.*

Washington, D.C.: Bureau of Adult, Vocational and Technical Education, U.S. Office of Education. 1972.

DeCrow, K. "Look, Jane, Look! See Dick Run and Jump! Admire Him!" In Anderson, S., *Sex Differences and Discrimination in Education*. Worthington, Ohio: Charles A. Jones Co. 1972.

Educational Research Service, National Education Association. *State Graduation Requirements*. Washington, D.C.: Educational Research Service, National Education Association. 1972.

Farquhar, Norma; and Mohlman, Carol. "Life Competence: A Non-sexist Introduction to Practical Arts." *Social Education* (Oct. 1973), vol. 37, no. 6.

Graebner, D. B. "A Decade of Sexism in Readers." *The Reading Teacher* (Oct. 1972), vol. 26.

Kelly, J. M.; and Simon, A. J. "The Mentally Handicapped as Workers." *Personnel* (1969), vol. 46, no. 5.

Trecker, Janice. "Women in U.S. History High School Text Books." In *Report on Sex Bias in the Public Schools*. New York: National Organization for Women. 1971.

U'Ren, M. B. "The Images of Women in Textbooks." In Gornick, U., and Moran, B. K. (eds.), *Women in Sexist Society: Studies in Power to Powerless*. New York: Basic Books. 1971.

Willard, Emma. *Sexism in Education*. Minneapolis, Minn.: Task Force on Education. 1972.

Women on Words and Images. *Dick and Jane as Victims: Sex Stereotyping in Children's Readers*. Princeton, N.J.: Women on Words and Images. 1972.

# 5

# Transition
# to Work

No high school student arrives at graduation day without having had work experience. All have extended experience with the disciplines of schoolwork. Most are familiar with home chores. A great many have held some type of job on a part-time or summer basis. Some have even been self-employed in their own business, engaged in newspaper delivery or similar activities. Those who live on farms or whose parents are small business entrepreneurs have probably worked in the family enterprise.

Nevertheless, for the majority of students the last closing of the high school doors behind them marks the transition from full-time school to full-time work or career. This highly significant event places the student into a new statistical category; he or she is now part of the full-time work force.

As the result of the post-World War II "baby boom," U.S. labor markets were flooded with extraordinary numbers of new entrants during the last half of the 1960s and most of the '70s. On the average, 3.8 million Americans celebrate their eighteenth birthdays during each year of the 1970s. However, that pace will slow substantially during the 1980s as the result of the birthrates which began to level off after 1957 and have been on a low plateau since 1967. Sometime during the two years prior to their eighteenth birthdays, all but a handful of those young people will have left the shelter of the high school; the remainder will do so shortly after their eighteenth birthdays. About 20 percent will drop out of school before receiving a high school diploma. Some 43 percent of all young persons (58 percent of high school graduates) register for some type of post-secondary education or training, although only about one youth out of five will ultimately receive a bachelor's degree beyond the high school. Thus an average of 2.2 million youth each year make a permanent transition from the world of the school to the world of work upon leaving high school. To this number is added those individuals who have previously continued into post-secondary education and are either completing their course of study or dropping out of post-secondary institutions. This includes those who will seek full-time employment, or who will accept unpaid work as a homemaker or volunteer, or who will work in some other way outside the labor market. By any count, then, the total volume of school-to-work transitions currently involves an average of between three million and four million persons each year.

A basic premise of career education is that the education system should not be relieved of responsibility for the career progress of a youth until the feet of that youth are firmly planted on the rungs of a career ladder. Even then, the schools should retain some residual responsibility for assistance when a foot slips or when there is a desire to change ladders. This book need not explore the dimension of that responsibility at the post-secondary level, but we are concerned with how the high school and other institutions of the community can cooperate in aiding the transition which occurs at the point when students exit from school at the secondary level.

### Patterns of Transition

Information about the actual patterns of transition from school to work is limited, but we can profitably summarize what is known about that transition process. For example, studies have shown that the transition is easier for those who graduate than for those who do not graduate from high school. Although this may seem obvious, the exact reasons for it are not entirely clear. All educators have heard the argument that schooling has little relevance to employment performance in occupations other than those in which academic subject matter is an important component of the job content. Nevertheless, unemployment rates and levels of educational attainment show a strong negative correlation, with school dropouts typically suffering twice the unemployment rates of high school graduates. Those with more education not only tend to have lower rates of unemployment, they also tend to be unemployed for shorter periods of time.

Some critics of the schools argue that only because employers are so convinced of education's value will they pay the necessary premium to compensate the worker who stayed longer in school. Such critics maintain that the employer looks to the schools to screen out those persons unwilling to accept classroom discipline as persons also unlikely to be good prospects for discipline and productivity in the workplace. They suggest that those who will make the best workers are simply the types who are willing to endure longer school attendance.

The career educator has a ready answer for this argument: Schoolwork is work too! It has essentially the same job content as white-collar jobs. For most jobs in the modern labor market, education's content — whether from academic, fine arts, or practical arts courses — has some relevance. But what is more often ignored by the critics is that the same values, attitudes, work habits, and human relations skills which account for success in school are also the major criteria for success on many jobs. The schools reward, encourage, and reinforce those who exhibit these attributes. They also should and (where career education is practiced) do both motivate and teach these essential keys to career success.

It is also a fact that skills training, rather than being an alternative to educational attainment, strongly correlates with it. Given that vocational education in high schools occurs primarily during the junior and senior years, those who drop out are likely to miss vocational as well as academic education. Those who graduate from high school are three times as likely to pursue further occupational training beyond high school as are those who drop out of school. Continuing in school, the graduates were also more likely to have obtained vocational guidance and counseling.

That these school-based experiences are enjoyed to a higher degree by graduates than by dropouts is less surprising than the fact that the graduates also tend to gain more work experience during the school years. Despite rising educational attainment, the proportion of youth who work or look for work during their teenage years is persistently rising. To be either employed or looking for work is the definition of labor force participation. Labor force participation rates of teenagers, both male and female, declined persistently through the 1950s and into the early '60's but have trended upward just as persistently since that time. Whereas only 42.7 percent of the sixteen- and seventeen-year-old boys were working or looking for work in 1963, 51 percent were so engaged in 1974. For girls the same age, the comparable figures were 27 percent and 40 percent. The same pattern prevails for eighteen- and nineteen-year-olds but the participation rates are higher.

Participation rates of fourteen- and fifteen-year-old females are also rising, but that is not true of fourteen- and fifteen-year-old males. However, these are average rates at any point in time during a year. Actually, 60 percent of the sixteen- and seventeen-year-olds, and 81 percent of the eighteen- and nineteen-year-olds worked for pay or looked for work at some time during 1974. These figures are significant not only because they illustrate the high proportion of high school students who do work either part time or during the summer, but because studies have shown that those with work experiences prior to leaving school find the ultimate transition from school to work easier. For instance, a Labor Department study showed that three out of ten (30 percent) of those who worked while in high school had jobs waiting for them when they left school, compared to 17 percent of those who had not worked earlier. Graduates were even more successful than the total of school leavers, with 44 percent of those with work experience going directly to jobs, compared with 17 percent of those without work experience (Perrella and Bogan, 1964).

In all, nearly three out of ten students had jobs waiting for them upon leaving school, over half were looking for a job, and only a small proportion of the young men and a quarter of the girls did not seek paid work. Of those who looked for work, 54 percent found their first job within five weeks. An additional 19 percent found employment in less than fourteen weeks, while 13 percent took from fifteen to 27 weeks, and 13 percent had been unsuccessful in finding jobs at the time of the survey. All of this occurred in a year when the average level of unemployment for young and old was 5.7 percent.

Those individuals with some post-secondary education were only slightly more likely than high school graduates to have a job waiting for them when they left school; 22 percent of the high school dropouts, 33 percent of the high school graduates, and 35 percent of those with some college training had jobs waiting for them. However, among those who looked for employment, the more educated found jobs sooner, particularly the college trained; 71 percent of those with college training found employment in less than five weeks, compared to 54 percent of high school graduates and 52 percent of dropouts who found jobs within that period.

The procedures used to find the first full-time job varied. Of those surveyed, 41 percent made direct application to employers, 35 percent received help from friends or relatives, and 14 percent were aided by institutional referrals from schools or employment offices. By education level, little difference was noted in the use of direct application, although the more educated job seekers evidenced a slightly greater initiative in this connection. One important point is that dropouts tend to place greater dependence upon friends and relatives (with the more limited range of choices thus provided), compared to high school graduates and those with some college training; while the latter two groups rely more on institutional sources. Some 19 percent of high school graduates and 25 percent of the college trained sought institutional help in job seeking, compared to only 6 percent of dropouts who found their first job through these sources.

## Pathologies in Transition

The stark fact of school-to-work transition is that the unemployment level of youth is persistently triple that of adults. Since the unemployment rate for blacks is persistently double that of whites, black youth suffer six times the average unemployment rate. Data for other minority youth are less available, but the ratios are similar. And unemployment statistics measure only those actively seeking work. On the average during 1974, some 4.6 million fourteen- to 24-year-olds at any one time were not in school, or working, or seeking work. (This does not count those out of school during summers.) We don't know whether this was because these individuals were not interested in working, did not know how to seek work, or had found the search unrewarding. For the young women in the group, homemaking may be an explanation, but there is no obvious explanation why seven hundred thousand school-age young men (fourteen to eighteen years of age) would not be in school, at work, or seeking work.

The extraordinary high birthrate extending from the end of the Second World War into the early 1960s is a major factor in the youth problems which have prevailed until now. For instance, 3.5 million youth turned eighteen years of age in 1965, compared to 2.5 million in 1964. The number is even higher today. The labor market was certain to experience difficulty in absorbing those swollen numbers. Nevertheless, teenage unemployment was already at least double the adult averages before the products of the baby boom struck the labor market to triple the ratio. Thus declining birthrates are not likely to solve all of the problems involved in the transition from school to work.

## Improving the Transition

The American manpower development system has been criticized for dumping its school leavers into a labor market pool in contrast to the European system which places them on a ladder. However, most knowledgeable Americans have not been anxious to adopt the more structured European alterna-

tives. They recognize that the ladder abroad tends to be short
and limiting, while in America the alternatives are many and
the opportunities are generally considerable for those American
youth who manage to scramble up the slippery bank on their
own or who receive a special assist in moving from the labor
pool into employment.

One of the primary assumptions of career education is
that the school can and should concern itself with more than
preparation for labor market participation; it should also
participate in the placement process. However, to argue that
the schools should retain responsibility for each youth until
he or she has a safe foothold on a career ladder is not to say that
the school must provide either the ladder or the steadying hand.
Many labor market intermediaries are available. The school
may meet its responsibilities by orchestrating other sources
of assistance as well as by providing direct placement services.
The essential requirements for successful school-to-work transition are information, decision-making skills, job access, placement, and follow-up. Some of these terms include more than
appears on the surface. Their nature and source require
explanation.

### Sources of Job Information

Students need several kinds of job market information to
facilitate the transition from school to work. As they begin
seriously exploring various broad career alternatives, they need
general information about the outlook for opportunities. Each
student needs answers to certain basic questions. Which occupations are likely to grow rapidly, which slowly, and which not
at all? Where will that growth occur, in my community or
region, or elsewhere? How much competition will I have? What
will be my chances of job security and advancement? Where
will I live depending on the choices I make?

General data to aid in answering these questions would
be adequate for decision making during the first years of high
school as the career development process begins to mature from
exploration to occupational choice. But these data must include information about skill content, entrance requirements,
pay, life-style, and so forth, for a wide range of occupations.

However, when school's end nears and job search time approaches, the questions become more specific: How many jobs are there *now*? Where are they? How can I get access to them?

Career choice information is quite adequate and generally available on a national basis for the U.S. economy. The *Occupational Outlook Handbook*, published by the U.S. Department of Labor, is available in nearly every library, and any school counselor with the most rudimentary knowledge of careers has one. It described over 850 occupations in thirty industries. Of course, over thirty thousand names of occupations are listed in the *Dictionary of Occupational Titles,* but some of these are dual titles for the same basic job so that only about 22,000 different occupations are listed. However, many of these occupations employ few people, and many others of the occupations need little description because they are so low skilled as to have no entrance requirements. Therefore, we find that the *Occupational Outlook Handbook* is the basic source of information since it describes most of the major occupations which require substantial preparation and many newly emerging but potentially important ones. The occupations covered employ 97 percent of all sales workers, 95 percent of those in professional and related occupations, two-thirds of all skilled, clerical, and service workers, and two-fifths of operatives. The main farming occupations are covered, but few managerial and common labor tasks are covered.

The handbook describes the job duties of each occupation and notes geographic concentration of employment, proportions of women and part-time workers, educational training, licensure and other qualifications required, pay, and opportunities for advancement. Job characteristics which relate to personal characteristics are also noted to aid the reader in judging the appropriateness of the occupation. One shortcoming of the book is the absence of description of the life-style which is likely to accompany each occupation. (The student needs to be reminded that not only income but neighborhood location, friends, dress, recreation, family life, and other aspects of the individual's way of life are affected and often determined by an occupational choice.) The primary purpose of the handbook is to forecast the employment outlook for each occupation. It does this with reasonable accuracy in the only terms that are useful to the student. It describes employment growth for an occupation as "very rapid," "rapid moderate," "slow," and "little or no change"; and it describes the status of job opportunities as "excellent," "very good," "good," "may face keen competition," or "keen competition." The concern of the student is not the number to be employed but the prospects for finding a job and for continuing job security.

This bienniel *Occupational Outlook Handbook* and its accompanying *Occupational Outlook Quarterly* generally provide adequate information on current national trends for existing occupations. The publication is carefully done and has a justified reputation for being relatively accurate. But the future is always opaque. Projections require assumptions. One can only examine past trends, observe how the present differs from the past, identify impending developments which will change it even more, and make judgments about the future. Those judgments can be wrong, but those individuals in the Bureau of Labor Statistics who make the judgments are the best experts we have. They must assume no major catastrophes such as wars or depressions. Such things will happen, but a student cannot base his or her lifelong career plans on the extraordinary.

Projecting the numbers to be employed is difficult, but the direction and magnitude of change is all that is needed. The "batting average" of the handbook is high. Its major errors have been excessive conservatism about the employment-creating ability of major new products and technologies, such as was the case with television in the late 1940s and '50s. Projection from a short-trend line is a chancy thing. Fortunately, occupations do not disappear as rapidly as they appear, and thus there is less chance of unforeseen obsolescence. Jobs are more likely to disappear from declining economic demand than from technological change. Technological obsolescence does not occur without years of warning; still, those warnings are too often ignored.

Those students who have chosen a profession as their career may not care where they practice it and may not be concerned with less than national projections. However, most students will be as concerned with "Where am I going to live?" as with "What am I going to do for a living?" There the data are grossly inadequate. Making national predictions is not too difficult because broad forces of investment, government spending, and consumer tastes are somewhat foreseeable. It is much more difficult to foresee exactly where the jobs will emerge which these developments create.

Some state departments of employment security make statewide projections, and all are endeavoring to develop such a series. Chambers of commerce and universities sometimes make local projections, and trade associations may know the outlook for their industries. The new state and local manpower planning agencies which were mandated under the Comprehensive Employment and Training Act of 1973 are being forced to develop state and local data and projections in order to do their planning job. Vocational educators are currently pressing for greater availability of such data. Nevertheless, school counselors or students seeking the local occupational outlook for a community must display considerable initiative and innovativeness if they are to find the necessary information. Every possible local source should be covered. National data should be studied for projections in industries and occupations of particular importance to the locality. Representatives of the employment services, major industries, labor organizations, and chambers of commerce can be invited to work with the school.

Despite the apparent dearth of published material, the counselor or student can usually find more information than is currently being used. In fact, lack of use is more a problem than lack of information. Government documents are generally unattractive. Cold print may not "turn one on" or become a major factor in decision making. A job cannot be visualized from words, and even pictures are of little help until one actually tries a job for size and fit. For that reason, commercial publishers have produced a wide variety of attractive materials designed less to give information about job availability than about the nature of jobs. Where outlook information is included, it is generally taken from official sources. Among the contributions of the commercial sources are story-type publications which give the reader a word picture of what it might be like to spend one's life in a particular occupation. Visual materials show job content and work setting, illustrate accompanying life-styles, and stress preparation and entrance requirements.

Here again the volume of materials is greater than its utilization.

A high school which is really concerned with easing the transition from school to work will have available at least four information capabilities:

(1) It will have available counselors, somewhat adequate in number for the student body size, who are trained in vocational guidance and knowledgeable about local labor markets as well as national published data.

(2) It will have a library of guidance materials, both printed and audiovisual, available for any student to browse through in a self-exploring search for a possible career fit. (Many schools now have computerized data available for this purpose.)

(3) The counselors, teachers, and other school officials will have contacted institutions outside the school — major employers, unions, employment services, state and local manpower planning offices, civic clubs, and others in an organized effort to tap their information and assistance.

(4) The high school will be aware that job opportunities and job content are only the demand side of the career choice. A more vital question for the student may be: How do they relate to my values, talents, and preferred life-style? Reading about jobs and even observing them provide no adequate answer. Ultimately, the job must be "tried for size" before a realistic choice can be made, and that need imposes a work experience responsibility in the transition process.

*Work Experience Needs*

Chapter 10 explores thoroughly the need for and some techniques providing practical work experience at the high school level. Here, we need only to place the subject in the perspective of the transition period. Much of the threshing around which youth experience in their first few years of labor market participation is a tryout process through which they search for an occupation to which they want to commit themselves for a major portion of their careers. To have not only learned about and observed work but to have also experienced employment prior to graduation will shortcut and regularize this process to some degree. In addition, as noted at the beginning of this chapter, those who have had work experiences during their school years have a much easier time finding jobs upon leaving school. Best of all is school-supervised cooperative education in the occupational field which the student is considering.

### Decision-Making Skills

Both occupational information and in-school work experience are inputs to a decision-making process. The most important contribution of the emergence of career development theory over the past quarter-century is recognition that there are no one-time career choices. A long series of experiences beginning at birth influences the drift and the decisions and results ultimately in some type of career commitment which itself is never final. Therefore, if the career choice process is to be rational, rational decision making must begin early. The test of rationality in decision making is whether goals and objectives are thought through and deliberately chosen, and whether decisions and actions are consistent with those desired ends. Awareness of the nature of the world of work, understanding of the derivation of work values, and exploration of preferred life-styles and alternative occupational possibilities are all part of the goal-setting phase. However, every value which is developed, every choice of occupational clusters to be explored, and every life experience predispose and therefore have some effect on further choice.

Before high school, few of those decisions are binding, but at the high school level hard, more binding choices begin. In too many high schools, students are forced early to choose from among the vocational, general, or academic tracks, and they are penalized by extra coursework if they subsequently change their minds. Students who choose college preparation — the academic track — retain wide options for later occupational choice. Those who choose the general track tend to cut themselves off from those occupations which require college education. In fact, two-thirds of high school dropouts are from among the 25 percent enrolled in the general curriculum. Students in the vocational track tend to cut out professional options and to narrow their choices to the specific occupations directly related to the vocational courses taken. Even shifting from one vocational curriculum to another is difficult in many high schools.

Career education concepts argue for two modifications in the much maligned high school structure: (1) students should never be encouraged to make choices until they have been taught decision-making skills, and (2) particular career doors should not be closed before the end of high school.

Decision-making skills can be taught, as the curriculum of any graduate school of business will attest. The skills are the identification of problems, the marshaling of information, the exploration of alternative goals, the listing of alternative measures for goal achievement and the selection of the most promising, the fixing of interim objectives, and the development and implementation of a program to achieve them, followed by monitoring and evaluation of progress, with appropriate modification of program as experience indicates. These are the skills taught in business management, urban planning, or any other activity where substantial resources are committed and mistakes are costly. They are no less necessary when the commitment affects one's own worklife and all that goes with it. Such skills can be taught in the abstract and applied to any planning and decision-making process. They are more meaningful when taught in relation to concrete decisions which are of importance to the learner.

A career planning course could teach such skills with favorable impact, not only upon career decisions but upon any other personal or professional decisions subsequently made by the learner. At the same time, decision-making skills taught within other courses are useful for career decisions. For instance, decision-making skills can also be integrated into social studies, business, or personal finance courses where social and personal issues can be explored in a problem-solving mode. A by-product will be a deeper understanding and sense of involvement in the issues as well as experience with a generaliz-

able set of planning, problem-solving, and decision-making
techniques. (Decision making is discussed more thoroughly in
chapter 6.)

## Job Search Techniques

At least as important as the acquisition of job skills is the
acquisition of the skills involved in finding a job where those
job skills can be applied. Many labor market intermediaries
exist to aid potential employees and employers in finding each
other. Still, most hiring transactions take place with no formal
third-party intervention. Job seekers search out employers or
hear of job opportunities. Employers put out the word through
current employees. A web of informal networks always exists,
but the uninformed may not know how to use those networks.

We can easily examine the steps involved in searching for
a job. First, effective job search presupposes some choice among
occupations to pursue. Next, a knowledge of alternative sources
of job opportunity information is required. Then, the job seeker
needs to know the access routes into the desired employment.
This involves answering such questions as: Who are the gate-
keepers — personnel offices, unions, and so on — who must be
given the appropriate password? What are the prerequisites,
and what are the ports of entry? How can employers be approached, and how can they be sufficiently impressed to offer
the job?

The skills necessary to accomplish these steps can be
taught — and have been taught by remedial manpower programs — but they are rarely included in the high school curriculum. These skills should be added to a career planning
course or become a component of some other course available
for all and required or strongly recommended for all those who
are not either definitely college bound or on a track to virtually
guaranteed post-high school employment, such as in a family
business or a full-time extension of a part-time job already
held. Most of those who plan to go to college should receive
this instruction, both because few colleges teach it and because
a high proportion of college students seek part-time employment in tight labor markets.

The content to be taught in such a course should include sources of job information and the nature and availability of labor market intermediaries. Students should be instructed in the workings of labor markets and the interface between the external labor market of the local, regional, and national economy and the internal labor market of the particular employing establishment. Each internal labor market has its own port, or ports, of entry through which the individual must enter to become employed. Some employing establishments can only be entered by formal examination (e.g., most civil service jobs). Many require a license, an educational credential, or union membership. Some employers hire only at the bottom of a promotion ladder and fill all other requirements from within. Some hire only those referred through a union hiring hall. Only frustration can result from a student preparing or trying to enter through other than these prescribed ports of entry.

Different employers have different means of recruitment, selection, and hiring, and prospects for an employee differ markedly once he or she is inside the establishment. Discrimination is also a reality, and students should be prepared to avoid, circumvent, or deliberately confront any such barriers which may be imposed. Employers are prone to reject certain job seekers with specific habits, personalities, and grooming, and to be attracted to others. The student may be entitled to a personal style, but each should know the costs of being "different," and each should be aware of how to influence the employer favorably. Instruction in the skills of job search — skills which may last a lifetime — may be of even more value than a placement service in providing access to the first job.

Some jobs offer steady and stable employment, good and increasing pay, promotion opportunities, and fringe benefits. Others are unstable, poorly paid, and "dead end." The former are often described as the primary labor market, and the latter as the secondary labor market. Many youth begin their working careers in the secondary labor market and move laterally or vertically into the primary market. It is important to a successful career that potential labor market participants learn the difference and how to traverse the path. The placement officer, described at the end of this chapter, is the most appropriate among school personnel to teach job search techniques. Where no such officer exists, a counselor may be the appropriate person. In addition to conceptual and factual knowledge about the labor market and its intermediaries, role playing, television feedback, and visits to employment services and company personnel departments can add an air of reality.

### Labor Market Intermediaries

The successful labor market participant is conscious of the available labor market intermediaries and knows how to use them. These intermediaries are a variety of organizations and institutions which operate between employers and employees and facilitate the process of matching people and jobs. For the student to be familiar with these aids at the exit point from school, someone in the school should be available to pass on that knowledge.

The most ubiquitous of these is the public employment service, now being renamed Job Service, with some 2,300 offices spread across the nation. These are state agencies fully supported by federal funds. Their primary function is to accept employer job orders and applications from job seekers and attempt to match the two. Among the services they offer job seekers are: (1) applicant interviews to record experiences, (2) skills and desires testing to ascertain skills and aptitudes, (3) employment counseling, (4) referral to manpower training and other programs to improve employability, (5) payment of unemployment compensation to those who are eligible, and (6) "job development" to sell employers on hiring those whose qualifications may not precisely meet their preferences. To employers they offer a cost-free source of employees and some statistical services. They also provide to the general public, including employers and employees, considerable labor market data and analysis.

The most progressive of these offices have computerized their job applications and orders for quicker and more accurate matching. They also provide to potential job seekers information about employers who might hire workers with the applicants' skills, even though no job order was submitted. Thus the job seeker can focus more sharply his or her own job search efforts. A few of the offices — but only a few — have also experimented successfully with teaching job search techniques. As public agencies, eager for public support, many public employment service offices actively seek opportunities to visit the schools, explain their services, and provide testing and employment counseling to students at the schools. Most would welcome appropriately scheduled visits to their offices to explain and demonstrate available services.

The private employment agency is another labor market intermediary. These agencies are increasing rapidly in number. They charge fees for their services, and each agency ordinarily specializes in a broad occupational area, such as clerical occupations. They charge a finder's fee to the employer or a proportion of wages for some period to the employee. It is rather remarkable that a fee-charging service can compete so successfully with one that is offered free. Public employment service personnel often believe that this is because the private agencies will cater to the employer's racial, ethnic, or age prejudices, whereas the public agency is committed to equal economic opportunity. The private agencies deny this and counter by arguing that they merely provide a higher quality service and offer better jobs. At any rate, job-seeking students should be taught to assess carefully the fees they will be charged, whether or not they keep the job, and to accept the service if it is worth the price.

Industrial unions which represent all of the employees in large unionized establishments rarely participate in the hiring process, and thus do not act as labor market intermediaries. Their role is to represent employees in setting the rules of the workplace, including pay, and to protect the employee's rights under the labor management agreement. However, craft unions which represent only those with a particular skill or which represent employees in industries in which employment is temporary and fluctuating, such as the construction, longshoring, and maritime fields, often operate union hiring halls. Employers agree to refer all job orders to these union-operated services. Union hiring halls are forbidden to discriminate in placement against nonmembers, but there are many ways to give preference to union members.

Students interested in preparing for these jobs should be cognizant of the need to gain union membership as well as the required job skills. Apprenticeship programs, operated jointly by unions and employers, offer both union membership and skills training, as well as employment and incomes. Entrance may be limited by labor market conditions, but objective examinations provide either entrance or a place on the waiting list.

Not really an intermediary but an important and expanding part of the placement process is the company personnel department. Large companies have one or more departments responsible for recruitment, selection, hiring, training, promotion, and other personnel functions. Even when there are no current job openings, they may accept applications for referral as openings occur.

The most readily available of all labor market intermediaries is the help wanted section of the newspaper classified ads. However, these are limited in the information provided by the employer. Many of the ads are from outside the area; others are misleading in that they are from placement agencies rather than employers, represent high-turnover jobs, or seek door-to-door sales representatives rather than salaried employees. Nevertheless, they are a useful place to start a job search (Walsh *et al.*, 1975).

Although they do not provide placement services, an important new development on the labor market scene is the manpower planning offices now emerging in every state and in large- and medium-size cities and counties. They study the area's manpower needs and the job needs of the residents, particularly of the disadvantaged who suffer the most unemployment and poverty. They then are responsible to design and operate programs to correct imbalances. These planning offices are an important source of labor market information, if not of jobs.

Most colleges have their own placement offices and, as will be discussed below, some high schools are becoming involved in placement activities. Some churches and civic clubs operate referral and placement services for their members. Professional associations often provide labor exchanges for those already in the profession or those attaining professional degrees. In recent years, a variety of what are called "community-based organizations" has emerged to represent various minority ethnic and disadvantaged socioeconomic groups. These also often provide labor market services for their members. The school must be aware of, have access to, and be able to advise students about all of these if they are to adequately facilitate the school-to-work transition.

Of course, schools face difficulty in finding or developing staff with this knowledge. However, it need not come from the school staff. Employment service staff would react eagerly to an invitation to come into the schools to display their knowledge. Staff of personnel departments of local employers, private and public, are generally willing to serve as visiting lecturers or host field trips. Local union officials also welcome opportunities to explain their services. A major skill of the school staff can be that of tapping community resources.

### School-to-Work Transition as a Simulation Exercise

To establish a working career which is based on a choice of the least undesirable of the jobs immediately available upon leaving school or leaving another job is a formula for mediocrity or less in career satisfaction. Yet that is the standard practice for youth and adults. Ignorance of the range of job opportunities available is an important constraint. But it is less a limiting factor than one's failure to analyze his or her own strengths or weaknesses and preferred life-styles in the attempt to identify what employment fields one should pursue. Employment services tend to make the same mistake. For those with work experience, they seek to match job openings with jobs which the job seeker has held in the past or for which she or he has had specific training. That formula inevitably restricts the job seeker to a narrow range.

Tests such as the Kuder Interest Inventory and the General Aptitude Test Battery (GATB), both of which are used by the public employment service, are useful. They are readily available and easily administered, and every youth should take them. Nevertheless, they are limited tests. Interest inventories suggest broad areas in which an individual might have an interest. The GATB assesses not interests but broad ranges of skill, such as manual dexterity.

But as we have already pointed out, the best predictor of future achievement is past accomplishment, and the best way to discover what people are interested in and enjoy is to ask them. However, because people are not accustomed to such self-analysis, appropriate techniques are necessary which may be best applied with the help of a skilled counselor or teacher.

A variety of books and instructional programs is emerging to assist adults who are faced with the necessity of career change or who are dissatisfied with present career patterns to replan their lives for more attractive careers. These have not been especially adapted to the needs of high school youth, but that can be done with reasonable ease by a dedicated counselor or teacher. Especially recommended are: (1) *Where Do I Go from Here with My Life?* (Crystal and Bolles, 1974), (2) *What Color Is Your Parachute?* (Bolles, 1973), (3) *Go Hire Yourself an Employer* (Irish, 1973), (4) *Career Satisfaction and Success* (Haldane, 1974), and (5) *Making Vocational Choices: A Theory of Careers* (Holland, 1973). The first four are helpful, practical guides, and the book by Holland provides desirable theoretical underpinnings.

Drawing upon these sources and the work of Pearson (1974), we synthesized the following career planning exercise. It is designed to meet each of the criteria we have discussed and, in addition, to support a variety of academic learnings. The exercise can be accomplished by a counselor or a teacher, but it will be more effective if undertaken by an interdisciplinary team, perhaps coordinated by a counselor. The key concept is to build on past successful experiences as evidence of both capability and interest.

STUDENTS ARE FIRST asked to think of an experience which meets three criteria:

    (1) Something I did well.

    (2) Something I enjoyed doing.

    (3) Something of which I am proud.

It might be a school assignment, a part-time or summer work experience, a hobby, an act of personal service, or any active experience. At first, some students will have difficulty, perhaps complaining that they can think of no such experience, but a little probing by the counselor or teacher will identify some such activity in every person's life.

Then the student is assigned to write out in the greatest possible detail, as if describing the process to a four- or five-year-old child who had never seen it done, exactly what was done and how it was accomplished. For instance, a description of a piano lesson might consist of several pages describing the process of finding the appropriate teacher, meeting and becoming acquainted with the teacher, receiving or obtaining instruction manuals, studying them, setting times for practice and following that schedule, observing proper posture, learning notes and the corresponding keyboard, learning rudimentary music theory, exercising finger dexterity, counting beats, regulating a metronome, keeping time with it, and so forth. An English teacher could very well be recruited to make this an exercise in written communication. However, the student should be encouraged to ramble freely and not to value brevity in this particular written exercise.

Students should be assigned to work in small groups of two or three to probe and ask questions leading to greater descriptive detail. Here, the students exercise skills in questioning, in analysis, in oral communication, and in human relations. The essays should then be rewritten on the basis of the added detail which emerges from the questioning. The purpose of the detail is to identify every possible skill used by the student in this successful and enjoyable activity.

THE NEXT STEP is to begin identifying the skills used. Here the student can learn some vital points about the nature of skills. To the students, the term "skill" may imply an entire occupation spoken of as a "skilled craft," such as electrician or plumber. In fact, the term "skill" is used in the *Dictionary of Occupational Titles* in a much more fundamental sense which is far better adapted for personal analysis. For instance, the dictionary generalizes skills in three categories — working with data, with people, and with things — and then lists under each a hierarchy of skills descending from the highest to the least. For example:

*Data*

| | |
|---|---|
| synthesizing (1) | computing-compiling (4) |
| coordinating (2) | copying (5) |
| analyzing (3) | comparing (6) |

*People*

| mentoring | coaching |
| negotiating | persuading |
| supervising | diverting |
| consulting | exchanging information |
| instructing | taking instructions |
| directing | helping, serving |

*Things*

| precision working | driving |
| setting up | handling |
| manipulating | feeding |
| operating | offbearing |
| controlling | tending |

Each of these terms has a fairly precise definition as used in the *Dictionary of Occupational Titles* to analyze the skills required on a job. The hierarchy, it will be noted, is established by the degree of discretion exercised by the workers. For analysis of the students' capabilities and interests, no such hierarchy is necessary; nor is it desirable to be limited to these few descriptors. Literally hundreds are possible, each of which will allude to some mental or physical action.

THE SECOND STEP of the exercise, therefore, is for the small groups to analyze each of their activity descriptions and identify all of the skills used. The list for each activity will be extensive and will include skills which a casual review of the activity would never identify. For instance, the piano lesson may have been unsuccessful in terms of musical talent, yet persistence, consistency, self-discipline, manual dexterity, the ability to accept instruction, and a variety of other skills having little or much to do with music may have been demonstrated.

These steps should be repeated several times with different activities until a skill profile for the individual begins to emerge. Those who have held part-time or summer jobs should be particularly encouraged to analyze every work experience in this manner. Class time need not be taken for subsequent activities analysis. Once the students have learned the techniques, further analysis can be a homework assignment. In fact, career development of other family members may be enhanced by encouraging the student to demonstrate the same analysis at home.

NEXT, THE STUDENTS individually and in their small groups might be assigned to analyze each list of skills and arrange skills in clusters according to ways in which the skills are related. These should not be occupationally or industrially related clusters, but those which appear to have some skill commonality, such as a preference for working with people or data or things, for working alone or in large or small groups, for being self-motivated or working better under supervision, for preferring the indoors to the outdoors, for problem solving, for mechanical skills, for manual dexterity, for persuasiveness, and so on. Deriving their own clustering system is itself an important learning experience.

Now the exercise might continue to the identification of occupational areas which use these skills. However, it may be more instructive to detour at this point to considerations of labor market analysis and further self-analysis before returning to identification of occupational areas.

"WHERE WOULD YOU like to live?" might be the next question to explore, with a social studies teacher leading the students into the study of economic and social geography. A values clarification exercise might result from each student asking these important questions of herself or himself:

(1) What is most important for me, where I live or what I do?

(2) Shall I choose where I want to live and then find out what I can do to make a living there, or shall I decide what occupations I want to pursue and then decide where opportunities like that are most likely to be found?

(3) Is some optimum combination of both possible by considering a range of several from each?

As the student identifies potential locations, the assignment should include a carefully written defense of why that particular place was chosen and, perhaps, why others were rejected. Each student then should choose some particular location and study it carefully from a personal, social, and economic viewpoint. What living conditions are characteristic of the area, including climate, recreation, rural or urban structure, city size, cultural attributes, educational institutions, environment, industry mix, region, and so on? What is its industrial structure? What are the interrelationships among climate, natural resource availability, transportation, communications, power sources, labor force, and the industrial structure? In what ways does the nature of the industries determine the occupational structure? What is happening to population, labor force growth, economic growth, employment and unemployment, income trends, and other indicators, and why? Again the analysis can involve the English instructor as well as the social studies instructor in the preparation and grading of written or oral reports.

THE NEXT STEP might be a return to self-analysis with the question: What do I want to do with my life? Of course, this is a value-laden question to which many of the values-clarification questions of chapter 3 can contribute understanding. Here, the student might be assigned an essay on his or her philosophy of life, seeking personal answers to vital questions. What should be the broad goals of society and self? What are the student's views on social, political, and business ethics? What is the ideal character one might set as a personal goal? How is that accomplished? A humanities teacher can use this as an exercise in exploring the major philosophical and ethical systems and their meaning for personal ethics and values.

The exercise might lead to the question: What in society most needs doing? This topic is particularly appropriate for a group report, discussed and written by several students. The individual might then turn to the question: What would I like to accomplish in my life? The student's written answer might be submitted to small group discussion before being submitted in final form.

The student should then be led to explore the income needs of his or her preferred life-style. Techniques of accounting and principles of personal finance can be used to help students come to a realization of the income required for any chosen life-style. Family size, education requirements, ambitions for children, retirement needs, insurance, the impact of inflation over time, and other practical consideration should be introduced. The subject of income structure by occupational area could then be introduced, along with the economic principles responsible for wage and income differentials.

At this point, the student will have developed — or at least thought about — a list of demonstrated skills and interests, a preferred geographical location and its economic opportunities, a value structure related to social needs and personal philosophy, and a notion of the income requirements of a preferred life-style. Now she or he can begin trying to harmonize the varied and often conflicting criteria into a range of possible occupational and career choices. What are the occupations suggested by the skills list? In what industries do they occur?

To what extent are they available in the preferred location? Would I rather change occupational preferences or locational preferences? What is the hierarchical structure in each of the attractive occupational fields? To what extent do these indicated occupations square with ethical values, social needs, and ultimate life goals? How far up the occupational hierarchy would it be necessary to go in order to have the preferred income? Would I rather compromise my income goals or various of my other goals?

The very complexity of the considerations will prevent the student from making a premature choice. In fact, the experience may be so confusing that it will be necessary to point out that these decisions will be made by accident and by default if not done deliberately. The decisions will either be made or they will make themselves.

The skills list will not point to one particular occupational area but to many which may have little or no relationship except for these skill commonalities. The students in small group settings will want to examine each clustered skills list and come up with a series of possible occupations which each individual will order by rank in accordance with his or her perceived preferences. Figure 2 illustrates the combination of these and other considerations into ten occupational areas leading to the choice of an immediate job search objective.

Identifying the range of possible occupations which fit all of the criteria leads the learning experience back to considerations of the labor market. Which firms in the desired location offer such occupations? What do they pay? Why do wage differentials exist within the same occupations in the same community? What are the fringe benefits, social insurance taxes, and other programs involved in the pay structure? Are the occupations unionized? What is the role of the labor union in modern industrial society? What other labor market intermediaries exist for these occupations? What are the education and training requirements? Where can the education or training be acquired and at what cost? What are the most effective job search techniques for these occupations? What is the long-run outlook? Where does it lead?

To make this part of the exercise as practical as possible, the student should list everyone he or she knows who is engaged

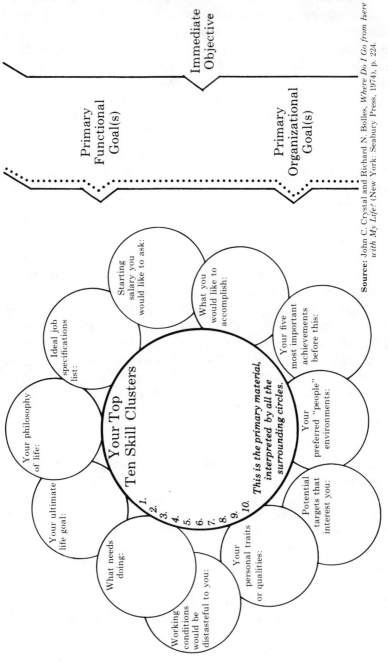

Immediate Objective

Primary Functional Goal(s)

Primary Organizational Goal(s)

Starting salary you would like to ask:

Ideal job specifications list:

What you would like to accomplish:

Your philosophy of life:

Your Top Ten Skill Clusters

*This is the primary material, interpreted by all the surrounding circles.*

Your five most important achievements before this:

Your preferred "people" environments:

Your ultimate life goal:

1.
2.
3.
4.
5.
6.
7.
8.
9.
10.

Potential targets that interest you:

What needs doing:

Your personal traits or qualities:

Working conditions would be distasteful to you:

**Source:** John C. Crystal and Richard N. Bolles, *Where Do I Go from Here with My Life?* (New York: Seabury Press, 1974). p. 224.

**Figure 2.** Combining Skill Lists into Occupational Areas for Selection of Job Search Objectives

in the selected occupations or closely related occupations, as well as every known employer of workers in these occupations. The list should be added to by parents, relatives, or friends who can provide introductions to persons working in these occupations. The student should then interview a substantial number of these persons to learn more of what these jobs are like and how to obtain them.

This is an exercise which might be undertaken several times during the high school years. It might be repeated annually or added to step by step over these years. The same process can be used to choose part-time and summer jobs, thus simulating the process which will ultimately be done "for real." All the way along, the students should be reminded that they are learning decision-making skills. As the student draws nearer school leaving age, the experience will progress from simulation to reality. For the student leaving formal education after high school, whether permanently or temporarily, the interviews with participants in the occupations of interest become, in fact, a job search technique. By interviewing employers and supervisors as an aid to career decision making, the students will be contacting potential employers who should be impressed by the rational approach to decision making and the employment potential of these young people. Job offers or opportunities to return for job applications will be opened up. Interviews with union officials and officials of other labor market intermediaries will have the same effect.

In addition to this exercise and other types of activities designed to help students plan and become acquainted with the labor market, both job-seeking and job-getting skills should be taught as part of the career education process. Young persons should be fully aware by the time they begin thinking seriously about seeking employment that although one has a right to personal values and a personal life-style, those values which clash with the preferences of employers and other power sources in society may be costly. Discussion of these value considerations should probably become a part of the exercise. Students should be able to understand that such preferences on the part of employers are not necessarily efforts to force conformity; they are simply expressions of the employers' experiences with other workers and their work habits as they relate to personal

individuals when they apply such standards. Because they can choose their employees from among a fairly large number of applicants they are naturally going to select those who evidence values which the employer feels are most likely to result in good work habits.

For these reasons, students should be aware of the impact of grooming, dress, language, and other aspects of comportment which become factors in job seeking. The object is not to present a false image, but to present the best possible image of a person who, after all, the employer has never seen before. These same considerations apply to other job-seeking skills, such as résumé writing, making personal contacts with employers, making follow-up contacts, completing application forms, and interviewing. Teachers will find that role playing and television feedback experiences in these situations will be helpful to students in developing these skills and will provide meaningful learning situations.

The exercise we have offered above as an example may be shortened, lengthened, repeated, or modified at will, according to the preferences of students, counselors, or teachers. Labor market differences in various communities will dictate some variations. The exercise can involve as many or as few of the school staff as desired. However, we highly recommend that every student go through this or a similar exercise at least once during the high school years, with the counselor and teacher adapting it to their own prevailing situation. The important thing is to acquaint the student with the process of job seeking; the specific answers which the student derives from the exercise are not as crucial as the fact that the student be given the opportunity to ask the necessary questions.

Having gone through such an exercise one or more times during the school years, the school leaver should know a great deal about the personal attributes and interests which will determine the jobs to be sought, the sources of those jobs, and the techniques for finding them. But we strongly advise even more help for students. The school's responsibility cannot be fulfilled by throwing students out into the working world unaided. The school has some responsibility to provide the type of assistance normally associated with job placement service.

## *The School Placement Service*

Having accepted the career education commitment to maintain responsibility until each student has achieved successful labor market entry, the high school still faces the issue of whether to undertake placement activities itself or merely to steer students to existing services. We believe that whichever posture the school assumes along this scale of possible alternatives, a career education program is not complete unless some attention is given to this vital step in the transition process.

As we have demonstrated above, a variety of helps is available in the community, and school personnel can provide a valuable service by instructing students about such services and guiding them in the direction of those service organizations. After all, no matter how good the service might be, it is of little value if the student does not know about its existence. This type of guidance to existing services is the minimum level of placement assistance which should be available in the high school. However, all of these community service organizations have a broader constituency to serve than merely high school students. Also, they are typically job or employer oriented, whereas the school can show greater concern for the educational alternatives involved in the work experience and for the longer term career progress of the individual student.

Thus the school can provide a more exclusive, more effective, and more durable service for its particular constituents if it undertakes its own placement activity. The basic considerations in providing such a service are: (1) the costs, (2) the relative effectiveness, (3) the extent to which the school can obtain job orders, and (4) the extent to which the school is prepared to maintain interest in the student's career after he or she exits the school door. If the school can afford the cost, and if it can convince a substantial body of employers to give the school's "product" preference in hiring, then it may be worth the effort. Two by-products will be a repeated test of the school's effectiveness and the development of a communication link to learn the skill needs of employers.

Of course, the primary effect of a placement service should be to ease significantly the process of transition from school to work. Indeed, studies of existing high school placement services indicate that they are effective. A study of three such services in Pennsylvania noted that "the three schools consistently had higher placement percentages and lower unemployment rates than any comparable group located in the literature review" (Meehan and Franchak, 1976, p. vi).

As mentioned above, a wide range of placement program approaches is available to the school or school district. Two particularly promising approaches are discussed in some depth below. But no school should be discouraged from some sort of placement assistance because the programs discussed here seem too ambitious. These programs can be modified to suit the particular needs of each school. Furthermore, many different kinds of approaches have been tried with some success. For example, in the Sheboygan public schools of Wisconsin, the state employment service makes available to the schools a computerized job bank of microfiche. The job bank is used at various levels of the career education program, but one valuable use is at the twelfth grade level as a placement tool (Seifert, 1975, p. 1). Another example which might be adapted for high school use comes from a community college in Illinois. The college operates a series of placement seminars which are designed to assist students in the placement process (Fowler, 1975, p. 1).

These examples and many others indicate how a school can enter the placement field easily and inexpensively. The following are more complete and more effective models.

## The Cooperative Model

The first model depends upon extensive cooperation with and by existing sources, primarily the public employment service. In this instance, one school staff member is assigned responsibility for liaison with the community. That person might be a counselor or a cooperative education coordinator, whichever has or can develop the best rapport with the community. In this model, direct contacts with employers are confined primarily to seeking opportunities for site visits, obtaining speakers for school classes, and arranging for cooperative education slots. The coordinator actively seeks the assistance of placement agencies and the services they provide. The public employment service is urged to send counseling staff members to the high school to administer aptitude tests, to lecture on local and regional labor market conditions, to provide labor market information, to describe the services available at the employment service, to arrange for students to tour the facilities, and to arrange for a "dry run" through those facilities. This activity can begin for students during their first year of high school and can continue at various intervals until graduation.

The coordinator can arrange with the employment service to have the agency establish a specific "desk" and particular staff to specialize in service to those in school and those leaving school as labor market entrants. The employment service can also supply periodic labor market information and instruction in job search techniques. Where the public employment service has a computerized job bank, a computer printout or microfilm of its available job orders can be delivered to the high school daily.

All of the evidence of past experience is that most public employment service offices are eager to establish such relationships. It adds to the agency's role in the community and to its security as an institution. In addition, the school liaison officer can invite to the school and establish relationships with reputable private placement agencies and with ethnic and other community organizations involved in placement. Nevertheless, in this model the public employment agency serves as the school's primary placement arm.

There can be little doubt that a school placement service adds significantly to the initial career success probabilities for the student. After all, the school placement service is an addition to, not a replacement for, the other available placement services.

## The Independent Service Model

Title I, Part D, Section 143 of the vocational education amendments of 1968 authorized programs or projects for intensive occupational guidance and counseling during the last years of school and for initial job placement. Few local education agencies and schools have responded to that invitation, but the number and the interest appear to be increasing with the career education emphasis. The National Association for Industry–Education Cooperation, under contract with the U.S. Office of Education, has prepared an as yet unpublished placement services training curriculum manual (National Association for Secondary Education Cooperation, 1975). It cites school placement services in Georgia, New Jersey, Michigan, Massachusetts, Ohio, New York, and Florida, and it provides its own recommended model for a districtwide job development and placement service. Each of the systems studied differs in some ways from the others, but from their commonalities emerge a preferred model.

(1) An integrated program is needed which involves:

   (a) Job development — not only contacting employers to obtain job orders but working with them to adjust jobs and the occupational structure so that youth are offered more opportunities.

   (b) Teaching students the skills of job search and the prerequisites for job getting and job holding, as well as specific job skills.

   (c) Assisting youth to choose among alternative opportunities.

   (d) Providing access to part-time and summer jobs and apprenticeship and other nonschool training programs, as well as full-time post-school jobs.

   (e) Placing students in full- or part-time jobs commensurate with their desires and abilities.

   (f) Follow-up to assure that the student performs well and is successful and that the employer is not unrealistic in expectations, and to obtain feedback about the quality of and changes needed in the school's programs.

(2) Districtwide programs are preferred. While each school must have its placement staff who can know the youth personally, there are economies of scale in design and

supervision of programs in doing job development at a multischool level.

(3) Active and committed advisory committees involving public and private employers, labor organizations, other placement organizations, manpower agencies, and community-based organizations representing minorities are a must.

(4) Counselors, cooperative education coordinators, and vocational education teachers should all be involved in the school placement service, but full-time staff who are not tied to desks, classrooms, and office routine are necessary to carry it out.

(5) Those involved in the school placement service should be familiar with and able to administer and interpret all of the major kinds of ability, achievement, aptitude, interest, and personality tests, but they should also be capable of using test results with judgment as one of many aids to decision making.

(6) Rather than competing with other labor market intermediaries and placement agencies, the school placement service should use them all and share generously any. credit for student placements.

(7) An extensive structure of appropriate forms to describe students and jobs and accumulations of national, regional, and local labor market information is necessary.

(8) Special capability, concern, and commitment are required for the placement of disadvantaged and handicapped students and for breaking out of sex stereotypes in employment.

(9) A school placement service must differ from all other placement agencies in its depth of concern for the educational nature of jobs and their long-term career contributions.

(10) Contact with employer and employee following placement is as important as the initial placement. Inex-

perienced youth have much to learn about the necessary discipline of the workplace. Employers may need a special understanding which is unnecessary with adult workers. Follow-up coaching of the student and the supervisors can lengthen job tenure and the satisfactions of both employer and employee. A satisfied employer will be the source of further job orders and contacts. By-products will be general support for the schools and the availability of friendly employers to participate in career education instruction. In search for accountability measures, none could be a more convincing test for a career education program than successfully placed graduates, many along their chosen career paths.

On the other hand, there can be no surer signal of weakness in the school's program than if students prove to be unready for work, have poor work attitudes, are irresponsible, or otherwise displease their employers. The school should instigate a follow-up process to follow students into their careers and a feedback system to determine changes needed to improve the program's effectiveness.

Establishing an effective school placement service is no minor undertaking, but the school system which has the resources and the commitment to carry it off will be well rewarded through student success, parental support, and community reputation.


## Job Access and Barriers

The school-to-work transition will require special attention to the needs of school dropouts, minorities, and the handicapped. Major barriers to job access are race discrimination, sex and age discrimination, lack of education and skills required by employers, reluctance of employers to accept the disadvantaged, and conflicts between the personality and attitudes of youth and of employers. Providing appropriate skills training and aiding the youth in personality adjustment and the development of values and attitudes are the essence of career education. However, if the school is convinced that its career education job does not end short of placement in a job or another school, then the career educator must be concerned about removal of job barriers throughout the community. There can be no general prescription, but probably no institution in the community is better structured in the long run to work for the elimination of those barriers existing in every labor market which have nothing to do with productive capacity. The school can be an important moral agent, educating the community away from such discriminatory actions. At the same time the school is in a position to identify discrimination against its students and also to educate them regarding appropriate recourse.

## *Summary*

A prime concept of career education is that schools accept the responsibility for the school-to-work transition and test the effectiveness of education programs by following students through and past the transition into the first stages of promising work careers. An average of 3.5 million to four million young Americans per year must pursue that transition for the remainder of the 1970s and into the '80s. In recent years, the transition has been a painful one. Improving it will require the skills and abilities provided by an active career education program beginning in the elementary school, as well as the following:

(1) Current, accurate, and localized labor market and job information

(2) Realistic exploration of job content and prospects in relation to preferred life-styles

(3) Actual work experience

(4) Decision-making skills

(5) Familiarity with labor market institutions

(6) Instruction in job search techniques

(7) Job placement services

(8) Continued student advocacy

The school must make careful decisions, based upon relative costs and effectiveness, about which services it will perform and which it will seek to obtain from other sources in the community. Whatever the choices, the *successful* transition of students from school to work is the capstone of effective career education.

## *References*

Bolles, Richard Nelson. *What Color Is Your Parachute?* Berkeley, California: Ten Speed Press. 1973.

Crystal, John C.; and Bolles, Richard N. *Where Do I Go from Here with My Life?* New York: Seabury Press. 1974.

Fowler, Jack R. "Placement Seminars — A Practical Approach." *Inform* (November 1975), vol. 4, no. 4.

Haldane, Bernard. *Career Satisfaction and Success.* New York: American Management Association. 1974.

Holland, John L. *Making Vocational Choices: A Theory of Careers.* New York: Prentice-Hall, Inc. 1973.

Irish, Richard K. *Go Hire Yourself an Employer.* Garden City, New York: Anchor Books. 1973.

Levitan, Sar. *Work Is Here to Stay, Alas.* Salt Lake City: Olympus Publishing Company. 1974.

Meehan, Merrill L.; and Franchak, Stephen J. *Evaluation of Three School-Based Job Placement Projects in Pennsylvania.* Philadelphia: Pennsylvania State Department of Education, Bureau of Vocational Education, Research Coordinating Unit. February 1976.

National Association for Industry-Education Cooperation. *Placement Services Training Curriculum Manual.* Washington, D.C.: National Association for Industry-Education Cooperation. (Mimeographed.) 1975.

Pearson, H. G. *Career Concepts.* Wayland, Massachusetts: privately printed. 1974.

Perrella, Vera C.; and Bogan, Forrest A. "Out of School Youth." *Monthly Labor Review* (Nov. 1964). See also Swanstrom, Thomas E., "Out School Youth — Part II," *Monthly Labor Review* (Dec. 1964), and Perrella, Vera C., and Waldman,

Elizabeth, "Out of School Youth — Two Years Later," *Monthly Labor Review* (Aug. 1966). (Apparently no comparable study has been done since that time.)

Seifert, Terry. "Use of Job Bank in Career Exploration and Placement in the Secondary School." *Inform* (April 1975), vol. 3, no. 9.

Walsh, Jack; *et al. Help Wanted: Case Studies of Classified Ads.* Salt Lake City: Olympus Publishing Co. 1975.

# 6

# Decision
# Making

Life might be characterized as being a series of decisions —
some major, some minor, but all interdependent. Two of the
most striking realizations about those decisions are (1) that
each of us must make such an incredibly large number of decisions, and (2) that the interrelationships between those myriad
decisions are so infinitely complex. As an illustration, think
back to the decision you made this morning about which shirt
or blouse to wear. Surely that was an uncomplicated decision.
But a whole complex of decisions preceded and conditioned
that simple decision. Your mood of today was perhaps conditioned by decisions you made yesterday about what to eat or
when to go to bed, and your mood may have been a factor in
deciding which color or style to wear. You decided what the
weather would likely be for the day before you selected your
clothing. Some time ago you decided you liked those particular
blouses or shirts or ties now hanging in your closet well enough
to purchase them instead of others. Yesterday, you decided to
wear blue, so you don't want to wear blue again today. A week
ago you decided to make an appointment for lunch today, so
you wanted to wear your most attractive outfit. Two days ago

you decided to have your black shoes repaired, and so you had
to select something which would look good with your brown
shoes. When you were a sophomore in high school, a friend said
you looked good in green, and on that basis you decided green
was your "best" color. But you decided to wear the green blouse
or shirt last week, and it's a little wrinkled, and since you
decided to sleep five minutes longer this morning, there isn't
time to get it pressed.

This kind of interrelationship between decisions goes on
and on. It is so complex with regard to even the easiest kinds
of decisions that we cannot comprehend it. And if the complexity is so great with such simple decisions, imagine how
intricate the network of relationships is likely to be for such
major decisions as those involved in career selection.

If decisions are that frequent and complex for the adult
teacher or educational administrator who has made and left
behind many crucial life decisions, think how overpowering and
even frightening are the decisions to be confronted daily by the
high school student. Yet think also of the limited experience
and data upon which to base those crucial decisions and how
little formal training in decision making any of us have. Decision making is a necessary component of any adequate career
education program at the high school level. The process taught
may or may not be directly related to career choice, though it
will probably be most meaningful to most youth. The process
is not appreciably different whether it is deciding which clothes
to wear, which class to take, which girl or boy to date, whether
to prepare for college of job, or which of either to choose. However, before the decision-making process is taught, it must be
understood by the teacher. To direct that it be taught requires
the administrator to understand how it can be taught. The
subject is too complex to be satisfactorily treated in one chapter. But some techniques can be introduced and some references
provided for further study.

### The Decision Tree

In our discussion of decision making, a growing tree serves
as a useful simile. Imagine a tiny ant embarking on a seventy-

or eighty-year exploration of an already large and still growing tree. At each fork in the tree, at each branching of limbs and leaves, the ant must make a decision about which limb to follow or which leaf stem to explore. Sometimes the ant has only two alternatives, sometimes many alternatives. Of course, it is possible for the ant to change its mind and go back along one limb or stem to a junction point, from which to embark on another path. But if a decision is made to retrace, then the farther the ant has traveled on the branch, the more time must be consumed in retracing and the less time can be spent in exploring new territory.

There is another possibility for change which does not involve backtracking. One branch may overlap another in such a fashion that the ant can change from one to the other without retracing its path, but such occurrences are rare and strictly accidental. When this happens, there is no way for the ant to establish a solid understanding about the "foundations" of the new branch. Furthermore, since the tree is always growing it is impossible for the ant to stand back and get an overall picture of the territory, and it is also impossible to obtain such a view from other observers, since they too can only observe the tree at the moment and cannot accurately predict how it will grow.

Obviously, our ant could benefit from communication with other ants ahead of it, or with ants retracing their steps after making unhappy or confused decisions, but at no time will it be possible to know about all of the branches from all of the limbs ahead. When the ant begins exploration of the tree, the task appears challenging but not impossible. As the ant continues along the chosen branches, the tree grows, spreads out, becomes more complex — and the frustration of the explorer increases. Even in seventy or eighty years it is not possible to explore the entire tree, and our ant may look across the way at others which have selected different branches to explore and which seem to be making more progress. This may tempt our ant to give up or to turn back, but the commitment of earlier decisions makes such a move inadvisable. The limb along which the ant has traveled has grown fat and secure and crusted with the convoluted bark of age.

The simile can be carried on at length, but the comparison between the exploring ant and the exploring human being is obvious. Like the tree itself, our simile has its strengths and weaknesses. It does illustrate the interdependence of decisions, but perhaps it is too fatalistic and does not permit sufficient flexibility for the individual. After all, true freedom of choice presupposes both the existence and knowledge of a wide range of alternatives. It is the availability of choice which is important, not all of the factors which influence it. Choice is neither illusory nor powerless. "Choice or decision is creative in face of limited uncertainty; it is a sudden, spontaneous emergence of novelty which appears when we contemplate a range of imagined outcomes of an immediate action" (Cohen, 1964, p. 39).

But our simile of the ant and the tree will serve us well if we use it to illustrate the importance of making wise decisions because so many of the decisions we make move us along our chosen "branch" toward the next set of alternatives. As Robert Frost so eloquently put it in "The Road Not Taken" (Matthiessen, 1950, p. 557):

> I shall be telling this with a sigh
> Somewhere ages and ages hence:
> Two roads diverged in a wood, and I —
> I took the one less traveled by,
> And that has made all the difference.

One additional concept should be mentioned in connection with the "decision tree" simile. Many of the decisions in life do not offer a "no-go" alternative. We cannot avoid such decisions; we must move one way or another. If we do not make our own decisions, then those decisions will inevitably be made for us by the exigencies of time and necessity. This is particularly true for career decisions. They may be delayed, but they cannot be avoided. No living organism can do nothing. And if the individual does not "opt" for his or her own choices, then forces outside the individual will "co-opt" those choices and move the individual along the path (or branch) of least resistance. In simpler words, not to decide is to decide.

Accepting the necessity of making decisions can become a part of the challenge and the joy of living; avoiding it or fearing it contributes to the frustrations and unhappiness of life.

## The Challenge of Uncertainty

Is there anyone who has not wished for Aladdin's magic lamp or, better yet, for a crystal ball which could reveal the future? Decisions would be much easier, we think, if we could only see into the future and *know* what would happen as a result of our decisions. Of course, the key to *good* decision making is to remove as much as possible of the unknown from the future by intelligent analysis of the present and rational projections of future developments based on that analysis. But no amount of intelligence can remove all of the uncertainty from the future.

And how dull life would be without uncertainty! Uncertainty adds excitement, suspense, adventure, intrigue! But it also adds fear and irresolution and doubt and acquiescence.

Imagine Janice Junior on a Friday morning in the fall. She's worried because she doesn't have a date to the Saturday night stomp, and it's "boy's choice." She's depressed. She doesn't pay attention to her teachers. She wonders if anyone will ask her. As each class period ends she becomes more unhappy and frustrated. She blames it on her hair style, the shape of her legs, her mother's strict rules. Finally, just before school adjourns for the football game, Sammy Senior asks Janice to the stomp. She is relieved, but already worrying about what to wear and how she will look on Saturday night.

At the football game, Janice enters completely into the frenzy of rooting for the school team. She screams, yells, sings, jumps up and down, and refuses to admit that the team might lose, even when they're behind by sixteen points. There's always a chance they can come from behind, Janice thinks, and everthing she does is in anticipation of a victory. When the game is over, and the team has lost, she is disappointed and perhaps depressed... but not for long. Other activities intervene to cheer her up.

In both cases our heroine was confronted with uncertainty. In one instance the uncertainty almost defeated her; in the other instance the uncertainty challenged her, excited her, and even changed her body chemistry to give her renewed energy.

We all face uncertainty in many things we do or attempt to do. Even if we could do so, it probably would be a mistake for most of us to try to eliminate all of that uncertainty, because it can be the source of great motivation, desire, and success, just as it is the source of excitement for the millions of spectators at sporting events. In fact, uncertainty may be essential to success in our endeavors. According to Cohen (1964, p. 119):

> It acts...as an inner stimulus, it excites the daredevil spirit, and mobilizes all the skill and agility of which the performer is capable. Without it, insufficient effort might be forthcoming. If you are totally and absolutely convinced that you will succeed in a task you will, paradoxically, exert less (and perhaps insufficient) effort than if you do not feel this absolute assurance. The suspicion of possible failure serves to marshal all one's reserves. At the same time the element of doubt induces the performer to take every possible precaution, and he never trusts to luck. For when a performer begins to rely on luck, the rot sets in.

There is some reason to suspect that successful individuals in many walks of life *use* uncertainty rather than allowing uncertainty to *use* them. Psychological studies of risk taking indicate at least two distinct types of individuals. One type is intent upon the possibilities of success and has a tendency to ignore the possibilities of failure; the other type is intent upon discovering a path which has the fewest possibilities of failure. This difference must distinguished from the difference between optimism and pessimism. On the one hand, the individual wants to maximize his or her hope of success, and on the other hand the individual wants to minimize the possibility of failure. Both are optimistic, but they choose different ways of expressing optimism. The distinction is important in consideration of decision making, because these two differing attitudes doubtless act as motivators in any situation involving choice. Some people are more eager to avoid failure than to achieve success, and others are more eager to achieve success than to avoid failure. Studies indicate more of us belong to the first category than to the second (Atkinson, 1957, pp. 359–72).

In approaching the subject of decision making, teachers can point out the benefits of uncertainty and help students understand how uncertainty can be a challenge rather than a

danger. The decision-making process is designed not to eliminate all uncertainties (that is impossible) but to provide means
of improving the potential for calculating probabilities of both
success and failure.

## *Theoretical Foundations*

The theory of decision making is extremely complex, and it
occupies the time and efforts of many psychologists, sociologists,
communications experts, and management theorists. Here,
we are not so concerned with the theory as we are with the
practical aspects of decision making, particularly with respect
to decisions about work and careers. However, the theorists
provide us with a few concepts which will make the subject
more comprehensible and utilitarian.

For one thing, the experts divide the variables which
influence decision making into two main categories or classes.
The first is called "utility," and the second is called "probability" (Edwards and Tversky, 1967, p. 7). Once again, we over-
simplify greatly, but "utility" decisions are those based on the
attractiveness of various alternatives, and "probability" decisions are those based on the probability of events occurring.
For example, one decides to pursue a career in mechanics
because one finds that activity more attractive than accounting.
This is a utility decision. On the other hand, one may decide
to seek a career in management because there is high likelihood
of an above-average income in that field. This is a probability
decision. Obviously, most career decisions are derived from
combinations of utility and probability variables, but some
understanding of these two different classes can be most useful
in working toward important decisions. Utility decisions tend
to be emotional or value decisions, not subject to arguments
of reason, while probability decisions tend to be arrived at on
rational grounds.

Another concept which deserves stating, even though it
may be obvious to most educators, is the individual variability
which exists in making decisions. Given the same information
and the same opportunities, different individuals will make
different decisions. Furthermore, a single individual will make

different decisions at different times, even though the alternatives appear to be exactly the same. None of this is surprising in view of the previously discussed fact that there are at least two types of basic attitudes about decision making, and in view of the fact that decisions have a cumulative nature. Individual differences affect decision making in many ways. Creative persons are likely to be much more imaginative and divergent in analyzing data; they will be much "looser" in making decisions, and their decisions may appear to the observer as unwarranted in relation to more common perceptions of the facts. Conversely, convergent thinkers — the noncreative — will follow distinct patterns in their decision making.

The implications of the concept of variability are that the teacher or counselor should encourage varied decisions by students, and that individuals should not be discouraged by the fact that their decisions tend to change from time to time. This is not a sign of weakness or of being wishy-washy; it is entirely normal and necessary for personal growth.

The decision-making curriculum introduced in 1972 by the College Entrance Exam Board has shown that decision making is a skill that can be taught. Educators and students have responded to the program with a high degree of enthusiasm and a consistent expression that this is something that individuals in school or anywhere else need. In addition to the research that has been conducted by the college board on the "Deciding/Decisions and Outcomes" program, the initial work on Donald Super's Career Development Inventory has proved promising. As curriculum and programs are developed and evaluated, one can be assured that more and more people in the educational community will be able to help individuals learn to make well-considered, well-informed decisions.

Still another concept comes not from decision making theorists but from the developmental theory of Jean Piaget. According to Piaget (Bolton, 1972, p. 71), at some time near the age of twelve years, a child enters the period of "formal operations." This involves a reorientation to reality, and it constitutes the major advance of formal over concrete thinking. This period of development is characterized by (1) the ability to think in terms of possibilities or "what might be," (2) the ability to think propositionally or to make logical extensions of the relations between objects and events, and (3) the ability to think in terms of systematic combinations and the analysis of those combinations. In other words, about the time a student enters high school he or she first reaches the stage in development when long-range decision making becomes possible. Prior to that time the child is essentially limited to thinking only in terms of the concrete operations of classification and relation of objects and events. This situation has two important implications for career education and decision making. First, the process of propositional decision making may be relatively new to students, and its scope and complexity may be somewhat intimidating. Second, some students may be reluctant to make the kinds of commitments which career decision making implies, since they are accustomed to dealing with decisions of much shorter duration.

However, the skills required for formal thinking and decision making can be taught, and the motivation to use those skills can be learned through practice and through increased understanding of both the purpose and the process of decision making.

## The Decision-Making Process

We know considerably more about the process of decision making than we do about the act itself. This is because we can break the process down into its various tasks and examine each of the tasks independently. Such task analysis has been conducted extensively, particularly with group activity and particularly as it applies to business organizations. However, the same task breakdown is applicable to decisions of individuals. The principles and process of decision making can be taught but, like every other behavioral topic, it must be practiced to be really learned. High school courses on almost any topic can provide opportunities to learn and practice decision making. Contract learning is a good approach, allowing students to decide exactly what projects they will undertake and when they will do and complete them. Group projects and class assignments that allow students a choice help teach the key skills of decision making. They also help students learn that few decisions need be lonely decisions, and input from others is almost always helpful. We strongly recommend that students who are involved in decision making use the resources, the reactions, and the support of their teachers, counselors, parents, peers, and any others with whom they can discuss such matters.

To successfully teach decision making, one must first identify the steps in making any decision, and then try to make the steps as rational as possible. These steps are:

(1) Identifying the decision to be made

(2) Gathering information for decision

(3) Identifying the available alternatives

(4) Weighing the evidence

(5) Choosing among the alternatives

(6) Implementing the decision

(7) Reviewing and modifying the decision

To break a decision — irrespective of its simplicity — into these seven steps may seem cumbersome. Yet consider the steps incorporated into the relatively simple decision of what to wear for the day. The decision must be made. Consciously or unconsciously one must marshal information needed for the decisions: What is the weather? What are the activities to be undertaken during the day? What is the impression one desires to make? What clothes does one own? One then looks into the closet and observes the alternatives available, weighs them against the data concerning weather, activities and so forth, and then makes the choice and dons the clothing. Upon looking in the mirror, the tie does not match the suit or the blouse isn't right for the skirt. A change is quickly made and one is off to school or to work.

### Identifying the Decisions to be Made

To know what decisions must be made, what ones are best delayed, which can be made now or later, and which are inter-related to what others is the beginning of wisdom. Some decisions are moral decisions of right and wrong, based on one's value system, religion, or law of the land. More are pragmatic decisions of "better" and "worse." Seldom can they be described simply as "good" or "bad." Few decisions are clean-cut. There are pros and cons, advantages and disadvantages. It is more useful to think of those which, on balance, have positive results as satisfying decisions and those which balance out in the negative as unsatisfying. Every decision is impeded by complex constraints of risk, their impact on others, and lack of information upon which to base decisions or lack of resources to carry them out. Therefore, to make a decision is the first decision. Many youth will be unaware that, as stated before, to decide not to decide is a decision in itself. Many will be reluctant to make decisions and should be aware of the reasons for their reluctance. These constraints on making decisions are usefully divided between the internal and the external (Epperley, *et al.*, p. 13). Internal constraints may be fear of failure, risk or change, lack of self-confidence, ambivalence, stereotyped notions of oneself and one's prospects, or procrastination. External constraints are those such as family expectations and responsibilities, societal stereotyping, peer pressure, or laws. Every student should be aware of the inherent tendency to blame internal reluctance on external constraints, rather than to face one's own fears or lack of self-discipline.

Every student must understand that any decision involves risk and uncertainty. No one has a crystal ball to know "what will happen if"? One reason for following a coherent decision-making process is to reduce those risks and uncertainties. Gathering all possible information and examining all alternatives can do that, but risk and uncertainty can never be eliminated. Some decisions are inherently more risky than others, and one must assess the degree of uncertainty and the potential loss from a wrong decision in order to decide how much time and resources to invest to reduce that uncertainty. Having counted the costs of deciding and not deciding and having reduced the risks by gathering information, one generally has greater confidence in the decision. However, some people, as a result of personality and experiences, are inherently more fearful of risk than others. Because such personality factors are so ingrained by the time a student reaches high school, they are difficult, but not impossible, to change. Students can be helped to build their self-confidence by inventorying their strengths and by noting the number of decisions, no matter how minor, that they make successfully each day.

The potential decision maker should also be brought to realize the values of sharing impending decisions with others, getting all of the advice possible, but ultimately making and taking the responsibility for one's own decisions. High school students, particularly, should be aware that the key measure of maturity is one's willingness to make decisions and accept the consequences of one's own decisions without trying to shift them or the blame for them to others.

It is also useful to recognize that some decisions are irreversible and, once made, should not be looked back upon, but that one must go on from there. However, most are not irreversible, and one should not be reluctant to reverse oneself or change course when there is evidence to justify it.

To decide what decisions must be made, one should be clear about one's goals and objectives. This is particularly true when the decisions to be made are long run, such as those related to careers.

Goals are the broad and ultimate ends, and objectives are the more specific milestones which bring the goals into reach. Career goals should start with the overall life-style the individual would like to pursue, and they should identify the array of career paths which are consistent with that life-style. Considerations such as job content, employment prospects, employment stability, pay and income promotion possibilities, and all of the usual list of career prospects are meaningful only in the context of the life-style to which they contribute. This is true whether one is disposed to be a "workaholic" or one who works mainly to afford leisure-time activities.

One's goals are also the only meaningful test of rationality. A decision is rational which contributes to the achievement of one's goals. An individual who desires a long life is irrational to jump over a cliff but one who is deliberately set on suicide may be acting rationally. It is much easier to determine rationality by this test than it is to criticize someone else's goals.

Having identified career paths consistent with his or her preferred life-style, the decision maker than explores them, hoping to minimize the uncertainties surrounding the goals.

These uncertainties can be lessened by the individual coming to an understanding of the personal values and needs underlying that life-style preference. In doing so, it is important that the student extend his or her career horizons beyond that which is familiar because of family and community surroundings. These, more than obstacles to education and training or discrimination in employment, tend to lock youth into narrow career tracks. They can explore only those alternatives that seem realistic to them. A student whose parent is a beautician may choose the same occupation because the educational needs, job requirements, working conditions, and life-style are familiar. For the same student to consider becoming an attorney would require exploration of an entirely new range of qualifications, opportunities, and life-styles.

Having chosen a goal, one can then set forth a series of objectives, achievement of which will bring one closer and closer to one's long-range goals.

Goals are often vague and difficult to define. Objectives, to be useful, must be desirable, achievable, and measurable. One must be able to establish a plan for achieving them and then measure the progress being made toward them. Only then can one know whether a plan is working or needs modification.

## Gathering Information for Decisions

Having decided upon an area for a decision, in this case career choice, whether tentative or final, one gathers the information for decision. All of the comments above are germane to knowing what information to gather. An important principle is that information has costs. One decides how much to invest in accumulating information based on the importance of the decision, the costs of a wrong decision, and the irreversibility of the decision.

One must know what information will be useful — where to find it, how to accumulate it, and how to use it. For career decision making, the most important information needed concerns oneself — values, goals, likes and dislikes, talents, and abilities. Then one must consider the impact on and reaction of family and friends most significant in one's life. These considerations must then be compared to the opportunities that are and will be available, to the present and future employment prospects, to the preparation and training requirements, the content of the various jobs that will likely make up the career, the income and stability prospects, the implied life-style (on and off the job), and the risks of failure and success. Therefore, the information gathering process begins with facts about oneself.

### Exploring Oneself

Each student should participate in some sort of self-analysis in which she or he makes a realistic inventory of personal characteristics. The inventory must include a system of values and evolve values classification activities (see chapter 3), an assessment of interests, an honest appraisal of personality traits, a listing of both abilities and capabilities, an estimation of motivation and desire, and some consideration of pressures from outside sources such as parents, friends, teachers, and relatives. A simple self-analysis can be constructed by having the student list (1) personal strengths (the things I do well and enjoy), (2) leisure-time activities I enjoy most and do best, (3) the subjects I enjoy most in school, (4) the qualities I admire most in myself and others, and (5) the occupational areas I find most interesting.

Ideally, this inventorying process should begin earlier than high school and should continue throughout life. It is a process which requires the thinking skills of Piaget's "formal operations" period; and thus it will not be easy for those students who are just moving into that stage of development. As a matter of fact, it will not be easy for any student, because self-analysis is never an easy thing to accomplish. Frequently, it is a painful process, but it is not nearly so painful as the consternation which may occur later in life if early self-inventory and self-analysis are not completed. Personal judgment on self-evaluation can be supplemented by asking friends, parents, teachers, or classmates to participate in the self-appraisal exercise.

In this regard, teachers and counselors must be extremely careful as they assist students in acquiring self-analysis skills. A positive self-concept can be developed by building on personal strengths rather than emphasizing personal limitations. It is important to realize that the same decision-making process applies to the concept of turning a negative quality into a positive quality by identifying goals and objectives designed to meet those goals. The student must feel free to explore his or her personal traits without fear that these traits will be subjected to harsh judgment by peers or teachers. Students who fear criticism of particular traits will quite naturally try to hide them from the group and, more importantly, from themselves. Teachers must emphasize that the process is one of exploration and discovery, not judgment and comparison.

Many tools are available to assist with the accumulation of inventory items. As mentioned in chapter 5, most state Job Service offices are prepared to administer various types of interest inventory "tests." In many instances, representatives of the employment service will come to the school and administer the tests if arrangements are completed far enough in advance. Much has been written in criticism of these test instruments, and most educators are aware of the limitations of such tests. However, they do provide a base from which to build a more meaningful inventory of interests. New instruments are being designed and tested, and we feel that they are particularly useful in indicating those areas where current interests are expressed. Once again, the best indicators of present and future interests are past activities. Students should examine the ways in which they spend their time. They should make lists of things they most like to do and things they least like to do. By analyzing those lists for patterns of interest and by comparing them with the results of interest tests, they can begin to place interests in some order of priority.

Similar exercises should occur with regard to values. The process of value clarification and related activities is discussed in chapter 3. New literature on values clarification is readily available to most educators, and contains numerous exercises designed to help students assess their own value systems. Some of these exercises involve group activity and some are based on individual activities in writing and speaking. Some depend on student-teacher interactions to divulge value orientations. The point is that a sufficient number and variety of values clarification exercises are available so that one or more might be productively included in the work outline of almost any course.

They provide a means for students to identify their personal values and recognize value conflicts as they relate to career decisions. Conflict resolutions can be accomplished by using the same decision-making process referred to earlier in this chapter. Some of the activities included in the Human Potential Seminars conducted by James McHolland would be appropriate for high school use.

Personality characteristics should also be inventoried. One way to conduct a personality inventory is for the instructor to provide a list of fifteen or twenty personal characteristics. These should be varied enough to cover such things as interpersonal relationships, grooming and personal habits, and attitudes. Each student rates himself or herself for each trait on a scale of 1 to 10, and then asks five others to do the same. Raters should include peers, parents, and at least one "outside" acquaintance. The student can make a profile or inventory, arranging the traits in order from strong to weak. We emphasize once again that no value judgments should be implied concerning the listed traits. The extrovert is no more valuable to himself or herself — or to society — then the introvert. Each is important, and each can find a work role which is equally satisfying.

With some guidance, the student can also complete inventories of abilities and capabilities, of desire, and of motivation as measured by such things as energy, attention to detail, patience, attendance and promptness, follow through, and conscientiousness in such experiences as music lessons or athletic practice sessions. The student should be able to determine factors which are personally satisfying from work experience, leisure activities, school activities or subjects, and with part-time or summer jobs. This is a good time to introduce the concept discussed above that some individuals seek success while others seek to avoid failure. Most individuals respond to reward motivation, but some seem to require pre-task pressure. Some individuals are self-motivators; others are more comfortable in a structured situation. Some can sustain motivation through to completion of long-range tasks; others prefer tasks which can be completed quickly. Some seem to take pleasure in detailed work; others become nervous and unproductive when attention to detail is an important part of the task.

As in all of the categories of personal inventory, the descriptors selected must be based upon past experience, not on future hopes. The objective is to find out what actually motivates the student, not what the student wishes would motivate her or him. If a student expresses a desire to act in a service capacity but has never shown any proclivity toward this type of activity in the past, chances are that "service" should not be placed too high on the list of motivators. It's admirable to want to serve, but students must begin to face the reality that they will be much more comfortable and productive in fields for which personal motivation exists. Despite the protestations of some observers, the young girl who has more patience with the neighbor's children than with her mathematics assignment will probably find more satisfaction as a mother than as an accountant. Of course, one of the primary goals of career education is to give that young lady both the information and the opportunity to choose from among a number of occupations, including motherhood.

One final bit of information ought to be included on each student's personal inventory, and that is some consideration of the outside pressures which are part of every student's life. This should be entered as "present life circumstances" because it is not really a part of the student's character, but is a reality of factors to be considered in the decision-making process. These pressures need to be recognized by both the student and his associates. They cannot be dealt with if they are hidden or ignored. All students are under pressure from parents, teachers, and peers to behave in certain ways and to move in certain career directions. Students will respond to those pressures, based on their values and life circumstances and they need to be aware of them.

As the personal inventory information is gathered — and analyzed over a period of several days or a semester — each student should write it down in some orderly fashion. The decision data sheet in Figure 3 is one suggestion for a personal inventory profile. Naturally, these entries can and will change and priorities will shift as the student matures. However, most students will evidence a surprising degree of consistency and will begin to see patterns emerge which will help them identify

Decision Data Sheet
(Personal inventory profile)

In each column, list items in order of priority or importance.

| Values | Interests | Abilities and Capabilities | Character Traits | Motivators |
|--------|-----------|----------------------------|------------------|------------|
|        |           |                            |                  |            |

Outside pressures (Include a one- or two-sentence summary of the pressures you feel from parents, friends, and others with regard to career expectations):

_____

_____

**Figure 3.** Summary Sheet for Data from Personal Analysis Inventory

their career area interests and enable them to make the appropriate career decision.

## Occupational and Labor Market Information

Prepared with a deepened understanding of one's values, preferred life-style, likes, dislikes, and abilities, the decision maker can accumulate information about the occupational and career alternatives compatible with self-perception. The information must be ordered in some meaningful fashion. Careers themselves can be grouped in occupational clusters' or some other logical grouping. The twelve to sixteen career cluster areas as identified by USOE and other researchers in career education will be useful to the high school student. Some states have also designed career clusters related to high school subjects. Information about each potential career alternative can be segregated into such categories as "life-style," "income," "training required," "geographic location of opportunities," "skills required," and so on. This is one reason that an exercise revolving round this second step in the decision-making process is such an ideal exercise for a class in English composition: It required students not only to research information but to organize it in a written presentation, and organization is one of the keys to good writing.

Those students who have had the benefits of career education programs throughout the early school years have a distinct advantage when they reach this stage of decision making. They have been accumulating information about careers throughout their school years. They are familiar with work values and how they apply to various career opportunities. They have explored a wide range of career possibilities, either on a cluster basis or through some other organized system. They understand such things as job stratification, career ladders, and life-styles, and they know about "people" jobs, "data" jobs, and "thing" jobs.

Such students have an advantage, and this is why career education is necessary for all ages. Students who have had no experience with career education in the lower grades can still work at the marshaling of information in high school if they are provided sufficient guidance by teachers and counselors.

The process is one of focusing on those careers which fit within the limits established by the self-identification. For most students, many occupations will fit within these limits, but the number should probably be narrowed to three or four as the information gathering proceeds. Naturally, the more knowledge a student has about the breadth of opportunities, the better are his or her chances of identifying those careers which hold the most promise. Career educators advocate an extensive program of career exploration in the junior high school to provide the broadest possible vision of career potential for each student.

Many sources of information about occupations and careers are available. School counselors are aware of those sources, and in most cases counselors will have a career information file. A primary source of career information is the *Occupational Outlook Handbook*, but that is only a beginning. Additional information should be sought from persons already employed in the specific occupations under study, from the thousands of trade associations whose job is partially to promote worker interest in the trade or occupation, from government agencies which keep track of employment statistics, from education groups which maintain information about training specialties of various educational institutions, and from magazine and newspaper accounts of activities within specific occupations. Information about local, state, and national careers and job opportunities can be developed by students to establish a "Career Resources File" in the school library where this information can be collected and made available for easy reference.

When the student's own inventory of self is compared with complete information about career alternatives, considerable uncertainty about "job fit" can be eliminated. This is particularly valuable in reducing the chance that a student will work toward a career goal which can provide nothing but frustration and unhappiness for that particular student. The process will not eliminate all uncertainty, but it can often point to a poor career choice which the student will want to avoid.

However, no matter how pleasing the "fit" may be, the student should accept the age-old caution about not putting all the eggs in one basket, and he or she should explore alternatives.

### *Weighing the Evidence and Choosing among Alternatives*

Choosing among alternatives involves exploration of alternative life goals, alternative career patterns, alternative occupational choices, and alternative priorities of preparation and access to those occupations. No business person would tackle a problem or make a decision without establishing some alternative goals, because like the ant in our decision tree simile, it is possible to end up "out on a limb," no matter how much uncertainty may have been eliminated. Future events are difficult to predict, as well as that which one will really find fulfilling. With regard to career goals, three basic unpredictables exist:

(1) The goal may prove to be unattainable, because the job market may change; or the individual may run out of time, money, or motivation; or outside forces such as marriage and family may intervene.

(2) The goal, once reached, may prove to be unfulfilling or only temporarily satisfying.

(3) The individual may simply want to change careers at some future time in life. Research indicates that this is rapidly becoming not only a possibility in our society but a probability.

Therefore, one should have begun by expanding the alternatives before beginning to narrow them. The student must also learn to be intensely practical in identifying the obstacles which might stand in the way of achieving any goal. Yet one must be careful that personal and social stereotypes do not unduly limit one's conception of available alternatives. The wise decision maker weighs the pros and cons of each alternative, considering both the short- and long-run implications and analyzes the risks involved in each in contrast to the risks he or she feels comfortable in taking.

Having narrowed the possible career areas of interest, one is wise to explore the alternative occupations which might serve the said purposes. For example, the young woman who wants to be a physician might also investigate related career areas such as nursing or physical therapy. The potential automobile mechanic might also look into refrigeration mechanics and diesel mechanics. But some special effort should be made to investigate alternative careers which are unrelated to the primary goals but which meet the criteria established in the self-exploration phase. For instance, the student who is attracted by the routine of an assembly-line job may find the criteria established in his or her personal inventory are met equally well by certain types of accounting work. In other words, students should attempt to augment their utility-based goals with some probability-based goals. The sooner one can identify these disparate alternatives, the more likely one is able to shift gears and prepare for "options" in later life.

This is a good point at which to mention the burdens of occupational freedom. As with all forms of freedom, occupational freedom brings with it the burden of responsibility. When options are narrow or nonexistent, one has no responsibility to choose wisely or carefully, because the choices are made *for* the individual by outside forces. As the freedom of choice expands to include a wide range of potential occupations, then the responsibility to make wise choices becomes increasingly burdensome. This includes responsibility to self as well as responsibility to others. While the concern should be to find and establish a career pattern satisfying to oneself, few can be happy without the approval of others, and much of career satisfaction emanates from the feeling that one is being of service to others.

Let us examine this question with regard to the ongoing "liberation" of women in our society. When every woman was "supposed" to be a mother and a wife, with few other options, then the responsibility for choice by women in our society was practically nonexistent. A woman simply learned to cook, to raise children, and to smile benignly at her husband as she obeyed his every command. And if she was unhappy in that role, she could always blame it on society, or on her husband. After all, it was not her decision. (In deference to males, their choices were limited, also; they *had* to be breadwinners.) Now we are into an era when women have freedom to choose. In fact, their freedom of choice may be even more broad than that of men for a certain period of history while we make adjustment to a more open society. Girls and women can still choose to be mothers and housewives, or to pursue a working career, or to become heavily involved in volunteer work, or any combination of these alternatives. The point is that women now have freedom of choice, with all the responsibilities that accompany such freedom. Furthermore, since men still act as breadwinners in many instances, the choices of women need not always be economically motivated. This places a heavy responsibility on young women of high school age. They must make rational decisions about life-styles and career goals, and frequently they must anticipate changing career goals one or more times in their lives. Thus the exploration of alternative career goals may be even more important for female students than for male students.

An important part of the collection of information about specific careers is the investigation of entry procedures and training requirements, discussed in chapter 5. For some occupations, the access paths are well defined. The professions require certain educational training and licensing. Most craft trades require apprenticeship and union membership. But other occupations may permit many different routes of entry. For example, one may achieve a management position from several directions. One may work from the bottom up, although this route is more romantic than real in our current system. One may study management in a school of business and enter a firm on the junior executive or middle executive level. One may study marketing or law or engineering and enter a firm in those specialties, hoping to grow into a management position. Finally, one may achieve a management position through the organization of one's own company, in which case the accumulation of capital or credit sources is a prerequisite.

In the process of decision making, all of these alternative approaches must be listed for the major career goals under consideration, as well as for those alternative goals discussed above. Of course, no listing of approaches is complete without detailed statements about the time and energy involved, the training institutions available, the locations of such institutions, the costs of training or capital acquisition, the academic and skills levels required to complete training, and the competition for openings in the training institutions.

Education and training are not the only preparations necessary for entry into occupations. Those in some occupations require adjustment of attitudes — the clergy, for example— or changes in life-style which can be "phased in" over a period of time. The person whose ambition involves farming, horticulture, or gardening may have to learn to change a pattern of summer recreational activities to one of winter recreation.

The accumulation of information about alternative measures for goal achievement can best be achieved by reading, by conversations with others, by communications with those already in the field, and by discussions with career counselors. Once the alternative routes are listed and thoroughly considered, the student should select the most promising one. However, information about the alternatives should not be discarded, for it may prove valuable if future modifications of goals or objectives should occur.

Having weighed all of the evidence and chosen among the alternatives, the student as decision maker is ready to move to implementation of the decision. As this occurs, it is important that the student recognize three other facts about decisions: (1) the test of maturity is the extent to which one takes responsibility for his or her decisions; (2) decisions of this nature are highly personal and, right or wrong, only for the person who makes them and must live with them; (3) few decisions are irreversible, but some are. The wise decision maker knows the difference and acts accordingly.

### Implementing the Decision of a Program

Decisions should be implemented according to a preconceived plan which includes a timetable for the accomplishment and a periodic review of the progress being made. The student should realize that there should be no reluctance or embarrassment in making changes in that plan as experience indicates the need for modifications.

Quite obviously, by the time a student has reached this step in the decision-making process, the career goal has been selected. The student knows, at least tentatively, where she or he wants to go and how to get there. What remains is to set a timetable and identify interim objectives. It does no good whatsoever to set a goal without dividing the path toward that goal into achievable, measurable objectives. In football, the goal is to move the ball across the goal line. But the team which is most likely to win the most games is the one which does not depend on the occasional "long bomb," but sets its interim objectives at making five yards at a time to earn a series of first downs.

Interim objectives serve at least three functions: First, they motivate because it is easier to plan and accomplish for short-range tasks than for long-range goals. Second, they provide a sense of accomplishment and progress as each interim objective is reached. Third, they provide a measure against which to test progress and see if movement toward the goal is continuing on schedule.

In the case of career goals, each occupation provides a different set of interim objectives. They may include acquisition of certain skills or competencies, completion of certain courses, graduation from high school or other institutions, completion of various work experience programs, accumulation of a certain level of wealth or credit, entry into a work situation, or receipt of certain certificates of recognition. Whatever the nature of the objectives, they should be detailed as completely as possible and attached to a realistic time schedule.

Once that is done, the student has effectively implemented a program designed to lead toward a career goal. At this point, it may appear that the decision-making process is complete, that the decision has been made. But no decision is final until the goal is either achieved, modified, or discarded.

### Reviewing and Modifying the Decision

Ideally, by the time students leave high school they will be well aware that decision making is a *process*, not an *event*. They will have set goals and will be working toward those goals, but they will understand that as more information is accumulated, the goals may change. Almost assuredly, the goals *will* change for everyone; for some, the goals will change drastically.

Those changes may be a function of the monitoring and evaluation which students must be prepared to do. Preparation for ongoing evaluation of career goals should be a part of high school career education. This step involves measuring progress against that timetable of interim objectives. It is the easiest step of all, although perhaps one of the most painful. In a sense, it is a test of how much uncertainty was removed at previous steps in the decision process, how well the student evaluated himself or herself, how carefully career information was accumulated, and how reasonably objectives were identified and scheduled.

However, the primary purpose of monitoring and evaluation is a protective one. To return to the decision tree simile once again – this step is designed to protect against traveling too far out on that limb before turning back, or against traveling too fast...or not fast enough.

The monitoring and evaluation step should divulge any obvious weaknesses in the original program. If progress is not being made according to plan, then one must either change the plan or change the level of performance. The program might be stretched over a longer period of time, or it might be modified to include additional objectives, or it might be discarded altogether. Discarding the original program may not mean discarding the goal (although that, too, is a possibility). It may simply mean activitating one of the alternative plans.

If all goes according to plan, the student – at this point a young or not-so-young adult – will find herself or himself well on the way toward implementing a career plan and accomplishing a goal, two components of the same process. As life circumstances change, the individual will continually update the personal inventory, expand the horizons of career possibilities, and explore new career goals. In all likelihood, career decision making, like career education, is a process which will continue throughout a lifetime.


### Scope of the Process

At first glance, it may appear that career decision making is a long and difficult process. Indeed, it is not a simple thing, and as we said in the beginning, even this complex explanation is an oversimplification. But spread over the full span of the high school years, the process is not nearly so intimidating as it may appear in this condensed description. Most of the skills involved are skills which every citizen must develop.

Here, we advocate a more formalized approach with the vital practice of putting information down on paper instead of trying to handle the total process in the mind. Career educators are convinced that a minimal amount of training in these skills will contribute great dividends for individual students and for society.

Furthermore, the evidence is clear that incorporation of this type of skill training in the classroom — all classrooms — brings benefits to both teacher and student. It will help motivate students, and it will add relevance and interest to course materials. The next chapter will explore some of the ways in which career education can be incorporated into the academic classroom.

## References

Atkinson, J. W. "Motivational Determinants of Risk-Taking Behavior." *Psychological Review* (1957), vol. 64.

Berdie, Ralph F.; and Hood, Albert. *Decisions for Tomorrow: Plans for High School Seniors after Graduation.* Minneapolis: University of Minnesota Press. 1965.

Bolton, Neil. *The Psychology of Thinking.* London: Methuen & Co. 1972.

Cohen, John. *Behavior in Uncertainty.* New York: Basic Books. 1964.

Edwards, Ward; and Tversky, Amos. Editors. *Decision Making.* Middlesex, England: Penguin Books. 1967.

Epperley, Jane R.; *et al. Emphasis: Decisions.* Annandale: Northern Virginia Community College. 1976.

Gelatt, H. B.; *et al. Deciding.* New York: College Entrance Examination Board. 1972.
_____; *et al. Decisions and Outcomes.* New York: College Entrance Examination Board. 1973.

Herr, Edwin L. *Decision Making and Vocational Development.* Boston: Houghton Mifflin. No date.

Hoyt, Kenneth B.; and Hebeler, Jean R. Editors. *Career Education for Gifted and Talented Students.* Salt Lake City: Olympus Publishing Company. 1974.

Katz, Martin. *Decisions and Values*. New York: College Entrance Examination Board. 1963.

Levitan, Sar A.; and Johnston, William B. *Work Is Here to Stay, Alas*. Salt Lake City: Olympus Publishing Company. 1973.

Matthiessen, F. O. Editor. *The Oxford Book of American Verse*. New York: Oxford University Press. 1950.

McHolland, James. *Decision Making Resource Manual*. Evanston, Illinois: Human Potential Seminars. 1972.

Newell, Allen; and Simon, Herbert A. *Human Problem Solving*. Englewood Cliffs, New Jersey: Prentice-Hall. 1972.

# 7

# Academic Foundations

The proponents of career education are wholly convinced that a natural affinity exists between the goals of career education and the goals of those academic disciplines traditionally associated with a "liberal education" — such subjects as English, mathematics, foreign languages, social sciences, the arts, and physical education. In simplified terms, these goals are: first, to help the student develop an understanding of self and society; second, to assist the student in becoming a contributing member of that society; third, to help the student develop self-awareness and self-esteem; and fourth, to provide motivation for the learning of academic subject matter.

Furthermore, proponents of career education are just as convinced that career education is totally dependent upon solid academic foundations and that the academic classroom can receive material benefits if it actively relates subject matter to career goals and needs. This natural symbiosis provides one of the key strengths of the career education movement, for it means that not only does career education pose *no* threat to traditional academic subjects but it actually provides stimulus for added interest in those subjects. For example, it is unthinkable that a student would develop a meaningful value system (chapter 3) without some foundations in the social sciences and the physical sciences. It is unreasonable to expect a student to deal with labor market statistics (chapter 5) without first providing some foundation in library research, arithmetic, and English composition.

This need for solid academic foundations becomes even more pronounced when it is related to careers themselves. We are no longer a nation of farmers, laborers, and production-line workers — if indeed we ever were. Those occupations are still vitally important. But we are also now a nation of teachers, accountants, secretaries, professional men and women, mechanics and cashiers. As Levitan and Johnston note (1973, p. 83):

> From the bird's eye view, employment has changed during the century from agrarian to industrial to "white collar." Farming was the most common occupation in 1880; by 1940, blue-collar workers were the most numerous in the labor force; in 1970, white-collar occupations *outnumbered both of these combined.* (Emphasis added.)

Thus most occupations today require some capability for dealing with figures, ideas, words, people or some combination of those things. Even the skills required of the farmer and the laborer and the production-line worker now include computation, communication, and conceptualization of mechanical functions.

Virtually all workers in today's work force must be able to read and complete various written forms, to compute mathematical problems for reports or billings, and to deal socially with others on the job. Moreover, research indicates that those individuals who advance in any work situation — those who receive the promotions — are likely to be those who have developed communication, social, or computation skills in addition to job skills that are required for the particular occupation. A recent study noted that the qualities shared by successful persons in the management field include (1) oral persuasiveness, (2) social boldness, (3) self-confidence, (4) energy, and (5) sociability. According to the researcher who produced this list of qualities (Costello, 1976 p. 6):

> ...[The] successful manager is primarily an effective speaker. He likes to talk. He is willing to call on a customer

> cold, even if there is a distinct possibility that he may be
> thrown out. In other words, he is interested in persuading
> others to his point of view.... While oral communication
> is the most important factor in success, the ability to
> communicate in written form is probably important as well.

Other studies also indicate that specific job skills are often
only a small (although still necessary) part of the requirements
for success in any work situation. The acquisition of general
skills which are usable in many occupations can only increase
in importance as workers become more and more mobile, and
as frequent job changes during a lifetime become the rule instead of the exception.

Few would question the fact that students need to learn
English, mathematics, science, the arts, and other subject
matter in order to prepare themselves for life and for whatever
work they will do. But knowledge of that fact — even by students themselves — is not sufficient to motivate young people
to apply full effort toward the acquisition of skills in those
basic academic fields. As mentioned in the previous chapter,
students of high school age are just reaching the developmental
stage where they are able to think in terms of long-range planning and current preparation for future events. This type of
associational thinking is new to them, and they are not always
comfortable with it. The difficulty is compounded when the
associations they are asked to make are totally abstract associations. Little value is achieved by telling a student, "When
you get a job you will need to know how to write a complete
sentence." The student is more likely to be motivated if the
reference is a concrete one: "Salesmen must complete a sales
report daily or weekly. In order to do so, they must know how to
organize thoughts and write them in complete sentences. For
example,..."

Some may argue that high school students are not thinking
seriously about careers and that the inclusion of a career component in the academic classroom will not appeal to student
interests. The evidence is quite the contrary. As mentioned
earlier, at a recent series of career education miniconferences,
teachers themselves ranked "motivation of students" as the
number one benefit to be derived from including a career education component in academic subjects at the high school level.

Research indicates that students are thinking quite seriously about their careers as early as the eighth grade (Flores and Olsen, 1967, p. 112).

Students of high school age *are* thinking about careers, and they *are* motivated by perceived career needs. This is particularly true if students have had the benefits of career education activities in the early grades. However, for almost all students, the high school years are extremely difficult years as far as career planning is concerned. The period is a highly volatile one, and while most students will come to high school with specific career goals, those goals will change for the majority of students before they graduate (Super, 1969, p. 5). The problem is a complex one, which probably accounts in part for our propensity to avoid it. Conversely, however, avoiding it increases its complexity.

Students come to high school at various stages of development. Some are capable of thinking in terms of long-range planning; others have not yet reached that stage or are just learning to deal with it. Most are concerned about careers because they are asked to make choices among course offerings and because they are thinking about some type of work activity, either part time or during the summers. The more advanced students have already selected specific career goals and are working toward them with commitment and motivation. Students who are not yet capable of setting such specific goals may feel confused, worthless, even guilty. They may lack motivation and may be tempted to run away from the responsibility of decision making by dropping out of school. They may be extremely volatile in their interests as their career goals shift, and the good mathematics student one semester may fail mathematics the next.

It is a difficult time for students, and a difficult time for teachers. But we are confident that some of the difficulty can be alleviated through the incorporation of career education practices in the classroom. As discussed in the previous chapter, career education can help the student understand that decision making is a process, and that it continues not only through high school but through life. Students who have not set hard and fast goals need not feel inferior. Career education can help the teacher motivate students by showing them that some courses — particularly the academic courses — have application for almost all occupations, and that students who have not identified specific career goals can be accumulating meaningful skills just as surely as students who have identified their goals.

When approached in this fashion, career education loses all of the "threatening" proportions which some have attributed to it. Career education is an aid to the student and the teacher. The primary responsibility of the teacher is still the effective teaching of the subject matter; career education offers one way to enhance that effectiveness. The individual teacher is the key to the success of any educational program; career education merely provides an additional tool for that teacher, a tool with proven potential.

Since the proponents of career education envision *no* course in the curriculum titled "career education," and since they campaign for *no* career education unit within any course, the entire career education movement is dependent upon the willingness of all teachers to incorporate career education practices in the daily routine of the classroom. Teachers of English, mathematics, social sciences, physical sciences, foreign languages, and physical education are especially important, because the subject matter with which they deal has far-ranging application for virtually all occupations, as well as for the self-discovery process so necessary to effective career decision making.

## *Techniques for Practicing Career Education*

Any consideration of techniques for incorporating career education into the classroom must be based upon the reality of student orientation toward career development. As discussed above, the range of student needs will be extremely broad, particularly in high school. Students at lower levels of education tend to fall easily into recognizable categories: Elementary grade students are developing career awareness and work values; junior high students have reached the career exploration stage and are beginning to understand values. But in the high school, students cannot be so neatly categorized. Some are highly advanced in the career development stage and are consciously acquiring career skills; others have only recently narrowed the field and are just beginning to identify their own values and the skills they will need; still others have not moved beyond the exploration stage and are searching for a field of interest.

The teacher must take these varying levels of development into account. For example, a mathematics teacher may want to include a problem in which an automobile body repair worker is called upon to calculate an estimate for some body work. The teacher will naturally provide parts costs, hourly rates, percentage markups, and so on in order for the students to work out the problem. Conceivably, some students in the class may already have decided to pursue careers in auto body repair. Those students will understand the importance of the problem and the need to be able to solve it. But there may also be students who have never heard about such activity. They will benefit from a little extra information about that particular career, about the kinds of skills necessary for body repair work, and about the life-style usually associated with body repair workers. Perhaps the students who have already investigated such careers can be helpful in providing this type of information. In this way, the exercise assists with skill development as well as with career exploration and even values clarification.

As the career education movement continues to grow, more and more textbooks in all academic fields will be written to incorporate career education concepts. (Of course, the danger exists that some publishers will go too far and will produce textbooks in which academic content is sacrificed in a mistaken effort to capitalize on career education. Sophisticated teachers will recognize such materials and will guard against them.) But regardless of how well the textbooks absorb the principles of career education, the primary responsibility rests with the individual teacher. Only the teacher is in a position to identify the needs and the resources of the students in his or her class, and to respond to those needs by taking advantage of the unique "teaching moments" which arise in every classroom.

"Teaching moments" provide convenient, meaningful opportunities to include career education in daily learning activities. They are moments of digression, based upon previous events in the classroom, which allow the teaching of a concept or an idea in a short period of time. The time involved may be from five seconds to fifteen minutes, and the teaching moment can be spontaneous, contrived, or planned. A spontaneous teaching moment is exactly what the term implies. It may occur at any time, and it may originate in a question, a comment, or an action of a student, of a teacher, or of any other person or persons. For example, during a demonstration about photosynthesis, a student may ask a question about job opportunities in the field of biology. That provides the teacher an opportunity to mention the types of jobs available and the amount of training required, or to ask other members of the class what their career exploration activities have uncovered concerning such jobs. Or perhaps a paper airplane is launched from an unknown point in the classroom. It gives the mathematics teacher a chance to talk about aerodynamics and the field of aeronautical engineering. It gives the social studies teacher a chance to demonstrate the principles of organization by setting up one "production line" where each student makes one fold in a paper airplane without any design or management, and another "production line" where one individual is designated as "designer" and another as "manager." It gives the foreign languages teacher a chance to introduce such new words as the equivalents of "airplane," "pilot," "navigator," a "flight attendant," "mechanic," and so on.

A contrived teaching moment has the appearance of spontaneity, but its arrival has been prearranged. For example, the teacher (or a designated student) may come to class late and use that "moment" to discuss the effects of tardiness in the workplace. Another contrived teaching moment occurs when a student is primed to ask a particular question about work values or careers related to the subject under discussion, or when an "unexpected" visitor drops in at an opportune time to ask her or him questions about how the study of English (or mathematics or science) has helped in professional development.

A planned teaching moment requires a little more structuring than the previous examples. For instance, after the English class reads a short story by Faulkner, the teacher might discuss the way the author worked, the life-style he lived, the aloneness he frequently experienced, and some of the apocryphal tales which have grown up round him and his work. (Of course, the same subject might be assigned to a student.) The mathematics teacher might take ten minutes at the end of a class period to ask students to list all occupations or work tasks in which the lesson of the day might have practical application. These planned teaching moments might be extended into mini-units if they prove to be effective.

Mini-units provide another technique for including career education in the classroom. A mini-unit requires from fifteen minutes to three class periods to complete, and it may be a unit by itself or part of a larger, regular unit. Mini-units can be designed to deal with career aspects of the topic being taught, and they can provide a change of pace, a motivational point of reference, and an opportunity for catch-up and review. These units can be programmed instructional units, individualized units, or independent study. An increasing amount of material is becoming available as the career education movement broadens its appeal to include manufacturers of audiovisual materials, government agencies, business organizations, labor unions, and professional associations. Many of these organizations produce films, books, cassettes, filmstrips, pamphlets and other materials which can form the basis of one or more mini-units. Field trips and interviews provide another resource for mini-unit design.

Perhaps the most effective way to use mini-units is to include them as part of a regular unit. This approach is more harmonious with the basic concepts of career education, since career education is not a separate discipline but should be incorporated into the existing curriculum of all courses. The best way to accomplish this is for every teacher to include "career implications" as a subtopic in each daily lesson plan and teaching unit. (A sample lesson plan format is shown in Figure 4.) The addition of this subtopic to the lesson plan serves as a gentle reminder to include career education concepts in appropriate lessons. Of course, not every lesson will have career implications, but it is surprising how many subjects can be related to work or careers, given a little creative imagination. Practically every lesson or unit provides a natural opportunity for some mention of work values, or career exploration and development, or decision making, or life-style. For example, a social studies unit about the "age of discovery" could include one or more discussion topics about work-related concepts associated with seagoing explorers such as Columbus, Magellan, or Drake. How many men were required to operate one of the ships? What kinds of skills were necessary? What was the division of labor aboard ship? What was the life-style of the offices as contrasted with that of the seamen? Who made decisions about what types of food and how much food to carry on a journey of indeterminate length? What kinds of values motivated men to "sign on" for such voyages? Who paid for salaries and provisions? Why? And of course a parallel situation could be constructed for modern times by stating a proposition such as: Suppose NASA were planning a large mission to Mars in three separate spacecraft—the Pinta, the Nina, and the Santa Maria. The mission would take three years, and ninety workers would be aboard the "ships." How many students would volunteer to go? Why? What jobs would they elect to perform aboard the spacecraft?

Obviously, only the limits of the teacher's imagination control how much or how little a particular lesson — any

Topic or concept:

Goals and objectives:

Ideas to be learned:

Career implications:

Resources:

Preassessment:

Learning activities:

        Teacher activities        Student activities

Evaluation:

**Figure 4.** Sample Lesson Plan Outline Which Includes "Career Implications" as a Subtopic

lesson – might be related to the important career considerations which are inevitably on the minds of students.

The teacher can also provide a meaningful "case study" of a career decision based upon personal experience. Within the career education concept, it is totally appropriate for the teacher to talk about her or his own career decisions. This should not be a "sales pitch" for teaching as a profession or for college education. The discussion should revolve round the particular values which influenced the decision, the life-style of a teacher (including both positive and negative factors), the doubts and disappointments which accompanied the long preparatory road, the satisfactions which have followed, and any other factors which might help students understand that career decision making is a lifelong activity and that academic training will be valuable preparation for all occupations.

The techniques for practicing career education are as many and as varied as the teachers and administrators who accept responsibility for this vital facet of high school education.

## Applications for Specific Subject Matter

The manner in which teachers apply the principles of career education to their own classrooms is individual. It depends upon the subject matter, the method of instruction employed, the particular student audience, and the predilections of the teacher. Literally thousands of examples are available in the form of newsletter reports, lesson plans, program analyses, conference reports, and other informal exchanges. Unfortunately, few of these examples have been documented. However, one excellent source has been compiled as a product of a national conference on career education in the academic classroom. The book is titled *Career Education in the Academic Classroom*, and it was put together by teachers and other representatives of national associations for various academic subjects (Mangum *et al.*, 1975).

The examples which follow are heavily abridged excerpts from that book. They are included to show the variety of approaches which are possible for those who want to provide that important career education dimension for students. Many of the approaches have applicability for several types of academic classrooms other than the one described.

## Science and Career Education

It is evident today that the nation needs a scientifically literate population. All youth must have a background in science so that they can interpret their world adequately, make decisions about its future, and use this knowledge in many other aspects of their lives. It is hard to conceive of a future citizenry that can afford ignorance about genetic manipulation, computers, pollution, energy shortages, extreme population growth, poor nutrition, and other science-related problems. On still another level, science is needed by the lay person less for its information than for its methodologies. In the study of science, attitudes and methods are developed which guide the student to gather related facts, organize them, select and try a procedure to solve the problem, and evaluate the results. This approach, unique to science, is useful in dealing with problems of all kinds.

When career education permeates regular classroom activities, it enhances the teacher's awareness of the lifetime needs of students, and it tends to heighten classroom interest in studies that once may have seemed dull and irrelevant to many students. The strong motivational power of career education stems from its application of learning to potential uses in the future work and other lifetime pursuits of students, and from its democratic recognition of each person's need to be recognized, considered, and readied for the responsibilities of adulthood.

In the science classroom, career education is an important tool. It can help teachers develop student interest in science careers and in the myriad careers related to science. It can motivate students to learn scientific procedures for use in other occupations and in their nonvocational pursuits. It can demonstrate the linkages among science studies and between science and other disciplines.

At the outset, teachers themselves must develop an awareness of all potential career possibilities, whether they are in a scientific or a related field. The introduction of newspaper and magazine articles about a variety of such careers should become a part of the way of life in science classes. In this approach, careers might be divided into two groups — those which are directly related to science, and those which are indirectly related to science. Two examples of classroom activities revolving round careers directly related to science follow.

### Example One — Science Activity

Have chemistry students do a study of labels on containers in the kitchen, the cleaning closet, the medicine cabinet, the garden shed, and the home workshop. The assignment would be to learn something about a limited number of these substances. This task requires considerable detective work, for not all ingredients can be fully identified. However, those that are identified will fall into a number of chemical categories and will open many channels for discussion. Students will find out about the interrelatedness of chemistry with everyday life and with a wide variety of products. Their needs to learn more about chemical nomenclature will also be identified.

### Example Two — Science Activity

Have science students examine occupations in the community to determine how those occupations relate to science. What do a pharmacy, a grocery store, a photographic studio, the highway department, a hearing aid dealer, a television station, the parks department, a print shop, a hospital, a petroleum refinery have to do with chemistry? Or biology? Or physics? Students should make their own arrangements to visit some business or industry in the community in small groups. Then they might present what they have learned to the class.

While many careers are *directly* related to science, as illustrated above, an infinitely large number are *indirectly* related. Indeed, all careers have a science component, from homemaker to mechanic, from attorney to piano tuner, from politician to creative writer. Classroom activities designed to demonstrate the relationship of science to varied careers might be included in the following examples.

### Example One — Indirect Science Activity

The music instructor might bring a number of musical instruments to science class during a study of acoustics in physics. A comparison of stringed, woodwind, percussion and brass instruments in terms of how sound is produced and modulated opens up many fields of discussion and investigation. It also shows students how science is related to leisure or occupational interests.

### Example Two — Indirect Science Activity

Motorcycles interest many of today's students. Although their maintenance can be delegated to experts who will keep a machine in good running order, a basic understanding of the working principles of a cycle allows even a novice to maintain the machine. Students in a motorcycle maintenance project might bring one of their cycles into the classroom where all students could help to:

(1) Identify the parts of the cycle and discuss their functions

(2) List these functions alongside pertinent scientific principles

(3) Investigate how each part can be adjusted to accomplish different results in the operation of a cycle

(4) Relate what has been learned to scientific knowledge (in terms of fuel, oxygen mixtures and combustion, metal parts versus plastic parts for certain purposes, function of lubricants and so on)

### Example Three — Indirect Science Activity

In relation to the above activity, the class might invite someone from a local motorcycle repair shop to the classroom to explain the cycle parts, their functions, and how one knows what to do in repairing motorcycles (hypotheses) and the reasons (experience) for making these decisions (facts).

Strategies of these kinds can bring into the science classroom a multitude of experiences that will enable students to feel the pulse of science and examine its insides in ways that largely were possible for only a few students — those who knew that they were heading into science careers — before the advent of career education.

## Mathematics and Career Education

Mathematics is concerned with ideas, processes, and reasoning. It is a way of thinking, of organizing logical proof. It is an organized structure of knowledge with well-defined terms, symbols, and processes which develops its own beauty with its harmony, order, and consistency. The good mathematics teacher develops mathematical ideas and skills that students can use for further study, for everyday problems, and for personal satisfaction. Some students will be charmed by the logical consistency and beauty of mathematics. Others will enjoy the manipulation of numbers. However, for most, if the teacher fails to show how mathematics applies to other studies and interests, students are unlikely to transfer their knowledge of mathematics to other settings and will have less interest in the subject. When students are shown how specific mathematical facts and skills can solve problems in the home and the community, in industry, in recreation, and in endless other ways, they are likely to try harder to learn. Career education is one way to motivate students and to provide linkages between the classroom and other life situations.

The world of work is rich with mathematical problems that can become laboratory exercises. To help students understand vectors, the teacher could relate mathematics to vectors involved in an airplane flight and used by navigators and flight controllers. If students are to learn to interpret statistical graphs, they might use data and newspaper graphs which encompass current public issues such as the relationship of employability and education. If students are to learn probability, they might look at how this applies to the work of insurance actuaries. Examples from the world of work can also help in the teaching of mathematical topics such as computation, measurement, statistical data, percentages, equations, geometric relations, ratio and proportion, estimation and approximation, and the use of computing machines. Another excellent way that career education can help in teaching mathematics is to have students identify mathematical problems related to the work of their parents, friends, or relatives.

Mathematics is the entry gate to many occupations and professions. Knowledge of mathematics and facility in its application can enhance or limit the freedom a person has in making career choices. In fact, discharging the responsibilities of an intelligent citizen is extremely difficult for anyone who lacks mathematical skills and concepts. At least three levels of mathematics competency are identifiable in terms of the career relevance of mathematics as taught in the high school. These are not totally discrete levels but tend to blend and merge as they approach one another. The lowest acceptable level of mathematics competency should include mastery of at least the basic computation skills needed to function as intelligent consumers and citizens. The second level of mathematics competency has more than a tint of individuality. It embraces both an understanding of mathematical concepts and capability in performing mathematical operations needed for satisfactory accomplishments of an occupation such as carpenter, bank teller, physician, or physicist. The third level of competency relates to mathematically oriented professions — engineer, mathematician, actuary, statistician, mathematics teacher. These professions require extended study of mathematics and a high level of performance.

Obviously, the process of making the teaching of mathematics relevant calls for attention to individual needs. This demands some flexibility on the part of the teacher as he or she adapts a personal style to the needs of various students. At least three models are available to be used in integrating career goals into the mathematics curriculum. In the first model, teacher and student attempt to relate a specific mathematics subject or topic to careers. For instance, one might explore those careers in which geometry is used, together with the ways in which it is used. Examples include architecture, navigation, astronomy, sheetmetal work, sports, electronics, interior design, and physics.

The second model basically reverses the process and examines the nature of mathematical skills required by a specific occupation. For example, an electronics technician must be able to read plans, blueprints, schematic drawings, and various instruments such as ohmmeters, ammeters and time indicators. He or she must be able to work algebraic problems in order to determine required resistances or voltages, and must be able to work with geometry in computations of surface illumination.

The third model expands upon the second to include an entire industry, or field of interest, or item of concern. One might look at the use of mathematics in the automobile industry, from manufacture to repair. Or one might examine applications of mathematics in environmental fields. Or one might begin with a ballpoint pen, trying to discover all the ways in which mathematics was employed in the design and manufacture of that instrument.

The following examples illustrate the approach used in the second model. They revolve round a specific career, that of interior designer. In order to work as an interior designer, an individual must have the basic computation skills of addition, subtraction, multiplication, division, fractions, ratio and proportion, decimals, scale drawing, areas, and percentages. If students plan to enter an architecture or engineering school, the mathematics requirement will be greater, and they should plan to take two years of high school algebra, geometry, and any other advanced courses that are offered in mathematics.

## Example One – Mathematics

The designer must be able to calculate the wall area in order to know how much material is needed for decorating.

(1) What is the cost of paint for four walls and ceiling of a room 30 by 26 feet, with a picture window of 9 by 6 feet in one wall and two door spaces 3 feet by 6 feet 8 inches? The paint to be used costs $10.49 a gallon, and each gallon will cover 400 square feet. (Fraction of a gallon cannot be bought.) The ceiling is the standard height of 8 feet.

(2) Suppose the room is 29 by 17 feet, but the long walls are 12 feet high in the center, sloping to 9 feet high at the ends. How much will the paint cost? (All other facts are the same as for the problem above.)

## Example Two – Mathematics

An industrial designer for an office furniture company compiles a specification sheet for a client. After talking to the client, the designer makes a rough sketch of the floor plan to scale, showing all wall placements or removals and the locations of all pieces of furniture necessary for the smooth operation of the business. Given a scale of ¼ inch to 1 foot, find the following:

| Item | Actual Measurement | Scale Measurement |
|---|---|---|
| Desk | 48″ by 36″ | _____ |
| Desk | 52″ by 42″ | _____ |
| Chair | 24″ by 18″ | _____ |

| Chair | 28" by 22" | _____ |
| Table | 72" by 36" | _____ |
| File | 14" by 36" | _____ |
| Bookshelves | 20" by 92" | _____ |
| Couch | 36" by 76" | _____ |
| End table | 36" by 18" | _____ |

## Example Three — Mathematics

Often it is necessary for an interior designer to decide how to cut fabric for an item to ensure minimum waste and the lowest cost in construction. This could include fabric for redoing furniture, for making draperies or for any number of items to be placed in a home. A customer wants a red, crushed velvet, hanging lampshade with gold swirl cord. The shade is 10 inches in diameter and 18 inches tall. The bolt of velvet fabric is 44 inches wide and costs $3.75 a yard. Should the shade be cut in one piece? Or would it be cheaper to cut it in two pieces and have two seams? Allow ¼ inch on each piece for each seam and ½ inch at the top and at the bottom to form an overlap to secure the fabric to the frame of the lampshade.

(Clue: Before cutting the fabric, the designer should draw a plan or make a pattern of less expensive material, such as bunting or paper. In this problem, the designer should visualize the fabric as "unwrapped" from the cylindrical shade and would therefore need a rectangle of pattern material to begin the mathematical calculations of the exact dimension he or she will need when cutting the velvet fabric.)

The role of the high school mathematics teacher is truly significant when the nation's students are attempting to make career choices. In addition to being a mode of thought and reasoning, mathematics will take on a broader dimension by incorporating the principles of career education — a system of thought and reasoning that has important, direct relationships to the lives and careers of most students.

## English and Career Education

A basic task of those who teach English is to reconcile the humane uses of English with the practical applications of English. The humane uses are to help students define and enhance the self and achieve healthy interaction with others. The practical uses are the means by which the self is presented and by which dynamic interaction with others is achieved. These are specific skills needed for functional, practical literacy — job applications, employment résumés, interviews, public speaking, and other forms of informational and persuasive communication. A career education emphasis in English can help clarify the interdependence that unites these humane and practical functions.

Since career education is a process by which individuals shape and control their destinies with some concurrent measures of personal satisfaction and societal contribution, English should become a valuable resource to everyone because of the power it bestows on individuals to see into themselves and others and to manage their affairs with competence and affability. English also contributes in a more specific way to career education through its emphasis on communication skills. Most productive activities involve communication among human beings. Most instructions in paid employment must flow through spoken and written language. All human relations are communication. And all jobs that are not primarily manual are almost entirely communicative — the transmission of ideas, orders and messages.

When career education in English studies is incorporated, certain goals should be established which are aimed at helping students achieve economic independence, appreciate the dignity of work, learn about the satisfactions and disatisfactions of work, and acquire the ability to make wise decisions about career options and choices. The following goals are stated in terms of students who complete the high school English program. These students should:

(1) Have the linguistic knowledge and skills necessary to become employable, to continue education throughout a lifetime, and to pursue developing vocational and avocational career interests

(2) Have increased self-awareness and direction, expanded career awareness and aspirations, and appropriate attitudes about the personal and social significance of work and careers as a result of clarifying their values through literature and other English disciplines

(3) Have decision-making skills necessary for future long-range career planning, particularly in English-related careers and in other careers where linguistic ability is an important skill

The following examples of learning activities may suggest to the English teacher how the content of the English program can carry out these goals for career education. The sample activities are designed to correspond with the goals enumerated above.

## Example One – English

Many different types of written communication are required by different occupations. These activities will help students learn to recognize the different kinds of communication.

(1) Students will study specific occupations to determine the amount and the kind of reading and writing skills which are needed; if possible, they should collect samples of writing by workers in these occupations.

(2) Students will demonstrate an understanding of a variety of written communications in the world of work by producing an array of these communications and identifying where they are used and why they are needed.

(3) Students will assemble and examine a variety of written communications from a single work site, such as a business office.

(4) Students will evaluate the written communications of their peers as a means of strengthening their understanding of what they and their fellow students know and what they still must learn.

## Example Two – English

In one sense, the study of literature is a process of identifying, developing and clarifying values. It increases self-awareness and direction. This process can easily be expanded to include career development and work values. Activities which will provide added awareness of the personal significance of work and careers include:

(1) Students will analyze anecdotal accounts, such as newspaper interviews with interesting persons, to learn the personal significance of work and careers for various people.

(2) Students will explore, through interviews, differing values held by individuals regarding their work, and will invite guest speakers to the classroom, see audiotapes made at work sites, and the like.

(3) Students will write essays or participate in a panel discussion on the role that a career plays in the development and nuturing of self-concepts.

### Example Three — English

In addition to being able to research information about various occupations and their life-styles, students must be capable of "researching" themselves in the sense that they can verbally express their own interests, capabilities, and experiences. Activities which will help students be able to use knowledge of themselves in the career decision-making process include:

(1) Students will prepare a résumé and portfolio about themselves, including creative or informative writing they have done and other types of communications (photo essays, cartoons, graphics) which may be useful in helping their parents, counselors, vocational educators, prospective employers, college entrance interviewers, and themselves to determine appropriate career channels and choices.

(2) Students will use language in classroom situations often enough to gain experience in talking effectively about their career interests and their personal strengths.

Career education, broadly defined, can penetrate the content and the methodology of the high school English program at a time when students are seeking clarification of their personal values and are facing the need to make career decisions. The English classroom can become a laboratory in which to explore communication in its many forms and to prepare for effective and satisfying communication with other people. These are vital skills, whether they are used in work, in leisure, or in both.

## Social Studies and Career Education

In a broad and profound sense, social studies and career education are intimately related. Both seek to prepare the young for a way of life that is not only constructive but offers personal fulfillment. A position statement in 1972 by the National Council for the Social Studies said: "Social studies education has a twofold purpose: the enhancement of human dignity through learning, and a commitment to rational processes as the principal means of attaining that end." That duality of purpose cannot be separated from career education, which is the totality of experiences through which one learns about and prepares to engage in work as part of her or his way of living. Both social studies and career education are concerned with helping the young become adults who can cope successfully with changing societal patterns and requirements, able to exert freedom of choice and able to accept responsibility. Both recognize the importance of personal development — the need to arrive at an understanding of self and a sense of personal worth which are grounded in the knowledge that each individual is important to society and can command the respect of his or her fellow humans.

The teacher is important in helping students achieve insights about their abilities, limitations, attitudes, aspirations, interests and potential, and in helping students see the congruency of these personal characteristics with needs in various occupations. Basic to all career education, the strengthening of skills for making such assessments can be a major contribution of social science teachers in the career preparation of their students. Social studies offers youth a broad background against which to measure personal decisions on occupational options and the life-styles that these may entail, while career education can introduce the relevancy of personal interest into the social studies classroom.

The real return to the student's career interests is less specific than what can be learned in auto mechanics or computer programming classes. Nevertheless, the return may be great. Many of the attitudes, values, and cognitive knowledge and skills that can be acquired in the social studies classroom are extremely important in the occupational life of most workers, as well as in their social, political, and family lives. This is because learning about work goes far beyond skills preparation for a particular job. It involves intellectual strategies that are a key part of the social studies approach — inquiry, value clarification, problem solving, and decision making. It involves questions about how individuals relate to their jobs, what they bring to it, what it does for them, what they see in it, and what they take from it.

As with all academic disciplines, career education should not be "added on" to social studies courses. It should be fused into courses in such a way that students can see the relationships between the subjects they study and the world of work. This requires the development of a carefully designed plan, based on an analysis of each course component, and decisions as to where fusion is suitable and how it is to be achieved. In most cases, the best way to help youth gain a better understanding of themselves, perceive their potential and understand their work opportunities is to draw information from a subject area and extend it to include related careers, thus helping students examine many life-styles and relate them to specific occupations. Discussions about personal, group, and societal values can help students make decisions. Also, a closer look at occupations in which social studies information is a necessary component can enrich student understanding of relationships between what is learned in school and the world outside the school.

Following are examples from each of the major social studies disciplines to show how teachers can plan career-related experiences within the context of existing social studies programs.

### Example One — History

One topic taught in history courses that can be related to career evaluation is technological change. From studying early history, the teacher can find simple forms of technological invention to serve as springboards for studying career implications — tools for gathering and producing food, the wheel, fire, and writing. Inventions appearing after the tenth century — the modern form of the clock, the printing press, the factory system, the ballpoint pen, automatic weapons, the telephone, and the computer — can be used to continue student awareness of careers. Students can examine the effects of these inventions on people's working lives and explore how such inventions terminated certain kinds of jobs and created other kinds.

Lessons or student projects could be developed to guide student study of an industry, of job clusters, of specific occupations, of career change over a period of years, of social implications, and of cross-cultural implications. The same approach can be used with such history topics as the agricultural revolution, emergency of complex living patterns, epidemics and catastrophes, ethnic studies, exploration and colonization, state history, wars, and other topics.

## Example Two — Geography

Modern geography courses have advanced beyond the "place" geography that was once taught. Today, geography studies aid students in developing thinking skills and in associating ideas. The study of a region, for example, provides many opportunities to examine spatial interaction and areal association. This can be an excellent starting point for a social studies teacher to introduce career implications of subject content. In the urban region, interesting career opportunities have emerged in urban planning, land use and resource allocation, building inspection, rehabilitation, and mass transportation. Many students could reinforce their understanding of geographic concepts while actively learning more about careers in these fields. The career implications of other topics in geography could include adaptation to the environment, economic geography, energy, urbanization, and others.

## Example Three — Economics

The teaching of economics offers many opportunities to stimulate career exploration by students. For example, a significant topic in many economic courses is the concept of scarcity, followed by the allocation of limited resources. Students exploring this topic learn of the relationship between economic decisions that individuals and society make and how these decisions affect the distribution of limited resources in the economic system. Scarcity of iron ore and its allocation could lead to the study of careers in the steel and mining industries and in those industries that produce metals that might serve as substitutes for iron and steel.

A shortage of doctors — with its consequent allocation of medical services — could lead to a study of the social and economic implications of health maintenance organizations, then to a study of the career opportunities in health care professions. Career implications can also be studied along with such topics as division of labor, distribution of goods, personal and consumer economics, employment and capital investment.

## Example Four — Political Science

Civics, government, and political science courses contain a number of concepts useful in developing career interests. For example, the concept of law — the fact that every society has laws or rules that govern the conduct of its human behavior — is common in political science. This concept enables the teacher to offer learning experiences that open the eyes of students to a great many careers, including those in law-making structures at local, county, state and federal levels, in legislative support and lobbying. Other applications from the political science field are political party careers, government service, law enforcement, cultural exchange, and international trade.

## Example Five — Sociology and Anthropology

Human behavior in groups and institutions is a concern of these two broad areas. However, abstract normative or functional concepts often are studied in social studies classes without revealing ways that students can gain even an elementary awareness of career opportunities related to the concepts that are presented. One example of how relatively abstract concepts in these subjects can be more readily understood in terms of careers is in the study of social and technological change. If a teacher introduces the concept of automation through discussion of the invention of the computer, there is a good opportunity to analyze resulting social changes and career implications. Careers which are related to standard course topics include such things as crisis intervention careers (conflict), family counseling (family), child development and personnel careers (human relationships), recreation (leisure), religious careers (religion), organizational design and analysis (social structure).

## Example Six — Philosophy and Psychology

Although courses in philosophy and psychology are not offered universally, many schools now provide minicourses or units in these fields. Teachers have an excellent opportunity to develop student interest in the improvement of the human condition through human service occupations if career implications are studied when topics such as interpersonal and intergroup relationships are discussed. Concepts of these relationships involve the study of conflict and conflict resolution (coping) skills.

Careers in human relations, counseling, and psychiatric treatment are natural avenues for career exploration that can accompany the study of these concepts in a philosophy or psychology course or unit. In a philosophy course or unit, the study of the human search for meaning in life also offers an opportunity to bring career education into the classroom. This applies particularly to the investigation of values and values-related topics.

Social studies teachers have a particular opportunity to help students in appraising their individual capabilities, interests, and needs. Numerous test instruments are available to help teachers and students inventory these personal characteristics. Teachers who are qualified to administer and interpret such test instruments should do so. In any case, the classroom teacher and the school counselor can work as a team to help students make realistic decisions, based on information provided by such tests.

## Visual Arts and Career Education

Art education and art production have many elements that have great relevance and value in the work aspects of most people's lives. This is because they require the manipulation of materials and forms, the organization of ideas, and creative approaches to new kinds of problems. What is produced is not just art that can be seen or heard but also many skills — composed of sensitivities, human understanding, and complex and creative problem-solving strategies — that are indispensable in trade and industry, international affairs, and personal relationships, as well as in the various professional art fields. To everyday tasks, art adds a meaningful human dimension to the functional requirements and satisfactions of jobs, and helps make work of all kinds more meaningful to the worker.

Building programs which will identify important relationships between the study and creation of art with the world of work and its vast occupational potentials demands that the teacher may have to alter any traditional biases that are present in the classroom. While the general field bias toward art for its own sake, which tends to separate even college programs into distinct tracks, may remain as a personal commitment on the part of the teacher, it is inappropriate for most adolescents in secondary school art programs. It is the responsibility of the art teacher to help students identify the values and benefits of other approaches to the use of art as well as those in art for its own sake. Then students can decide for themselves the directions in which they will go.

Along with recognizing, encouraging, and developing students who are likely to become professional artists, the art instructor must identify ways to help other students mesh their art education with their career education needs. For these students — and they are by far the majority in the art classroom — the teacher needs to make the art discipline relevant to the individual both through vocational opportunities and through many specific applications to all areas of human endeavor. By doing so, the teacher helps students make a transition from the abstract, the mystical, and the intangible qualities of art to relevant and meaningful personal applications in the world in which most of them will work. This not only makes art of interest to students who otherwise might not have participated in it, it enhances the value of art in their educational development and in society.

What is needed in most career education in art is not vocational education for art jobs. Indeed, the most effective program probably will emphasize the broad functions underlying success in a wide variety of occupations, rather than emphasizing all possible art-related occupations and the specific art skills each one requires. Career education may be incorporated in the art classroom using a number of different approaches. The following examples illustrate three such approaches. The first examines the relationship of art and art-related careers to the environment, using a student project approach. The second is a study of values, particularly those of various types of artists, using a study-discussion approach. The third is an exploration of careers related to art, using a combination of field trips and visiting resource persons.

**Example One — Art-Related Careers**

This activity is designed to help students explore such careers as exhibit designer, graphic designer, illustrator and display artist, together with such related careers as management, layout design, and color coordinator. These careers offer many satisfactions in discovering and working out solutions to visual communications problems, but in order to define the various career roles involved, it may be necessary to engage in interdisciplinary activities. These activities might include displays, bulletin boards, exhibits, and showcases.

In addition, there may be many areas in the school where the art department could enhance the environment. These might include courtyards, entryways, blank walls, poorly lit sections of the school, inadequate signs, library stacks, or just plain eyesores. Students could be asked to identify needs of these kinds throughout the school. Sometimes this may involve another content area and will require understanding the concepts and needs in that area. In exploring solutions, students might study color and other design applications in commercial displays, museum exhibits, and architectural super-graphics.

Then students can change an area by mounting an exhibit, designing a bulletin board, producing sculpture, or redesigning the use of space. Students who work in these areas learn that careers in this field involve working with the variable of human idiosyncrasies. The managerial function is necessary for these careers as well as the creative functions.

### Example Two — Study-Discussion Approach

This activity should take place in an art history, painting, drawing, or sculpture class. Precautions must be taken that art for its own sake not be disregarded, and art which is merely a tool to explore careers be emphasized. Students should be involved in expressing their ideas and emotions through the art media, not in just studying careers. However, this type of activity would give them a realistic view of what the artist does in performing as an artist, and what values operate as motivational forces upon the artist. Students can become aware of the role of the artist in the world of work by:

(1) Discussing the role of the artist in society as a painter or sculptor who seeks only self-fulfillment through his or her medium

(2) Discussing the role of the artist in society as a painter or sculptor who creates works of art as a service for others

(3) Having an artist visit the classroom to discuss his or her attitudes toward work and responsibilities to self, home, and society

### Example Three — Careers Related to Art

Frequently, students are not aware of the many careers which are associated with art and for which a knowledge of art is important.

Through museum field trips and discussions with art specialists, teachers can help students study careers in an art museum by:

(1) Having students explore careers involved in a work of art from its creation to its acquisition by a museum ("occupational lineage" of a work of art) —

    (a) Artist creating the work of art

    (b) Critic analyzing the work of art

    (c) Historian analyzing, evaluating, and interpreting the work of art

    (d) Museum director purchasing the work of art

    (e) Curator storing the work of art

    (f) Exhibit specialist displaying the work of art

    (g) Cataloguer recording the work of art for publication

    (h) Docent explaining the work of art to the public

    (i) Education specialist designing programs for students around the work of art

    (j) Teacher using the work of art as an original resource for classroom activities

    (k) Conservationist keeping the work of art in the proper environment and keeping it clean

    (l) Guard protecting the work of art from damage and theft

    (m) Gallery staff packing and shipping the work of art for other exhibits

(2) Having artists, critics, historians, and curators visit the classroom to discuss their specialist roles, preferably before the class makes a museum visit

(3) Having specialists, when possible, demonstrate their specialties

(4) Providing opportunities in which students can observe specialists at work in their studios and museums


It is clear today that art careers, art-related careers, and careers which are made more meaningful by acquaintance with art processes must be a significant focus of the art educator. Painting, sculpture, and other art activities, while vital and important in themselves, can be made far more meaningful to students if the art educator is sensitive to the needs all students will have when they enter the working world beyond the classroom.

### Foreign Languages and Career Education

During the past fifteen years, foreign language teaching in public schools has undergone a revolution of sorts. The earlier emphasis on teaching students to read and write other languages has given way to an emphasis on oral and aural skills — speaking and understanding a language with the purpose of achieving first those communication skills that are most useful in everyday life. As students progress in the study of a language, they build up their reading and writing skills, enabling them to explore in greater depth other models of thought and value systems and to learn more about the roots and linkages of languages.

Career education and foreign language instruction have many significant mutual interests. While career education is concerned with the total development of students in their preparation for adult working life, in the foreign language sector, it provides a way for students to relate their foreign language learning to their growing awareness of their own career goals and potential — and all without altering the traditional values of the discipline. Identification of learning goals with career goals can strengthen motivation and achievement while encouraging students to select and evaluate their curriculum on a rational basis. Career education also gives language educators an opportunity to reach a broader segment of the student population than they have attracted in years past.

So far as linguistic skills are concerned, most students — even those who have never studied a foreign language — can readily come to understand the relevance of these skills to real and potential careers. A substantial body of data has been compiled to demonstrate the value of supportive language skills in a wide variety of occupations. The humanistic values of language study are less obvious, and educators will need to seek ways to present and explicate these values to their current and potential students by providing a new rationale for language study in terms of students' career goals and developmental choices. The aims of career education are not at cross-purposes with the humanistic aims of foreign language study. Actually, the two parallel processes converge in shaping self-fulfilled individuals — people who understand the relationships between education and career opportunities, and who are interested in their own and other cultures, in all of the many heritages that make up their own and other cultures, and in all of the many heritages that make up the humanities.

Essentially, the study of foreign languages helps students define and pursue their own life values, whether vocational or avocational, or both. Thus the relationship of foreign language competency to careers may be viewed as a continuum, spanning the need for foreign languages as a primary skill, as a co-equal skill, as an adjunct skill, or as valuable background. Students should be made aware of this continuum through direct teaching and through activities that enable them to discover these relationships.

There are a number of ways to relate career education to foreign language studies. One of the most useful is to correlate regular textbook materials and classroom techniques with career development concepts. First, teachers and students should be aware of the potential and the limitations in careers for which knowledge of a second language is a primary skill — chiefly teaching, translating, and oral interpreting. Second, teachers and students should discuss career uses of language skills in that broad range of positions for which knowledge of a foreign language is an important ancillary or supportive skill. The list of such positions extends from the entry level to executive or professional status, and it covers such diverse fields as business and industry, civil service, communication media, science, health services, social sciences, and travel or tourism. Examples of jobs range from taxi driver or hotel receptionist to foreign correspondents and executives in multinational corporations. In each case, language skills enhance and extend the job seeker's specialized preparation and enable him or her to apply for a wider range of positions.

Third, teachers should make students aware that acquiring second language skills will broaden their options in numerous career areas and in many cases will increase their earning capacity as well. A recent survey by the Modern Language Association found that more than 70 percent of U.S. business firms report that second language skills are important in some way in their business operations.

These three objectives can be accomplished in many different ways and at many different levels. The following examples were selected to show activities which range from the fairly simple to the complex. In each case, these activities have been employed in the classroom with noticeable success.

### Example One — Foreign Language Activity

This exercise offers an easy way to help students explore career possibilities while at the same time building career-related vocabularies and providing an important listening experience. The exercise is called "Listen and Guess." The teacher prepares an audio cassette in the target language on which various jobs or occupations are described. These cassettes might be obtained from other language teachers and from native speakers from the community in order to give variety to the messages. Students listen to each statement and guess which occupation has been described.

Be sure to include a variety of jobs, from unskilled to professional, and try to include a sentence or two about the life-style of the worker. If visual aids are desired, flash cards picturing various occupations and giving job titles in foreign languages are available from commercial firms.

### Example Two — Foreign Language Activity

Depending on the size and nature of the community, a language-use survey of local businesses can be useful in encouraging foreign language study and in motivating those currently involved in such study. Students design and prepare a survey form and then visit the personnel managers or other executives of local firms to determine the language needs of those organizations. (Where possible, students should interview persons in a field which coincides with their own interests.) In class, students compile the results of their survey and attempt to construct a profile of language needs in the area.

The survey questionnaire should not be too complex, but it should include such questions as: Do any of your customers or clients use or speak a foreign language? Do you presently employ people with

foreign language skills? Are applicants with foreign language skills
preferable? What percentage of your employees have at least one
foreign language skill? Which skill is most important to your operation: listening, speaking, reading or writing? At which job levels are
language skills most important? List the languages which are most
beneficial to your business setting in order of importance.

**Example Three — Foreign Language Activity**

Many language teachers find that role playing is a useful tool
for language training, and a number of teachers build their simula-
tions round career roles. In one instance, the teacher has videotaped
short scenes in actual situations involving medical careers, public
service careers, and business careers. The teacher shows the class the
videotape — perhaps a hospital admission scene, or taking a blood
test, or visiting a dentist. Class members receive a written transcription
of the dialog, together with a list of new vocabulary words, a grammatical review, and some questions related to activities from the
scene.

The class reviews the scene once again, this time on audio cassette. The cassette includes pronunciation practice and additional
grammatical exercises built round the vocabulary of the scene. Finally,
students themselves simulate the scene before the class, using the
vocabulary but not necessarily the same sequencing of events. The
teacher provides certain aids for the simulation exercise. For example,
in the hospital admission scene a mimeographed copy of a standard
hospital admission form is provided to the student acting as admis-
sions interviewer.

This is an ambitious program and a very successful one. However, it can be modified to suit local conditions and the availability
of support equipment. For example, an illustration of a scene in a
dentist's office might be substituted for the videotape. The primary
thing is that the career orientation of the simulation adds interest
and motivation for students.

Teachers should not postpone offering career-oriented
instruction simply because few materials may have been published for a foreign language program with a career education
focus. Start with materials at hand, and find ways to use them
in the classroom. An enthusiastic teacher will find that students
are willing to share the responsibility for locating resources
as part of their learning experience. Activities in which students
discover relationships for themselves and learn to do other
independent work are, after all, an important part of education.

Career emphasis implies a new focus, some redirection in the classroom, and greater integration with other disciplines. Therefore, the foreign language teacher must reevaluate traditional components of the language course and decide which terms are essential in meeting new goals. At times it may be necessary to stress functional objectives at the expense of some traditional topics. Fortunately, the current emphasis being given in foreign language instruction to the teaching of literature and culture as a way of life allows for a here-and-now approach, and it is well suited to the purposes of career education. Using this approach, the foreign language teacher can answer more adequately the questions that have been raised by many students: "Why am I studying a *foreign* language?" and "Where am I going to use my knowledge of a foreign language?"

## Health Sciences, Recreation, and Physical Education

Historically, career concerns have been an integral part of education in health, physical education, and recreation. Students have generally been attracted to these fields for two reasons: because they found great pleasure in them, and because they saw the potential for a career. Those interested in careers usually wanted to become health and physical education teachers, coaches, recreation leaders, or professional performers. Students still are attracted to health, physical education, and recreation programs for the enjoyment they offer and for career reasons, but there are significant changes. Increasingly, the focus in these programs is on improving the quality of life for all students, not just those who are the most highly skilled.

There are many important ways in which career education can continue to broaden the appeal of health, physical education, and recreation subjects and link subject content to the growing awareness by students of personal needs throughout their lives. First, there is the fact that good mental and physical health, knowledge of bodily functions, and wise use of leisure have much to do with career success. Second, the three disciplines now offer a wide variety of direct and indirect routes into future careers.

*Health Sciences and Career Education*

Because any career choices that people make are influenced heavily by their value systems, some of the content in health education should help students examine their values as these relate to their future work, their future lives, their community, and their world. Do these values include the desire for economic independence, pride in accomplishment, and occupational satisfaction — and are these values supportive of good health? Health education must also give students an opportunity to examine their personal strengths and limitations in all aspects of emotional and physical health and the influence these factors may have on career choice.

But it is not only what a person brings to a career that is important. Equally important is what a career may do to that person. For this reason, a health education course should also encourage students to consider the influence that different careers might have on their health in terms of years of hard physical labor or years of sedentary work. Information on stress associated with various careers should be included.

Health education must also deal with the unexpected. No one expects an accident to happen, yet large numbers of people are disabled each year from automobile, home, and work-related accidents. This may force an individual to make a new career decision. Finally, at each stage of life there may be new limitations as a result of the continuing process of physical aging. But there may be new options as well. Knowing the role that good physical and mental health plays as one grows older may motivate students to maintain health so that future choices will not be limited.

The above considerations are part of most health education programs. Their value can be increased by simply including the subtopic "career implications" in each lesson plan, as suggested previously. In addition, specific activities can be incorporated which will give students opportunities to develop career understanding with regard to careers in the health care industry as well as careers in health-related work.

**Example One — Health Sciences**

Field trips provide a rich firsthand experience for gleaning information about health careers. These should be planned round specific learning objectives, and they should not attempt to serve too many students at one time. Possible sites for field trips include a medical research center, a public health department, a physician's office, a water treatment plant, an industrial safety office, an out-reach health center, a prosthetic limb manufacture and fitting center, a hospital, a volunteer health agency, the school nurse's office, an artificial organ "bank," and others.

### Example Two — Health Sciences

Students may become interested in careers through school food services, including management, purchasing, nutrition, menu planning, and the storage, processing, preparation, and distribution of food. A school health instructor can team nutrition learning with career education by presenting a problem-solving lesson to help students understand these various facets of food service.

If the cafeteria happens to be one that resembles a battlefield, with food used as ammunition, or if there are boycotts of the lunch line because students complain about the food, the problem solving might focus on this. Students could examine the tasks of each food service worker, the pay and any career ladder opportunities — or lack of them — in the food service field. If students are dissatisfied with the food they are offered, they might give special attention to the tasks in menu selection, food purchase, and food preparation in terms of the persons who are most responsible for each of these elements. Then, on the basis of their research, students might propose feasible changes to improve the school lunch menu or the lunchroom atmosphere.

### *Physical Education and Career Education*

Traditionally, physical education in secondary schools has been geared toward development of skills in sports and physical fitness. Too often, performance standards have been imposed externally without recognition of an individual's personal motivations and aspirations. While external performance standards do motivate some students, they cause others to withdraw from experiencing their own individual levels of excellence. Awareness of this problem, and the desire to serve all students well, is bringing change into physical education. The trend is toward enriching the curriculum with a variety of one- and two-person sports, and the adoption of a view of sport as many forms of movement rather than as a contest to be won or lost. Career education has an important place in this changing environment because it emphasizes the need of all students for career development in all areas of school instruction, and it helps to make physical educators aware of the rich resources they have to offer every student who enters their classes.

Movement serves to fulfill the societal needs of man by providing relief from other pursuits and by offering a universal language and common point of communication. The more complex and industrial a society becomes, and the more remote the physical demands on the individual, the more crucial and supportive the role of physical activity becomes. The increasingly sedentary life-style of a large part of our population often is attended by emotional and mental strain. Thus voluntary and planned involvement in movement activities becomes an essential ingredient in maintaining a balance in one's life.

The development of career awareness across this span of student interests does not require the displacement of physical education subject matter. Rather, career education is largely a matter of focus, and it enriches course content and increases student interest by helping all students discover personal rewards that they can carry away from their physical education classes. Skills acquired in physical education classes are frequently valuable in career activities. Everyone is aware of the social importance for business people of such physical activities as golf and tennis. In addition, young persons who are eager to become doctors, engineers, electricians, or artists can help develop the fine motor skills needed in those occupations through physical exercise and games.

Other activities, such as those below, can be incorporated into the curriculum to assist students in career development related to physical education.

### Example One — Physical Education

Students interested in physical education teaching as a career can be encouraged through a planned program of observation and assistance. Experience as a gymnasium supervisor, intramural assistant, equipment manager, or leader of the sports club provides training in organizing and handling administrative duties. Other ways to help students explore the nature of the occupation include giving them responsibility for locker room supervision, roll checks, equipment issue, facility safety checks, instructional assistance, and athletic team management.

**Example Two — Physical Education**

In the communication field, there is increasing interest in people who know sports and can communicate that knowledge in an interesting and informed way. Students interested in such careers can benefit by having the opportunity to interview local radio, television, and newspaper reporters, either in class or by appointment, and by being given responsibility for sports reports in the school paper or over the public address system. Students can also gain valuable experience through score keeping, sports photography, maintaining bulletin boards, and other activities related to physical education.

### Recreation and Career Education

There has been a massive surge in recent years in the field of discretionary time activities. Leisure and recreation now constitute a $150 billion industry that has great potential for continuing expansion. Occupational opportunities are broad in the field of leisure-time pursuits. The National Recreation and Park Association has identified more than seven hundred kinds of occupations which call for knowledge and skills in the areas of leisure-time activities.

Most of the employment opportunities in recreation can be classified under one of four occupational headings: Recreation services, recreation resources, tourism, and amusement and entertainment.

For those students who are not contemplating careers in the recreation field, the career education component of recreation classes might revolve round how to use leisure time in a productive way and how to locate and make use of leisure-time facilities for personal and family enjoyment. Since the wise use of leisure time can enhance work performance, students should explore various ways in which such time can be used.

**Example One — Recreation**

Have students plan a number of recreational activities to fit within certain limitations. For example, the time span may vary from one afternoon to two weeks; the number of persons involved may vary from one to five, with ages varying accordingly; the travel facilities may vary from bicycle to jet plane; the available funds may range from a few dollars to several hundred dollars a day. The objective is to encourage students to think about and plan recreational activities with which they are *not* familiar. This will require research, interviews, discussion, and other avenues of information gathering.

### Example Two — Recreation

Have students design recreational activities for children, based on one or more of the following categories: dance, drama, music, art, nature exploration, sports or games, and animal study. The design should include such factors as cost, time required, amount of supervision required, motivational techniques, facilities and equipment, size of group, and other considerations. This will provide valuable experience for those who are interested in recreation careers as well as for those students who will use their understanding of recreational activities for their personal and family leisure time.

### Example Three — Recreation

Have students interview workers to see how they spend their leisure time. Ask them to speculate about the reasons for relationships between types of recreation activities and (a) occupations, (b) age, (c) sex, and (d) previous involvement in sports.

Career education in recreation and leisure-time areas should not lose sight of the fact that it is important for all future adults to develop interests, skills, and awareness of the uses to which leisure time can be put. This is true whether students become homemakers, lawyers, or construction workers, or whether they enter some occupation outside the leisure field. Leisure is more than a host of occupations; it is a resource that all students should learn to use well, and it is the responsibility of the schools to prepare them to do so.

### References

Costello, John. "What You Need to Climb the Business Ladder." *Nation's Business* (June 1976), vol. 64, no. 6.

Flores, T.; and Olsen, L. "Stability and Realism of Occupational Aspiration in Eighth and Twelfth Grade Males." *Vocational Guidance Quarterly* (1967), vol. 16.

Levitan, Sar A.; and Johnston, William B. *Work Is Here to Stay, Alas.* Salt Lake City: Olympus Publishing Company. 1973.

Mangum, Garth L.; *et al. Career Education in the Academic Classroom.* Salt Lake City: Olympus Publishing Company. 1975.

Super, Donald E. "Vocational Development Theory: Persons, Positions, and Processes." *The Counseling Psychologist* (1969), vol. 1.

# 8

# Vocational Education

Vocational education has been present in American high schools since the Smith-Hughes Act of 1917 and even before. Instruction in practical arts of handicraft and homemaking has an even longer history. Vocational skills training is one of the key components of career education from the beginning, and vocational educators have been among the strongest advocates and supporters of career education. However, career educators argue that the high school has not conceived its vocational education responsibilities broadly enough. The occupations considered to be within the scope of high school vocational education are too few. In fact, without explicitly recognizing it, high schools are providing the basic skill requirements for many more occupations than they list among their vocational offerings. Career educators also see the practical arts as useful but sometimes deficient. Too many of these courses tend to concentrate on handicraft skills which are largely outmoded in the modern world of work, and they fail to point up the career implications of even that which is being taught. However, the trend is clearly in the direction of an understanding of the processes of modern industry and of career opportunities within them.

To the career educator, the term "vocational skills train-ing" is not limited to those courses authorized for financial support under federal vocational education legislation. This term refers to specific job skills, whether attained in the voca-tional education lab, in the academic classroom, in the univer-sity, or on the job. Success in the labor market requires job seeking, job getting, and job holding skills, as noted earlier. To the extent that practical arts and vocational education affect attitudes toward work, general understanding of business and industrial processes, and familiarity with work settings and work discipline, they contribute to general education in all three types of job skills for the entire world of work. To the extent that they offer specific skills useful in performing occu-pational tasks, they are part of vocational skills training along with other education activities that do the same thing. Thus a music class is as much vocational skills training to the pro-spective musician, art to the artist, and math to the engineer, as is typing to the prospective secretary.

Since these traditional activities of vocational education are so much a part of the career education concept, we must examine the relationship of career education to vocational education within the context of the high school's role in career development. Following that review of points made in chapter 2, this chapter describes vocational education and the practical arts as they now exist and then suggests some improvements which might enhance their contribution to career education.

### The Current Status of Career Preparation

Career decision making and career preparation are two of the primary responsibilities of the high school in career education. Long before the student is ready to leave high school, the process of making career decisions has inevitably begun. It cannot be avoided. Whether to remain to graduate, how dili-gently to apply oneself, what electives to take, how hard to apply oneself in each class, what extracurricular activities to pursue — are all decisions with indelible career imprints. Beyond the high school, the student will continue education, or enter the labor market, or fall into some other nonschool, non-employment status. The decision to follow one of these routes will be made, whether or not the student has been prepared to make it wisely.

Though the student may put off until after high school learning the skills of the occupation for which he or she chooses to prepare, the attitudes and habits with which the job market will be approached are being developed willy-nilly. The student who does not choose vocational skills training in the high school or to pursue such training at the post-secondary level has decided deliberately or by default to pursue occupations which require no preentry training — where formal training is either not required or is obtained on the job. This is a legitimate choice, but it should be a deliberate one. All of this helps explain why preparation is so much a part of the responsibility of the high school within the career education concept. The high school does not have sole preparation responsibility, of course. Other institutions which must share some of the burden include parents, employers, trade associations, chambers of commerce, employee groups (unions and professional associations), and government agencies. Many students, after making a decision, will delay specific career preparation beyond the high school. But the high school must accept a key preparation role because it serves almost every young person in our society and because it is the final step in the formal education process for a majority of our citizens.

In preparing students for the world of work, the high school should assume responsibility for at least three major tasks:

(1) Ensuring that every student has the general intellectual skills — reading, writing, oral communication, basic science, practical arts, and so forth — that are necessary for success in every field of work

(2) Providing opportunities for cooperative education programs which use the most effective career preparation capabilities of the school and other institutions of society

(3) Providing in-school career preparation activities which (a) are most efficiently provided in a school setting, or (b) supplement or replace the career preparation activities which should logically be performed by other

agencies of society but which are not being performed for reasons such as sex, social, age, or racial prejudice, economic perturbations, or geographic distance from the school

In addition to these major responsibilities, the high school should also be concerned with providing continued opportunities for the career awareness and career exploration activities which were begun at the elementary and junior high school levels.

These three phases — career awareness, career exploration, and career preparation — are "in process" during the high school years, whether out of design or out of necessity. Career awareness and career exploration have come to be widely accepted goals of the education system; career preparation is still subject to a considerable amount of discussion.

## Vocational Education and the Awareness of Exploration Phases of Career Education

There is no better way of being aware of the meaning of work and careers than having worked. There is no more adequate way of exploring occupations than having "tried them on." Therefore, some vocational educators who have not had contact with career education programs in the elementary and junior high schools assume that career awareness and exploration are simple matters which can be handled by a course or two taught by vocational educators in high school. Several things are wrong with this attitude:

(1) Attitudes are learned early in life, and attitudes toward work are difficult to change by the time a student has reached high school age.

(2) A "course" (or even two courses) is not a very effective way of teaching people to become aware of or to explore the world of work. Thousands of students during the 1920s suffered through "occupation" courses which consisted of the teacher reading long lists of job descriptions, pay scales, and job-entry requirements. This type of course cannot substitute for observation,

simulation, and discussion which are best spread over several years and are best presented in relationship to other types of school learning.

(3) The vocational educator is not necessarily the best person to teach career awareness and exploration. As a specialist in one part of career preparation, he or she is apt to seek recruits for that specialty and may have little patience with those who are not interested in or qualified for that specialty. And, because nonprofessional careers are emphasized in vocational education, the vocational educator may be suspected of not giving adequate attention to professional careers. As with academic teachers and guidance counselors, vocational educators need special training to do the best possible job of helping students to develop career awareness and to explore a wide variety of careers.

Nevertheless, participation in vocational education can make a vital contribution to increasing awareness and to exploration of alternative careers and their meanings in each student's life-style, so long as these tasks are not left to the vocational educator alone.

### Arguments for Career Preparation in the High School

Many persons have difficulty in understanding the role of the school in preparing young people for occupations. Most of these same individuals have no problem in accepting the need to provide opportunities to develop awareness of self or to explore the many opportunities for careers in our society. Many of them also accept the need to teach awareness of the importance of work in the survival of society and to encourage youth to explore their own abilities and interests in an occupational context. But when it comes to actual preparation for work, these individuals draw the line.

Perhaps it is because they fear that career preparation will conflict with the responsibilities of the school to educate for civic, leisure, family, consumer, and other responsibilities which are common to all people, and which should form the core of general education. In response, we contend that work is also a responsibility – a responsibility to self and to society. In fact, without work it is practically impossible to fulfill the other responsibilities with which the school curriculum is concerned. The superintendent of schools in one large city has put it in even stronger terms. He says that a high school should have only two exits: one leading to work and the other leading to further education. He makes it clear that the high school should not and cannot avoid responsibility for preparing its students for one or both of these exits. The student who graduates from high school without such preparation is as much a failure of the school as the student who drops out without it.

Some interpret the "two-exit" goal as advocating the continuation of two separate "tracks" in high school – college preparatory and vocational curriculums – with little or no interchange between them. That means eliminating the third "track" – the general curriculum – which does not lead to one of the two recommended exits. And that, some contend, is enough reform to expect in one generation.

But most advocates of career education want to go even farther. They want to break down the walls between the college preparatory curriculum and the vocational curriculum, and they want to facilitate movement within and between these two curriculums. One of the motives for advocating this restructuring is a social concern: The vocational curriculum appears to foster discrimination in that it serves mostly students from lower class homes in sex-stereotyped classifications; it fails to serve nonconformists; and it is not called upon to serve certain classes of students. The same is true of the college preparatory curriculum, only in reverse. Both curriculums have failed to serve dropouts. Thus career education advocates argue that there should be no "tracking" based on discrimination, and that high school should concentrate on preparing all students for careers, whether that preparation can be completed before high school graduation or whether it is begun in the high school years and continued in post-high school training. Of course, many critics disagree with this point of view.

## *Criticisms of High School Career Preparation*

The criticisms of career preparation in the high school usually fall into one of four categories, typified by these statements:

(1) It ought not be done at all.

(2) It ought to be done later.

(3) It ought to be done by some other agency.

(4) It ought to be done more effectively by the high school than has ever been the case in the past.

Each of these criticisms can be examined against the facts, beginning with the belief that career preparation ought not be done at all.

The persons who argue that career preparation is not needed rarely go all the way with their argument. Usually they agree that certain of the professions have some content for which preparation is needed. A few of these critics seem to be elitists who argue that preparation is needed for leaders but feel that followers will be more easily led if they know that they owe their opportunities for career preparation to the paternalism of their employers. However, a far larger group of such critics opposes career preparation because of a lack of understanding of the need for it. Typically, the argument of this latter group is as follows: Most jobs can be learned in a very few minutes (e.g., work on an assembly line may require learning how to tighten one bolt), and so spending school time on preparation for a job is a waste of money. Besides, jobs are changing rapidly, so preparing a student for a job is almost certain to ensure that student's obsolescence and hence decrease the options open to him or her.

These arguments do not recognize the following facts about the world of work:

(1) Fewer than 2 percent of the labor force in this country is employed on assembly line jobs, and jobs requiring semiskilled operatives and unskilled laborers are a declining 25 percent of total employment (Levitan and Johnson, 1973, pp. 84, 100).

(2) The jobs increasing most rapidly in number are exactly those which have the most education-related content.

(3) The simpler the job, the more likely it is to be low in pay and tenuous in job security. Those who have formal preparation for jobs earn more per year, have less unemployment, and have higher job satisfaction than those who leave school without such preparation.

(4) Attitudes toward work, human relations skills, knowledge of the work environment, and an understanding of the importance of work for the preservation of society — all of which can be taught in school — are often as important for job success as are specific job skills. These skills, knowledge, and attitudes are difficult to teach in a vacuum, however, and high school career preparation programs can provide a setting which enables them to be taught realistically.

The second argument, that career preparation ought to begin in college, ignores the facts that only about 80 percent of the population completes high school, only half enter a post-secondary school, and only a quarter complete post-secondary school. Thus postponement of career preparation until after high school completion would short-change three-fourths of the school population.

The third argument, that some agency other than the public school should be responsible for career preparation, simply opens the question: Who? No one would argue with the fact that other agencies have major responsibilities for job preparation. But to place sole reliance on them also seems indefensible. Private trade schools cannot serve the poor unless they receive subsidies. Apprenticeships produce less than 5 percent of the annual supply of new workers and are concentrated in two sectors of the labor force — construction and metal working. Employers in small firms cannot afford extensive training programs. And most employers regard training of workers as an objective which is secondary to producing goods and services at a profit.

The remaining objection, that high schools ought to do a more effective job of career preparation, is what this chapter is about.

## *Vocational Education and the "Preparation" Phase of Career Education*

Because vocational education constitutes an indispensable part of the preparation phase of career education, an understanding of this phase is necessary to an understanding of the relationship of vocational and career education. "Awareness" and "exploration" precede "preparation," the phase in which:

(1) Students acquire career decision-making skills, work seeking skills, and work evaluation skills

(2) They perfect skills in communication, computation, and human relations which are needed by everyone

(3) They acquire additional salable skills which apply more to some types of work than to others

The preparation phase of career education can be (and once was) conducted entirely on the job. However, there has been a continuing trend toward a combination of preparation in school and training on the job. This combination may be done *sequentially* (as is the case when a person goes to engineering school for four years, and follows this with two years of experience on the job), or *concurrently* (as in a part-time cooperative education program, in which the student engages in alternating periods of study and work under the supervision of the school). Both the sequential and the concurrent methods of instruction are usually accompanied by a certain amount of general education. (Most commonly, 50 percent of the school time in any one school year is spent in general education and 50 percent in specialized instruction.)

The length of the in-school preparation phase varies considerably from one type of career to another. For convenience, careers can be divided into four categories of length of specialized preparation:

(1) *Professional* — Forty to a hundred semester hours

spread over four to seven years of full-time schooling, usually in a university.

(2) *Technical* — Thirty to 45 semester hours spread over two years of full-time schooling, usually in a community college.

(3) *Vocational, skilled* — Twenty to 35 semester hours in one year of full-time schooling, usually in a community college; or approximately the same amount of instruction (four to six Carnegie units) spread over two to four years of high school.

(4) *Vocational, specialized* — One day to six months of intensive instruction, usually offered to adults by high schools, proprietary schools (e.g., trade and business schools), community colleges, or universities. Specialized preparation is usually completed by persons who are already employed and hence does not provide additional entrants to the labor force.

When one studies the data on the percentage of people employed in various types of occupations and the proportion of students in different types of occupational education programs, some interesting comparisons emerge:

(1) Professional preparation is useful for about 20 percent of the labor market and is completed by about 20 percent of students.

(2) Technical preparation is useful for about 15 percent of the labor market, but less than 10 percent of students complete it.

(3) Vocational preparation is useful for about 40 percent of the labor market, but less than 30 percent of students complete it, and about a third of its graduates go on to technical or professional preparation.

There are no in-school programs preparing people for job entry to approximately 20 percent of the careers in the labor market, and about 50 percent of new entrants to the labor force have not participated in career preparation programs of any type.

It is a common assumption that vocational education is synonymous with the career preparation phase of career education. This assumption is not quite accurate. Vocational education is concerned with preparation for the large numbers of vocational and technical careers which are nonprofessional and require less than a college degree for entrance, but which require more knowledge and skill than is possessed by the typical high school graduate from the general curriculum.

Career preparation includes (but vocational education usually omits):

(1) Preparation for the professions and for similar careers requiring a baccalaureate for entry (about 20 percent of the labor force)

(2) Preparation for nonpaid work such as homemaking (once a full-fledge part of vocational education, but now half-in, half-out due to evaluation specialists who convinced Congress that placement of vocational graduates in homemaking was equivalent to unemployment) and volunteer work (both of these major types of work are, of course, outside the paid labor force)

(3) Education which is needed for more effective involvement in all types of work; e.g., work seeking skills, personal and work evaluation skills, and knowledge of how work is organized and carried out (preparation for all work inside and outside the labor force)

It is a common mistake to say that the vocational education curriculum prepares people for 80 percent of the jobs, while the college preparatory curriculum in the secondary school prepares people for only 20 percent of the jobs. It would be more accurate to say that at least 50 percent of high school students are not now prepared for work of any type, and that traditional programs of vocational education, which are designed to prepare people for skilled occupations, are unlikely to meet this need. Career education programs which emphasize preparation for nonpaid work and preparation which is useful for all types of work (2 and 3 above) offer real promise of meeting some of the needs of this 50 percent. Vocational educators can expand their contributions to the career education of all students by stressing their offerings as opportunities for career exploration by those not ready for a career choice and therefore not ready to undertake vocational education as career preparation.

## *Current Programs of Vocational Education*

The majority of high schools in this country is small. Half of them have less than four hundred students. These schools are usually in rural areas or small towns, and they typically have three vocational programs: (1) home economics for girls, (2) business education for girls, and (3) agriculture for boys. Another program designed primarily for boys, industrial arts, has only recently become eligible to receive federal vocational funds. Usually, industrial arts serves an exploratory career education function and teaches a few skills in the use of tools, skills which have limited preparatory value for today's world of work. The large number of high schools which have less than two hundred students usually are unable to offer business education or industrial arts, and they may have no vocational programs whatsoever. Although they call themselves "comprehensive" high schools, the college preparatory curriculum comprises most of their offerings.

Comprehensive high schools with enrollments of more than a thousand usually add distributive education (mostly retail sales), an introduction to health occupations, such additional business education courses as bookkeeping and shorthand, and more variety in the home economics offerings. However, the major changes are likely to be the addition of one or more part-time cooperative education programs (in which students work half-time in business and industry under the eye of a school-employed coordinator) and trade and industrial education programs in fields such as drafting, electronics, auto mechanics, machine shop, and carpentry.

Very large comprehensive high schools (three thousand to five thousand students) offer a greater variety in each of these fields, adding courses in such fields as data processing, ornamental horticulture, cosmetology, quantity food cookery, automobile body repair, welding, and cabinetmaking.

Parochial high schools rarely have extensive vocational education programs because of the relatively high cost of such offerings. Some parochial schools send students to nearby public high schools for vocational courses.

A third type of high school specializes in the vocational curriculum and does not pretend to offer college preparatory or general curriculums. In very large cities, these are called trade or vocational high schools, and they may be so specialized that they offer only business occupations curriculums or trade and industrial curriculums. For example, New York City has one school which specializes in marine occupations.

Medium-size communities have been encouraged by Congress to establish area vocational schools, and many states have urged that these area schools operate at the high school level. Such schools often draw students from half a dozen or more "home" high schools. Vocational students typically spend half of each day studying academic courses in their "home" high school and then travel to the area vocational school for the remaining half-day.

In theory, each local community builds its own vocational curriculums, based on a study of the needs of the local community. In practice, however, the size of the high school is a far more potent factor in determining the range of vocational offerings than is the type of community in which it is situated. And it would appear that the preferences of students and their parents are the most important factor in determining whether a program will survive. It is rare for a school to continue offering a program in which only five or ten students are willing to enroll.

There are modest differences in the types of vocational courses from one high school to another, based on employment opportunities in the community or on the presence of an unusually popular teacher. But each vocational subject tends to have its own index of popularity. One can expect that about 5 to 10 percent of the senior class of a comprehensive high school will be willing to enroll in business education classes, 2 to 5 percent will enroll in vocational machine shop, and less than 1 percent will enroll in welding. Thus the size of the school has an enormous effect on the breadth of program which can be offered (assuming that fifteen to 25 students are needed in any one class to make it economically feasible).

These percentages are based on a typical comprehensive high school which has three curriculums: college preparatory, enrolling half of the students; general, enrolling a quarter of the students; and vocational, enrolling the remaining quarter. An area vocational high school which offers only vocational programs will find that the percentages of its student body willing to enroll in each of the vocational specialties increases about fourfold.

## Limitations of the Typical High School Vocational Education Program

It is part of the conventional wisdom that the basic limitations of vocational education revolve round the teaching of obsolete skills on obsolete equipment in occupations that are obsolete or about to become obsolete. Anyone who has made a thorough study of what actually goes on in vocational education programs could cite extreme examples of such obsolescence, but they are not typical. These are not the most frequent or serious problems. In skills centers where the Manpower Development and Training Act required every program to be certified by state employment service personnel as offering training in occupations where there was a reasonable expectation of employment, the occupations taught have been almost identical to those offered in urban vocational education programs.

While it is true that students and employers alike place high value on up-to-date equipment, a survey of vocational curriculum graduates found that, on the average, they had been able to shift in less than half an hour from the type of equipment used in the school to that used in employment (Eninger, 1965, p. 5). The fact that high school vocational graduates have approximately a third the unemployment of comparable graduates of nonvocational curriculums would seem to indicate that the teaching of obsolete skills is not a significant problem.

The real problems of vocational education in the high school are quite different. They revolve round:

(1) Sex stereotyping in vocational programs

(2) Overemphasis on blue-collar jobs for children from blue-collar families

(3) Offering programs only in the junior and senior years, too late to meet the needs of most dropouts

(4) Preparation for too few occupational fields

(5) Overemphasis on securing employment in the field for which the student was prepared, and underemphasis on careers in general

Perhaps the worst of these problems is the last one listed. It sounds sensible to evaluate a vocational program in a given occupational field on the basis of how many of its graduates find employment in that occupation. Obviously, if none of the graduates could find such employment, something must be wrong. The overemphasis comes in expecting every student to take such employment. A third of the high school graduates of vocational education programs go on to post-secondary education. Few would classify them as failures. Nor are those students failures who learn during the program that they would enjoy some other occupational field more than the one they have studied.

Overemphasis on placement "in the occupation for which trained" leads to the selection of the most qualified applicants for vocational programs instead of the selection of those students who can profit most from the instruction. It also leads to restrictions on transfers from one vocational program to another on the grounds that it is better to prepare a student thoroughly, even for an occupation which he or she has learned is not personally satisfying, than to allow the student to shift goals to a different occupational field if there is not enough time remaining during the high school years to allow thorough occupational preparation. Furthermore, it leads to emphasis on entry-level job preparation, rather than to more basic preparation which would be useful in each of a succession of jobs on a career ladder.

### Role of Youth Clubs in Career Education

One cannot discuss vocational education without also considering the youth clubs which are so closely related to the major vocational education offerings. Almost two million high school and post-secondary students participate in five vocational youth organizations: Future Farmers of America, Future Homemakers of America, Distributive Education Clubs of America, Future Business Leaders of America, and Vocational-Industrial Clubs of America. All five of the groups have local, state, and national organizations and officers, and they provide excellent opportunities for the development of leadership skills. Each of these five national organizations holds local, regional, and national conferences, and most of them conduct competitive contests in a wide variety of activities. The organizations publish well-prepared materials for student information and use. Their principal emphasis is on the development of leadership skills, and the results are impressive. State and national officers of these organizations are perhaps the best "lobbyists" for vocational education in Congress and before business and industry groups.

In the health occupations field, the Student Nurses ASsociation serves somewhat the same function, but it is limited to post-secondary students of nursing. Some state and local schools have clubs which cover all of the health occupations, and in each local organization a vocational teacher is usually the club adviser.

Other youth organizations are available in some areas for high school youth who wish to explore one or more of several professions. Three of the larger national groups are the Future Teachers of America, the Junior Engineering Technical Society, and the Junior Academy of Science. National or local counterparts also exist in theater, journalism, music, and many other professions. The adult sponsor of a local club may be a teacher or a local practitioner who has expertise in the field with which the club is concerned.

There is a distinct difference between the vocational youth groups and the pre-professional youth groups. Vocational youth groups usually require that the student member be enrolled in the related vocational program. This means that the student has made at least a nominal career choice and is in the preparation phase of career education. Consequently, the club emphasizes proficiency in a limited range of occupations rather than exploration of careers. In contrast, the students in pre-professional youth groups are encouraged to explore careers (but only within the professions), and there usually is an open-entry, open-exit membership policy which is unrelated to the student's major field of study in the high school. Frequently, a local pre-professional youth club serves as a recruiting agent for a particular college which provides the necessary preparation for that particular career or careers.

The undisputed value of youth clubs in developing positive attitudes and leadership skills leads one to enquire why there are so few career education clubs, or at least prevocational clubs. Such groups could play a major role in developing career awareness and in assisting with career exploration. Some industrial arts and home economics clubs do play this role, but the former are more likely to emphasize exploration of avocational interests, and the latter frequently emphasize preparation for homemaking.

The youth groups with the most extensive career exploration programs usually operate outside the schools. Explorers (formerly Explorer Scouts) have an extremely well-developed career exploration program which encompasses all types of careers. Somewhat less extensive career exploration is offered by 4-H Clubs, Scouts, and similar youth service clubs, and by Junior Achievement.

## Status of the Fine and Practical Arts

Almost every high school has teachers who are specialists in the fine and practical arts. Art, music, home economics, industrial arts, and business are the most common subjects, but in the larger high schools each of these fields is further subdivided. For example, the art department may have specialists in ceramics, painting, and crafts, while music may have vocal and instrumental specialists. Similarly, some home economics departments have teachers of textiles, nutrition, and family living, while industrial arts departments have specialists in woods, metals, graphic arts, and power mechanics. In the business field, personal typing, note-hand, and family economics are popular specialties. Some schools have practical arts instruction in agriculture, health, and distribution of goods and services.

None of these programs has career preparation as a major goal, but they all have significant contributions to make toward advanced levels of career awareness and exploration. Their principal goal is general education in fields about which every student should know but which are not treated adequately by the "academic" subjects. For example, every person should know something about how food is produced and distributed and how it affects our health and well-being. Presumably, parts of this knowledge could and should come from economics and physical education teachers, but practical arts specialists frequently are more effective in such instruction. Because the practical arts are a part of general education, they attempt to teach content which *every* person should learn, rather than to teach that which is needed by only a fraction of the populace. Thus their content covers both work and leisure-time activities; it is concerned with societal as well as individual effects; and it emphasizes the study of efficient action (sometimes called "praxiology").

There is no question but that an effective practical arts program could provide a major part of the instruction needed for career awareness and career preparation. Unfortunately, few schools have practical arts programs which extend beyond home economics and industrial arts. Moreover, few females study industrial arts and few males study home economics, although both are needed by all students.

This general education should be a part of the instruction of every student, irrespective of curriculum. Students in the vocational curriculum typically spend only one-fourth of their high school time on vocational education subjects, one-fourth on practical arts subjects, and the remaining half on other general education subjects such as English, mathematics, and social studies. They rarely enroll in fine arts courses. Students in the college preparatory curriculum typically have little or no instruction in the practical arts, receive more general education than do vocational students, and spend a fourth or more of their time in pre-professional or advanced level mathematics, foreign languages, English, and other subjects which are not required of all students. The general curriculum is described by Project TALENT as a curriculum which "does not prepare you either for college or for work, but consists of courses required for graduation plus subjects that you like" (Flanagan, *et al.*, 1964, p. 5).

Unfortunately, a number of writers have failed to distinguish between the general curriculum and general education, and they have recommended that the latter be abolished, although it is clear that they mean to abolish the former. General education should be a part of every curriculum, and the fine and practical arts are an integral part of general education. However, it makes no sense educationally to prescribe the fine arts as "general education" for the upper strata of the population and the practical arts as "general education" for students from the lower socioeconomic level.

The fine and practical arts share an emphasis on activity which offers the adolescent student a welcome change from the heavy emphasis on classroom work which is characteristic of most other high school subjects. Moreover, since only a few community colleges and universities require entering students to demonstrate proficiency in the fine or practical arts, high school instructors can design those courses to meet the needs of their students, rather than to meet the demands of an external agency. This relative freedom of setting and of content allows unusual opportunities for teaching career education concepts.

Some problems do exist, however. One major problem is that, despite legal rulings which discourage it, segregation by sex is common in home economics, industrial arts, and physical education. A second problem is lack of coordination between similar programs in the junior high school and high school. For example, it is not at all uncommon for high school freshmen to be considered insufficiently mature to operate equipment which they have already used successfully in the junior high school. A third difficulty is that teachers in some fine and practical arts programs have overemphasized avocational goals at the expense of vocational goals. A principal reason for this is that they rightfully have wanted to emphasize the utility of their subject for every student. They have seen that every student should have an avocation, but sometimes they have failed to see that every student also needs to explore careers along with exploration of self, and needs to acquire salable skills which will increase the options available after he or she leaves school.

In spite of these problems, it seems likely that teachers of the fine and practical arts have been among the most successful of all teachers in helping students to know themselves in relationship to the real world. This is due in large part to the afore-mentioned freedoms of curriculum and physical setting. But it is also due to the opportunity teachers have to work closely with students who are frank, curious, ready for independent work, and aware of and interested in knowing the consequence of rapid personal changes.

Another major factor has been teacher willingness to deal with their load of 120 or more students each day by getting to know each student's strengths and weaknesses, attitudes and desires, not only in the cognitive, but also in the affective, psychomotor and perceptual domains. Career education in the high school seeks not only to capitalize on this teacher knowledge of the individual student, but to aid the teacher in making it even more thorough and complete.

### Unfilled Assignments in High School Vocational Skills Training

Whatever the limitations and strengths of vocational education as it currently exists in America's high schools, there are a number of aspects of vocational skills training which the high schools are ignoring or pursuing halfheartedly because they fail to perceive the full implications of the career education responsibility. We will examine a few of those "unfilled assignments," including occupational education, career preparation for the professions, nonspecific career preparation, and vocational education as general education for work.

### Occupational Education in the High School

Occupational education is a phrase sometimes used to describe preparation for and upgrading in all kinds and levels of work. In contrast, federal legislation limits vocational education to occupations which are not "professional" and which do not require a baccalaureate degree for entrance. Thus federal vocational education funds cannot, by law, be used to prepare a person in becoming an actor or actress (because acting is a profession). Nor can federally funded vocational education prepare one to become an attorney (because an attorney usually must have at least a bachelor's degree). To make this distinction clear, the federal government publishes a list of occupations for which vocational education funds may not be used.

The reason for this distinction between occupational and vocational education was the recognition more than fifty years ago that the nation was willing to spend large amounts of time and effort on preparation of students for the professions through college education in a variety of fields, while at the same time public schools paid virtually no attention to the vocations in which more than 80 percent of the nation's population was working. Congress wanted to expand the latter type of education and to prevent educators from spending all of the limited funds available on further expansion of education for the professions; and thus Congress forbade the expenditure of vocational education funds for this purpose.

The reasons for limiting the use of vocational education funds to certain occupations are easy to understand, but there is no doubt that the application of this policy has caused numerous difficulties, especially in the high school. For example, some states have refused to provide federal funds for high school classes from which a sizable proportion of students have gone to college. Several widely cited evaluations of vocational education count all graduates who have gone to college in the same category as students who are dropouts, who are unemployed, or who have chosen an occupation different from the one they studied in high school.

The separation of jobs into "professional" or "not professional" is nonsensical from the viewpoint of the career educator, even if the separation makes sense to a government auditor or to an evaluator in that same category. It is a basic concept of career education that every student should have the right to make a personal decision as to how far up the career ladder he or she will attempt to climb. It is nonsense to tell a student of drafting that she must drop out of the class the moment she decides that becoming an engineer might be more interesting to her than becoming a draftsman.

Most vocational educators decry this type of separation of "vocational" and "nonvocational" careers, and are active at the local school level in encouraging the development of career preparation programs. They are particularly interested in building ties between occupational education programs in the high school and those in the community college.

### Career Preparation for the Professions

Because Congress wanted to be sure that its vocational funds would be used to prepare people for occupations with which most schools were unconcerned, it restricted the use of these funds to occupations which are nonprofessional and which require less than a baccalaureate degree for entry. However, career education is concerned with preparation for *all* occupations which are useful in society.

It has been usual to delay preparation for these "non-reimbursable" (nonvocational) occupations until after high school graduation. But what about the high school student in a vocational class who chooses to prepare for a professional career which is related to the vocational subject being studied? It hardly seems reasonable to expel the student from the vocational class or to insist that the changed occupational goal be repressed until after high school graduation. Besides, most professionals would perform more adequately if they had a sound knowledge of the activities of the nonprofessionals in related occupations. For example, the architect is likely to be a better architect if he or she knows something of the work of the carpenter. Thus it does not appear unreasonable to allow a student of carpentry, who decides to become an architect, at least to finish out the school year in the carpentry class.

But what about the high school student who desires to become an architect (or other professional) and has had no contact with vocational education? Which courses should that student select? Usually, the high school solicits the advice of a post-secondary school which is designed to prepare people for that profession and asks for advice as to appropriate high school courses and other activities. More recently, it has been recognized that part-time "cooperative" placement in a professional's office is desirable while the student is still in high school. It may be argued that this is exploration, rather than preparation, but an examination of the activities of students in such professional co-op programs indicates some elements of each.

The point is that many students are ready to begin preparation for careers while they are still in high school. If they are ready they should begin. In addition to preparation in an appropriate class or on the job, preparation can begin through clubs (e.g., Future Teachers of America or Junior Engineering Technical Society) or through periodic discussions with a "model" (a professional in the community to whom the student can look for guidance).

Principal efforts in the nonvocational (professional) phase of occupational education have come from the fine arts, English, and foreign language departments. Classes in journalism and theater are found in most medium-size high schools. Similar occupational emphasis is sometimes found in advanced instrumental music classes and in advanced painting, sculpture, and crafts instruction. Emphasis on preparing for vocal music careers seems to come principally from individual instruction, often outside regular school hours. The recent shift in emphasis in foreign language from translation of written words to oral communication has been accompanied by acknowledgment of career opportunities for translators.

In spite of these few exceptions, it is doubtless true that most of the emphasis on "nonvocational" careers in the high school is placed on exploration of careers, rather than preparation for them. Where the careers require a baccalaureate degree for entrance, this is as it should be. It is a basic principle of teaching that specific instruction should be provided shortly before the time when it is needed. If a baccalaureate degree is needed for entry into an occupation, most of the preparation for that occupation should be concentrated in the last two years of the college program. In these cases, it is obvious that exploration is needed during high school so that the individual has a better basis for selection of a career before making the mistake of dropping out of school too soon or of continuing into college for the wrong reasons.

However, those professions which do not require a baccalaureate for entry are quite different. These doubtless are
the careers with which high schools have been least well prepared to cope. And as is the case with all professions, these
activities are not eligible for vocational education funds; nor
have they been accorded full status in many community colleges or universities. Dancing, announcing, production control,
and time study are examples. Selling, practical nursing, and
bookkeeping were in this same class until they were accepted
by Congress as being legitimate subjects for vocational education. Preparation for careers in professional athletics is half
accepted by high schools and colleges, primarily for public
relations purposes rather than for educational reasons.

Exploration of professional and other nonvocational
careers in the high school is extensive in a few fields, minimal
in a few more, and nonexistent in most. The best examples are
found in programs which explore an entire occupational cluster,
with no attempt to limit exploration to the vocational level or
to the professional level. One of the earliest and best examples
is Project Feast, which explores the entire foods industry from
busboy to executive chef and can refer youths to jobs after
high school or send them on to community colleges or universities in the same field. This program has been aided greatly
by the excellent career ladder studies conducted by the National Restaurant Association.

Similar activities have begun in the health field, with the
organization of health occupations clubs such as the one at
Columbus High School in Columbus, Indiana. The entire
range of health occupations is explored, from orderly to physician, and related careers in fields such as pharmacy and
hospital administration are not overlooked. The student who
completes a thorough exploration of an entire career cluster is
much less likely to be thrust by family, friends, or the school
into a career level that does not accord with her or his desired
life-style. Nor is such a person as likely to be dismayed after
completing a premedical program in college only to find that
there is no chance of acceptance into a medical or veterinary
school. Nor is there as great a likelihood of completing a year of
medical school only to learn that this field requires activities
which the student abhors.

Less comprehensive, but still desirable, are the exploration activities which cover only one level of one or two career clusters. The Junior Engineering Technical Society (JETS) was established more than twenty years ago to help school students explore careers in engineering. Its genesis was based on the fact that many students enroll in engineering colleges with little or no knowledge of what an engineer does. The result is that a high proportion of students transfer out of engineering after spending two or three college years in a curriculum for which they have little interest or aptitude. The resultant waste of the time of students and of professors is enormous. Unfortunately, few high schools have an engineer on the staff to serve as a JETS sponsor. The best solution seems to be to have the club be sponsored by an interested physical science teacher. Club activities include interviews with nearby engineers and visits to the places where they work. Major colleges of engineering provide liaison with JETS clubs as a means of identifying outstanding students.

Some schools have science clubs which serve a similar function of exploring professional careers in science. (Because careers in science and engineering require similar talents but different interests, it would be interesting to explore the extent to which the science teachers who sponsor clubs in both fields tend to influence the most capable students to enter science rather than engineering.)

Drama clubs, dance clubs, foreign language clubs, and other clubs organized round particular subject matter may or may not place emphasis upon career exploration. Careers in social science professions, such as psychology, economics, and sociology, rarely receive much attention in the high school. Nor are careers in the humanities frequently addressed. The result is thousands of students who major in one of these fields in college with never a thought as to the type of career to be followed when the bachelor's degree has been completed. Few people would argue about the value of college majors in the social sciences and humanities. However, it would seem reasonable to suppose that instruction in psychology might be more useful if it points out that a career in psychology is virtually impossible if one has only a baccalaureate degree.

### Nonspecific Career Preparation

Each program in vocational, technical, and professional education is designed to prepare persons for successful careers in a specific group of occupations. These occupations may employ millions of people — as in the secretarial field — or a few hundred — as in musicology. One specific training program may prepare a person for as many as two hundred job titles — as in vocational machine shop — or for as few as two or three — as in veterinary medicine. They may range in length from a few hours of instruction — as in some phase of retailing — to six or more years for a specialized profession.

No more than 20 percent of careers are in professional fields, and current programs of technical and vocational education prepare no more than 30 percent of the population for entrance into the occupations they represent. Approximately a third of all jobs can be performed successfully without a formal preparation by any reasonably intelligent and presentable person who can read, write, and do simple arithmetic, drive an automobile, and evidence reasonable manual dexterity. Another third are learned on the job, and the final third require some pre-entry preparation.

By increasing the size of high schools through school consolidation, a wider variety of vocational skills training courses can be offered to students. Expansion of the part-time cooperative education program has even greater potential for increasing the breadth of vocational programs available to high school students. However, when all is said and done, it is unlikely that more than half of high school students could be expected to complete a vocational education program and to enter the occupational field for which that program was designed. There are more than thirty thousand job titles in the *Dictionary of Occupational Titles*, but less than three hundred different vocational, technical, or professional programs are offered with any frequency in the nation's schools and colleges. Many of these educational programs relate to dozens or even hundreds of job titles, and the *Occupational Outlook Handbook* indicates that its similar list encompasses over two-thirds of the existing jobs. Nevertheless, a quick review of the *Dictionary of Occupational Titles* will reveal hundreds of job titles for which there is no training offered in schools in any part of the country, and thousands of job titles for which training is not available in any one school, no matter how large or well equipped that school may be.

Cooperative education programs do not offer a complete answer, either, for they can offer education only in occupations which exist in the community. It is apparent that schools cannot and should not offer vocational skills training in every field. More efficient methods for acquiring skills are available in many occupational fields. But the key question remains: What is the school's obligation for career preparation to those who will neither attend college nor enroll in a high school vocational class?

One of the major problems of career preparation in the high school revolves round the question of what the school should do to prepare students for the approximately two-thirds of all jobs which require little or no specific preparation prior to employment. Among these are jobs which a person of average intelligence can do immediately or can learn on the job in a week or two, provided that he or she has had typical experiences in the home and school. Almost all unskilled and semiskilled work is of this type, as are the lowest levels of clerical and service work. Most of these jobs require low levels of performance in tasks of one or both of two types:

(1) Tasks involving the use of paper, pencil, and books, which the school has for years sought to teach to everyone. These skills include reading, writing, and simple arithmetic. Jobs of this type include some mailing and messenger jobs which require little more skill than the ability to read and write addresses.

(2) Tasks which do not require the use of paper, but which the home (and more recently the school) has sought to teach to nearly everyone. Such skills include speaking, driving an automobile, handling simple tools, following directions and detailed orders, and measuring and mixing ingredients according to a recipe. Many simple delivery, service, and manufacturing jobs are of this type.

One should not make the mistake of assuming that these jobs require *no* skill. Anyone who has seen attempts to establish certain very simple types of manufacturing or construction enterprises in developing countries is struck by the difficulties which arise as a result of the absence of skills which we assume that everyone acquires naturally in a developed country such as the United States. "Unskilled" work is basically work which requires little more skill than is acquired by most people in our country in school or at home. Those who have not had this experience will have difficulty in performing even unskilled work.

An important problem is that some people require far more time than others to learn even the simplest skills. Some 5 to 10 percent of the school population have severe learning difficulties. A skill which the average student can learn in minutes may require months for a "trainable" student to acquire.

Thus it should be obvious that special attention needs to be paid to those students whose early learning in home and school have been neglected, and to those students who have severe learning difficulties as a result of physical, mental, or emotional problems. Less obvious, but not less real, is the obligation to provide some career preparation for normal persons who choose occupations which require little or no specific skills training.

### *Vocational Education as General Education for Work*

It is a general phenomenon that only about half of the persons who complete a vocational or professional curriculum actually work in the field for which they are prepared or in some closely related field. This is as true of collegiate professional programs as it is of high school vocational programs. The principal exceptions are temporary, and they seem to depend in part on the current state of the labor market and in part on the amount of time and money spent in training. At the moment, physicians are in great demand, and thus about 95 percent of new doctors of medicine enter the practice of medicine. But currently, less than a third of those prepared to be teachers of history actually take jobs in that field, because there is a much greater supply than demand.

In other times, however, it is probable that both of these groups have been much nearer the typical 50 percent placement figure. Occupational areas such as law, accounting, and engineering have always had large proportions of their graduates using their preparation in relatively unrelated employment in business and government. In fields such as psychology, where the baccalaureate program is unrelated to the entry job market, and in fields such as music, where the demand is chronically smaller than the supply, the placement rate falls regularly well below the 50 percent mark. In fact, if graduates are followed over a lifetime, a substantial portion of every occupational group makes major career shifts.

Evaluators of vocational education have tended to feel that a 50 percent placement rate in the occupation for which the person was trained is far too low. In fact, however, sometimes it may be too high.

There is an obvious discrepancy if a person enters a given vocational education program but does not go to work in a career for which this program is preparatory. This discrepancy may be due to one or more of a variety of reasons. Some of these reasons are undesirable, and are at least partially under the control of the school. For example:

(1) The student had inadequate knowledge of the goals of the program.

(2) The program did not prepare students adequately for entry into the world of work.

(3) There were inadequate efforts to place the student properly.

Other reasons are undesirable, but may *not* be under the control of the school. For example:

(1) Employment opportunities suddenly decreased before the student could get a job in the field for which he or she was trained.

(2) Available jobs in the occupational field went to those who had friends or relatives in key posts.

(3) Pay was greater in a nonrelated occupational field which was otherwise less desirable from the student's standpoint.

(4) So few students in the community were interested in this type of training that it was not feasible to offer the program.

Still other reasons for employment in an occupation other than the one for which the student was prepared may be desirable reasons. For example:

(1) The student discovered during the educational program that this kind of work was personally distasteful, or that another type of work was personally more desirable.

(2) The student knew that employment opportunities would be low, but chose after careful deliberation to take a chance that he or she would be exceptionally lucky.

(3) The school was unable to offer the vocational program desired by the student, and so he or she took the most similar course available.

Those persons who are unable to enroll in precisely the vocational programs they desire can learn much which is applicable to all or part of the world of work by enrolling in a less desired vocational program. In an earlier chapter we indicated that students need to acquire:

(1) Basic academic skills

(2) General vocational skill

(3) Good work habits

(4) Job seeking, getting, and holding skills

(5) Occupational skills

All students receive instruction in the first of these five types of skills, and the second, third, and fourth can be learned nearly as well in a vocational education program which is the second choice of the student as they can be in the program which she or he would have preferred. Even more important, however, is the fact that these three types of skills can best be taught and learned in a program designed for this purpose. They cannot be learned in a vacuum; nor does a statement that they are needed suffice. Vocational education classes are among the logical places in which to teach and learn general vocational skills, good work habits, and job seeking, getting, and holding skills. The vocational graduates who acquire these skills and use them to find work in a field which is different from the one which served as a vehicle for their learning have nevertheless been well served by the school.

The final category — that is, the specific skill content of an occupation — can often be learned either in a classroom situation or on the job. That method which is most efficient depends upon the nature of the skills required, the costs and difficulties of simulating the environment of the workplace in the classroom, safety factors, the relative demands for theoretical and manipulative content, and the volume of persons available to be trained in the occupations. It is the tendency to focus on the final occupational content rather than the more general skills which has most confused the issues between vocational education which is offered in school and that which is offered on the job.

## Installing Career Education in Practical Arts and Vocational Education

When a career education program is proposed in a high school, almost invariably the majority of the practical arts and vocational instructors supports it. However, it is also true that after the program is installed, the practical arts and vocational instructors are likely to change their own offerings very little. The principal reason for this lack of change seems to be a feeling of these teachers that they have been implementing career education all along, and hence there is no reason to change. Discussion of the differences and similarities between career and vocational education indicates that there is some justification for this feeling on the part of vocational educators, but that some important parts of career education are not likely to be present in vocational education.

When vocational education teachers are asked to prepare lesson plans for career education, a typical reaction is for them to prepare plans which teach the performance of specific skills. Perhaps they make the common mistake of assuming that because the teacher sees the relevance of particular subject matter, all students will also see this relevance. But why should we expect that students will believe that learning to cut threads on a lathe is any more relevant than learning to solve a quadratic equation, or that learning to dress properly for a white-collar job is any more important than learning about the history of the American Revolution? Some students will learn all four of these because the teacher tells them to learn it; other students will learn all four because of an urge to learn or an urge to excel; still other students will be unwilling to learn some or all of the four because they fail to see relevance to their personal lives. Vocational education teachers should not assume — no more than academic teachers should assume — that because they see the relevance of what they are teaching, all of their students will also see it.

A major purpose of this chapter is to point out some ways in which these missing pieces can be addressed in the high school. Another purpose is to show how vocational educators and practical arts instructors can and should be actively involved in career education.

## Problems in the Relationship of Career and Vocational Education

Career education has had its greatest successes in the elementary school. It now appears that its introduction into junior high schools is well under way; but in high schools, there is little to be seen of career education except for vocational education. This can be explained in a variety of ways:

(1) Some persons feel that vocational education and the preparation phase of career education are synonymous; thus if their high school has the former, they feel that the latter is accomplished.

(2) Parents want career education to be available in high school, but don't necessarily want their children to enroll in it, especially not in its career preparation phase.

(3) The curriculum in high school is mandated by colleges and by accrediting associations.

(4) High school teachers who accept career education goals feel that little can be done until awareness and exploration activities are well under way in the lower grades.

(5) Some of the high school teachers who accept career education goals know that they have only a limited awareness of the vast range of career options existing in the world of work, and are uncomfortable with the thought that they will be involved in preparing students for careers with which they are unfamiliar.

(6) Some persons who accept awareness and exploration of careers as legitimate school activities feel that preparation is the job of private trade schools or employers rather than of the schools.

Everyone agrees that vocational education is an essential element in career education. But this should not be interpreted to mean that vocational education needs no changes if it is to fill its role in career education completely. The most frequently needed changes include the following:

(1) Flexibility for all students to change career goals, and modification of sequence and major field graduation requirements so that students who change vocational goals are not delayed in high school graduation

(2) Emphasis on preparation for careers rather than just for an entry-level job

(3) Evaluation on the basis of satisfaction with and from work, rather than on the basis of the proportion of students who are employed in the occupation for which they were prepared

(4) Emphasis on preparation for work roles which require

coping with people, data, and things, rather than just on skills in performing work processes

(5) Instruction in the economics of work so that students know the effects of absenteeism, low productivity, unsafe actions, and poor quality of work

(6) Knowledge of labor market mechanisms for securing and changing jobs, for improving working conditions, and coping with practices which tend to exclude some people from certain work roles

(7) Encouragement for nonvocational education students to enroll in vocational education classes for career exploration purposes

The following are some activities which teachers will find useful in handling career education improvements of the vocational education students.

## Activities for Vocational Education Classes

(1) Set up an advisory committee made of up employers and employees from all parts of the field for which you are preparing students (with advice from their group on curriculum content, equipment purchases or donations, and placement opportunities).

(2) Use your advisory committee members as resource persons to tell or demonstrate actions which led to unusual success or failure on the job.

(3) Ask recent graduates or dropouts to describe their experiences in the world of work. Or ask students to interview them.

(4) Prepare a map showing the geographic distribution of your graduates or dropouts. This will necessitate a follow-up study. While you are at it, get data on job titles, further education, pay ranges, and job satisfaction. Communicate these findings to students and prospective students.

(5) Prepare a map showing every employer of persons in your field and in your geographic area. Identify discrepancies between this list of employers and the one used above. Learn why some employers do not employ your former students.

(6) Conduct field trips to work sites where obsolete, conventional, and advanced practices are employed. Ask students to contrast them in terms of pay, job satisfaction, and opportunity.

(7) Set up a cooperative education program for your most advanced students while you give more intensive instruction to slower students.

(8) Teach students to perform equipment maintenance activities as well as teaching them how to use the equipment.

(9) Have each student prepare a résumé and go through a simulated employment interview.

(10) Identify each common source of employment information and catalog each one's costs and benefits.

(11) Strive for a balance of "live jobs" (tasks which come from outside your class, and which have obvious relevance) and practice a simulated activity (which teach skills not usually found in "live jobs").

(12) Outline typical career ladders and lattices in your field and put them on the bulletin board.

(13) Seek part-time work or attend classes which will keep you up-to-date in your occupational field or will round out your previous work experience.

(14) Set up a production line so that students can experience the advantages and disadvantages of job specialization.

(15) Ask a small employer to describe how he or she became an entrepreneur and to identify the advantages and disadvantages of being an employer.

(16) Ask a white-collar worker and a blue-collar worker to describe the advantages and disadvantages of their work roles.

(17) Identify a common product or service in your field. Have students role-play a management decision as to whether to produce this with their own work force or purchase it from outside. If proponents of one or the other action become too pervasive, ask the proponents and opponents to exchange roles.

(18) Administer an occupational competency test (written and

performance) to your advanced class. If you can't find such a test in your field, construct one.

(19) Identify which pieces of equipment in your laboratory are too obsolete and which are too complex for effective instruction. Set up a priority list for instruction.

(20) Keep a log of the amounts of time you are spending on laboratory work and classroom instruction. Is this the balance that you really want?

(21) Count the number of males and females enrolled in your classes. How does this compare with male and female employment in your field? What are the employment opportunities now and in the near future? (Very often employment opportunities are very good for persons of the opposite sex in a field which has been dominated by one sex.) Are potential students aware of this fact? If most of your students are of one sex, prepare a plan to include more of the second gender.

(22) List the course prerequisites for your program. To what extent do these prerequisites exclude students who have changed career goals recently? What changes are needed?

(23) Review the selection criteria that you use for admission to your course. To what extent are they related to occupational success? Do you admit students who have almost no chance for success in employment, e.g., defective color vision in electronics or printing? Do students who have little chance of occupational success know it and do they know what they can do to change this factor? Do you choose students who are docile, rather than those who are enthusiastic? Do you seek the "best" students, rather than those who can gain most from your instruction? Have other experts in your field reviewed your selection criteria to see if they are sound?

(24) Ask students to list the occupations of their parents and grandparents (go farther back if they can). Discuss the inheritability of occupations and occupational levels. What factors affect this type of inheritability?

(25) Review your exit and entry procedures. Can students who drop out of your program reenter at any time? Can they begin again where they had left off, providing that they are still proficient in what they learned earlier?

(26) Look for overlaps in content between your course and other related courses. What overlaps in content are there between prerequisite courses, your course, and subsequent courses? What post-secondary programs are your students most likely to enter? What credit do they receive for completing your course?

(27) If licensing is common in your field, determine how well your students do on licensing examinations. Do you pride yourself on having high average scores, rather than on the percentage who pass? In what examination areas do your students do least well?

(28) If apprenticeships are available in your field, determine how many of your students secure them. If the percentage is low, why? Do they receive credit for their work in your program? If not, what can be done to enable them to receive credit?

(29) If professional organizations or unions are active in your field, review how much your students know about them. How did they acquire that knowledge? What can you do to increase the amount and accuracy of their knowledge?

(30) Prepare a list of all of the skills you teach. Ask former students employed in your occupational field to check those which they use, and to check those they are expected to be able to do in an emergency, even if they seldom use them. Also ask students to list tasks which they regularly perform which are not on your list. Consider adding instruction from the latter list and deleting instruction skills which are used by less than half of your former students.

(31) Consider establishing a career education club which is open to all students who wish to learn more about your occupational field. Or consider adding another class of membership in your existing club, which would be open to students who are not enrolled in your program but wish to know more about it.

(32) Explore the possibility of a local federation of career education clubs which could sponsor career days, field trips, and programs on employment agencies, job interviewing, and other general vocational skills.

(33) Write an article for a professional magazine in your field, describing career education activities which have been successful and unsuccessful for you.

(34)  Confer with the staff of your guidance department and with teachers in other school departments to explore ways in which you can reinforce each other's instructions.

Vocational skills training is a vital component of career education. The high school is the logical preparation point for many but not all occupations. Vocational education, as presently conceived, is a vital part but only part of the vocational skills training capability of the high school. Many career decisions are unavoidable at the high school level. A great deal of innovative thought and accommodation is still needed to adjust vocational education's strengths to the broader concept of career education.

### *Postscript: A Test of Knowledge of the World of Work*

As an unconventional closing to this chapter, we offer the following "test" of the current level of understanding of your students about the world of work for both teachers and students. It provides interesting indicators of both the need for career education and the need for some revisions in the typical content of vocational education courses.

(1)  *Earnings:* Give the students a list, in random order, of job titles from each of the following levels: unskilled, semiskilled, skilled, technical, and professional. After each job title, list five categories of annual earnings (e.g., less than $5,000; $6,000 to $8,000; $10,000 to $12,000; $15,000 to $17,000; more than $20,000). Ask the students to choose typical annual earnings for each job title.

(2)  *Educational requirements:* Following each of the job titles, list six levels and types of education (e.g., less than high school; high school graduation; two years of specialized post-secondary education; four years of nonspecialized college education; four years of specialized college education; graduate study). Ask students to choose the level which is most likely to be required for each job title.

(3) *Other requirements:* For each job title, give students a list of the following job-entry requirements: experience in a lower level job; membership in a union or professional association; willingness to join a union or professional association; recommendation of a relative or friend already employed in the field; payment of an employment fee; ability to read a help wanted ad. Ask students to check *all* which are required for each of the job titles.

(4) *Working conditions:* For each job title, provide several bipolar descriptors of working conditions (i.e., indoor, outdoor; active, sedentary; hot, cold; monotonous, constantly changing; low responsibility, high responsibility; few accidents, many accidents; low noise level, high noise level, and so forth). Ask students to check *all* those which apply to each of the job titles.

Check with your advisory committee or the state employment agency or with a vocational guidance counselor to be certain you agree on the correct answers.

This test can be designed to cover a wide range of occupations, or it can cover only one career ladder. In either case, you and your students are likely to be unpleasantly surprised at the results unless a conscious effort has been made to teach this content. This type of test also works well as a pre- and post-test built round a specific unit of instruction.

Don't be surprised if you find that middle-class students score better than those from homes with low income, even after instruction. One clue to the reasons for this difference in scores may be discovered if another question is added to the test:

(5) *Influence of luck:* For each job title, ask the following: Which is most important in securing employment on this type of job — luck, willingness to work long and hard, influence of friends and relatives, or possession of educational and other entry requirements of the types listed in questions 2 and 3 above?

Other clues may be provided by comparing the students' abilities to read, their experiences in observing and talking to workers in a career field, and their previous experiences in career education programs.

## *References*

Eninger, Max. *The Process and Product of Trade and Industrial High School Level Vocational Education.* Pittsburgh: American Institute of Research. 1965.

Evans, Rupert E.; *et al. Career Education in the Middle/Junior High School.* Salt Lake City: Olympus Publishing Company. 1973.

Flanagan, John; *et al. The American High School Student.* Pittsburgh: University of Pittsburgh Project TALENT. 1968.

Hoyt, Kenneth B.; *et al. Career Education and the Elementary School Teacher.* Salt Lake City: Olympus Publishing Company. 1973.

Levitan, Sar; and William B. Johnston. *Work Is Here to Stay, Alas.* Salt Lake City: Olympus Publishing Company. 1973.

# 9

# Practical
# Applications

If vocational educators are to achieve and dispense the full values of an approach, they must examine their own classroom and laboratory activities with the same singleness of purpose as the teachers of academic subjects: to make certain that the principles of career education are incorporated as part of the daily educational experience. In this spirit, we offer the following examples of how teachers from all parts of the country have attempted to incorporate career education into the practical arts and vocational education classrooms. These examples were culled from literally thousands of experiences reported in the literature, at conferences, by letter, or by conversation. They are grouped according to the six major practical arts and vocational programs currently operating, and they are intended to show as much variety of approach as possible. In each case, the activities have been edited down from the original version in order to illustrate basic principles, rather than complete programs. These activities should be used simply as points of departure for the creative teacher who wants to provide that important career education dimension in his or her own classroom.

## *Home Economics*

The U.S. Office of Education reports that 95.5 percent of all public secondary schools offer some kind of home economics program. The reason for this near universality of offering is that home economics is partly general education and partly vocational education. "General home economics" refers to those courses which are applicable to almost everyone's need; e.g., beginning cooking and sewing, elementary instruction in human nutrition, and preparation for parenthood. "Vocational home economics" refers to those courses where the goal is career preparation for those persons interested in entering specific careers related to the skills of home economics.

Career educators tend not to make a sharp distinction between general and vocational classes in home economics. To them, homemaking, parenting, and the use of home economics skills all represent valid career activities, whether those skills are used in the home, in paid employment, in volunteer work, or in any combination of such outlets. Career educators are much more concerned about the sex stereotyping which tends to occur in such classes than with the particular role in which the skills will be used. The important criterion is that the choice be made openly, without bias and with adequate information and opportunity for subsequent change of direction — whether that choice is the taking of a single course or total immersion in occupational preparation.

## *Occupations from Home Economics Education*

Education in home economics can help prepare students for many different careers, including, of course, homemaking itself. Subject areas in home economics include child development, clothing and textiles, food and nutrition, home and institutional management, home furnishings and equipment, and consumer buying. Frequently, courses in these fields provide important "related instruction" for students — male and female — whose occupational interests are not in home economics fields. For example, the student interested in advertising should have an understanding of consumer buying, and the prospective cabinet maker could gain insights from a study of home furnishings. Of course, virtually everyone could benefit from more knowledge of foods and nutrition.

But we are concerned here more with the specific programs and the specific career fields related to home economics. They include:

(1) *General studies of home economics* — This program offers a variety of choices in career preparation and is designed for the person who will live two lives — a career individual and a homemaker. (We must begin thinking in terms of men as "homemakers" — or at least adjunct homemakers — with as much facility as we have traditionally thought of women as homemakers.) The integrated body of technical skills and economic social understanding gained through these programs will prepare graduates to enter employment in an occupation of their choice and at the same time maintain successful family activities. In this regard, it is important to realize that many changes have taken place in the structure of the family unit. Our society has a high incidence of singles, young adults, widows, widowers, and others who live alone or with peers in large metropolitan areas. The United States now has about 7.4 million single-parent families with children, seven million of them headed by women and half a million by men. The curriculum should include information for the single homemaker, men as well as women, perhaps to the extent that courses in "bachelor living" could be provided.

(2) *Design and sewing* — Preparatory programs in this field range from one school quarter in length for power-machine sewing to two years in length for such things as tailoring and apparel design and construction. The program usually includes courses in sewing with electric machines, (such as found in the home) to "power machines" (such as found in the manufacturing establishments), apparel design, tailoring, and trade sewing.

(3) *Foods* — The two major divisions of the restaurant food service industry are preparation and service.

Preparation includes cooking, baking, kitchen management, meal planning, and budget control. Service programs cover principles of marketing, accounting, dining service and operation, cashiering, and human relations. The foods program usually includes courses in food preparation, food service, and food supervision technology.

(4) *Housekeeping aide* — These short-term courses prepare students for employment as hotel, motel, or institutional housekeeping aides.

(5) *Early childhood education and instruction aide* — Programs in these two fields are designed for persons who are interested in working with children.

(6) *Other careers* — The number and variety of possible careers in the home economics field are extensive. The following partial listing shows the range of options:

| | |
|---|---|
| Power sewing machine operator | Extension agent |
| Tailor or seamstress | Apparel designer |
| Home demonstration agent | Milliner |
| Price control agent | Drapery maker |
| Credit interviewer | Model |
| Restaurant supervisor | Homemaker |
| Fashion coordinator | Home economist |
| Appliance demonstrator | Nutritionist |
| Interior decorator | Hostess or host |

## *Career Education Activities for Home Economics Classes*

Since home economics classes are already career oriented, in a sense, the types of career education activities which we recommend are intended primarily to expand understanding and awareness of career possibilities, to explore the relation of home economics to other careers, and to assist the student in developing self-awareness and acquiring better understanding of himself or herself.

### Self-Awareness: A Collage

In this activity, students acquire an awareness of line and color as they relate to interior design by making a collage of pictures. At the same time, students will become aware of their own feelings toward line and color and will discover how those feelings relate to the feelings of others. The materials required are a large piece of tagboard for each student, together with glue, scissors, and discarded magazines and catalogs. With or without prior discussion, students scan through magazines and cut or tear out any pictures that appeal to them, without weighing quality or value. Each student glues his or her pictures to the tagboard in any fashion to make a collage. When the collages are completed, they are displayed about the room. Each student selects the one collage which most appeals to him or her. This creates a series of partnerships based on mutual appreciation. The partners then discuss what appeals to the sense of color and line about the collage selected by both of them. (Caution students to look at color and line, not at specific subject matter of the pictures.)

When the partners have discussed their own responses to the collages, then an evaluation is conducted through a class sharing time in which particular attention is paid to likenesses and contrasts in the color and line of the various collages. This allows students to compare their own perceptions with those of other students and thus become more aware of both likenesses and differences.

## Appreciation and Attitudes: I Spy

This exercise is designed to help students become aware of purposive behavior through the observation of children, and to be able to identify those behaviors in children and themselves. To introduce this activity, the teacher discusses with the class the meaning and elements of purposive behavior as outlined in any one of several resource books (e.g., *Psychology in the Classroom, Discipline without Tears, or Maintaining Sanity in the Classroom*). A class discussion follows in which each of the elements of purposive behavior is clearly identified (attention-getting, power, revenge, and assumed disability). Then each student visits a kindergarten classroom or other place where children interact and observes one child for a given period of time. Using a purposive behavior chart (sometimes called a "child's mistaken goals" chart), the student notes the various behaviors of the child and their appropriate goal or element orientation.

Following the observations, the teacher leads the class in a summary discussion of purposive behavior, asking class members to relate examples from their observations. Students should also be asked to write a paragraph or two about their observations as a form of activity evaluation.

## Employability Skills: Comparison Trips

This activity requires that students visit stores or factories which sell or use sewing machines in order to identify the major differences between domestic and commercial machines. (Similar field trips can be used to demonstrate differences between domestic food preparation and commercial preparation, or between decorating for home and decorating for business, or between consumer buying and institutional buying.) The project begins in class with the teacher discussing the fact that domestic and commercial sewing machines have many attributes in common, but that there are several major differences. The discussion centers on why such differences exist and how they will become important to students who choose occupations in the sewing field. Following the discussion, students arrange themselves into groups of four or five each and decide which businesses would be appropriate to visit. With the help of the teacher, each group makes preliminary arrangements for visiting a particular business. The groups tour the designated sites, looking for and noting which machines are used for particular tasks and why.

Following the field trips, the class discusses what has been learned, listing differences between machines on the board and examining other factors about the two types of sewing machines. This activity is an excellent preliminary activity for a cooperative work program.

## Beginning Competency: M-m-m Good

This activity develops an understanding of the relationship between cooking skills and the commercial aspects of distributing baked goods to consumers. The teacher suggests the idea of making pastries and conducting a "Goodie Bazaar" for teachers. If the class reaction is favorable, a planning session is conducted in which students decide the tasks to be assigned, the date and place of the bazaar, and the prices to be charged for the items. Some students are delegated to confer with the school administration about the feasibility of the project and to arrange for the necessary facilities. Others are assigned the responsibility for advertising the bazaar to teachers. Students bake the pastries on the designed day and conduct the sale.

The teachers who participate in the bazaar are asked to comment on the goods they bought. The class should discuss these comments and relate their own feelings about the project. Of course, the money collected should be used to pay for the ingredients, and if any "profit" is left over, the class can decide what to do with it. This activity can also take the form of an auction, perhaps during the student lunch hour, and it can be coupled with in-class demonstration by a professional baker or field trips to local bakeries.

**Random Activities**

The activities below were selected to give some indication of the kinds of activities which could take place in various classes to provide additional career education perspective. The designation of specific classes is suggested only; similar activities can occur in a variety of classes.

(1) *Marriage and family living* — Discuss and define "self-direction," and have students list individuals whom they regard as self-directed. Survey various television programs to analyze the validity of family structures portrayed. Arrange a talk by a counselor concerning the relationships of family life-style and careers.

(2) *Personal relationships* — Conduct a class discussion based on the topic: "Has the concept of work changed?" Ask a management consultant to discuss the positive and negative values of addressing company executives (or teachers) by their first names.

(3) *Consumer education* — Have students produce something in an assembly line, such as syrup or paper flowers. Arrange a field trip to a modern factory or business. Have a hospital administrator discuss the cost factors involved in a typical hospital bill.

(4) *Foods and nutrition* — Place a food in a closed box and ask students to guess the food by asking questions related only to nutrition which can be answered "yes" or "no." Prepare a "game board" of various food items and have students shop for food using various amounts of game money; the winner is the student who buys the most nutritious assortment of foods.

## *Agriculture and Applied Biology*

Career education in agriculture is not limited to farming and to the production of food and fiber, as important as these are. The wide range and variety of agriculture-related career opportunities, as well as the primary importance of agriculture in the lives of all, is an important education concept. We strongly recommend some type of unit in vocational agriculture courses which revolves round orientation to occupational opportunities in the field, even for those students who have had the career exploration benefits of career education in the middle school years. Hemp and Walker (1973) developed a twelve-week unit which is well worth studying as an example (see "References," this chapter). Naturally, this type of exploratory unit should be available to students as early as possible during their school years, preferably in the ninth or tenth grades.

Agricultural education revolves basically round six major job families: (1) production agribusiness, (2) agricultural mechanics, (3) supplies and services, (4) agricultural products, (5) horticulture, and (6) forestry. The variety of vocational offerings and the depth of the instruction should be limited only by the interests and aptitudes of students, by the limitations of the school's facilities, by the competencies of the instructional staff, and by the employment opportunities in the area.

The number of occupations included in the agricultural field is extensive. The following are just a few, and they are included here only to indicate the variety of occupations which are available.

| | |
|---|---|
| Landscape architect | Florist |
| Petroleum engineer | Farmer |
| Wildlife manager | Rancher |
| Fish and game manager | Tree surgeon |
| Agricultural engineer | Dairy farmer |
| Golf course manager | Veterinarian |
| Soil conservationist | Butcher |
| Water systems service representative | Miner |
| Equipment service representative | Farm manager |
| Feed store manager | Agronomist |
| Machinery salesman | Extension agent |
| Livestock buyer | Forest ranger |

## Career Education Activities for Agriculture and Applied Biology Classes

By the time the student reaches vocational agriculture classes in the high school, he or she has likely selected a specific course of study, and career education will have reached the "preparation" stage. Therefore, career education will consist of the normal coursework in vocational agriculture classes, with perhaps some form of cooperative vocational education in addition. Nevertheless, additional activities which are exploratory in nature should be included even during the final year in high school for several reasons. First, although students may be involved in vocational agriculture courses, some may not have made up their minds about the specific occupations they will pursue. Second, some students may have selected occupations but may also wish to consider preparation for alternative occupations in order to provide wider options for employment. Third, some students may never have had the opportunity to explore the wide variety of career possibilities in the agriculture field.

Accordingly, the following are but a few activities which can be included in various vocational agriculture courses to (1) assist students in understanding the nature of agriculture occupations, (2) relate the meaning of those occupations to the economic structure, and (3) to explore occupational alternatives.

### The Situational Question

As a class "opener," or even near the end of a class hour, the teacher might structure a situational question for student response. For example:

> Johnnie is a young man who lives in an urban area. He lives in a subdivision, beautifully landscaped, and he attends a new school which won a grounds beautification award in the annual citywide competition. This morning Johnnie's mother insisted that he drink two glasses of milk and eat one sausage or two pieces of bacon. How has Johnnie been involved in agribusiness during the day? Which agribusiness occupations have affected his life?

Obviously, this question is intended for a class of students from an urban area, but similar situational questions can be used to relate agribusiness to inner city or rural students. Develop a series of such situational questions and see how many occupations students can list in a given amount of time.

### What's My Job Family

In order to participate in this activity, students must be familiar with the six job families listed earlier. The object of the activity is to develop facility in "fitting" specific jobs into the six job families. The teacher may want to divide the class into groups and award prizes to the winning team. First, the names of the six job families are listed on the board or are presented to team members on cards. The teacher selects key characteristics of specific jobs and reads those characteristics to the class, one characteristic at a time. The first team to identify the job family in which the job belongs wins the point.

As students become more familiar with job families and job titles, the contest can be altered slightly by calling it "What's my job title?" and working toward specific occupational titles instead of families. This form of involvement activity encourages students to think about job titles and job responsibilities over a wide range of careers.

### How Much Did Johnnie Make?

This activity relates agriculture careers to studies of academic subjects, particularly mathematics. It can be coupled with a situation question concerning the problem in order to indicate the economic interrelationships of various careers in agriculture. The problem which follows is only an example. The teacher can develop additional examples which relate to the particular subject matter under discussion at the time.

Johnnie raised one acre of tobacco this year. He is now trying to figure his net income after deducting all of his expenses. He sold 3,000 pounds of tobacco at an average of 85 cents per pound. (On the day Johnnie sold his crop, he was the top man at the sale, and his name was mentioned on the television news that evenings.)

However, Johnnie had quite a few expenses. They included one ton of 5-10-15 fertilizer at $60 per ton, 200 pounds of ammonium nitrate at $65 per ton, $25 worth of materials for plant bed preparation, crop insurance at $70 per acre, the cost of operating machinery for 25 hours at $2 per hour, marketing costs of $150, taxes of $50, and 200 hours of labor at $2 per hour.

Since Johnnie was raising the tobacco on a neighbor's farm, he received only half of the income. What was Johnnie's net income from one acre of tobacco?

## Role Playing

Assign students to play the roles of the various customers of a farm supply firm as indicated below. Also have students play the roles of the store clerk, the store manager, and the store owner. Have each of the students involved react to the situations as if he or she were actually participating in that particular situation. The rest of the class can comment upon the actions of each individual after the simulation is completed.

(1) A customer remarks, "I am just looking."

(2) A man comes into the store and says, "I want to see the best lawn spray you stock."

(3) A woman asks, "What will you do if this weed killer doesn't kill the weeds in my lawn?"

(4) A customer brings a chainsaw back and says, "The warranty on my chainsaw ran out three days ago and my saw quit yesterday. What are you going to do about it?"

(5) A woman asks, "How do you start a charge account in this store?"

(6) A customer wants to know: "Why don't you keep all brands of tractor oil in stock?"

## Field Trips

Field trips to various locations where a variety of workers performing various job tasks can be observed are always a valuable learning experience, provided that sufficient preparation takes place before the actual visit and provided that adequate time is set aside after the visit to allow discussion of the experience. Select locations and times which are convenient to students, where the full cooperation of the firm or operation can be prearranged, and where a number of different occupations and activities can be observed. Before the trip, assign one student to research and describe the operation to the class or, if that is not possible, the teacher can describe the operation. In class discussion, list the names of all occupations that will be observed in the field trip, and discuss some of the tasks persons in those occupations perform. Have students develop in discussion a list of questions they want to ask workers they meet at the operation to be visited.

Make sure questions include inquiries about life-style, tasks, and career preparation. Sometimes it is desirable to have the owner or manager of the operation visit with the class before the field trip takes place.

Following the field trip. arrange for an adequate "de-briefing" session in the classroom. This de-briefing can take many forms, from straight class discussion, to presentation of papers by class members, to having class members "role play" the parts of workers they observed and asking the same list of questions as those developed prior to the visit.

## Brainstorming for Occupations

Valuable understanding of agriculture careers and the inter-relationships between various occupations within the field can be learned through a process of "brainstorming." It also allows for significant class interaction and gives students an opportunity to test their own knowledge about occupations.

On the chalkboard, list three or four types of crops or livestock produced by farmers in the community. Select one of these products and ask students to name the different items the farmer must purchase in order to produce the product. For example, if corn is selected, the farmer must buy seed, fertilizer, chemicals, machinery, and so on. List such items to the right of the product selected. (For increased understanding, it is helpful also to name a local firm from which the various items might be purchased, although it is not necessary to write firm names on the board.) Add to the list of items a list of processes and services which must be performed on the crop. Finally, to the right of the items and services list, write down as many occupations as possible which deal with each of the items and services listed. Obviously, the list of occupations will be extensive, and it will not be possible to list *all* occupations involved. But this exercise can give students some idea of the variety of occupations available and how interrelated they are.

## *Business Education*

Business education in the high school performs three important career education functions: first, it provides general education in business and business skills appropriate for all students. Second, it provides extensive career exploration opportunities for those students who will pursue advanced business education at the post-secondary level. Third, it provides career preparation activities for those students who will enter business occupations after graduation or for those who seek basic preparation prior to post-secondary training in business.

Therefore, a well-planned curriculum requires a balance of vocational business education and basic business education. Such a curriculum will provide ample opportunities for career exploration, general skills training, and career preparation.

The relationship between business education and general education is obvious. Since a large proportion of available occupations involves working within a business firm, it is important that students acquire some understanding of the economic and social structure of the business community. A person who understands the structure and operation of business is better prepared to function within a business firm. In addition to this general knowledge, certain specific skills are important to many students. Typing, operating a small calculator, and performing simple bookkeeping functions are skills which are useful to many persons in our society, both vocationally and avocationally. For example, an interesting demonstration can be incorporated in a beginning typing class to indicate the value of typing skills. Ask students to type out a list of things they like to do. Set a fifteen minute time limit. Students who are not familiar with the typewriter will use the "hunt and peck" method and will find the chore laborious. At the end of fifteen minutes, ask how many students listed twenty items, then fifteen, then ten. Open a short discussion by asking students whether they were more concerned with finding the right keys or determining which items to put on the list. Were they more frustrated by the machine or the list of items? Then explain that the value of developing typing skill is to make the list — the content — more important than the process. The typewriter becomes an extension of the individual, a tool. It is more efficient than handwriting in much the same way that a hammer is more efficient than a rock. It is a skill which will be useful throughout life in many applications.

With regard to career exploration activities, business education teachers can provide a great deal of assistance to students, both in the classroom and through other channels. Frequently, students have had little experience with business operations. Even those students whose parents are employed in business often do not understand the variety of occupations available. After all, where some children visit the parents' workplace to view the activities which take place there, few children can learn much from visiting a business office and watching men and women sit behind desks, talk on the telephone, or operate typewriters. Of course, business education deals with a vast variety of skills and occupations. Included are:

| | |
|---|---|
| Accountant | Keypunch operator |
| Secretary | Sales person |
| Office manager | Bookkeeper |
| Personnel director | File clerk |
| Advertising worker | Purchasing agent |
| Computer operator | Computer programmer |
| Public relations worker | Stenographer |
| Bank manager | Bank teller |

Business education is concerned with teaching the skills which are requisites for employment in these occupations. In the career education vocabulary, this skills training comes under the heading of career preparation. At the high school level, preparation for careers in business may be designed to provide job-entry skills at the time of graduation, or it may be designed to provide a base upon which to build in post-secondary training or in college degree programs. Whatever the primary objectives of the program, it should also include such career education considerations as values clarification, decision making, and job-seeking skills.

### Career Education Activities for Business Education Classes

Many jobs in the business office require an ability to get along with others and to understand one's own attitudes and responses. Therefore, it is appropriate in business education classes to conduct activities designed for social interaction and social development.

## Appreciation and Attitudes: Everybody's Different

This activity is designed to give students an opportunity to explore and recognize individual differences by acting as a group of supervisors who have met to discuss how to handle different types of employees; i.e., "sensitive," "slow," "timid," "careless," "bold," "lazy," "stubborn." The teacher begins the activity by asking the class to name and describe several different types of employees who might be encountered on the job. The teacher might suggest one type from the list above as a starter, giving some characteristics of that type of employee. (Several resources are available to assist with compilation of such descriptive material, including literature from the fields of career guidance and personnel administration.) After a sufficient number of employee types have been listed and their characteristics have been described, divide the class into groups — one group for each employee type named. Describe a specific employee situation. (For example, one employee in the typing pool is not keeping up with the others.) Have each student group arrive at a consensus about how it would handle this employee if he or she was of the particular type they have been assigned. After an allotted period of group discussion, have the group present its solutions to the class as a whole.

This is a good exercise to assist in values clarification and self-assessment. Students might also be asked to write a paper in which they discuss how they might respond if they were the employee in the situation.

## Employability Skills: Race-Role Confusion

Through this activity, students will develop an understanding of interpersonal skills within the class group. Later, they can transfer these skills to occupational situations. The instructor introduces the activity by discussing situations which have occurred in the classroom or around the school as a result of race or sex differences. Then students are divided into groups of five to seven, and they relate to each other embarrassing moments they have experienced because of feelings of prejudice. Each group selects one such moment to dramatize before the class. Paper bag masks are provided for each member of the dramatization group, and each mask clearly indicates by coloring or decoration that it represents a black person or a white person, a male or a female, or other group representative. The dramatizations should not be elaborate. After each dramatization, the role-playing individuals discuss their reactions to the situations and respond to pertinent questions by the instructor.

Teacher and students should make some attempt to relate each situation to actual on-the-job situations. At the conclusion of the activity, the teacher and students can discuss how they can make use of the self-knowledge they have gained as a result of the activity. This same activity can be used to develop insight or self-awareness regarding situations in which an individual feels others are "talking about" him or her, or those in which individuals from different socio-economic groups interact and generate possible value conflicts.

## Economic Awareness: Budgeting

This is an ongoing activity which can be used in conjunction with a bookkeeping class, a consumer education class, a personal finance class, or almost any other type of business education class. It will help students develop a sense of economic awareness in terms of goal-setting, budgeting, and evaluation. Have students secure or rule out sufficient columnar sheets to allow one sheet for each week of the quarter or semester. The sheets should have at least three vertical columns for "budgeted," "actual expenditure," and "accumulated credit or deficit."

Have each student predict his or her weekly income and allocate it in the "budgeted" column to such ordinary student expenditures as clothes, food, entertainment, transportation, savings, and so on. Have the student fill out all of the weekly "budgeted" columns at the beginning of the period, making the breakdown as complete as possible, and leaving only a marginal amount for expenditures labeled "miscellaneous." At the beginning of each week during the quarter or semester, have the students fill in the actual expenditures for each item made during the previous week, together with the accumulated deficit or credit. Allow class time for discussion of budgetary problems and for discussions of how students might be able to "get more for their money" through wise purchases. Students should not be *forced* to divulge their own financial activities, but in most cases enough students will be willing to discuss problems to make the exercise worthwhile.

Do not allow students to change their original budget allocations. However, during the period in which the activity is undertaken, introduce occasional hypothetical situations which might alter student budgets. For example, during one discussion suggest that students might set a goal for accumulating funds by the end of the period. Perhaps they want to take a trip, or purchase a gift, or make a substantial personal purchase. Ask how they would adjust their budgets to accommodate that goal. During another discussion, the teacher might suggest that each student has received a $100 windfall and ask how they would distribute it on their budgets. In another case, an unexpected expense — an accident or a forgotten assessment of some kind — demands that each student raise $50 before the week is over. How would they handle this emergency?

This is an excellent activity, but one which must be handled with care and sensitivity. The objective is not to change the way in which students are currently handling their own funds but to point out how planning and budgeting function in personal and business economics. The same goals can be achieved with simulated funds and situations, but the exercise takes on more interest if the students' own income and expenditure figures are used.

## Business Decision Making: Simulations

More and more firms are involved these days in creating and marketing simulation games for classroom use. The creation of such games has developed into a science based on strict rules of design and founded on the principles of educational psychology. We recommend that teachers in business education courses investigate some of these simulation games which are related to business decision making. As with books and other types of educational materials, the value of simulation games can be ascertained by examining the credentials of the author and by searching the literature for formal reviews of the materials.

## *Distributive Education*

High school distributive education is a program of instruction in distribution and marketing. The term "distribution" refers to those activities that direct the flow of goods and services from producer to consumer. Distributive activities include marketing functions such as sales promotion, buying, operations, market research, and management. In the past, secondary school curriculums in distributive education have concentrated primarily on cooperative education as the method of instruction, but an increasing number of schools are now broadening their approach to distributive education. This new approach provides a sequence of courses or instructional experiences which is concerned with specific areas of subject matter. The course structure may be modified somewhat to accommodate the career goals of students in different localities or different groups.

The field of distributive education covers a number of specific activities, including selling, sales promotion, buying, operations involved in handling customers and products, market research, and management. These activities require a variety of skills, such as dealing with people, writing, designing, planning, organizing, researching, and analyzing. The occupations which fall within the purview of distributive education are wide ranging and varied. Following are just a few of the distribution and marketing occupations, selected to indicate the variety of opportunities:

| | |
|---|---|
| Economist | Sales supervisor |
| Sales representative | Sales engineer |
| Statistician | Systems analyst |
| Advertising representative | Hotel-motel manager |
| Bank teller | Media buyer |
| Transportation manager | Credit manager |
| Marketing researcher | Finance manager |
| Packaging designer | Realtor |
| Production and control manager | Insurance agent |
| Customer service agent | Cashier |

Marketing and distribution jobs have been identified in at least 21 occupational areas in the *Dictionary of Occupational Titles,* and each of those areas contains dozens of specific occupational titles for which distributive education can help prepare students.

Since many of the occupations which are of concern to distributive education involve dealing with others, a high proportion of the activities employed in the teaching process are participation-type activities. That is, the teaching activities in distributive education frequently attempt to involve the student directly through such techniques as discussions, case problems, role-playing, surveys, and creative projects. In the jargon of teaching methods, these are sometimes called "student-centered" teaching techniques.

For this reason — and because marketing and distribution are so important to all business activities — distributive education can make a significant contribution to the career education activities of a great many students. A course in sales methods would add an important contribution to the education of students who will pursue careers in the production of goods or the providing of services. For that matter, it would be most useful to all consumers to have some understanding of the types of sales techniques with which they might be confronted.

## *Career Education Activities for*
## *Distributive Education Classes*

Few fields of education are provided with a "laboratory" which is as pervasive and as available as the distributive education "lab." It is virtually impossible to go through a single day without confronting the activities of marketing and distribution specialists. The average person is exposed to over fifteen hundred advertising messages per day. Goods and services are sold through the mail, at the door, on the corner, and in the school. Items are "stocked" by the grocery store, the candy machine, the newspaper delivery person, and the warehouse. And goods are distributed by truck, bicycle, train, and plane. In short, the subject matter of distributive education is familiar to all of us; career education activities in distributive education need only make the familiar meaningful.

### Career Exploration: To Market, To Market

This activity is designed to stimulate students to think about the many distribution and marketing occupations involved with any product or service and to indicate how important these occupations may be. The activity works best when it is spread out over a day or two to allow students to discuss the problem with parents, peers, and others, and to relate what they regularly see and hear to the operations of the marketplace. Near the end of a class period, ask students to select by consensus a common item from the classroom environment. It may be a desk, a pencil, a picture on the wall, or any other specific item. Tell students that the following day they will trace that item from its origins to its place in the classroom by naming every occupation which is necessary to bring it there. Ask them to think about the problem overnight, to talk to others about it, and to jot down some specific ideas so that they can construct a complete occupational flow chart. They should try to determine the raw materials which go into the product and the processes involved in producing it.

The following day, open the discussion and begin listing all of the occupations involved. They need not be in order, but some kind of chronological organization is helpful. Insist that students be specific in naming occupations. For example, if the item selected is a pencil, they should not be satisfied with the generic term "sales representative" but should include the lumber salesman who sold the wood to the manufacturer, the paint saleswoman, the eraser salesman, the graphite saleswoman, and so on. It will not be possible to develop a complete list, but it should be extensive. When the list has grown to respectable proportions, ask students to identify all of those occupations on the list which are directly connected with marketing and distribution. Circle or star these occupations. This may stimulate suggestions for additional occupations from the class. Be sure that advertising, transportation, warehousing, and selling are included wherever appropriate.

### Advertising: The Creative Team

This activity helps students understand the various specialties which are part of advertising campaigns. Students can select three or four student activities scheduled during coming weeks. Divide the class into "creative teams" and assign each team one of the student activities. (These should be general activities such as sports events or dances, as opposed to group activities such as club meetings.) Each team will develop an advertising campaign for the activity to which it is assigned. Have the team members designate various task responsibilities to specific individuals. For example, each team will need an account executive, a copywriter, an art director, a media "buyer," a production manager, and so on. The team can create posters, handouts, "radio" commercials, and other types of advertisements.

If possible, the campaign should actually take place and should be tied to the event. In any case, some sort of post-event analysis should take place, with the various teams comparing their campaigns and discussing the duties of specific occupations within the team. This activity can be expanded to include market research and other related tasks if the teacher so desires. Remember, the important part of the activity is not the quality of the product or products but the experience students have in learning about the various occupations employed in advertising, in working under the creative team concept, and in understanding the division of responsibilities in a group effort.

### Role-Playing: Pick a Number

This activity places students in role situations which will help them understand direct sales problems from a variety of points of view.

Have each student describe a sales situation in writing on one side of a sheet of paper. The description should tell about the item being sold, the location of the sales effort, and the individuals who are involved. The description of the individuals should be as complete as possible, including ages, sex, mood or type of character, buying habits, and so on.

For example, a student might set a scene in which a young man recently employed as a shoe salesman in a department store is selling shoes to a middle-aged lady who has spent most of the day shopping and is somewhat tired and irritable. Wherever possible, the description should be based on a real situation which has been experienced or observed by the student or by acquaintances of the student. (Encourage students to think beyond the strict retail selling situation to include industrial sales, door-to-door sales, and other direct sales situations.)

Attach a number to each of the student papers and display them in a convenient location. Using some form of random selection, form a series of two-member "teams" in the class. At periodic intervals during the semester, have the teams draw a number from a "hat." This number will indicate the sales situation which the team is to act out before the class. Give the team a day or two to think about the situation, but discourage team members from working together to perfect a performance; the object is to fully accept the roles of sales representative and customer, based on the descriptions provided.

Give each team five or ten minutes to perform, and then ask for class discussion about how the sales representative might have done a more effective job. This is particularly useful if students are learning sales techniques and can relate the performance they have witnessed to the sales techniques they have learned. This activity is primarily a career preparation activity, but it is also useful as a consumer education tool.

## Industrial Arts Education

The broad field of industrial education includes both industrial arts and trade and industrial education. Industrial arts usually refers to the general education portion, whereas trade and industrial education refers to the vocation portion of industrial education. Some industrial educators feel that technical education forms a third part of their field, but it is now generally agreed that technical education represents a *level* of education and employment intermediate between the levels of professionals and skilled white-collar or blue-collar workers.

A well-planned industrial arts program can offer secondary school students opportunities to engage in learning activities which are relevant to their roles as members of an industrial-technical society. These activities are relevant whether the student decides to concentrate upon preparation for a specific career in the industrial field, or upon increasing understanding and ability to handle materials (i.e., woods, metals, plastics, ceramics), or upon improving capabilities for dealing with processes such as planning, designing, constructing, organizing, operating, and servicing. Quite obviously, the career preparation which takes place in industrial education courses can be short-term preparation which readies a student for employment upon graduation from high school. It can also be long-term preparation as part of a career goal which includes post-secondary education, building on an industrial education base acquired in the high school. Or it can be adjunct preparation which is ancillary to a primary career goal of a professional nature such as engineering or architecture or industrial management. And of course, it can also be a "defensive" skill tool which all students can use in their "careers" as consumers.

The field of industrial arts education encompasses the broad aspects of such industrial areas as construction, transportation, communication, manufacturing, and resource development. The specific subject matter offered in industrial arts courses includes such things as automotives, ceramics, design, drawing, power mechanics, electricity, electronics, graphic arts, leather crafts, lapidary, metal working, plastics, textiles, and wood working. The direction of specific programs in various parts of the country depends largely upon the interests of students and the nature of the economic base in those areas. Some programs are industry-centered in that they concentrate on an overview of industry with such subjects as "industry today," "the evolution of industry organization and enterprise," "operating an enterprise," "distributing products and services," and "student business ventures." Specific skills training relates to this overview. Other programs offer a technology-centered approach in which industrial arts are used to develop an understanding of technology and its disciplines. Some programs are career or occupation centered and include a considerable amount of career exploration through field trips, vocational counseling, and cooperative education. Finally, some programs approach industrial arts strictly from the standpoint of materials and processes, where the skills training is an end in itself and is not a part of a more comprehensive structure.

These are all valid approaches. Obviously, some lend themselves to career preparation, some to career exploration, and some to general education, all of which are viable career education components.

In its pure form, trade and industrial education involves training for occupations that are skilled or semiskilled and are concerned with layout designing, producing, processing, assembling, testing, maintaining, servicing, or repairing any product or commodity. Usually, instruction is provided in basic manipulative skills, safety judgment, and related occupational information in mathematics, drafting, and science. This is done through a combination of shop or laboratory experiences which simulate those found in industry. As will be discussed in chapter 10, these same objectives are also accomplished through cooperative education in which actual on-the-job experineces are combined with in-school training.

As an indication of the variety of occupations for which training can be provided in industrial arts programs, we offer the following brief list:

| | |
|---|---|
| Machine operator | Mobile home assembler |
| Industrial designer | Sheet metal worker |
| Chemical engineer | Electrician |
| Machine maintenance worker | Tool and die maker |
| Electronic engineer | Welder |
| Assembly line operator | Mechanical engineer |
| Industrial traffic manager | Job printer |
| Inspector | Bookbinder |
| Bricklayer | Detailer |
| Auto mechanic | Typesetter |

## *Teaching Techniques for Industrial Arts*

Instruction in the industrial arts must be designed so that it enables students to *experience* the organized body of content.

It emphasizes the "hands-on" approach to teaching, but that can include role-playing in situations such as applying for a job, as well as learning to operate a planer, a joiner, or a printing press. Other effective techniques include the use of demonstration films, field trips, extensive use of wall charts and displays, guest technicians, and the use of video tape equipment for instant analysis.

## Career Education Activities for Industrial Arts Classes

As is the case with most vocational education classes, industrial arts courses lean heavily toward the career preparation phase of career education. Thus most of what occurs in these classes could rightly be classified as career education. However, additional activities can be incorporated into such classes which will expand their career education value to students. For example, the activities might relate to the job finding, getting, and holding skills which are so important to all students.

### Decision Making: Exploring Apprenticeship Programs

The purpose of this activity is to acquaint the student with the apprenticeship system and the local labor market. The materials needed for the activity include as much printed information as possible about apprenticeships and training in the local area. Often this type of material can be obtained from the local employment security office, from labor unions, and from the U.S. Department of Labor. (For instance, a bulletin of the Labor Department titled *Occupational Manpower and Training Needs* is a valuable resource tool.)

The activity begins when the instructor explains what an apprentice is and what he or she does. This explanation can include a short history of the apprenticeship concept dating from early times. The instructor then asks each student to list five possible career choices which are of interest to him or her. Students can then use the resource material to determine which of the careers each has listed have apprenticeship programs in the area. (Where possible, students might also examine the current job situation for the chosen career areas, including availability of jobs and average pay scales. Much of this information is available through the local employment security office and other sources.)

After this information has been compiled, the instructor can then select volunteers to begin further discussion of major career fields. It is helpful to list on the chalkboard the qualifications of the apprenticeship programs such as age, education level, minimum entry requirements, and skills. The bulletin mentioned above is a valuable tool for researching future prospects for employment in specific career fields. The activity is not complete until it has been "tied together" with a discussion about how resource materials and resource agencies can be helpful in the process of career decision making.

As an additional part of this same activity, the instructor might consider inviting representatives from local apprenticeship programs or from the local employment security office to speak to the class, either as individuals or as a panel.

## Economic Awareness: Where the Jobs Are

Students — particularly those interested in industrial arts — need to know how their interests and plans relate to present and future job trends in their community, state, and nation. This activity will help students realize that such information is available and will help them to learn how to acquire it. Two resource items are required: the *Occupational Outlook Handbook* and a list of businesses in the community which employ workers in industrial arts fields.

The activity begins with a discussion of the occupations found within the community which relate to student interests. As specific occupations are discussed, the instructor lists possible sites for visits to observe workers in these occupational areas. Students indicate first, second, and third choices for on-site observation. The instructor can then make arrangements for a field trip. (If possible, a student committee should be assigned responsibility for making arrangements, including contacts with businesses, arrangements for transportation, and clearances from the school administration.) As with any field trip, the visit should be preceded by a class discussion to determine just what students should look for.

Students can evaluate their job-site visits by analyzing how much they have learned about the particular occupation or occupations they observed, with particular attention to salary, life-style, work hours, likes and dislikes, and advantages and disadvantages. The primary objective is to increase student knowledge of job opportunities in the community.

## Attitudes: Learning to Work Together

The purpose of this activity is to encourage students to think about their responsibilities to themselves and others when accepting a a job or task. The activity involves placing students in an actual work situation which requires students to work together to complete a project. The instructor should prepare a list of projects which lend themselves to small group effort or which could be undertaken by the entire class as an organized group. The instructor should explain the purpose of the activity and should indicate why it is included in the course. Then the instructor should relate the activity to the world of work and, where possible, allow students to role-play "real life" situations that might occur when individuals must work together to accomplish some task.

Following this introductory portion of the activity, students should be asked to determine whether they want to divide into small groups and have each group work on a project, or work as a class on a single project and set it up on an assembly-line basis. The exact procedure can vary, so long as the students work together to produce the final product or accomplish the assigned task. Allow two weeks or more for completion of the task, and then have each group write an evaluation with particular attention to problems encountered in working together. For example, did they perceive personality conflicts between members of the group? Did they judge some persons as being lazy or lacking efficiency and, if so, what effect did that have on the total project? How did the group go about working out its problems? How could the task be approached differently for more positive results?

The emphasis throughout the entire activity should *not* be on the product or task itself but on the manner in which a group of individuals work together to accomplish a task. The discussion should center round such things as leadership, interpersonal relationships, division of responsibility, and personal reactions to group involvement.

## *Health Occupations*

Health occupations education programs at the secondary school level should be designed to satisfy essential community and individual needs in the most efficient manner. Graduate follow-up studies, student interest surveys, and consultations with the state employment service and the health occupations advisory council can be useful in identifying and verifying needs for health occupation programs in the school.

The major purpose of health occupations education programs is to provide experiences so that students will have sufficient competency to obtain and perform adequately in at least a lower level-entry job. In the health field, this would usually be at the aide level. However, the need exists for additional programs which will assist students with career exploration activities and in which students may begin the first part of a health occupations program in the secondary school and continue to completion of the program at a post-secondary institution. For many careers in the health occupations field, students will be required to invest large amounts of time and energy in preparatory training. Students can benefit greatly by beginning some of that training as early as high school and by acquiring a full understanding of the preparation required for health occupation. In addition, since the demand for positions in some segments of the health industry is much higher than the number of positions available, many students will not be able to complete the long preparatory training. Those students will benefit from an understanding of and some prepartion for alternative careers within the health field, careers in which the number of available jobs is more in balance with the number of persons desiring those positions.

Therefore, the objectives of health education occupations programs at the senior high school level should be fairly broad and should include at least the following:

(1) Describe the training required for various health occupations.

(2) Give students an opportunity to evaluate hands-on work experiences in health occupations in terms of personal interests, capabilities, life-styles, and career goals.

(3) Provide a systematic means for tracing student progress toward health occupations goals which includes a record of steps to be completed as well as steps already completed.

(4) Describe the various ways a health occupations employee can move upward in health occupations employment.

(5) Give students knowledge of and experience in identify-

ing and using information sources concerning post-secondary education in health occupations

In the health occupations field, the number of career possibilities is rapidly expanding as the health industry itself changes to meet increasing demands for health care. Teachers in health occupations education should have some knowledge of this wide range of available careers and should attempt to keep abreast of the various problems in health care delivery which are likely to spur development of additional career opportunities. The following list provides a few job choices as an illustration of the wide range of careers available:

| | |
|---|---|
| Dental aide | Medical technologist |
| Practical nurse | Orderly |
| Health aide | X-ray aide |
| Radiologic assistant | Physical therapy aide |
| Mental health aide | Medical assistant |
| Biomedical electronics technician | Laboratory equipment cleaner |
| Medical artist | Dental hygienist |
| Medical secretary | Inhalation therapist |
| Psychiatric technician | Registered nurse |
| Physician | Operating room assistant |
| Ambulance attendant | Hospital administrator |
| Child care attendant | Nursing home aide |
| Patient counselor | Geriatric aide |

As mentioned in the previous chapter, several schools and school districts have benefited from the formation of student health careers clubs. These clubs help students explore opportunities and share common interests. They also develop leadership and assist students in establishing realistic career goals. Both the New York State Department of Education and the New Jersey Department of Education have produced guidebooks for assisting in the organization and operation of health career clubs (see "References"). These guidebooks might be helpful to schools considering the formation of such clubs.

## Career Education Activities for
### Health Education Classes

As discussed above, career education in the health occupations field at the secondary level must be a combination of career exploration, skills training, and preparation for advanced education. It should include classroom work, rudimentary library research, and hands-on experience. The following activities represent each of those forms of learning.

### Career Exploration: Emergency!

This activity is designed to help students explore the range of health occupations involved in a somewhat ordinary health care situation. The instructor describes a situation of emergency health care. It should be something that is not too unusual and not beyond the understanding of students, such as an emergency appendectomy or the birth of a baby, but it ought to involve an operative procedure and a short hospital stay. Describe the situation in terms of human need. Then ask students through discussion to develop a list of all health occupations involved in the situation, from the first report of the emergency to final examination in the doctor's office. Encourage students to discuss the duties of the various participants as the list of occupations is developed on the chalkboard.

The list will never be complete, but once it has been developed to fairly comprehensive form, then return to the original situation and restate it. This time ask each student to consider himself or herself as the patient. Pose a question about how much training and preparation the patient would like each of those individuals in the occupations listed to have prior to this emergency situation. Rate the desired training for each occupation on a scale of 1 to 5 or some other convenient scale. Be certain to indicate that each of the occupations is necessary — even critical — to the successful performance of the emergency service, and no single one can be considered more important than another. However, there are levels of skills involved in the situation, and the point is to develop some understanding of the nature of those skills and the amount of preparation and training necessary in order to acquire them.

### The Road Ahead: A Research Paper

This exercise is designed to bring students face to face with the realities of preparation for health occupations careers. It will require some library research as well as at least one interview with a person in a health occupation. The instructor should ask students to select one specific health occupation for study from a list provided. Some effort should be made to avoid duplication so that insofar as possible each student will research a different occupation. In some situations it may be possible for students to work in groups of three, with responsibilities divided according to the main divisions of the project, as described below.

The object is for students to write a paper or make a verbal presentation to the class concerning three basic aspects of career preparation for a specific career:

(1) According to the literature, how much preparation is required, where can it be obtained, and what is its nature (i.e., academic training, on-the-job training, or skills training in a specialized institution)?

(2) What is the life-style of a person in that occupation? What does that person think about the preparation required?

(3) What does the future hold for a person in this particular occupation as indicated by the literature and as perceived by the individual interviewed?

This activity is a fairly straightforward assignment based on research, but it is calculated to point out at least two things. First, preparation for some health careers can be extensive and difficult. Second, many alternative ways are available to enter the health field, some of which provide considerable potential for future growth and advancement.

**Hands-On Experience: The Volunteer**

This is not an organized activity in the sense that other career education activities are organized and managed by the school or the teacher. Instead, it is simply bringing to the attention of students the many ways in which they can acquire experience in health occupations through volunteer service. Virtually all hospitals have active volunteer organizations to place high school students and others in hospital service positions. Similarly, many such opportunities exist in nursing homes, recreational centers for senior citizens, and child care centers. The teacher of health occupations should be familiar with all such volunteer programs in the community and should encourage students to participate as a part of their educational experience. Of course, the value of such participation can be shared with other class members through reports, papers, and other activities.

## *Summary*

Practical arts teachers at the secondary school level have always been involved in some kind of career education activity. However, too often the emphasis has been on entry-level jobs rather than on careers, and on a limited group of occupations rather than on the full range of work, from unskilled to professional and from volunteer to paid employment. Careful planning which involves all of the home economics, agriculture, business education, distributive education, health occupations, industrial arts, and trade and industrial teachers at the high school level is essential. By involving teachers of other subjects and by involving the community, a unified program can be developed with emphasis on career awareness, career exploration, and especially career preparation. Leadership of practical arts teachers in building a unified program can be instrumental in getting such a program under way more quickly and in helping to make it more useful.

## *References*

Coordinating Council for Occupational Education. *Career Choice and Career Preparation.* Olympia, Washington. 1972.

Curriculum Development Center, Vocational Education. *Exploring Careers in Agribusiness: A Guide for Teachers.* Lexington: University of Kentucky. July 1974.

Dawson, Kenneth E. "Industrial Arts and the World of Work." *Educational Leadership* (January 1965), no. 22.

Division of Agricultural Education, Department of Vocational and Technical Education. *A Teaching Guide for Career Orientation in Applied Biological and Agricultural Occupations.* Urbana-Champaign: University of Illinois. February 1973.

Donaldson, Roy J. "An Evaluative Study of Federally Reimbursed Cooperative Distributive Education Programs in the Public Schools of Illinois." University of Iowa. 1958. Doctoral dissertation.

Doneth, John R. "Teaching Beliefs and Classroom Methodology of Selected Project and Cooperative Plan Distributive Education Teacher-Coordinators." Northern Illinois University. 1969. Doctoral dissertation.

Eninger, Max W. *The Process and Product of Trade and Industrial High School Level Vocational Education in the United States.* Pittsburgh: American Institute for Research. 1965.

Even, Brenda B.; and Newlon, Betty J. *Career Education Activities: A Counselor's Handbook.* University of Arizona. 1974.

Hemp, Paul E.; and Walker, Robert W. *The Development of an Occupational Orientation Unit in Applied Biological Agricultural Occupations Using a Job Cluster Approach.* Urbana: University of Illinois, Division of Agricultural Education, Department of Vocational and Technical Education. February 1973.

Mason, Ralph E.; and Haines, Peter G. *Cooperative Occupational Education.* Danville, Illinois: Interstate Printers of Publishers, Inc. 1972.

Mather, Mary. "What Will the Seventies Require of Home Economics?" *Illinois Teacher for Contemporary Roles* (January-February 1971), vol. xiv, no. 3.

McGhee, Max B. "Career Preparation in Ornamental Horticulture: A Curriculum Guide for High School Vocational Agriculture." In *Career Education in Agribusiness, Natural Resources, and Environmental Protection.* Columbus: Ohio State University. 1974.

Meisenheimer, Nancy. "Single Young Adults." *Illinois Teacher for Contemporary Roles* (January-February 1971), vol. xiv, no. 3.

Meyer, Warren G. "Outcomes in Developing Vocational Competence in Distributive Occupation." In *New Perspectives in Education for Business.* Washington, D.C.: National Business Education Association. 1963.

New York State Department of Education. *Career Orientation/Health Occupations: Ideas for Local Development Grades K-12.* Albany: University of the State of New York, Bureau of Health Occupations Education. February 1972.

_____. *Health Career Clubs: A Guide to Organization.* Albany: University of the State of New York, Bureau of Health Occupations Education. February 1973.

_____. *Health Occupations Education Program Development Guide No. 6: Medical Assisting.* Albany: University of the State of New York, Bureau of Health Occupations Education. March 1971.

Roman, Jama. *School Subject — Career Cluster: Idea Units.* Toledo Public Schools. Toledo, Ohio. No date.

Rowe, John L. "The Case for Business Education in the Secondary School." In *Selected Readings.* Edited by Frank L. Steve. New York: Odyssey Press, Inc. 1968.

Samson, Harland E. "The Critical Requirements for Distributive Education Teacher-Coordinators." University of Minnesota. 1964. Doctoral dissertation.

Sheboygan Public Schools. *K–14 Career Education Guide.* Sheboygan, Wisconsin: Lakeshore Technical Institute. 1971.

State of Illinois, Board of Vocational Education and Rehabilitation, Division of Vocational and Technical Education. *An Aid for Planning Programs in Career Education.* Springfield, Illinois. No date.

_____. *A Systems Approach: Health Occupations Education at the Secondary Level.* Springfield, Illinois. No date.

_____, Office of Superintendent of Public Instruction. *Business Education for the Seventies.* Springfield, Illinois. 1972.

State of New Jersey, Department of Education. *Health Careers Clubs of New Jersey.* Trenton, New Jersey. 1972.

Stovall, Ruth. "Education in a World of Change: Secondary Education." *Journal of Home Economics* (September 1962), vol. 54.

Tomlinson, Robert M.; *et al. Guidelines for Health Occupations Education Programs.* Washington, D.C.: U.S. Government Printing Office. June 1971.

U.S. Department of Health, Education, and Welfare. *Distributive Education in the High School.* Washington, D.C.: U.S. Government Printing Office. 1969.

_____, Office of Education. *Guidelines for Industrial Arts in Career Education: Implications for Curriculum Development and Program Implementation.* Pittsburgh, Pennsylvania: University of Pittsburgh. No date.

_____; and U.S. Department of Labor. *Vocational Education and Occupations.* Washington, D.C.: U.S. Government Printing Office. 1969.

Weale, W. Bruce. "A Curriculum Guide for Distributive Education Students in New York State." New York: Columbia University. 1950. Doctoral dissertation.

Yoder, Edgar P. "Career Education in Agricultural Equipment and Mechanics: A Curriculum Guide for High School Vocational Agriculture." In *Career Education in Agribusiness, Natural Resources, and Environmental Protection.* Columbus: Ohio State University. 1974.

# 10

# Work Experience

There is no better place to learn about work than at work. Students in school learn a great deal about school work, but any in-school instruction about other types of work is of necessity somewhat abstract and artificial. No book, lecture, or classroom experience can possibly give an adequate feeling and understanding of the environment and description of the workplace, the job content, the tedium, or the challenge of work. But classroom skills, theory, and intellectual analysis and content are necessary in learning to understand work, because no student can conceivably experience all of the jobs which might be of interest.

Therefore, career education seeks to develop an optimum "mix" for each student — ample academic and theoretical background coupled with adequate learning about work from actual work experiences. While seeking this mix as a major goal, the career educator must keep in mind that educational institutions and their students use work or the work environment to accomplish a variety of purposes, including (Mason and Haines, 1972):

(1) To keep students in school part time while they obtain needed general education

315

(2) To help students explore the world of work and to assist them in occupational choice making

(3) To help maladjusted students with personality and behavior problems

(4) To help students earn money they may need to remain in school

(5) To provide practice in what has been learned in the classroom, and to assist in the transition from school to job

(6) To develop general and specific occupational skills, knowledge, and attitudes, particularly those not readily available in the school's laboratory

The proponents of career education have no argument with any of these purposes. Indeed, we would add a considerable number of items to this list of purposes, beginning with the development of social skills and, not by any means, ending with self-discovery. The main point is that whatever functions work experience may provide for students and institutions, it can and should fulfill an *educational* purpose which is complementary to and coordinated with the school experience.

Our purpose here is to examine how this is being accomplished now and to make some suggestions about how improvements might come about. The overriding concept which guides our comments is that every student can benefit from work experience outside the classroom. This benefit can be enhanced by active participation of the school in arranging work experience. And the work experience can include "volunteer" work as well as compensated work.

Three basic types of work programs illustrate the possibilities for use in the high school: (1) work-study, (2) cooperative vocational education, and (3) experience-based career education (EBCE). Each of these programs has advantages in certain settings, and the demarcation lines between them are not always clear.

## Work-Study Programs

Work-study programs provide economically disadvantaged students with an opportunity to obtain and hold paid, part-time jobs while they are enrolled full time in vocational education studies. A primary purpose is to prevent school dropouts by providing students from low-income families with supplemental income as an incentive to stay in school or as a means for meeting the expenses involved in continuing school. Some work-study programs use other names, but the characteristics are the same: The program is designed for students from low-income families, and those students who participate must be enrolled in a vocational education curriculum. The jobs in which work-study students work may be in the same family of occupations as the students' vocational training, or they may be unrelated to the vocational training. (Similar programs for nonvocational students are more properly called "work experience programs.")

Since work-study programs rarely provide students with classroom instruction related to their work, such programs cannot be considered cooperative education. The missing essential is the correlation of school and job learning, along with some well-defined career objectives. Also missing in such programs is a proper amount of coordination between employers and the school. Employers have no explicit responsibility to further the education of the students or to place the students in jobs appropriate to the skills they are obtaining in their vocational education studies. Nevertheless, the experience can be a positive one, in addition to being merely remunerative. A teacher or counselor dedicated to the concepts of career education can assist the student in drawing from his or her work activities understanding of the relevance of classroom studies, of the necessity for good work habits, and of the clarification of work values.

## Cooperative Education

The cooperative plan of instruction has been in existence in the secondary schools and colleges of the United States for over forty years. It has contributed to the development of a variety of programs which depend on the cooperation of business and education. These programs require an active working relationship between employers and educators, and they typically provide that half of participating students' time be spent in school and half be spent on the job.

Colleges make greater use of "co-op" than high schools. It is not easy to define what is and is not a co-op program. However, present estimates of the number of high school participants range from a low of 29,000 students to a high of 160,000 students. Co-op programs are most frequently called cooperative vocational education because they are funded in part from federal vocational education moneys. However, that has the unfortunate limitation to those occupations eligible for that funding (as mentioned in chapter 8). Cooperative education still carries the implication of combined study and employment but without occupational restriction.

The cooperative plan has received support from virtually every group which has examined it. It has been endorsed by Congress, by the education departments of every state, by a wide variety of local citizen groups, and by many business and industry leaders. It also has the "endorsement" of success, because more than 80 percent of the cooperative education graduates are placed in the occupations for which they were prepared (Evans, 1969).

It is not our purpose here to provide a detailed analysis of cooperative education. (For readers who are interested in more detail about such programs, we recommend the materials cited in "References" at the end of this chapter, with particular attention to the University of Minnesota publication, *A Guide for Cooperative Career Education*, and to the work by Mason and Haines, *Cooperative Occupational Education*.) But since career education and cooperative education are closely related in many respects, and since that relationship is most pronounced at the high school level, it is important to examine this relationship with some care. Perhaps the suggestions which follow will stimulate enough interest in both career education and cooperative education so that *all* students who desire to do so will have the opportunity to participate in on-the-job experiences in conjunction with high school education.

## Advantages of Cooperative Education Programs

Cooperative education involves agreements between the school and employers which enable students to receive general education and job-related instruction in the school and on-the-job training through part-time employment. The primary goal is to prepare students for satisfying and useful employment, but the programs offer the added advantage of permitting occupational exploration in real-life situations.

Career educators have a natural affinity for cooperative education programs, because such programs harmonize so well with the goals of career education. They allow students not only to learn about work values, career exploration, and job preparation, but to experience them. Thus such programs increase the relevance of education. Of course, all work experience programs accomplish this purpose to some extent, but cooperative education offers some particular advantages which are attractive to career educators. Those advantages are listed in *A Guide for Cooperative Career Education* as: (1) greater relevance of curriculum and instruction, (2) better application of learning, (3) balanced vocational capabilities, (4) extension of training to additional occupations and students, (5) built-in manpower control, (6) closer relationship with the community, and (7) career guidance. These advantages deserve closer examination.

### Greater Relevance of Curriculum and Instruction

Cooperative education has some built-in features that almost ensure relevant instruction when properly used. First, students are always "placed" in occupations which are in harmony with the students' interests and abilities, and then students follow a written plan of work experiences based on occupational requirements and individual needs. Second, classroom instruction, on-the-job training, and youth organization activities are all articulated in the development of clearly identified skills and competencies.

Third, students have an active role in the choice of content and methods and because of their work experiences, students seek out education that is helpful in developing personal needs. Also, students can evaluate more adequately the contributions of general education and career education in terms of their own needs and aspirations. Fourth, the teacher is not the sole authority; institutional activities are supplemented by information from employers, professionals in the field, and fellow workers in the occupational environment.

Fifth, students encounter daily situations in an adult environment which cause them to examine their values and reappraise their potential on a continuing basis. This allows the transition from school to work to occur gradually instead of with the sudden shock of the traditional transition.

### Better Application of Learning

Occupations vary widely in their reliance on job experience for teaching the required technical competencies, but the combination of classroom and on-the-job instruction provides for better application of learning in almost every type of work than does either classroom instruction or on-the-job training alone. With the combination approach, students are able to test their occupational learning voluntarily and independently in real-life situations. At the same time, the job functions as a learning laboratory where the structured assignments received in the classroom can be carried out without interfering with production. The classroom offers the opportunity for students to discuss with the group the problems they encounter on the job, to analyze those problems, and to acquire a better understanding of problem solving, using the scientific method. In this process of free interchange, students begin to see the values of general education.

### Improved Balance in Career Capabilities

In-school vocational education has done a commendable job of developing technical skills and knowledge in the traditional vocational fields. But these skills are only a part of what is needed for successful adaptation to the world of work. High school students must also acquire the work attitudes and the personal confidence which will allow them to maximize their career capabilities. Work attitudes are difficult to teach in most school settings, and so the best way to achieve balance between technical skills, values or attitudes, and self-respect is on the job.

Cooperative education allows students to observe and assess the importance of personal traits so necessary for employment — such things as punctuality, dress, regular attendance, and responsibility for completing assigned tasks. It allows students to consider the values of other adults of various ages and to relate those values to work performance and to life-style. It helps students clarify relationships between education, employment, and earnings, and it expands the students' contacts with the world outside the controlled environment of youth.

### Extension of Training to Additional Occupations and Students

Cooperative education can furnish the essential elements needed to complement classwork and to provide training programs desired by many different types of students in a wide variety of occupations. By definition, cooperative education is limited to those occupations in which complementary in-school activities are available. But that limitation provides surprisingly few restrictions on students in the average high school if the cooperative education program is coordinated by a person of vision and imagination. For example, students who are interested in advertising careers can find complementary instruction in both English and fine arts departments.

Thus cooperative education is able to provide for the needs of occupations which draw on more than one discipline, and it is able to accommodate students of all abilities. It also provides the same type of remunerative support to students from low-income families and to potential dropouts as do other work experience programs.

### Built-In Manpower Training Control

Cooperative education could never result in too many workers entering an occupation, since it depends upon the number of training stations, which in turn is related to employer needs. This manpower control feature is attractive to Congress, and it appeals to other groups dealing with manpower problems. It is also a feature which is important to both the school and the community.

It is important to the school because the cooperative education advisory committee — representing both employers and employees in the community — counsels the school on the manpower supply-and-demand problem and helps the school design appropriate fields. It is important to the community because cooperative education consistently yields high placement records, high employment stability, and high job satisfaction.

### Closer Relationship with the Community

Through cooperative education, the school and the community automatically develop closer ties. Members of the advisory committee are brought into contact with the school and its needs, while at the same time school administrators and teachers come to understand the needs of the community a little better.

As the program expands to accommodate new groups of students, the need for wider community support grows, and new groups are involved which introduce fresh perspectives on established policies and procedures. Business and industry spokesmen carry the message of the school to the community, and teachers are able to help students understand the problems of the community and its businesses.

### Improved Career Guidance

Through cooperative education, students are provided early occupational experiences which are vital in making immediate and long-range career decisions. Students may even try out a variety of work situations under the direction of trained teacher-coordinators before they leave high school. Furthermore, students can share these experiences with one another in classes and in youth clubs in order to assist in the clarification of personal values and in the development of career goals.

These and other advantages of cooperative education make it an attractive program for those who support the principles of career education. Obviously, not all students can participate in cooperative education programs, but all students can benefit from such programs if they exist in the high school and if adequate provision is made for the discussion of learning experiences gained under such programs.

## Role of the Teacher-Coordinator in Cooperative Education Programs

The success of any cooperative vocational education program depends largely upon the commitment and competence of the teacher-coordinator. The assignment involves three major activities: (1) coordinating on-the-job instruction related to career goals, (2) teaching a class which is "cooperative" with occupational experience, and (3) counseling students, employers, training sponsors, and other faculty members. This means that the teacher-coordinator must be able to communicate effectively, must have the ability to design and coordinate a variety of offerings, and must be intellectually equipped to perform periodic evaluations of student and program performance. Such individuals should understand student needs as well as the needs of the business community, and should have sufficient occupational experience to be able to earn and maintain the respect of students, employers, school personnel, and community leaders.

## Requirements for a Successful Program

The success of the cooperative education program will hinge upon how well the designers of the program succeed in: (1) meeting student needs, (2) meeting community needs, and (3) organizing an active advisory committee.

### Meeting Student Needs

The need for a cooperative education program begins with a group of students who need education to prepare themselves for employment in an occupation or an occupational field. The cooperative arrangement of combining on-the-job training with classroom instruction is chosen by them as the means of achieving this goal. In order to design a program which is appropriate for the students to be served, their needs and characteristics must be clearly defined. Program coordinators must know what skills and knowledge the students possess, what their interests are, and what attitudes and characteristics they exhibit. Only with this kind of information about students is it possible to place them in meaningful jobs and to plan appropriate related vocational instruction. It is vital to the success of the program that students be placed in positions in which they will experience a sense of achievement and will find satisfaction.

The most important data will be the expressed needs of the students themselves, provided that valid and reliable methods are used in the collection of that information. Care must be taken to ensure that the opinions of students are not unduly influenced by parents, peer groups, or faculty members, and that the expressed vocational desires are not based upon considerations of occupational prestige or popularity. Follow-up of previous students and interviews to determine their reactions to their own experiences are another important source. With careful administration of the data-gathering process, one could possibly develop a fairly accurate profile of student needs.

Not all students will be ready for cooperative education programs. As discussed in previous chapters, high school students are likely to be at a variety of stages in the career decision-making process. Cooperative education programs are designed primarily for those students who have already progressed far enough to have some idea of their career goals, if not in a specific occupation within a well-defined occupational field. Cooperative education can be useful in the career exploration process, but its primary function is in career preparation and career development.

Thus cooperative education programs begin with students who need education to prepare themselves for employment and employers who are willing to assist in the training of workers. The cooperative arrangement of combining on-the-job training with classroom instruction is chosen by both as the means for achieving these goals. The teacher-coordinator must match students to programs by comparing student characteristics with training demands. And regardless of student ability levels, there should be agreement between the school and employers about the program entry criteria and standards. Employers must be aware of the characteristics of the students they employ.

Some of the characteristics of potential participants which should be examined include academic ability and grades, vocational interests, educational background and qualifications, emotional stability, personality factors, character, physical characteristics, aptitudes and talents, parental aspirations for their child, socioeconomic background, and vocational maturity. Home visits and parental conference are an integral part of the selection process, and emphasis should be placed on positive characteristics to avoid using student data as a means of screening out potential enrollees. The goal is to develop students rather than to select those who least need development.

### Meeting Community Needs

Employer interest and support are essential to the success of cooperative education programs, and thus the needs of the community must be considered when planning such programs. Employers must perceive the program as offering at least two benefits to them: (1) a source of potential trained manpower for full-time jobs, and (2) an opportunity to fulfill a social obligation. (They must *not* consider the program to be a way of getting inexpensive part-time help.) For these reasons, the training must be for occupations which are related to existing career opportunities and which are susceptible to promotion and advancement. Employers can often be convinced that cooperative education programs will be helpful if they examine their own work forces and analyze such data as the number of persons employed in specific kinds of occupations, the short- and long-range need for workers, the training needs for particular occupations, and the number of students for whom specific employers could readily provide training.

The cooperation and support of organized labor is especially essential to the success of cooperative programs, and union support should be sought. Teacher-coordinators should seek to obtain the services of such community groups as service clubs, religious organizations, welfare agencies, manpower agencies, and civic action groups. The involvement of these groups at all stages of program planning and execution will be invaluable in making certain that the program meets community needs.

## Organizing an Active Advisory Committee

All career education programs and all cooperative education programs should have direct lines of communication with the community if these programs are going to serve the manpower needs of society. The advisory committee serves a vital role in keeping these lines of communication open. Perhaps that is its main function, although its purpose is to advise and counsel the education system's administration and instructional staffs in planning, implementing, and maintaining cooperative education programs.

These advisory committees include representatives from all interested parties — employers, community leaders, teachers, parents, administrators, and students. As such, they are comparable to the "community career education action councils" recommended in chapter 11, and the cooperative education adviser function should be subsumed under the latter group. As with any committee, the value of any advisory group is directly related to the degree of involvement in program planning, development, and promotion. This involvement can be maximized by making certain that regular meetings are held, that each meeting has a prepared agenda, that the opinions of all committee members are given equal consideration, that each member has specific duties and specific assignments, that a continuing communication program is conducted with committee members, that the committee receives formal recognition from appropriate authorities, that bylaws and goals are agreed upon and clearly stated in writing, and that evaluations of committee performance take place on a regular basis.

### In-School Instructional Plan

Cooperative education programs allow for maximum learning by correlating the in-school learning experiences with the learning that takes place at the on-the-job training station. In order to accomplish this, the teacher-coordinator is called upon to design the necessary learning experiences that will enable each student to progress toward his or her career objectives. When providing instruction for a group of students enrolled in cooperative education programs, one should give consideration to the capabilities and competencies needed by all workers, those competencies which are common to specific occupational fields, and those competencies which are specific to the jobs that students learn to perform at their training stations.

As is the case with any new worker, the student participants in cooperative education must learn many tasks in relation to their "jobs." Some of those tasks can best be learned at the training station, others lend themselves to in-school instruction, and many require learning reinforcement from both sources. The basic learning tasks can be summarized as follows (Mason and Haines, 1972):

(1) Student-learners must learn well the skills, technical information, and attitudes necessary to each one's job at the training station. This is a primary learning task for them.

(2) Student-learners must learn those concepts and operational techniques applicable to the general occupational field which they have chosen. Some of these cannot be applied at the training station because they are of a higher order than is demanded by the training station job assignment. On the other hand, many of these concepts and skills can be learned in school and applied to each one's present job to test their validity and to help point out the differences in application to businesses somewhat different from her or his own.

(3) Student-learners must meet those needs which are unique to each student as an individual and are unlike those of most (or any) classmates. This uniqueness of need stems from the fact that each student-learner works in a specific firm on a specific job and with a specific goal, each of which is likely to be different from those of other student-learners.

In order to assist the student-learner in the accomplishment of these learning tasks, the teacher-coordinator must plan in-school instruction with these guidelines in mind:

(1) Define the sets of learning tasks facing each student.

(2) Emphasize the career development approach.

(3) Define the appropriate educational objectives.

(4) Determine the sequence of instruction.

(5) Employ suitable methods, media, and materials.

The teacher-coordinator is usually expected to use innovative methods of instruction. Learnings should be presented in such a way that they will persist when the students enter full-time employment.

Learning activities and projects must also aim at developing the multiple capabilities and competencies which are necessary in most employment situations. This includes such capabilities and competencies as communicating, giving and following instructions, organizing work, working in groups, creating good will, making decisions, evaluating one's own performance, seeking needed information, and working with figures. In such a fashion, students once again learn the value of general education through their direct application in the workplace.

### Community Laboratory Instruction Plan

In a true cooperative education program, the workplace becomes an extension of the school, just as the school becomes an extension of the workplace. Therefore, great care must be exercised in the identification and selection of participating businesses and appropriate training stations within those business operations. What is more, this concern for proper selection is not a one-time effort; it must be on a continuing basis throughout the lifetime of the cooperative education program. This means that the teacher-coordinator must be as aware of the needs — and the performance — of participating businesses as he or she is of the needs of students and the career training potentials within the school.

Since business enterprises must be prepared to justify their activities to stockholders, owners, or in some cases absentee corporate management, the first step in obtaining full cooperation of business is to make certain the local management, as well as training sponsors, understand the benefits of cooperative education to business and industry. Among those benefits are (Harms, *et al.*, 1972):

(1) The program is a source of loyal, competent employees.

(2) The backing of the school ensures that the employer will have the student-trainee for the entire school year, providing an opportunity to develop skills in greater depth.

(3) Participating businesses make a civic contribution by helping the school and the student-trainee.

(4) Employers have the assistance of the school and the coordinator in training a worker.

(5) Workers are prepared for the entire industry, as well as for an individual business.

(6) Workers have a career interest rather than just an interest in a part-time job.

In cooperative education programs, businesses must be prepared to provide training stations and training sponsors in adequate numbers to make each program meaningful. The training station is a work position, and the training sponsor is the individual within the business who is responsible to oversee the activities of the student-learner on the job. Training stations must meet certain criteria. They must provide activities in the type of occupation (or occupations) which are relevant to the career goals of students. They should provide opportunity for some type of "rotation" of activities and duties. They should offer safe working conditions and adequate supervision. They should provide sufficient hours of work (about fifteen hours per week) to accomplish training without overloading the student. They should be located within a reasonable distance from the school. And they should provide for an adequate compensation scale.

## Evaluation of Cooperative Education Programs

Cooperative education programs are usually evaluated in terms of their effects on the employability of graduates, student retention and dropout rates, and the job performance of those who receive the training as compared to those who do not.

These are important criteria, but they examine only one aspect of the effort. Evaluation should also be concerned with such factors as increased student motivation, expanded interest in and understanding of work values, improved relations between business and education, and other considerations based upon the original goals of the cooperative program.

## Experience-Based Career Education

In the early days of career education the U.S. Office of Education specified three competing models: the school-based model, the home-based model, and the employer-based model. The school-based model became the dominant one. The home-based model gradually became transformed into a program which supplements the efforts of the school, transmitting career information to the home by means of television and printed materials.

The original concept of the employer-based model conceived of a total educational approach occurring within the employing establishment. However, employers were not willing to accept this responsibility, and the employer-based model was transformed into experience-based career education (EBCE). The EBCE concept was then given substance through implementation by four different educational laboratories. These laboratories will attempt to disseminate their approaches among school districts across the land. Because of the newness of the EBCE approach, there cannot be the detailed and standardized analysis available for cooperative education. So that the potential of EBCE can be assessed, it is necessary to describe each of the four approaches briefly.

### Appalachian Education Laboratory

The AEL/EBCE approach has the students spending 70 to 80 percent of their time at community sites of their choice. The curriculum is designed round courses and credit of the home high school in four major areas: career education, English and communications, mathematics and natural science, and social science. Students identify their career interests and aptitudes, using self-assessment exercises and tests. They identify their academic needs and interests through transcripts of past courses and through basic skills inventories. With the help of a learning coordinator they then select specific EBCE courses, job titles, experience sites, and academic themes based on these academic and career assessments.

The learning coordinator is a staff person who fills jointly the role of teacher, tutor, and counselor. Through personalized counseling, discussion, and negotiation sessions between the student and the learning coordinator, short-term learning projects are developed which identify in clear measurable terms precisely what learning will occur as well as where, when, and how. These individual student learning plans are then implemented by assignment of the student to various learning sites worked out cooperatively with community institutions or by activities in an off-campus learning center or at the high school. For instance, a student expressing an interest in working with children might be placed temporarily in the pediatric ward of a local hospital and will continue with frequent conferences with the learning coordinator to see that the learning plan is being accomplished while that is occurring. Another student might be assigned for a few weeks to a local agency or private business to help with the bookkeeping to fulfill math requirements.

The Appalachian laboratory strategy revolves round the conviction that the process of learning must be as carefully and completely taught as the content of learning. Therefore, the activities are designed to develop critical thinking and inquiry skills in the student, irrespective of the specific content of the project. Each short-term project, whether academic or career oriented, is planned to help students gain skills in five clearly specified levels of inquiry: planning the problem, gathering the data, organizing and analyzing data, generalizing and making inferences, and communicating the results. For each activity developed between the student and the learning coordinator, an activity sheet is developed, which is filled in as the activities are completed. When the activity sheet is evaluated, it is done according to the extent to which the student is making progress in using these inquiry or critical thinking skills, as well as the extent to which the student has mastered the content that was the academic objective of the activity.

Each of the AEL students is enrolled in a career planning and decision-making course during each semester. However, these are not courses that meet daily in the classroom in the traditional manner. Three aspects of career planning and decision making are emphasized throughout the students' experiences: self-knowledge (aptitudes, interest, temperaments, skills), knowledge of specific careers and jobs, and generalized world-of-work information. Throughout the school year students apply several career-related self-assessment instruments, the results of which are entered in a student program guide and referenced to the Labor Department's 114 worker trait group classifications to help the students identify various career clusters and career types which might merit investigation by them. Placement in experience sites then are designed round these expressions of interests to involve the students in gaining information about the specific job, the job environment, and the general nature of the world of work. The student and the learning coordinator continuously reconsider, at short intervals throughout the year, whether the student's initial assessment of personal career aptitudes and interests actually matches the resultant real work experiences.

As the result of parental or student requests or evidence of need as discovered by basic proficiency tests, special courses in reading, math proficiency, or other needed subjects are added on an individualized basis. Students may also enroll in local community colleges, vocational centers, or other available facilities and receive high school credit, or they may take some regular high school courses which also give them their opportunities for such courses as foreign languages, music, and athletics.

Depending upon agreement between the student and the learning coordinator, the student may participate in a variety of small group activities with other students who have common interests. These may be academic groups to share common problems and interests and enrich learning by participating cooperatively in a variety of academic projects; they may be career groups in which students share information and insights about their site placement and learning experiences, obtain information about training and job search, or in which they practice assessing and applying individual career aptitudes and skills. They may also be guidance and counseling groups which provide opportunity for students to develop and promote self-awareness, self-confidence, problem solving, or values clarification, and build their skills in human relations and communications.

The key persons in the students educational experiences are the learning coordinator and various community resource persons who volunteer to be assistants. These may be employers, public officials, staff of local museums or of neighboring vocational schools or community colleges, employees of various establishments, or any individual within the community with a special knowledge to impart.

Obviously, this system requires a high staff-to-student ratio and extensive cooperation from the community. Written reports of student activities and each one's progress are provided to parents on a quarterly basis. There are special periodical conferences with students and their parents who are also invited to participate in career-oriented seminars and special presentations. There is an EBCE community advisory council which includes parents as well as other community figures. All activities are carefully analyzed and the learning assessed and recorded. All of the accumulative materials, reports, forms, and the reactions of involved resource persons are continuously evaluated, recorded, and translated into standard course credits and grades and entered on the student's high school transcripts as if he or she were completing standard courses in the classroom. Upon satisfactory completion of the EBCE program, each student then receives a regular diploma in the home high school as well as a career education certificate documenting the career-oriented experiences and learning.

## Far West Laboratory

The Far West Laboratory EBCE program is also based upon one-to-one and small group interaction with volunteer resource persons from the community. Students plan and carry out their own individual and small group projects designed according to program guidelines and approved by the program staff and the resource persons to whom the students are assigned. Projects blend career development with basic skills, life skills, and academic learning through which the students earn course credit in the standard areas through research, experience, and related reading and discussion. The career development includes career awareness and self-development. The basic skills are specifically reading, writing, oral communication, and computational skills. The life skills are interpersonal inquiry, problem solving, and decision making. These are blended with learning opportunities in life science, physical science, social science, commerce, and communications and media. The resource sites are developed and analyzed for learning potential in these areas.

Drawing on these core curriculum goals and the learning potential offered by the various community resources, staff members help students work out individual goals and objectives, organized in a project plan. Students are required to put in 25 to thirty hours of program activity each week, with 50 percent of the time in project activities and 30 percent at resource sites. Each student project must involve at least one resource person or organization, along with related reading and at least one tangible product. Students are not required to complete any standard number of projects. Rather, the number, scope, and depth of student projects may vary widely, depending upon the student's interests, needs, and abilities. The student must satisfy minimum competency requirements in reading, writing, oral communications, career awareness, and career decision making. However, competence in these areas is assessed by the staff observing the performance of the students in real situations rather than by standardized testing. Students learn by planning, questioning, doing, and evaluating their own experiences and performances.

Independent study, using program materials, tutorials, small group workshops, or enrollment in regular community high school or college courses, is available to the students and staff in building the individual student's learning program. However, most of the students receive their instructions through the combination of individualized research projects and weekly seminars with other students working in the same fields. When constructing their project plans, students indicate the type and amount of high school credit they hope to earn, subject to the approval of their learning coordinators. Each completed project is evaluated by the learning coordinators, the resource persons, and other staff members. When a project is successfully completed, regular high school credit is assigned in the subject area designated and entered on the official transcript.

Staff members recruit volunteer resource people or gain commitments from resource organizations and then from individual volunteers within those organizations. The staff determines from examination of the students and their experience with their past students the kinds of resources needed and then pursues those through community contacts. Learning activities are tailored to the resource person's interests, expertise, work, and schedule. Whether he or she is business administrator, a lawyer, an arc welder, a public official, or a person expert in a particular avocational area such as poetry, gardening, or photography, the students are expected to learn primarily from direct one-to-one contacts.

The contacts may be short or long term. At the short-term level students spend one to three half-days to become acquanted with resource persons in their organizations and discover what can be learned there. If the mutual interest seems to develop, then an exploration of five to ten half-days allows the student to arrange several more visits to survey a career or area of study. Finally, the investigation level may last from twenty half-days to the full school term as students focus on in-depth research or on mastering selected career or academic skills.

The learning coordinator performs a combined teacher-counselor function, helping students make informed decisions about their own education on a daily basis and helping them develop the skills they need to pursue their own goals. Therefore, the learning coordinator is responsible for an ongoing assessment of the student's learning needs, interest capabilities, and goals; for long- and short-term program planning, including individualized projects using employer and community resources; for monitoring the student's activities and growth to identify and resolve problems, to assess competency and reevaluate interest and needs, and to apply criteria and procedures for awarding credit for completed student work.

Parents are invited to program orientations and to regularly scheduled individual parent conferences with staff members so that they can become aware of student progress. Parents
are also recruited to serve as resource persons, and parent
representatives sit on the program policy advisory board along
with representative resource persons from the community.
Once again, the approach obviously depends upon a skilled
staff with a high staff-to-student ratio, the cooperation of the
community, and students who respond well to the individualized
and self-starting approach.

### *Northwest Regional Education Laboratory*

The students in this program developed in Oregon spend
about 50 percent of their program time at learning sites, working directly with community instructors. These are individuals
who have volunteered to take part in the program and receive
some training from program staff. The program uses a detailed
task analysis procedure to identify the full learning potential
of each employer or community site and to translate this
potential into learning objectives. The objectives then become
the basis for individualized projects which students complete
in the community. The curriculum is divided into three content areas: life skills, basic skills, and career development.

The five life skills categories are (1) creative development,
(2) critical thinking, (3) personal and social development,
(4) science, and (5) functional citizenship. Lifelong learning,
personal growth, and relationship of individuals to broader
community, national, and world concerns are emphasized. The
life skills content area also includes a set of "survival skills"
such as knowledge of checking accounts, insurance, budgeting,
auto maintenance, and so forth. The EBCE students must
demonstrate competence in these areas as part of their program
requirements. The basic skills components concentrate on
reading, mathematics, writing, and listening and speaking skills
needed to perform tasks and functions in the program and in
adulthood. The career development component focuses on

identifying career interests, understanding the world of work, general employability skills, and career knowledge.

Each year, individual students must complete ten projects, two in each life skills area. A set of thirteen survival skills or competencies must be completed by all students in the program. Students must spend a minimum of fifteen hours a week at an employer or community site and complete a minimum of five career explorations per year.

Program staff survey employers and other community institutions to identify potential learning sites and learning activities, according to student need. Incoming students indicate career interests — the starting points for determining the type of sites needed for the program. Staff members recruit networks of community sites which represent a wide range of careers and occupations. Students then choose the sites they will visit, based upon assessed and expressed career interest. Students are encouraged to explore and compare as wide a range of careers and jobs as possible. They learn firsthand about particular occupations through individual career explorations and in-depth learning level experiences at the exploration sites of most interest to them. Although they must explore a minimum of five sites per year, the students are not required to explore a specified number of occupations in the particular category or cluster. Similarly, students are not asked to focus on potential future careers, but rather to expand their career interests through a variety of experiences.

An individual learning plan is negotiated between each student and the staff through a continuing cycle of assessment, prescription, evaluation, and integration of experiences. An initial assessment is made of the student's needs and interests. Each student then negotiates learning goals with the staff, and is helped to design a plan that prescribes a learning strategy to meet personal and program goals. As the student's work in the program progresses, each completed activity is evaluated by the students, staff, and appropriate community resource people. Students develop their own time lines for completing activities, and they meet regularly with staff members to report their progress. Student progress in the program is carefully monitored and recorded. Individualized problem-centered projects which the students complete at community sites encourage them to manage their own learning and perceive the relationship among personal goals, career options, and specific knowledge skills.

Each student is guided through a career exploration process of three- to five-day investigation of occupations of potential interest. The academic content is delivered primarily through actual community experiences based around a student's projects. In addition, however, students can include regular high school classes in their learning plans, if these are appropriate to their individual needs and goals. Similarly, they can enroll in selected classes at community colleges in the area. Program staff members contact each learning site at least once a week for routine site maintenance to assure that the community instructors are fulfilling their commitments and that the students are exercising appropriate diligence.

World-of-work seminars bring community adults to the learning center. Students meet weekly to share their experiences and plan coming events. At an annual retreat each fall, students and staff build group feelings and sharpen their group problem-solving skills. There are also evening gatherings with parents and community volunteers.

Grades are not assigned, but students are required to complete their work at performance levels appropriate to their abilities and goals. Evaluation criteria for each learning activity is individually negotiated between students and staff, and each completed learning experience is then evaluated and certified according to those criteria by the appropriate persons, including staff, parents, and the community resource persons.

When students leave the program they receive a certification portfolio that contains performance information needed by parents and high school placement officials, potential employers, and college registrars. Graduating students also receive a standard high school diploma.

### Research for Better Schools

The EBCE model of Research for Better Schools in Philadelphia, Pennsylvania, is much more school based than the other three models. Students spend approximately 20 percent of their schoolweek in the community. One career exploration component involves a series of minicourses designed round group and individual activities that are planned and conducted at community sites. Each mini-course, planned round a cluster of career areas, is offered either as an elective or as a substitute for required social studies courses.

Specialization provides students with in-depth individual project opportunities. The projects may be the results of assignments in an academic area, special student interests, or career exploration follow-up. In all cases, projects mix career and academic learning for required or elective school credit and involve student input on project design and hands-on student experience in the community. Career guidance uses both structured and informal group guidance activities to develop students' decision-making and problem-solving skills with respect to career planning. The academic resource center provides students with individually prescribed instruction in English and mathematics, complementing the career exploration and specialization activities.

Students remain on the rolls of the high school. They must meet the same course requirements as other students, but their credits must reflect career development, career guidance, and basic skills development, as well as the prescribed elective courses.

School staff functioning as counselors or coordinators help students plan their EBCE program. Students choose the career clusters they wish to explore by going through a career exploration catalog and making first, second, and third choices. Over the course of the year, a student usually explores three clusters. Students interested in career specialization must first negotiate with the coordinator to determine what they are prepared to do, then find the resource site to carry out their proposed activity.

The RBS model requires student access to regular school classes for all subjects other than English and math for basic skills development and the career exploration and specialization activities. Group instruction is stressed with groups of ten to fifteen students participating in the career exploration experiences. Students are also grouped in regularly scheduled guidance sessions. The academic resource center is individualized but uses small group instruction as one learning mode. The range of career options provided by RBS/EBCE depends on the number of employers and community resource sites required for the program. The program seeks to give students opportunities to sample as wide a range of careers, occupations, and job functions as possible. To do this, student exploration activities are organized within clusters of careers and occupations. Each term the student selects a career cluster for which employer–community site experiences have already been planned by program staff. To the student who becomes particularly interested in one job site or career while completing group exploratory experiences in a given cluster and individualized specialization, placement can be arranged to allow the student more substantive participation to those activities.

Students in the program are responsible for mastering the performance objectives in their individualized math and English program; for securing information about jobs, occupations, and careers while on resource sites; and for information processing, decision making, problem solving, and, finally, for self-evaluation.

The EBCE staff members help students understand the responsibilities in each of the three curriculum areas and follow regular school policies and procedures in dealing with problems. Guidance and counseling are delivered through the career guidance component of the curriculum. This component helps students acquire the self-evaluative problem-solving and decision-making skills they need to assess and relate their own experiences (in and outside the schools) to their own career development and to public issues.

The instructional components are part of the regular secondary school curriculum. Credit for courses students complete through field experiences can be determined at the discretion of the school administration. The RBS model is integrated with the regular school schedule, and the EBCE students graduate with their regular classes.

### Summary

Experience-based career education is a new and experimental approach that is currently emerging from pilot demonstration models and reaching a dissemination stage. The four models are described in the National Institute of Education Publication, *A Comparison of Four Experience-Based Career Education Programs* (National Institute of Education, 1976). Its limited application under innovative circumstances makes its applicability to general situations a question for future determination. How many schools will be able to afford the staffing and win the support of their communities remain to be seen. In contrast to cooperative education, it provides exploration opportunities rather than employment — breadth, not depth. Yet it is an exciting concept with which many school systems will and should want to experiment.

### *Weaknesses of Work Experience Programs*

Work experience programs offer important contributions toward the goals of career education, and every high school should include such programs as part of its career education effort. Obviously, many occupations do not lend themselves directly to work experience programs, but for a wide range of occupations, work experience offers a form of relevant career preparation activity which is not attainable through any other type of career education. And while work experience programs are not entirely new in American education, their potential has just barely been touched in terms of both depth and breadth. Nevertheless, there are also weaknesses in work experience programs which should be guarded against.

Cooperative education programs are not readily adaptable to some communities, such as those which are so small that they have a narrow range of available training stations, those which have declining population, or those in which most employment is in occupations for which there is a decreasing demand. Problems also occur in establishments which have strong employer-employee agreements. Some unions restrict entry; some agreements stipulate that no new workers can be hired until all "furloughed" workers have first been recalled; and some employers have a tradition of hiring relatives of present workers.

Work-study pursues income, and its career contribution is accidental. Cooperative education is limited in its career exploration potential in that it explores intensively one occupation but may restrict a student's opportunities to explore others. It is therefore most appropriate for those who have already narrowed their occupational choices, and have done so based upon knowledge of alternatives. Experience-based career education offers a wider range of exploration, but with less intensity and less likelihood of remaining in the employ of the owners at the experience site.

Other disadvantages are demographic and economic in nature. The number of students who can profit from work experience programs in any community is determined largely by the birthrate which occurred in that community sixteen to eighteen years earlier. The number who can be accommodated by the programs is determined in large part by the number of available employment opportunities at a particular time. Too often, the latter number is far smaller than the former. Any sort of economic instability affects the programs. Even minor recessions cause layoffs, and student-learners are often among the first to go because they can be returned to school for full-time study. (In this sense, the advantage listed above of adaptability to labor market demands becomes a disadvantage.) Once again, the skillful teacher-coordinator can often minimize the effects of recessionary periods on these programs by seeking alternatives which do not interfere with the goals of the program of the students.

The major limitations of EBCE appear at this early stage to be the costliness of a high staff-student ratio, the difficulty of attracting sufficient community resource volunteer individuals and organizations, and the uncertainty as to the quality of the learning. Only time and evaluation will tell how serious these are.

### Resolving the Problems

The advantages of work experience programs quite demonstrably overshadow the disadvantages, even when one considers the problems likely to be encountered in establishing such programs. Many of these problems can be overcome through careful planning and education of the school and the community. The three examples described here contrast work-study for which income is the primary objective and work experience is incidental, cooperative education which involves direct employment and often leads to permanent placement, and EBCE which stresses career exploration. All are valid approaches.

Work experience programs could become a tool for exploration and contributors to decision making, rather than being limited to preparation after an occupational choice is made. That would be tried only if work experience became a general educational methodology rather than a specific kind of educational program. It would need to be available for use, in varying ways, in the total teaching-learning process, beginning in the early elementary grades and continuing through all of higher education. To accomplish this, it would of course be essential that decision makers in education embrace both the concept of work and the importance of experiential learning. Unpaid volunteer work as well as paid employment must be involved. In fact, where career *exploration* is the goal, unpaid work experience in the world of paid employment may hold greater potential than does paid work experience. As the student moves closer to making bona fide occupational choices, paid work experience — including the responsibilities of being productive and fully accountable — become more important. Exploratory, unpaid work experience opportunities, involving frequent changes in work station assignment, should begin no later than the junior high school years and continue to be made available so long as students remain undecided about occupational choices.

One primary difficulty of work experience programs until now has been the shortage of qualified persons who can act in the role of teacher-coordinator. The Education Professions Development Act authorized substantial funds for the development of teachers and other leadership personnel for education, but only a small portion of this professional development program has been devoted to the education of teacher- coordinators. This situation will change as the career education movement continues and as more and more administrators see the advantages of work experience programs. In addition, as understanding of the values of career education is disseminated through the school system, local schools will encounter less resistance from vocational education teachers who fear work experience programs because they might reduce the demand on traditional vocational education. Various schools have employed different strategies to reduce this resistance, such as restricting cooperative education to occupations not taught in school laboratories. A better solution would be to link the two with initial preparation in the classrooms to make the student more productive and better prepared to learn at the work station. After all, the basic goals of both approaches are the same, and it is likely that in the long run vocational education will benefit from work experience programs, instead of being harmed by them.

Still another problem has to do with the phasing of work experience programs. Schools are accustomed to accepting students in September and graduating them in June. Business does not operate in this restricted sphere. Workers are needed year long. Educators must learn to phase cooperative education programs so that a steady supply of student-learners is available throughout the year and so that the program continues throughout the summer. This is not a difficult problem when it is examined carefully, because students learn at different rates. Thus some students are ready for their training stations in September, and some will not be ready until March or April. Acknowledgment of this fact tends to spread the need for job placements more evenly over the calendar year, and it seems only a matter of time until most school programs operate year-round.

Cooperative education and work experience are often opposed by some individuals who think instruction must be given solely inside school walls. Every administrator who has operated a cooperative program has had protesting phone calls from both teachers and lay citizens who do not understand why a faculty member should be off the school premises during school hours. The only solution to this problem seems to be a continuing program to educate the public about the rationale for career education and for cooperative education programs.

In some locations, work experience programs may be affected by wage-hour restrictions and youth employment safety regulations. However, the state education agencies which have tried to do so have generally been successful in obtaining exceptions to state laws and administrative rulings in order to permit such programs. These exceptions allow special consideration for cooperative education students with regard to wages, hours, safety regulations, and other restrictions designed to protect youth from exploitation. The basic rationale is that through the teacher-coordinator the school makes certain that the student is involved in a bona fide educational program and is not being exploited.

Other prohibitive regulations are common, and only the efforts and support of the entire education establishment will succeed in changing them. For example, many states prohibit the use of federal funds for coordination which extends across two or more of the traditional fields of vocational education. This eliminates such occupations as sales training for industrial supplies, which cuts across distributive education and trade and industrial education. Some states have solved this problem by assigning the coordination to the teacher who is most competent to handle the major portion of the occupation. In some states, regulations exclude such occupations as radio announcer because they have not been a part of traditional vocational education, even though they clearly meet all the criteria for inclusion. Equally oppressive regulations exclude from cooperative education those occupations which require less than two years for the "average worker" to learn. By definition, half of all students are below average in their ability to learn, and half are above average. To attempt to specify the length of time required by an "average" person to learn an occupation is an exercise in futility.

While small communities have their own problems with work experience education, as discussed above, large cities also have difficulties. Travel time for teacher-coordinators and for students is a major problem, since it is rarely possible to restrict students to employment or learning sites in a particular geographic sector of the city. Employers in large cities are more likely to be bound by seniority restrictions which inhibit introduction of student-learners, and teachers in large cities seem more likely to feel that the working day ends promptly at half past three unless overtime rates are paid. Despite these and other obstacles, many large city school systems are operating work experience programs successfully. In addition, urban districts are becoming increasingly aware that such programs offer an excellent means for aiding disadvantaged and educationally handicapped students who are disenchanted with full-time instruction in classrooms.

In this regard, we recognize the "advantages" of work-study programs to local school districts. After all, work-study programs do not require the employment of a teacher-coordinator or the organization of an educational program related to the students' work. Also, federal moneys are available for work-study, which means that the cost to the local school district is lower. Finally, students often elect work-study over cooperative education because earnings are slightly higher in jobs which emphasize production rather than learning. Work experience of any kind is important to career education, but cooperative education and EBCE are much more defensible from an educational point of view than work-study, and it is unwise for school districts to be "pennywise and pound foolish" where students — and society — are concerned. We are confident that Congress will eventually phase out support for work-study in favor of additional support for cooperative education.

Experience-based career education lacks the many years of experience and support but is a promising approach. In addition to direct support to schools and school districts, some portion of federal financial support should go to the development of curriculum and materials for cooperative education and EBCE programs. Such programs are currently hampered by a shortage of instructional materials of three basic types: (1) materials for the general instruction which applies to all of the occupations supervised by a particular coordinator, (2) materials directly related to each of these occupations, and (3) materials suitable for training the sponsors and community resource people.

Some efforts to develop work experience programs have been discouraged because of a shortage of training stations. Employers cite the high cost of developing such stations as the reason for their reluctance to provide them. One cannot deny that participation is costly to the employer. However, the cooperative education program is based on the notion that employers can recover these added costs through having a better supply of well-trained workers and through the recognition which comes from fulfilling a social responsibility. Nevertheless, if work experience education is to expand rapidly, it is unrealistic to expect employers to assume costs above those normally incurred in the training of new employees.

A good case can be made for full payment to the employer of all added costs of educational participation. This is already being done in many manpower training stations, and it is authorized by the Vocational Education amendments of 1968. Unfortunately, in the few states which have approved such payments, the expense to the employer of applying for and substantiating added costs are unreasonable in relation to the added costs of the training. This is an administrative problem which can be easily solved.

Ultimately, it must be recognized that no school-based work experience can ever carry the full flavor of a regular full-time job in the competitive labor market. They are at best substitutes for regular employment. However, no individual can ever hope to hold a sufficient variety of jobs to explore all of the important alternatives while still young enough to make the crucial career decisions. Cooperative education, experience-based career education, and other work experience programs provide an orchestrated substitute. Nevertheless, every youth needs the experience of getting and holding a job outside the protecting presence of teacher, coordinator, and program.

### References

*A Guide for Cooperative Career Education.* Minneapolis: Division of Vocational and Technical Education, College of Education, University of Minnesota. 1969.

American Council on Education. *Evaluative Criteria: The National Study of Secondary School Evaluation.* Washington, D.C.: American Council on Education, Publication Division. 1970.

Cotrell, D. J. "The Status and Future of Certification in Cooperative Vocational Education." In *Cooperative Occupational Education Programs: A Conference Seminar to Extend the Range of Vocational Education.*

Cushman, Harold R.; *et al. The Concerns and Expectations of*

*Prospective Participants in Directed Work Experience Programs*. Ithaca, New York: State University of New York. 1967.

ERIC Clearinghouse on Vocational Technical Education. *What State Leaders Should Know about Cooperative Vocational Education*. Information Series No. 38. August 1971.

Evans, Rupert N. "Cooperative Programs — Advantages, Disadvantages, and Factors in Development." *American Vocational Journal* (May 1969), vol. 44, no. 5.

Goldhammer, Keith. *Extending Career Education beyond the Schoolhouse Walls*. Columbus: Center for Vocational Education, Ohio State University. 1974.

Harms, Harm; *et al. Methods of Teaching Business and Distributive Education*. Cincinnati, Ohio: South-Western Publishing Co. 1972.

Haskyn, F. P. "Work Experience: Basic Issues," *Curriculum Journal* (January 1943).

Klaurens, Mary. "Co-op Plan or Cop-out Plan?" *D. E. Today* (Fall 1971), vol. 5, no. 1.

Koo, Po-Yen. *Controversies in Educational Evaluation: A Brief Clarification of a Few Basic Concepts of Evaluation Relating to Vocational and Technical Education*. Trenton: Division of Vocational Education, New Jersey State Department of Education. October 1970.

Kraft, Richard H. P. *Cost Effectiveness Analysis of Vocational-Technical Education Programs*. Tallahassee: Educational Systems and Planning Center, Florida State University. June 1969.

Mason, Ralph E.; and Haines, Peter G. *Cooperative Occupational Education*. Danville, Illinois: Interstate Printers and Publishers, Inc. 1972.

National Conference on Cooperative Vocational Education. *Implications of the 1968 Amendments*. Minneapolis, Minnesota, February 26–28, 1969. Notes and working papers.

National Institute of Education. *A Comparison of Four Experience-Based Career Education Programs*. Washington, D.C.: National Institute of Education. 1976.

Rowe, Kenneth. "Evaluation Models for Cooperative Programs." In *Cooperative Occupational Programs: A Con-*

*ference Seminar to Extend the Range of Vocational Education.*

"Sponsor Development Program." Report by the Richmond Professional Institute, Richmond, Virginia. 1956.

Starr, Harold; *et al. A System for State Evaluation of Vocational Education.* Columbus: Center for Vocational and Technical Education, Ohio State University. May 1970.

U.S. Office of Education, Vocational Division. *Work Experience Programs in American Secondary Schools,* Bulletin No. 5. Washington D.C.: U.S. Government Printing Office.

Warmbrod, J. Robert. *Review and Synthesis of Research on the Economics of Vocational Education.* Columbus: Center for Vocational and Technical Education, Ohio State University. November 1968.

# 11

# School Counselor

Despite the almost universal presence of professional counselors in the nation's high schools, remarkably little agreement exists about the role these counselors are expected to fill and the objectives they are to achieve. What counselors actually do is not so much in doubt: They give and interpret tests, they counsel students concerning personal and academic difficulties, they enforce attendance, they serve as liaison with juvenile authorities, they advise on college entrance requirements and choice of college, and sometimes they provide occupational information and assist in occupational choice. The disagreement over objectives occurs as counselors attempt to rationalize the role they play and give evidence that their efforts do make a difference.

Career education provides not only a more specific role for the high school counselor but also a more coherent rationale for that role. It is not reasonable to argue that career education will change entirely the useful roles counselors have always filled. Rather, we contend that the high school counselor can supply important contributions to career education and that those contributions will increase the counselor's job satisfaction and add significantly to his or her own career development.

Potential roles for counselors in career education have already been identified by the U.S. Office of Education, the American Personnel and Guidance Association, and school counselors already on the career education firing line. Essentially, their contributions fall into four functional areas: (1) the counselor as career development theorist, (2) the counselor as teacher of decision-making skills, (3) the counselor as provider of occupational information, and (4) the counselor as career education coordinator within the school. Discussion of these functions and the practical obstacles to their fulfillment comprise the bulk of this chapter. It begins by exploring the interaction of counseling theory and career education philosophy. It explores potential counselor roles in career education. It identifies obstacles counselors encounter when becoming involved in career education, and it ends by listing the competencies a counselor must acquire if he or she wants to attain the satisfactions offered by a key role in career education.

## Counseling Theory and Career Education Philosophy

The concepts of career development, the importance of decision making, and the career education emphasis on work, action, and collaboration interact to comprise the environment within which the counselor must participate in career education. It is necessary to understand these premises in order to determine the role the high school counselor must play and the preparation that will be necessary.

## The Counselor in Career Development Theory

The concept that career decision making is a lifelong process, beginning in infancy and continuing into old age, is a significant intellectual achievement. It is a vast improvement as a practical guide, in contrast to the outmoded attempts to match fixed individual traits to equally fixed job factors. It is also a key component of career education, along with the obligation of the teacher to point up the career relevance of the classroom topics, the obligation of the home and family to manifest positive work values, the obligation of employing and labor market institutions to offer stimulating and realistic learning environments, and the obligation of vocational educators to provide training in occupational skills. Career development is not the exclusive domain of the counselor, but it is an obvious domain. Career development is a natural process, whether guided or not. However, it is the guidance counselor who has the psychological training to best understand the career development process and to intervene in a positive way.

The career development process is usefully understood only if viewed as one aspect of broader human development. Human beings develop toward maturity physically, emotionally, intellectually, and socially — as well as in career terms — whether that development is guided or not, and whether or not maturity is achieved in any one or all of these aspects. The mature individual understands himself or herself in relation to society, shapes that self in harmony with a well-developed sense of values, and accepts responsibility for decisions and actions. In career terms, maturity is the ability to give reasoned and responsible answers to the questions: What is important to me? What is possible for me? What is probable for me? The mature person arrives at rational decisions based on answers to those questions, accepts responsibility for those decisions, and takes consistent action based on those decisions. Both heredity and environment are involved in career development, as they are in all human development. However, the mature individual rises above these limitations to a degree, and the mature career decision maker seeks information beyond the limitations on career horizons.

The profession of career guidance is based on the assumption that wise intervention strategies can enhance the normal career development process. Career guidance becomes useful and effective to the degree that it is based on intervention strategies which are in harmony with the normal process of career development. This assumes that career guidance starts in the very early years and continues at higher and higher levels of sopsistication throughout the life cycle. Intervention strategies designed to assist in the normal maturational stages of human development are more likely to succeed than those designed to provide remedial assistance to individuals whose development has been damaged or retarded. Economic, social, physical, educational, or psychological deprivation can serve to retard or impcdc optimal career development. All of this being the case, the high school counselor must evidence a high degree of sophistication in understanding the career development process and in enhancing and assisting the decision-making abilities of students who are faced with critical career decisions, many of whom have already been crucially damaged in their career development.

This emphasis on the counselor's role in career development often clashes with traditional training and with the "standard" approach of waiting in the counseling office for students to seek help one by one. Typically, counselors have been trained in a *process* of human relations and individual and group counseling. To intervene positively and effectively in the career development process requires *content* knowledge. The counselor must have an understanding of the school as a social system, of classroom practices and curriculum content, and of their impact upon the self-concepts, plans, and aspirations of the students.

Neither counseling sessions with individuals or groups, nor "career days," nor "occupations units" taught by the counselor can meet this need. Instead, someone who understands the career development process must transmit that understanding and its importance to parents, teachers, administrators, and school boards. This means in-service training for teachers in such career development principles and concepts as: the interrelationship of goals, values, and decision making in the self-development of youth; the changing nature of economic and labor market trends and the occupational structure of the economy; techniques for integrating career information, career relevance, and career development concepts into the subject matter of classes; and resources available to remake the curriculum to facilitate career development goals. Bridging the communication gaps between the academic educator and the vocational educator and between those who prefer abstract teaching methods and those who employ "hands on" teaching methods, and helping teachers create learning experiences which bring school, community, and the employment world into focus for the youth are difficult but necessary tasks for which the high school counselor may be a facilitator. In fact, no more positive contribution could be made than to help teachers, administrators, and parents understand their own career development processes — how they arrived at where they are, how they feel about their own careers, and what their current occupations are doing to their own self-concepts and life-styles. With that understanding of themselves and the patterns of their own career development, they will be better able to impact positively upon the lives of the youth they influence.

But this also means that counselors need retraining. They must themselves understand the career development process — their own and the generalized patterns for youth. The concepts of career education, the trends toward greater focus in the schools on human relations and the affective development of children and youth, new patterns of staffing (including teacher-counselor models and the use of paraprofessionals), new educational structures such as open schools, flexible scheduling, and team teaching — all must be part of the counselor's intellectual and practical equipment. And someone must be capable of choosing among and designing group counseling experiences, life planning laboratories where values can be clarified and ranked, actual and simulated work experiences, interviews with workers as role models, work observation, and other in-school and out-of-school experiences.

Admittedly, this is a tall order for the counselor, but according to Hansen (1972):

> ...if we believe in preventive education, and if we believe a primary task of the school is development of positive self-concepts, giving students a sense of control over their own lives, and maximizing their vocational possibilities, there is nothing more compatible with these objectives or with counselor roles than career development.... [P]art of a student's self-concept exploration is examining the meaning he wants work to have in his life — its social, personal, psychological, and economic implications. He needs assistance in evaluating his interests, aptitudes, and abilities, in reflecting on how work fits into his life and into the life-style he envisions — the needs he has for leisure, self-esteem, community involvement, for improving society, for family relationships, for security, for adventure, for status, for

power, for self-fulfillment...he needs counselors and teachers and a school system which asks, not "Where do Johnny and Janie best fit?" but "How does work fit into the kind of life Johnny and Janie want and the kinds of persons they perceive themselves to be?"

## The Counselor and Career Decision Making

A democratic society is rooted in the opportunity for free and informed choices by its citizens. It is the basic student need for freedom of choice coupled with the need for systematic assistance in reasoned decision making that combine to form the rationale for career guidance. The career guidance movement is rooted in the psychology of career development, the sociology of work in our culture, and the economic necessity of work for the survival of our system of government. It combines assistance in decision making with assistance in implementing decisions that persons have made.

The concept of *choice* is of central importance in the thinking of guidance personnel. The essential function of the counselor is to help people choose wisely from among the alternatives available to them. This the counselor does by encouraging the counselee to learn, think, consider, and decide about himself and his opportunities. It is not nearly so important *what* people choose as that they *choose* from the widest possible range of opportunities. It should not be so important to the counselor what the counselee decides about opportunities as what he or she decides about himself or herself in relation to these opportunities. The counselor does not *make* people do things; the counselor's role is to *let* them find ways of doing things. The counselor is not as interested in the *something* they become as in the *someone* they become.

This concept assumes that most persons are, by and large, rational individuals who will be making rational decisions based on the understandings they develop. The concern is not with trying to get more youth to enter certain occupations. Rather, the primary concern is with having individuals make choices based on increased self-knowledge and environmental understanding. If guidance is working properly, the students who choose vocational education or a job or college entrance should be those students who freely decided to move in those directions and who know the bases on which these decisions were made. This is one criterion which can be used in evaluating effectiveness of guidance services. Moreover, the students who have made a particular choice should be persons having reasonable chances for success in the programs for which they are enrolled. That is, if people make rational choices, most of these choices will take the probabilities of success into account. This, then, constitutes a second criterion on which effectiveness of guidance can be evaluated.

The primary allegiance of the counselor must be to his counselees, not to the particular choices they make. Philosophically, guidance counseling is based on the confident assumption that, given adequate information and time to choose from among alternatives, most people will choose wisely and sensibly. The counselor must uphold the right of the individual to lead his or her own life and must believe that most individuals can and will accept the responsibilities which accompany this right.

However, the belief that most choices at most times will be rational, based on available information, does not and should not imply that all or even most decisions will be — in some absolute sense — right.

It is vitally important that the career guidance function not be pictured as one of helping individuals "play it safe" by making decisions which hold high probabilities for successful implementation. Rather, the career guidance function must be pictured as helping individuals make decisions which take a risk factor into account as one of several elements entering into decision making. So long as and to the extent that counselors consider their function as one of helping individuals "play it safe," counselors will be rightfully accused of contributing to underdevelopment and underutilization of talent in our society.

Counselor success cannot realistically be measured by recording the proportion of individuals who successfuly implemented decisions reached in counseling. While recognizing the importance of the risk function, the counselor must also recognize that there are other important factors — including personal motivations of the individual and willingness of the individual to accept risk — which also need to be considered in evaluating the "goodness" of decisions reached in vocational guidance.

The commonly held perception that an individual should choose to do that in which he or she can be most successful should be rejected by guidance personnel. Everyone cannot "play it safe" — and not everyone wants to. Some students will elect the almost sure route to success, while others will elect the route involving the greater risk of failure. The function of the counselor is not to picture one decision as more desirable or more worthwhile than the other. Rather, the counselor's function is to help the individual understand fully and completely the alternatives with which he or she is faced.

As chapter 2 stressed, career guidance in the secondary school is only part of a broader process of career development. The process of career choice cannot be legitimately viewed as something which will or should occur only once in the lives of most individuals. It may be appropriate to counsel with students contemplating entry into high-level professional occupations in terms of career dimensions carrying through many years, but with a majority of high school students, such long-range career planning is neither appropriate nor defensible in terms of specific plans. If the school counselor can help the student formulate tentative plans for as much as from five to eight years after high school, that counselor should consider he or she has done well.

Because the counselor's influence may be limited in no way implies that it is not of vital importance. If the process of vocational choice is to be experienced for most students more than once after they leave the secondary school, it is essential that students learn a model for carrying through this process. The model provided by the counselor holds great potential for transfer value. Secondary school and immediate post-secondary experiences are powerful influences on self-perceptions of students. If the counselor can help a student begin movement toward entry into our occupational society in a positive and constructive manner, the student will be in a better position to continue such movement after he or she leaves the secondary school. The transfer value of knowledge regarding the process of occupational choice will be particularly important for those most likely to experience it more than once. With this segment of the high school population, the counselor's influence may be even more pervasive and vital than with those least likely to change occupations.

## The Counseling Significance of the Concept of Work

Several direct implications for change in counselor role and function are immediately apparent to those who recognize the centrality of work in the conceptualization of career education. Perhaps the most obvious is the degree to which the concept of work focuses on accomplishment — performance. For years, the research literature of guidance has clearly demonstrated that the best prediction of future performance is past performance. Yet typical student appraisal programs overlook the operational significance of this common research finding. For example, we know the best single predictor of future grades is past grades. Yet we continue to value various so-called "scholastic aptitude" tests more than we do grades. Holland (1972) has demonstrated that the best predictor of future vocational activities is to ask students about their vocational interests, not measure them with interest inventories. This, too, has had little apparent effect on practices.

One of career education's tenets is that, to a very large degree, a person is a product of his or her past accomplishments and experiences. When we ask an individual "Who are you?" the individual tells us primarily about his or her past accomplishments. True, they often begin answering the question by describing their characteristics — name, age, physical characteristics, interests, and values — because such descriptions help us differentiate one person from another; i.e., they serve as "identifiers." But this information does not help us greatly in our attempts to understand the person. We *predict* a person's behavior by the way in which we combine data concerning the person's characteristics. We *understand* another person only through behavioral expressions. The point is that in the past, we have put an undue emphasis on *describing* students by their characteristics and relatively little emphasis on *understanding* students through their *behavioral accomplishments*. Therefore, the emphasis on accomplishments which the word "work" brings to career education holds great potential for counselor use in better understanding those persons counselors seek to serve.

Further, an emphasis on accomplishment holds great potential for increasing meaningful student self-understanding. Educators have spent too much time *telling* students they are worthwhile and too little time letting students *discover* their own worth through successful accomplishments. Guidance literature is heavily burdened with normative approaches to increasing student self-understanding — with attempting to help students understand themselves through letting them know how they compare with others on some set of norms. The prime approach to self-understanding used in career education is one of helping the student see what he or she has accomplished, not in seeing what he or she has failed to accomplish. Success should be emphasized, not failure.

Finally, the emphasis on "work" found in career education holds great potential for helping individuals discover a personal meaning for work in their total life-styles. Too often counselors have spoken to students about "work" only in terms of the world of paid employment. Broader life-style implications, when discussed in conjunction with occupational decisions, have too often failed to consider either the desirability or the necessity many individuals have for work during part of their leisure time or in homemaking settings. This is particularly tragic for those individuals who find their roles in the world of paid employment dehumanizing, an involuntary set of activities the individual endures in order to gain enough economic benefits so that she or he can find some happiness when away from the place of paid employment.

Those who find themselves in such dehumanizing roles in the world of paid employment have no less a human need for work than does any other human being. A discussion of occupational goals devoid of discussion of the meaning and meaningfulness of work in the total life-style of the individual is incomplete indeed. It can only result in large numbers of individuals finding both their paid jobs and their total life-style largely lacking in significant personal meaning.

## The Counseling Significance of Action in Career Education

Career education is action centered and experience oriented. One who reads the career education literature must be impressed by the emphasis on such expressions as "hands on," "work experience," "field trips," and "work-study." Its emphasis on the project approach and on "learning by doing" has reminded many of the philosophy and the recommendations made many years ago by John Dewey. Insofar as this portion of career education is concerned, there is justification for the analogy.

This approach seems to have great appeal for the "now" generation of students. Rather than letting students talk about the future in abstract terms, career education allows them to experience what it would be like if, as adults, they were to engage in various forms of work. Because of the implications such activities hold for increasing student self-understanding and for decision making, it would seem worthwhile for counselors to "spend less time giving me sympathy and more time giving me help."

If counselors accept this challenge, they will spend relatively less time collecting and filing standardized test score data and relatively more time helping to design and use performance evaluation measures. They will spend less time talking with students about their need for part-time work and relatively more time helping students find it. They will spend relatively less time helping students gain admission to college and relatively more time helping students decide what they plan to do after they leave college. That is, going to college would not be a way of avoiding work but rather a way of preparing oneself for work. It would put a purpose in college attendance that, at present, is largely nonexistent for many of our so-called "college-bound" students.

In short, the action orientation of career education calls for more "action-oriented" counselors. If counselors change in this direction, they will be perceived by students in a more positive light. Maslow's needs structure has implications for change in counselor behavior. It may be that counselors have spent relatively too much time in attempting to meet student "self-actualization" needs and relatively too little time meeting their prior needs for "survival" and for "security."

## The Counseling Significance of Collaboration in Career Education

Career education emphasizes collaboration of efforts within the formal education system, between that system and the business-labor-industry-professional-government community, and between education and the home and family structure. Much of the rationale and organizational structure of career education is based on this basic principle of collaborative — not merely cooperative — effort. It is an emphasis that places high value on the total amount of help made available to any given individual and a relatively low value on assigning specific persons or organizations "credit" for such help.

This emphasis asks those teachers who have been called "academic" and those who have been called "vocational" to join together in making education, *as preparation for work*, both a prominent and a permanent goal of all who teach and of all who learn. It encourages a project approach to teaching that allows several teachers to be involved in a single project. It encourages the use of resource persons from the business-labor-industry-professional-government community in the classroom. It encourages the active involvement of parents in exposing youth to work values, in teaching good work habits, and in assisting youth in career decision making. It urges the classroom teacher to discuss the career implications of subject matter and to help students explore both the nature of various kinds of work and student aptitude for such work as regular classroom activities. In short, career education has proclaimed that career guidance, in its fullest sense, is the proper business and concern of the entire school staff, of the business-labor-industry-professional-government community, and of the home and family. By doing so, career education has denied that career guidance is the exclusive responsibility of the counselor.

Counselors can choose to react to this emphasis in a variety of ways. Some may very well react negatively by asserting that career guidance is one of the unique roles of the professional counselor. Others may react by pointing to the obvious lack of both skill and understanding in career guidance in many of those who work in career education. Still other counselors may profess to be disinterested in career guidance and busy themselves with other kinds of activities that they consider more properly to fit their role.

However, the most appropriate and productive role counselors can play is to enthusiastically endorse and enter into the collaborative efforts of the career education movement. Counselors should be actively seeking to help teachers discover and infuse career implications of their subject matter into the teaching-learning process. Counselors should be active participants in establishing and engaging in collaborative relationships with persons from the business-labor-industry-professional-government community. Counselors should seek to actively involve parents in the career decision-making process. In short, counselors will gain most if, instead of proclaiming career guidance as their unique role, they share their expertise in career guidance with all others involved in the career education program. Counselors will gain more status and acceptance by sharing their expertise than by "hoarding" it.

This would demand that counselors give a higher priority to career guidance than many now do. If this happens, both students and parents will be happier with counselors than many now are. It would demand that counselors spend relatively less time in their offices and relatively more time working directly with teachers. If this happens, counselors will be better accepted as members of the school staff. It will demand that counselors spend relatively more time outside the schoolbuilding interacting with parents and with members of the business-labor-industry-professional-government community. If this happens, students will receive more and better career guidance than if the counselor tries to be the primary person helping students in career decisions.

Career education's call for a collaborative emphasis holds high potential for increasing both the acceptability and the effectiveness of the professional counselor.

Those counselors who may be inclined to claim the career education movement as their own have missed the basic point of collaboration inherent in the career education concept. True, if career education is viewed as a *process* consisting of career awareness, exploration, decision making, preparation, entry and progression, then career education and career guidance have much in common. But when it is viewed as a collaborative *program effort,* they do not. Career development, like vocational education, is properly viewed as one programmatic component of career education. Career education is no more a simple extension of what has been known as career development than it is of what has been known as vocational education.

The days of educational isolationism are gone. Relationships between education and the larger society become closer each year. The assumption that the best way to ready students for the real world is to lock them up inside a schoolbuilding and keep them away from that world is an anachronism. That being the case, it is hoped the high school counselor will become part of the career education movement. The tasks discussed here are essential. Someone must do them. We believe it to be a logical extension of counselor role and findings.

The challenge of change in the career aspects of guidance are particularly great in the senior high school setting. This is true for many reasons, among which are:

(1) The general lack of integration of vocational education with the remainder of the curriculum

(2) The general misconception that senior high school students should choose between "going to college" and "going to work"

(3) The mistaken notion that career and vocational education in the senior high school is for students who cannot be admitted to college

(4) The fallacy that those contemplating college need not worry about career decision making

(5) The mistaken assumption that the prime purpose of the senior high school is preparing students for entry into college

The result of these mistakes has been a lack of true commitment to career education and to the career aspects of guidance. This has unfairly handicapped all secondary school students. In school after school, students are not really choosing college education or vocational education or a job. Instead, they are going to college because it is expected of them, settling for vocational education when they find discouragement in their attempts to participate in other parts of the total school curriculum, dropping out, or accepting whatever accidental sequences of jobs confronts them.

### Suggested Counselor Roles in Career Education

Bypassing the more philosophical arguments which have always separated counselors in pursuit of their own role, career educators, and particularly the counselors among them, have tended to focus directly upon the practical assistance counselors could give the career education process.

### Official Declarations

Counselor roles in career education have been the subject of policy declarations by the U.S. Office of Education and the American Personnel and Guidance Association. Opinions are also available from counselors with substantial experience in career education.

#### United States Office of Education

The official USOE policy paper, "An Introduction to Career Education," lists the following roles and functions for counseling and guidance personnel:

(1) Help classroom teachers implement career education in the classroom

(2) Serve, usually with other educational personnel, as liaison between the school and the business-industry-labor community

(3) Serve, usually with other educational personnel, in implementing career education concepts within the home and family structure

(4) Help students in the total career development process, including the making and implementation of career decisions

(5) Participate in part-time and full-time job placement programs and in followup studies of former students

*American Personnel and Guidance Association*

At its December 12–14, 1974, Board of Directors meeting, APGA adopted a policy statement titled "Career Guidance: Role and Functions of Counseling and Guidance Practitioners in Career Education." The following summary of both leadership and participatory functions for counselors in career education has been extracted from this much more comprehensive APGA policy statement:

### Leadership Functions

(1) Provide leadership in the identification and programmatic implementation of individual career development tasks

(2) Provide leadership in the identification, classification, and use of self, educational, and occupational information

(3) Provide leadership in the assimilation and application of career decision-making methods and materials

(4) Provide leadership in eliminating the influence of both racism and sexism as cultural restrictors of opportunities available to minority persons and to females

(5) Provide leadership in expanding the variety and appropriateness of assessment devices and procedures required for sound personal, educational, and occupational decision making

(6) Provide leadership in emphasizing the importance of and carrying out the functions of career counseling

### Participatory Functions

(1) Serving as liaison between the educational and community resource groups

(2) Conducting career guidance needs assessment surveys

(3) Conducting follow-up, follow-through, and job adjustment activities

(4) Organizing and operating part-time and full-time educational, occupational, and job placement programs

(5) Participating in curriculum revision

(6) Participating in efforts to involve the home and family in career education

(7) Participating in efforts to monitor and assess operations and communicating the results of those activities to other practitioners and clientele, as appropriate

Following this listing, the APGA policy statement closes with a strong set of implications for change in the counseling and guidance movement related to career education and with equally strong statements of support for career education as a total effort.

### School Counselors Now Participating in Career Education

During the USOE-sponsored seminar on "School Counselors and Career Education" held at the Ohio State University during the fall of 1975, the twelve experienced school counselors who served as seminar members "brainstormed" a number of ideas related to possible counselor roles and functions in career education. The listing they produced has been organized under a number of descriptive categories:

**Teaching Functions Possible for Counselors in Career Education**

(1) Teach self-awareness and socialization skills
(2) Teach career decision making and values clarification
(3) Teach students job getting, holding, and seeking skills

**Working with Teachers in Career Education**

(1) Assist teachers in relating subjects to careers
(2) Help teachers in career awareness activities in classes
(3) Provide and disseminate career education materials to teachers — along with counselor evaluation of the materials
(4) Invent and provide teachers with lists of creative career education activities they can try out in classes
(5) Construct homemade career education materials (film strips, slide tape presentations, and so forth) for teacher use in classes
(6) Serve as role models and in-service trainers of teachers who are interested in teaching decision making and values clarification
(7) Provide in-service education to teachers who want to use the group process
(8) Build and provide teachers a resource-person list for use as persons to be invited to classrooms
(9) Stimulate interaction between academic and vocational teachers

### Leadership Functions in Career Education

(1) Assist in coordination and implementation of career education

(2) Get principal to approve a counselor career education role plan for the year

(3) Assist administrators in understanding career education concepts

(4) Explain career education to parents — and to the broader community

(5) Manage the scope and sequence aspects of career education.

(6) Identify teachers ready for and amenable to career education in-service training

(7) Organize and manage a "teacher-adviser" system for career education

### Counselor Role in Career Education Curriculum Development

(1) Serve on total curriculum committee for the school

(2) Serve on departmental curriculum committees (to represent student needs)

(3) Reflect student needs to all curriculum planners

### Counselor Role in Evaluation of Career Education

(1) Collect self report data (students, teachers, administrators)

(2) Keep *process* records of counselor involvement in career education

(3) Participate in development of career education evaluation instruments and their selection from other sources

(4) Interpret career education evaluation findings

(5) Follow through with recommendations based on evaluation results

### Working Directly with Students in Career Education*

(1) Design and implement a work exploration program

(2) Place students in part-time work (paid and unpaid) while they are in high school

(3) Assist students in educational planning

(4) Serve as coordinator and implementer of career education field trips

---

*Other than teaching.

(5) Conduct student needs assessments for career education

(6) Administer student tests (aptitude, interest, values) needed in career education

(7) Establish and operate career education resource centers (for use by both students and by teachers)

When the three lists of possible school counselor role and function in career education are compared, their similarities are much more apparent than their differences. The group of experienced counselors, who have been actively involved in career education, formulated, as might be expected, the longest and most comprehensive list.

### Providing Professional Leadership for Career Education

Counselors experienced in career education acknowledge that they must play a leadership role, but seem to reject a connotation that they should be perceived as the "coordinators of career education." Instead, they would much prefer to think of themselves as the "orchestrators" of career education at the building level.

The difference between being perceived as a "coordinator," as opposed to an "orchestrator," is important to counselor practitioners. In general, it is the difference between one who has the "power of position" as opposed to one who has the "power of persuasion." Experienced counselors seem to generally agree that the "power of position," at the building level, cannot and should not be taken from the principal. They see that the effective implementation of career education will at times demand that teachers be actively encouraged — including being rewarded — for infusing a career education emphasis into the teaching-learning process. Counselors see meaningful teacher "rewards" coming much more often and much more easily if the building principal is responsible for operating the reward system.

While counselors generally agree that no one — including the building principal — can effectively implement career education through "ordering" teachers to participate, they also agree that the positive encouragement of building principals is a powerful and a needed force in effective implementation of career education. School counselors like to think of themselves as "teachers of teachers" for career education and as "helpers of teachers" in career education, but they resist a view that asks them to be the teachers' "boss."

Given this general view, what specific leadership roles do counselors who are experienced in career education believe the counselor should assume? First, there seems general consensus that the counselor should be concerned about scope and sequence problems in career education. Specifically, counselors are concerned that *some* scope and sequence plan be operating, and that the plan itself is consistent with what is known about the psychology of career development. It is important that career awareness and exploration be emphasized above the making of "final" occupational choices.

Those counselors who work on a regular basis with teachers in career education have multiple opportunities to discover and avoid unnecessary overlapping of and duplication in career education activities, as well as in the use of specific career education materials. Because counselors dedicated to career education may find themselves in more classrooms more often than any other staff member in the school, this is a natural leadership role to be played.

A second important, and very natural, career education leadership role for counselors lies in the identification and encouragement of teachers amenable to infusing career education concepts and approaches into the teaching-learning process. Experienced counselors seemed to be in general agreement with the "15-70-15" principle as an operational reality in most schools. That principle holds that, among any teaching faculty, about 15 percent of teachers, once a valid new idea is introduced, will find ways of incorporating it in their classrooms. A second 15 percent will ignore the new idea forever, but the remaining 70 percent are susceptible to change, given the proper role models and encouragement. Counselors now working in career education believe they can perform a valuable leadership function through encouraging the "turned on" 15 percent to share their ideas and enthusiasm with the 70 percent of "possible converts."

A third major leadership role possible for counselors to play in career education centers round using counselor background and expertise for purposes of conducting student needs assessments, identifying appropriate evaluation measures, and assistance in conducting and interpreting results of evaluations of effectiveness for career education. By and large, counselors have both more interest and more professional background in student appraisal procedures and in evaluation than do most other faculty members. By using such expertise for these purposes, counselors can provide a leadership role helpful in keeping the entire career education effort squarely centered about student needs.

Finally, a fourth very important leadership role for senior high school counselors in career education is participation in the "teacher-adviser" system. This system calls for selected teachers (usually at least one from each major department) to be assigned as teacher-advisers to students for at least one period per day. Their major function is to help students consider career options growing out of specialization in a given subject matter area. In effect, the teacher-adviser serves as a career counselor for students interested in careers related to particular subjects.

Given the right background, knowledge, interest, and commitment on the part of teachers, the teacher-adviser idea makes good sense in career education. The trick is to make sure teachers possess such competencies. The counselor role consists of providing teacher-advisers with appropriate information as well as in-service training. It may also include organization of topics for those who hold group sessions with students.

### Helping Teachers in Career Education

Experienced school counselors working in career education seem to feel that counselor-teacher relationships have improved because of the ways they have found to work with teachers as part of the collaborative career education effort. They seem to be in equally strong agreement that, if this kind of change in counselor role is to take place, it will probably be initiated by counselors, not by teachers. These roles differ from "leadership" roles in that they are most effective if done on a "sharing" rather than on a "showing" or "telling" basis. Also, these roles seem to be most effectively performed on a one-to-one relationship between counselor and teacher, not as a total group impact.

These counselors see themselves as sources and suppliers of innovative and creative ideas to teachers seeking to infuse a career education emphasis into the total teaching-learning process. Not that teachers are not capable of inventing such ideas for themselves. On the contrary, many of the innovative ideas counselors have put into teacher manuals are ones they have seen creative teachers using. However a *majority* of teachers, while capable of "inventing" career education activities for themselves, seems to need some "starter ideas" at the beginning; and the counselor working with many teachers is a natural communication link among teachers who may have few opportunities for exchange of ideas during the school day.

A second major way counselors see themselves as being helpful to teachers in career education is through serving, either alone or with the teacher, in actual classes being conducted at school to help provide occupational information, work values, and decision-making skills, particularly when work simulation is involved.

Third, counselors should be involved in helping classroom teachers emphasize career implications of their subject matter to students, including (1) counselor involvement in basic policy decisions regarding the way in which the general nature of the occupational world is to be pictured in career education, and (2) efforts to actually help teachers become familiar with the career implications of their subject matter. Many classroom teachers seem willing to incorporate career education into their teaching, but they do not know what the career implications of their subject matter are. The counselor can do much to provide teachers with data that will help them become aware of careers that require a background in their subject matter area. This can best be done by combining the expertise of the counselor in systems of occupational classification with the expertise of classroom teachers in their subject matter areas. Of course, this requires counselors to devote considerable time to working with teachers both in groups and on an individual basis.

Fourth, experienced counselors also see themselves as helpful to teachers in serving as a source of names of potential resource persons from the business-labor-industry community who are willing to come into the classroom and discuss their careers with students. This role, of course, depends upon the counselors being in systematic contact with members of that community.

A fifth way experienced counselors see themselves as being helpful to teachers in career education is through stimulating interaction between academic and vocational education teachers at the senior high school level. Career education seeks no fusion of these two kinds of program offerings, but it does seek a fusion of purpose in encouraging both academic and vocational education teachers to emphasize education, as preparation for both paid and unpaid work. By emphasizing this commonality of purpose, counselors can be effective facilitators of cooperative efforts between vocational education and academic teachers. Through emphasizing both the need for job-specific and for adaptability skills, they can also help both kinds of teachers better understand and appreciate the contributions each makes in emphasizing education as preparation for work.

## Working Directly with Students in Career Education

All professionals in career education seem to feel that they have important contributions to make in terms of their direct work with students. First, and most important as well as most obvious, is direct counseling with students. The career education literature is replete with examples of practices in the areas of career awareness, career exploration, values clarification, and career decision. If these functions, performed by a wide variety of persons, are to take place beginning early in the elementary school and continuing throughout public education, it is apparent that at some point in time students will logically be expected to use the skills and knowledge they have acquired in making career decisions.

At such points, whether these decisions are tentative or more specifically action oriented, there is a great need for high-quality, professional counseling. While career education calls for a variety of types of persons to be involved in the career guidance process, none can or should take the place of the professional counselor. One of the potential dangers of counselor involvement in comprehensive career education efforts is that some such activity may take place at the expense of time required for performing the professional counseling function. This must not be.

Second, experienced counselors also become involved directly in the teaching of students, either in the form of specific units or, at times, in the form of specific courses assigned to counselors. In some instances this has been built into the organizational framework for career education and simply assigned as a required counselor role. Conceptualizers of career education argue that it should be infused into existing courses, not added as a new course in the curriculum. This does not mean that career education units cannot be a part of existing courses, nor that career education lessons cannot occur frequently in all kinds of courses. Counselors experienced in career education report that they are frequently expected to teach such "units" or "lessons."

Third, some counselors working in career education report themselves actively engaged in job placement involving both part-time work experience activities and full-time job placement for students leaving the secondary school. The extent to which counselors in general will be asked to accept such responsibilities will depend heavily on the stance vocational educators in the school system take and, in addition, on whether or not the school system employs "work experience coordinators" in addition to "counselors." At present, there exist few work experience coordinators who do not function to some extent as counselors, but there are many "counselors" who apparently do not see themselves as work experience coordinators. If counselors experienced in career education are right, this will increasingly become a role counselors are asked to play.

Fourth, and finally, counselors experienced in career education report themselves deeply involved in field trip experiences for students. Teachers appear happy to turn over to school counselors the responsibility for organizing and conducting student field trips in the business-labor-industry community. On the whole, experienced counselors working in career education seem to be urging that this not become a common pattern. Few object to participating, along with teachers, in organizing and making student field trips. It is a valuable way of helping counselors make contacts with the broader community, to build a list of resource persons for career guidance, and to observe students as they participate in career awareness and career exploration activities. At the same time, experienced counselors seem to feel strongly that classroom teachers need this exposure as well. They seem to see this as a participatory, but not as an exclusive, function of the counselor.

### *Helping to Emphasize Vocational Skills Training*

The third major counselor function involves working with classroom teachers who are ignorant of the career education movement, are reluctant participants in it, or are active opponents of career education.

### *Helping to Emphasize Vocational Skills Training*

Counselors must be both willing and able to help emphasize vocational skills training in formal education. This involves three major counselor functions. The first is to influence curriculum change. It is safe to say that all counselors have worked with students who have need of some kind of vocational skills training. Yet in most high schools, vocational education programs are limited in both scope and availability, and neither the variety nor the flexibility in scheduling is such that the programs really meet student needs. As an individual concerned with the needs of all students, the counselor must speak out to advocate more vocational education, at more levels, and with greater variety. Vocational education is a proper concern of the counselor.

Second, counselors should become much better acquainted than most are today with the nature and variety of vocational education opportunities, including opportunities at the post-secondary level. It is important that counselors be able to picture such opportunities to students in ways that will truly enable them to choose vocational education if they are inclined to do so. This means that counselors and students must rid themselves of the false perception of vocational education as an alternative for those who cannot succeed in the college preparatory curriculum of the high school or in the four-year college.

The goal is to become at least as competent in helping students choose vocational education as in helping students choose educational offerings leading toward the college degree.

Third, counselors have a major role to play in helping "academic" teachers recognize that they, too, are engaged in vocational skills training. Too many have operated for too long as though they have no responsibilities in this area.

### Helping to Involve the Business-Labor-Industry Community

The business-labor-industry community contributes to the goals of career education in two major ways. First, it contributes by serving as a setting for work experience, work study, and work observation opportunities for students. Second, it assists students in making successful transitions from school to work. Thus if career education is to work, someone in the school must serve as liaison between the school system and the business-labor-industry community. This is a duty that logically could be assumed by professional school counselors, but even if counselors do not assume direct responsibility for these duties, they can hardly avoid involvement as they counsel students regarding various work experience programs and job placement. The next chapter outlines approaches for the high school to take in making use of these and other community resources.

Also, since counselors are frequently criticized for lacking recent significant experience in the world of work outside education, the opportunity to work with the business-labor-industry community offers potential for building a more favorable image for the counselor in the total community.

Most importantly, the professional counselor must accept some responsibility for helping students implement decisions they make in the counseling interview. The counselor's job is not completed if he or she considers responsibility ended at the point when the student has formulated a plan. The counselor must participate in the total program of transition from school to work, including job placement. Only then will career education achieve its full potential.

## Helping the Home and Family Participate

The home and family component of career education is viewed in three major segments: (1) teaching the values of the home, (2) teaching consumer education in the home, and (3) changing parental attitudes in ways that will support the goals of career education. Although some counselors doubtless will be working in all three tasks, the one that should be common to all counselors is that of working with parental attitudes. Counselors frequently find themselves hampered in their efforts to help students by parents who insist that their children go to college, even when students express interest in vocational school or technical school or occupational education in a community college. Rather than simply accepting this attitude on the part of parents, counselors must become active agents in changing it in ways that more accurately reflect the kind of occupational society now existing in the United States.

## Practical Problems Facing Counselors
## in Career Education

Those counselors with substantial experience in career education identify a number of practical problems which the high school counselor should anticipate. Many experienced counselors now actively engaged in career education reported that at some point in time after a career education effort has been initiated for classroom teachers they had gone to teachers and offered to help them infuse career education into their classroom activities.

The response of many teachers has been in effect to say, "Who needs you now? I'm doing just fine without your help." And the truth is, they may be. On the other hand, most teachers could probably benefit from counselor assistance. Proper role identification function for the counselor may be difficult to put into practice for a number of reasons: first, initial career education efforts were heavily influenced by federal vocational education funds. This meant that vocational educators, in many communities, assumed major leadership roles in career educa-

tion program development and addressed their attention to
the need for change among classroom teachers. It was almost
as though it was assumed that academic teachers, not counselors or vocational educators, were the ones that had to change
if career education was to be successful.

Second, many school counselors contributed to this
strategic error by assuming, either implicitly or explicitly, that
career education represented nothing more than an extension
of career development which, as counselors, they had been
doing all along. That is, like many vocational educators, they
also assumed that it was only academic teachers who had to
change.

Third, as a result, in many school systems, the major
emphasis on in-service education in career education was
placed on academic teachers. True, school counselors were often
included in such in-service activities, but the primary emphasis
was upon helping teachers, not counselors, change. Worse yet,
in school after school, when intensive discussions were held
concerning the nature and implications of career education,
only classroom teachers were involved. As a result, in many
schools across the country, teachers are more knowledgeable
about career education than are counselors.

To overcome this problem, counselors experienced in
career education have three major recommendations for other
counselors who have now decided they want to play an active
leadership role in this effort: (1) study career education concepts
in sufficient detail to understand how and in what ways they
represent more than a simple extension of career development
concepts, (2) recognize that career education calls for changes
in counselor role and function as well as changes in teachers,
and (3) take the initiative in working with teachers who are
already involved in career education. In doing so, the counselor
will learn from that minority of teachers who are already
"turned on" and operating in career education. They can then
use what is learned from them in efforts to "turn on" other
teachers in your school.

## The Counselor as a Teacher

As noted above, counselors experienced in career education
report that they frequently find themselves in classrooms

actively interacting with students in the teaching-learning process. Sometimes this involves team teaching with a classroom teacher. At other times it involves teaching only one lesson, or one series of lessons, within a unit or a course. At still other times it involves counselors being assigned as *the* teacher of a particular course. The problem, of course, is how counselors can be effective role models for both teachers and students as they perform the teaching function.

The problem is complicated by a conscious return to an emphasis on quality of instruction on the part of many of today's public schoolteachers. In recent years there has been an important resurgence of efforts by classroom teachers to improve the quality of instruction. Teachers are increasingly concerned about such matters as lesson objectives, activities, the use of resource persons and materials, and evaluating student outcomes from instruction. Counselors who offer to teach one or more class periods (while the regular teacher is in the room) must be aware of and able to function effectively and deal within this emphasis.

The problem of quality, in the teaching-learning process, is obviously much more complicated than the substantive content to be taught. Rather, it deals with the whole question of how that content is organized, presented, made meaningful, and assimilated by students. For example, it is not enough to point out that the counselor knows more about "values clarification" or "decision making" than the teacher. Unless the counselor is able to present the substantive content in ways consistent with the teachers' standards of excellence, the final effect may be more negative than positive. If the counselor is to have influence with teachers, it is imperative that the counselor be a good teacher.

Trends in school counselor certification over the last twenty years have worked against this emphasis. In some states, the former requirement that school counselors possess both a teaching certificate and demonstrate successful teaching experience has been completely removed from counselor certification requirements. Therefore, when counselors either volunteer or are asked to perform in a classroom, they must spend considerable time in preparation with the regular teacher of that class. The counselor should not use an approach that is inconsistent with that being used by the teacher. There is nothing wrong — and a great deal right — about recognizing the teacher as a consultant to the counselor, as well as recognizing the counselor as a consultant to the teacher. Both have much to learn from each other if career education is to be effective for students.

### The "Self" versus "Careers" Dilemma

One very popular conceptual model for career education pictures the major dimensions of career education represented by two words: "self" and "careers." There is always the danger that some school counselors will tend to regard "self" as their major emphasis while leaving "careers" to others. This is a "cop out." It relates to the trend in recent years to insert a psychological emphasis into counselor education programs and to play down the career guidance function. This trend appears to be reversing, but many of today's school counselors are products of counselor education programs that have such an emphasis. These counselors must recognize that they have been given a deficient educational background. There is no way a counselor can become involved as a *collaborative* member of a career education team if all the counselor can do is *cooperate* by supplying expertise in only one part of the career education equation.

A second factor has been the unwillingness, or inability, of many school counselors to recognize the profound implications for student appraisal procedures and for increasing student self-understanding which the action orientation of career education contains with its emphasis on the humanistic aspects of "work." The emphasis within career education on helping students discover both who and why they are in terms of what they have been and are able to accomplish is consistent, not contradictory, to much of the psychological education that many of today's school counselors have received. True, it does require some translation, but not a completely different set of understandings.

Third, it is essential that school counselors recognize that the word "career" in the term "career education" includes unpaid work as well as the entire world of paid employment.

As such, it includes an emphasis on lifelong learning, on volunteerism, on the wise and productive use of leisure time, and on social and occupational problems in our society that are associated with both racism and sexism. The school counselor who seeks to avoid becoming involved with the "career" part of "career education," thinking it has only to do with the world of paid employment, has missed a central part of its meaning.

Counselors experienced in career education appear unanimous in their plea for other school counselors to embrace both the "self" and the "careers" dimensions of career education as mutually important and supportive.

### Clerks or Consultants?

Many school counselors now involved in career education have reported themselves very active in supplying teachers with career information, with identifying and recruiting resource persons from the broader community to serve in career education, and with participating in organizing and conducting student field trips as part of the career education effort. As they do these kinds of things, the practical problem they face is whether they are functioning as clerical or subprofessional personnel or as professional consultants to career education. It will be no favor to either counselors or to career education if a different kind of clerical activity is substituted for the clerical record-keeping function that many of today's school counselors are already expected to perform.

This provision of information and materials needs supplementation in many ways that require the professional competence of the counselor as a consultant, not as a clerk. For instance, as career information is transmitted from counselor to teacher, it should include an evaluation of the worth, along with a set of suggestions, for proper use of the material. If the information is drawn from national sources, cautions regarding its local applicability are in order. If, on the other hand, the material has been locally generated through counselor effort, an interpretation of both the positive and the negative aspects of the material should be included.

Many classroom teachers need much more than the name of a career field, or a listing of occupations contained within that field, if they are to successfully infuse career material into their lesson plans. Counselors can, and should, help teachers understand careers — and their possible relationship to subject matter — in ways that go beyond the material itself. This kind of "bridging" function is one that, if performed well, will make it clear that the counselor is more than a "transmitter of information."

Apparently many teachers have been inclined to encourage counselors to assume responsibility for organizing and conducting field trips with the contention that the counselor can do this because she or he "doesn't have classes to teach." Of course, this problem is not too difficult to solve in those situations where an entire class is to be involved in a field trip. At such times, the teacher doesn't have a class to teach. By arranging such field trips in ways that allow the teacher to use a preparation period as well as a class period, teachers as well as counselors can accompany students on field trips. Many advantages for career education occur if the classroom teacher participates in the field trip, not the least of which is the new knowledge and additional motivation accruing to the teacher. Some counselors have found it desirable to teach the teacher's next period class so that the teacher can conduct the entire field trip.

A different problem arises in the increasingly popular career education practice of small group field trips. In such situations, the teacher obviously cannot accompany those students and leave the rest of the class sitting by themselves. Experienced counselors recommend that this is an instance where paraprofessional personnel and parents may make valuable contributions. Of course, the counselor will often be present, but it does not seem wise to make the mandatory presence of the school counselor a standard part of such field trips. The counselor's time is better spent in preliminary and in follow-up activities with both teachers and the community.

The prime recommendation counselors experienced in career education have for other school counselors is that they: (1) never provide information to teachers without some offer to explain or interpret such information, (2) agree to participate in field trips, but refuse to take total responsibility for them, and (3) continue to seek ways to be useful without being "used" to perform functions that could be done as well or better either by clerical or by support personnel.

## Career Education Resource Center

As career education efforts move toward maturity, it is becoming increasingly obvious that it will be impractical to place either full-time career education coordinators or career education resource centers in a school system at the building level. Yet both are needed for a truly quality career education effort. As a result, a career education coordinator for the school system is becoming more popular. So too is the concept of providing — somewhere within the community — a career education resource center designed to serve both currently enrolled students and out-of-school youth and adults. Such centers typically include as staff members professional specialists in career guidance, counseling, placement, and follow-up.

However, with professional guidance personnel in such centers, school counselors may attempt to use them as an excuse to avoid restructuring their duties to include a substantial emphasis on career guidance. A central systemwide career education resource center can operate in either of the following ways: (1) as a central physical facility to which students from throughout the school system are sent when in need of career guidance and counseling, or (2) as a central clearinghouse serving each school in the system, but with the basic career guidance function being decentralized in each school. However, students cannot be "dissected" in terms of career guidance problems as opposed to other kinds of problems. If today's school counselors are to help teachers effectively in career education, they must acquire a greater degree of competence in career guidance, counseling, placement, and follow-up. For all of these reasons, the concept of the career education resource center serving as a "clearinghouse" for schools within a given community is much preferred over such a center regarded as a place to which students with career guidance problems are to be referred.

### *Implications for Change in the Personnel and Guidance Movement*

The counselor role outlined above calls for significant behavioral changes on the part of professionals in the personnel and guidance field. Among these, the following are of greatest significance:

(1) A change toward emphasizing the counselor as a member of the career education team and away from an emphasis on the counselor as an isolated professional worker

(2) A change away from viewing the counselor as one who functions primarily within the physical framework of formal education and toward greater counselor involvement in the business-labor-industry community and in the home and family structure

(3) A change toward emphasizing career guidance in life-style terms and away from the narrowness of functioning that is inherent in the occupational guidance emphasis of the past

(4) A change toward emphasizing the counselor as a major influence on curriculum change and away from a view of the counselor as one who helps students adjust to the existing curriculum

(5) A change toward using the concept of work as a means of helping students acquire self-understanding and personal meaningfulness and away from viewing self-concept and self-actualization in more psychotherapeutic orientations

(6) A change toward helping others use some of the expertise and understandings developed by the personnel and guidance movement and away from attempting to make such data the exclusive province of the counselor

(7) A change toward counselor activity and involvement in the broader environment and away from an emphasis

on the counselor interacting with students in a counseling office as the single most important counselor
function to be performed

### Basic Competencies Required by Counselors

If counselors are to accomplish the functions outlined
above, they will require certain competencies, some of which
they usually possess at the present time and some of which they
will have to acquire. Active counselors will want to take the
initiative in expanding their own competencies through education, self-improvement, in-service programs, and other means.
However, in order to ensure these basic competencies in future
counselors, we advocate extensive restructuring in counselor
education programs. That restructuring should include training calculated to provide at least the following twenty
competencies:

(1) Competency in taking occupational and career information, regardless of the system used in presenting
it, and placing all of it into a comprehensive picture
of our occupational society consistent with the philosophy and organizational structure of any given career
education program

(2) Competency in helping teachers discover and become
knowledgeable about the career implications of their
subject matter

(3) Competency in helping classroom teachers devise,
formulate, and execute action plans for infusing career
implications of their subject matter into lesson plans

(4) Competency in helping teachers, school administrators,
curriculum specialists, parents, and the general public
understand the nature, mission, and goals of the career
education movement

(5) Competency in helping students view vocational education opportunities at the secondary school level as
differing in kind from other educational opportunities

available, to a degree that students will be able to make reasoned choices from among all such possible opportunities

(6) Competency in helping secondary school students view various forms of post-high school educational opportunities (including college, occupational education, on-the-job training, apprenticeship, and the armed forces) as differing in kind, to a degree that students will be able to make reasoned choices from among all such possible opportunities

(7) Competency in using the resources of the business-labor-industry community as aids to students in the career exploration and decision-making processes

(8) Competency in using the resources of the total community in helping all secondary school students (who desire to do so) engage in work experience and work-study programs

(9) Competency in using the resources of the business-labor-industry community and the public employment service in establishing and operating a part-time job placement program for secondary school students and a full-time job placement program for school leavers

(10) Competency in helping students, both individually and in groups, engage in the career decision-making process to a degree consistent with students' levels of career development

(11) Competency in helping students, both individually and in groups, become aware of and further develop work values as part of their personal value systems

(12) Competency in helping students, both individually and in groups, better understand their aptitudes and career interests through the use of both tests and nontesting student appraisal procedures

(13) Competencies in career counseling, occupational counseling, and job counseling to a degree that both counselor and client recognize the clear and distinct

differences existing among these three possible counseling topics

(14) Competency in using computerized career counseling systems, including those concerned with personal assessment, career information, job data banks, educational data banks, and career counseling

(15) Competency in providing data to parents in such a form and in such a way that parents have a clear and accurate understanding and acceptance of various kinds of educational and career opportunities that can be expected to be available to their children

(16) Competency in communicating career guidance needs (both educational and occupational) of students to curriculum experts and educational decision makers in ways that form a significant portion of the base data required for possible changes in curricular offerings that should be made available to youth

(17) Competency in providing data to those interested in combining racism and sexism in our educational society in ways that will make both educational and career opportunities more open and available to all youth, regardless of race or sex

(18) Competency in using the services and talents of support personnel in career guidance

(19) Competency in working with counselors from other settings in providing continuing career guidance services to both in-school and out-of-school youth and adults in the community

(20) Competency in establishing sound working relationships with community groups (such as the local chamber of commerce, service clubs, labor unions, and the like) who are interested in and concerned about career guidance and counseling

### Change in Counselor Attitudes

One final note of caution would seem to be in order. It is hoped that no one will set about to initiate any plan of action designed to provide counselors with some or all of these competencies — or with any others — until and unless the even harder problems of counselor attitudes and values are considered. Neither of these topics has been discussed here because attitudes and values are not properly seen as "competencies." Yet they will determine not only readiness for acquiring competencies, but the practical likelihood of having such competencies put to effective use in ways that provide concrete contributions to the career education movement. It is fruitless to embark on any sizable effort aimed at increasing counselor competencies unless simultaneous attention is paid to questions of counselor attitudes and personal value systems.

What we must strive for — in both counseling and career education — is a blend of understanding and knowledge, of *why* something needs to be done and *how* it can be done in a specific situation. If school counseling is to become a true profession, then counselors must learn to become professionally responsible — to take that which they have learned and make thoughtful, rational, and innovative applications to the school and community setting in which they are employed.

We feel strongly that one positive move in this direction is for the high school counselor to accept a primary role (or roles) in career education.

### *Summary*

It should be evident from the foregoing that proponents of career education regard the school counselor as an important — indeed, vital — participant in any career education activity, particularly at the high school level. However, this participation will require that counselors broaden their own concept of responsibility to include such things as greater participation in school curriculum planning, more involvement with students in the classroom as well as in other settings, and increased activity outside the school to build relationships with the business-labor-industrial community. Obviously, in order to accept these new responsibilities, some of the traditional duties of counselors will have to be eliminated or redefined.

Career education will make it necessary for counselors to acquire greater knowledge of such things as the labor market, decision making, career development, job placement, occupation classification systems, and job training information systems. In turn, this new thrust will doubtless necessitate rather extensive changes in the nation's counselor education program.

The goals and principles of career education are not far removed from the traditional goals of the school counselor. In career education these traditional goals are expanded to incorporate all of education, from the academic classroom to the vocational education lab to the counselor's office. The counselor can choose to play an important role in the design, planning, and implementation of career education activities. We very much hope that most will choose to do so.

### References

Hansen, Lorraine. *New Counselor Role in Career Development.* 1972.

Herr, Edwin L.; and Cramer, Stanley H. *Vocational Guidance and Career Development in the Schools: Toward a Systems Approach.* New York: Houghton-Mifflin. 1972.

Hoyt, Kenneth B.; *et al. Career Education and the Elementary School Teacher.* Salt Lake City: Olympus Publishing Company. 1973.

_____. *Career Education: What It Is and How to Do It.* Salt Lake City: Olympus Publishing Company. 1974.

Meyer, Robert S. "Career Education: An Opportunity for Counselors and Teachers to Work Together." *Guidelines for Pupil Services* (May 1973), vol. II, no. 3.

Super, Donald E. "A Theory of Vocational Development." *American Psychologist* (1953), vol. 8.

# 12

# Community
# Resources

It has been a basic concept from the beginning that career education cannot occur in the school alone. The classroom is an efficient but antiseptic learning environment. To be shut off from the world is not the best way to learn about the world. Figure 5 which is drawn from the original *Career Education: Handbook for Implementation* (U.S. Office of Education, 1972) illustrates the need for collaboration between the school and the community in pursuing the goals of career education. This chapter is designed to alert the high school career educator to the types of resources available in most communities and to suggest ways of making use of them.

### The Principle of Collaboration in Career Education

The term "collaboration" is used advisedly in relation to the community role in career education. Collaboration implies that the parties involved share responsibility and authority for policies, decisions, and actions contributing to the success (or lack of success) of the total effort. To "cooperate" with another agency or organization, on the other hand, carries

391

no implication that one either can, or should, affect the policies or operational practices of the others.

The concept of collaboration can be threatening and distasteful to many. Why should a local school board, a super-intendent, or a building principal listen to suggestions from the business-labor-industry community? Why should the president of a local corporation consider changing company policies, based on suggestions made by educators? Why should an established community organization, such as, for example, the Boy Scouts of America, listen to suggestions from the schools for changing its operational programs? Natural responses are, "They don't understand what we are up against," or "What we do is none of their business." It is this notion that career education seeks to eradicate through a collaborative community effort. To the extent that the schools and other community institutions share a common concern for helping youth and adults solve problems of education-work relationships, what each contributes to the solution of such problems becomes the "business" of all. The principle of collaboration calls for all relevant institutions to center their primary concern round the question, "How much help can be made available to the individual?" not round the question, "How much credit can we get for helping?"

## Collaboration: Issues and Responses

Collaboration among community resources concerned with the lifelong career success of current high school students requires answers to each of a number of operational questions such as:

(1) How are community resource people to be identified for the classroom?

(2) What procedures will be used for contacting community resource people? Who is to initiate the contact?

(3) Who arranges for field trips for students? For faculty members?

(4) How is agreement to be reached on development and selection of career education materials for use in the classroom?

(5) What emphasis should be placed on paid as opposed to unpaid work experience for students?

(6) Who evaluates the effectiveness of resource people in the classroom? How are such evaluations to be carried out? To whom are they reported?

(7) Who evaluates the effectiveness of student field trips into the community? Who conducts such evaluations? To whom are results reported?

(8) How should interested community agencies and organizations contact school officials with respect to career education–related activities?

(9) Under what arrangements should summer work experience opportunities for faculty members be arranged? What restrictions should be in place?

Even these few illustrative questions make it obvious that effective, workable answers require involvement of multiple

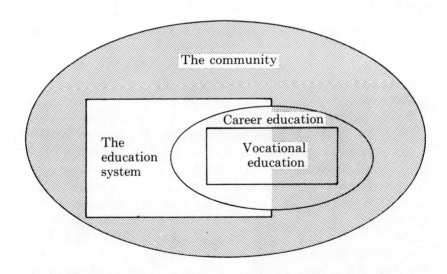

**Figure 5.** Career Education's Place in Education

segments of the community. Whenever questions involving school operations are involved, school officials must of course be part of the decision-making group. Yet if school officials try to make some of these decisions unilaterally without the collaborative involvement of other segments of the community, or by consulting some parts of the community while ignoring others, the decisions will simply not be implementable. For example, if basic policies regarding work experience programs for senior high school students are made between school officials and industry executives, local labor unions can be expected to object — and they should! It would not be wise for school officials to operate under a series of policies, each quite different in nature, that give an advantage to one community organization over another. The collaborative policies required for an effective community career education effort should apply to all segments of the community equally.

In each case — whether one is speaking about the local school system, the local unit of the Boy Scouts of America, the local chamber of commerce, the local labor union council, the local council of churches, employees, or any other community career education resource, it is obvious that the *total* goals of the organization extend considerably beyond career education. Thus, in addition to working out collaborative policies with other community agencies and organizations, it is also essential that each such agency or organization view commitments to career education within a broader set of goals and responsibilities. An essential understanding in any collaborative community career education effort must be the right of any partner to refuse to participate in implementing a specific decision reached by the group. Both legal and practical matters make this necessary. As the collaborative effort evolves, understandings of mutual problems should increase to a point where such refusals rarely become necessary. At the outset, however, they may be rather frequent and, unless they are recognized as a learning experience for all involved, may lead to abortion of the collaborative effort before it has a chance to work. All communities should be recognized and be prepared to deal with this problem. All of this argues for a community career education action council of some type, preferably with leadership emanating from the school district level.

## Career Education Activities Calling for Collaborative Efforts

There is no aspect of career education that cannot profit from a collaborative effort that uses a variety of community resources. A list of specific career education activities on which collaboration is possible would include the following:

(1) Identifying community career education resource persons

(2) Preparing career education materials for use in the classroom

(3) Conducting career education experiences for students in classrooms

(4) Providing observational experiences (including shadowing experiences) for students in the business-labor-industry community

(5) Providing career exploration experiences (including both unpaid work experience and internships) for students in the community

(6) Providing paid work experience opportunities for students

(7) Providing part-time and full-time job placement programs for students

(8) Providing unpaid work experience for students related to productive use of leisure time

(9) Developing vocational simulation equipment and exercises for students for use in discovering occupational interests and aptitudes

(10) Providing direct experiences for students in decision making

(11) Providing staff development materials and activities for educators designed to increase their knowledge and appreciation of the world of work

(12) Providing work experience opportunities (paid or unpaid) for staff persons in education within the business-labor-industry community

Community resources for these activities now exist in almost every community — both in rural and in urban America — for increasing the effectiveness of the total career education effort. A wide variety of kinds of organizations has been participating, oftentimes in isolation from the formal education system, in providing these kinds of activities to youth for many years. It is time that all such efforts be joined together, in a collaborative fashion, in ways that will maximize the helpfulness available to youth. It is neither wise nor prudent for local school officials to attempt to provide these kinds of activities by ignoring currently existing community efforts. Nor is it wise for such community efforts to continue to operate as though career education does not exist.

## Current Major National Programs Involved in Career Education

Each of the national efforts to be described here was involved in certain aspects of career education long before the term "career education" was coined. None needs the support of career education advocates in order to continue to exist. Each is a strong and viable effort in its own right. On the other hand, high school career educators will find there is much to learn from persons associated with these national efforts and many ways in which the effectiveness of local career education efforts can be enhanced by working with their local counterparts.

### Junior Achievement

Junior Achievement is the nation's oldest youth economic education program. Founded in 1919, it involved (during 1975) 192,000 senior high school students who directed and operated 7,500 small-scale businesses in more than a thousand communities in our nation. This program operates a systematic, planned effort through local business and industry executives which involves approximately 30 two-hour meetings per year for participating senior high school students. These students, working in groups of approximately twenty, form and operate small businesses under the guidance and leadership of business and industry executives. It is an intensive, "hands-on" experience involving all aspects of the business from product design to production to marketing, accounting, and personnel practices. Paid professional staff members organize Junior Achievement efforts in communities throughout the nation, but Junior Achievement advisers themselves are volunteers from the ranks of business and industry executives.

The stated prime purpose of Junior Achievement is economic education. It aims to help senior high school students discover, through actual participatory experiences, the nature and operations of the free enterprise system in the United States. In this sense, Junior Achievement holds great potential value for all senior high school students. A secondary goal is to provide career awareness and career exploration opportunities for those students considering careers in various aspects of business.

An increasing number of high schools are offering students elective credits toward high school graduation for successful participation in Junior Achievement programs. The surprising thing is that more are not doing so. Certainly, the Junior Achievement program provides an excellent opportunity for all high school students to learn the basic principles of economic education in an exciting and stimulating way. The opportunities for career exploration, inherent in the Junior Achievement approach, could be greatly expanded well beyond the area of business with very little effort. In any community having both an existing Junior Achievement program and a beginning career education effort, those responsible for career education should be seeking ways to work actively and collaboratively with Junior Achievement sponsors. Career education could, and should, stimulate more student interest in Junior Achievement.

In addition to the traditional Junior Achievement program for senior high school students, the Junior Achievement organization now operates several additional kinds of programs, each of which represents a valuable contribution to the total career education effort. These include:

(1) *Project business* — A program for junior high school students involving one class period per week for eighteen weeks in which a volunteer representative

from the business world serves as a resource person in existing social studies, economics, or mathematics classes. This program may be operational in as many as fifteen hundred classrooms during the 1976–77 school year.

(2) *Economic awareness* – An informative program in basic economics for students who do not sign up for Junior Achievement.

(3) *Job education* – A summer paid work experience program for disadvantaged inner-city youth.

Obviously, the Junior Achievement program, with its prime emphasis on economic understanding and careers in business, represents only a relatively small part of a total career education effort. Just as obviously, it represents a very large part in terms of active volunteer involvement of members of the business-industry community in the career development of those youths it serves. A truly collaborative career education effort, in any community where Junior Achievement exists, would surely involve representation on the community career education action council, active efforts of school personnel to assist the Junior Achievement program, and active efforts of that program to enhance the *total* career education effort.

Where Junior Achievement efforts are not now present in a given community, information regarding Junior Achievement can be obtained by writing to: Junior Achievement, Inc., 550 Summer Street, Camford, Connecticut 06901.

## *Boy Scouts of America*

The Boy Scouts of America have operated programs of cub scouting and scouting in communities throughout the nation for many years. In 1969 it established a new program called "Exploring" aimed specifically at helping youth, ages 15 to 21, make decisions regarding their personal and vocational lives. "Explorers" are *not* Scouts. Therefore, they are not correctly referred to as "Explorer Scouts." Open to both boys and girls, young women now comprise 34 percent of the total membership of 433,586 Explorers throughout the land. In 1975, the Exploring program consisted of 25,448 Explorer Posts and Ships and involved 112,748 volunteers and about four hundred professional executives.

The total Explorer program involves six major kinds of activities: (1) social, (2) vocation, (3) outdoor, (4) personal fitness, (5) service, and (6) citizenship. Concern is expressed for aiding youth in developing and making decisions about total life-style, not merely their probable roles in the world of paid employment. The emphasis on productivity and usefulness is entirely consistent with career education's emphasis on making work — paid or unpaid — a meaningful part of the individual's life-style in both the world of paid employment and in productive use of leisure time.

Each year, in cooperation with local high schools, the Exploring program seeks to survey occupational interests of high school-age youth (grade nine through eleven) by use of a "Student Career Interest Survey Card." Results of this effort are reported back to local communities along with encouragement to form Explorer Posts related to areas of strong expressed local student interest. An Explorer Post is typically formed round a particular area of vocational interest — e.g., health occupations, law enforcement, environmental education, and so on — often with help of funds supplied by professional associations or industrial organizations having special interest in encouraging youth to explore careers in that area.

Career exploration activities carried out as part of the Explorer program include the use of resource persons in group meetings, field trips, and exploratory work experience — basically the same kinds of activities one finds in any comprehensive career education effort. With the way the Explorer program is organized and operated from the national level, it is indeed possible to establish Explorer Posts, in any community, covering a wide range of occupational areas. At present, the opportunities for career exploration among the total range is limited by the kinds of emphases leading to formation of specific Explorer Posts.

The extensive involvement of volunteers from the business-industry community, the high degree of similarity in goals between the Exploring program and career education, and the use of after-school time for Exploring — all argue strongly for much closer collaborative efforts between the Exploring program and career education than have typically been evidenced. Local school officials could easily become much more active in urging an expansion of the Explorer program in ways that will more adequately cover the world of paid employment and be available to a greater proportion of the student body. Those members of the business-industry community now serving as volunteers in Exploring programs could be encouraged to involve themselves more fully in the total career education effort. Relationships between school counselors and Explorer Posts, as well as teachers in specific areas, could and should be greatly increased. If career education is thought of as a total community effort — and not simply as something run by the school system — then surely the Exploring program of the Boy Scouts of America should operate as an integral part of that effort.

It is important to note that at present plans are being developed for inserting a strong career awareness emphasis into the Cub Scout Program. This, too, would be entirely consistent with the goals of career education. Those wishing more information regarding the Explorer program should write to: Boy Scouts of America, North Brunswick, New Jersey 08902.

### Girl Scouts of the U.S.A.

Currently, there are about 3.5 million members of the Girl Scouts operating out of 350 Girl Scout Councils in this nation. Over 500,000 women currently serve, on a volunteer basis, as Girl Scout Leaders. In recent years, this organization has expressed a strong interest in and commitment to the problem of establishing a national coordinated effort aimed at beginning to solve the problem of reduction of occupational sex stereotyping as a deterrent to full freedom of occupational choice for women.

One model program in the area of health careers — titled "From Dreams to Reality" — has already been developed and is currently being used with Girl Scouts, ages twelve to seventeen, in many Girl Scout Councils. The manual for this program is exceptionally well developed and includes a number of fascinating approaches aimed at helping Girl Scouts explore their interests and aptitudes in the area of health occupations. Many of the ideas, self-analysis processes, and *kinds* of suggested exploratory activities found in this manual would be equally applicable to any occupational area a person — male or female — might wish to explore. To the extent that any local Girl Scout Council expresses interest in emphasizing career exploration for its members, local career education coordinators should find multiple ways of encouraging and assisting this effort. To do so would surely enhance both the comprehensiveness and the effectiveness of a total community career education effort.

Like the Boy Scouts of America, the Girl Scouts of the U.S.A. has also expressed interest in and made progress toward helping elementary school-age girls engage in the process of career awareness. The new handbook for Brownie Scouts will include a separate section on "The World of Work." Those wishing more information should write to: Girl Scouts of the U.S.A., Program Department, 830 Third Avenue, New York, N.Y. 10022.

## National Alliance of Businessmen

The National Alliance of Businessmen (NAB) was established in 1968 to aid in the effort to find jobs for the disadvantaged. Funded jointly by the U.S. Department of Labor and financial-personnel contributions from major industries, NAB metro boards now operate in 130 large urban communities throughout the United States. The potential of NAB for career education, however, extends considerably beyond these 130 metropolitan areas.

In recent years, NAB's Alliance Youth Program was established with a major goal of *preventing* unemployment among disadvantaged adults through a series of five major kinds of program efforts for youth: (1) summer employment, (2) career preparation, (3) motivation, (4) guidance, and (5) college-industry cooperation. Its summer employment program seeks to locate and place disadvantaged youth in full- or part-time summer jobs. Its primary purpose is to provide such youth with opportunity to earn money required for their use in returning to high school in the fall. Participation of the school's career education personnel — especially school counselors — is actively sought in discovering such youth and motivating them to participate in this program.

Career preparation is provided needy high school youth through the Guided Opportunities for Life Decisions (GOLD) Program. This is essentially a work-study program for disadvantaged youth which can, and often does, operate in conjunction with the school's own work-study program efforts. Participating employers provide youth in this program with career guidance as part of the effort.

The Youth Motivation Task Force (YMTF) Program brings successful businessmen and businesswomen from disadvantaged backgrounds together with disadvantaged high school students — usually as part of the school program during the schoolday. The major purpose is an "I made it, so can you" approach to motivating youth.

For several years, NAB has operated Career Guidance Institutes for high school counselors. In recent years, persons attending such institutes have been selected as teams from a local school, involving teachers and administrators as well as counselors. Activities include learning more about occupations and occupational opportunities through field trips and personal contacts with persons from the business-industry community. Participants are encouraged to develop and implement ways of infusing such knowledge into both the teaching-learning process and into the career guidance process in high school settings. The projects resulting from recent NAB Career Guidance Institutes are clearly career education infusion materials developed by classroom teachers along with an increased emphasis on career guidance by high school counselors. The Career Guidance Institutes of NAB have in effect become career education staff development efforts which, from our vantage point, might be more appropriately named "Career Education Institutes."

The College Cluster program of NAB is an effort to help colleges serving primarily minority youth better blend the liberal arts with professional specialization offerings that will improve ability of graduates from such institutions to enter and compete successfully in the labor market.

In each NAB metro, the Youth Program has encouraged the establishment and operation of an industry-education committee charged with responsibility for successfully implementing these various youth programs. Membership on this committee is seen as coming from the entire business-labor-industry community as well as from the formal school system. It is obvious that, conceptually, little difference exists between what NAB calls an "industry-education committee" and what we recommend as a "community career education action council." The essential difference, of course, is that the community career education action council would involve those concerned with *all* youth at all levels of education. The NAB industry-education council should either be strongly represented or, preferably, become an integral part of the community career education action council. The name is unimportant. What is important is a coordinated and unified community effort.

Those interested in learning more about the total NAB effort — including the NAB youth program — should write: National Alliance of Businessmen, 1730 K Street, N.W., Washington, D.C. 20006.

## Business and Professional Women's Foundation

As part of its national concern for encouraging and assisting women to enter business and professional occupations, the Business and Professional Women's Foundation, through its local chapters nationwide, has an active program providing career counseling for women 25 and over. Recently, through a Carnegie Foundation grant, the Business and Professional Women's Foundation embarked on a joint effort with the American Personnel and Guidance Association aimed at developing more effective career counseling for high school girls. With their main contacts being made with school counselors, this effort now extends into 250 to three hundred communities in various parts of the country.

There are a very large number of local business and professional women's clubs located in the United States. Members of such clubs could be valuable resources for assisting, particularly in that part of career education concerned with reduction of occupational sex stereotyping. They could also serve as valuable career role models, as key individuals in community career exploration experiences, and in community career guidance and counseling efforts. Local career education advocates have not to date made as much use of this resource as they should. Those interested in doing so can obtain further information from: Business and Professional Women's Foundation, 2012 Massachusetts Ave., N.W., Washington, D.C. 20036.

## National Association of Manufacturers

The National Association of Manufacturers was organized in 1905 with a major expressed goal of promoting and providing better education-industry cooperation. In 1969, the association started publishing a series of public policy reports on industry-education cooperation. One of these reports dealt with the desirability of appointing an industry-education coordinator at the federal, state, and local levels. One such person now serves in this role within the U.S. Office of Education — Mr. Louis Mendez, Bureau of Occupational and Adult Education. In addition, a state coordinator has been appointed in each of the fifty states. Unfortunately, most are on a part-time basis in various state educational agencies. This aspect of the National Association of Manufacturer's operation is in clearest evidence in New York State.

Recently, the association has been collecting data regarding what 150 of their member companies are doing in the area of industry-education cooperation. One hopes that this publication, when it appears, will contain numerous examples of how such councils are contributing directly to community career education efforts. Local career education people interested in learning more about how to work with industry could learn much from the past experiences of these members. Those interested in doing so should write: National Association of Manufacturers, 1776 F Street, N.W., Washington, D.C. 20006.

## National Association for Industry-Education Cooperation

The National Association for Industry-Education Cooperation (NAIEC) was established in 1964 with an avowed purpose of using the resources of education and of industry in ways that will enhance and improve the relevance and quality of education programs as preparation for work. Originally established as the business-industry section of the National Science Teachers Association, NAIEC broadened its scope and became an independent organization in 1964–65. In 1972, NAIEC merged with the National Community Resources Workshop Association.

The activities of NAIEC, like its interests, parallel those of career education very closely. Approximately twenty NAIEC local councils (eight in New York State) are operational and about 150 persons are now active members of NAIEC. One of these activities consists of community resources workshops designed to provide local educators with a means of analyzing all community resources, of learning more about the world of work in their community, and in devising ways of bringing a greater emphasis to education-work relationships in the classroom. Approximately fifty of these workshops, involving credit from cooperating colleges and universities, have been held in states such as Michigan, New Jersey, Ohio, New York, Indiana, and Washington.

As a result of its experiences, NAIEC has produced two publications, one concerned with how to establish an industry-education council and the other with how to conduct a community resources workshop. Career educators can learn much from studying these two publications and will find them entirely consistent with the goals and objectives of career education.

For years, NAIEC has been struggling as a small professional association of dedicated individuals from industry and education to establish ways of improving education-work relationships. When the term "career education" came along, NAIEC found essentially nothing new in its expressions of needs and concerns. As the career education concept has now evolved and broadened, it still includes the basic concerns that led to the formation of NAIEC in the first place. Where local NAIEC industry-education councils have been established, they should indeed be used by career education personnel. Where NAIEC seeks to establish new councils, they should find career education practitioners ready and eager to assist in this effort.

Those interested in learning more about this organization can do so by writing: Dr. Donald M. Clark, President, National Association for Industry-Education Cooperation, 235 Hendricks Blvd., Buffalo, New York 14226.

### U.S. Chamber of Commerce

The U.S. Chamber of Commerce has had career education as a top priority since 1971. During this time, it has taken the leadership in bringing together a wide variety of agencies and organizations, both within and outside formal education, to prepare, by consensus agreement, a major policy statement on career education. The resulting publication, titled *Career Education: What It Is and Why We Need It*, was published in 1975 and has received wide national distribution and discussion since that time.

The U.S. Chamber of Commerce has been active in support of career education and has also sponsored national career education conferences. The most significant work of the national organization, however, has been its efforts to interest and involve local chambers of commerce in community education efforts. At the present time, approximately a hundred such local chambers across the nation are working actively to help implement career education in their communities. Of course, some are more active than others. A prime example of an outstanding effort can be seen in the work of the Albuquerque Chamber of Commerce in New Mexico. It has been actively involved in identifying business-labor-industry resource persons for career education, in promoting part- and full-time job placement, and in working with educational officials in infusing career education throughout the school system.

As with many other national organizations, activities of local units of the U.S. Chamber of Commerce are not under the direction or control of the national organization. Each local chamber, while receiving information and suggestions from the national chamber, is free to develop its own initiatives. The actions of the national chamber in endorsing and supporting career education can and should serve as a model for local use — provided local education officials want this to happen. At the local level, the chamber of commerce cannot typically be expected to take the initiative. Given an invitation to participate in career education by top administrative officials in the school system, local chamber of commerce organizations in most communities can be expected to respond favorably.

The power and potential of the local chamber of commerce for supporting the career education concept and for taking a leadership role in assisting in its implementation as a collaborative community effort should be used wherever possible. For further information regarding activities of the U.S. Chamber of Commerce, write: Chamber of Commerce of the U.S.A., Education and Manpower Development Committee, 1615 H. Street, N.W., Washington, D.C. 20062.

### American Telephone & Telegraph Company

The American Telephone & Telegraph Company (AT&T) has for years had an established policy of cooperating with school systems on a wide variety of kinds of educational endeavors. Currently, about three hundred full-time AT&T professional people are assigned full time to the job of educational relations. Located throughout the United States, they work with local AT&T employees in helping them cooperate with local school systems.

Many of the AT&T programs are oriented primarily round classroom instruction rather than centering directly on career education. Included among these are the award winning Aids to Science Education programs, a special program designed to help students understand computers, and a variety of programs designed to acquaint students with good telephone usage techniques. These direct instructional aids have served to supplement other instructional materials in many school systems.

In recent years, AT&T has become directly and deeply involved in career education through a variety of efforts. One such effort is a career awareness book, designed for use in elementary school reading, social studies, and language arts classes, titled "Come Work with Us in a Telephone Company." At the secondary school level, another example illustrating careers in the telephone company is seen in a film titled "A Career Is Calling."

Recently, AT&T has made a concerted effort, at the secondary and post-secondary levels, to participate actively in the total career education effort. A large part of this has involved production of very high-quality films, each of which is accompanied by a good discussion guide. Included among these films is one designed to acquaint business people with career education, titled "Getting It Together: Our Kids, Our Schools, Our Business." A second film, titled "A World for Women in Engineering," shows women at work in traditionally male-dominated engineering jobs in the telephone company. Using a total life-style, rather than a narrow occupational approach, it is an excellent example of efforts to reduce occupational sex stereotyping. Recently, AT&T produced yet another film devoted to the problem of reducing occupational sex stereotyping which approaches both the potential for females to enter traditionally male-dominated occupations and for males to enter occupations traditionally dominated by females. The film, titled "Anything You Want to Be," is designed to be used as part of a multimedia curriculum package developed by AT&T for use in the senior high school. All of these materials are free on loan to schools and can be obtained through contact with local telephone company personnel.

At the national corporate level, AT&T has been among the leaders of major industry in seeking support for and active participation in career education. A part of this effort has been aimed at encouraging local career education practitioners to extend their scope of contacts with representatives from the business-labor-industry community beyond their local telephone company. For further information write: American Telephone & Telegraph Co., Manager of Educational Relations, Room 538, 195 Broadway, New York City, New York 10007.

## General Motors Corporation

In 1975, General Motors Corporation took a major national leadership role in career education through adoption of a policy statement and a set of implementation guidelines for use at local General Motors plants throughout the nation. Because of the nature of this policy statement, and its obvious implications for similar kinds of actions on the part of other major national corporations, it is reproduced here in full:

### General Motors and Career Education

General Motors' support of quality education includes the concept of career education in United States schools and colleges. By joining in this educational movement, GM seeks to help guide students to becoming better citizens with increased self-awareness, improved decision-making capabilities, and with better skills for work. This national career education effort should lead to more meaningful, worthwhile, satisfying careers for all American youth.

General Motors intends to help schools and colleges, particularly those in GM plant city communities, meet their career education objectives by actively participating in a number of ways to include:

— Providing classroom speakers and materials on specific careers and career areas

— Providing plant visits that emphasize people skills and work environment

— Cooperating with local school people in designing more realistic career curricula and teaching aids

— Cooperating in career orientation programs for counselors, teachers, and administrators

— Serving on industry-education advisory councils and coordinating GM's involvement with state and national organizations supporting the career education effort

General Motors joins with other business, organized labor, community organizations, parents, and educators in this effort to make preparation for an individual's life work a major goal of American education at all levels.

In implementing this policy statement, GM has established at its national headquarters an active program designed to encourage local GM plant personnel to work collaboratively with school systems in their career education efforts. Such activities are reported through a newsletter titled "Career Education Exchange." A recent issue of this newsletter reported an involvement of local GM plant officials with career education efforts of local school systems in Arlington, Texas, and in Dayton, Defiance, and Hudson, Ohio. It also provided these GM personnel with other sources of career education materials and activities.

General Motors has expressed interest in helping other corporations interested in formulating career education policy statements and has employed professional staff members who are both interested in and qualified to furthering both the conceptualization and the implementation of career education. Persons interested in taking advantage of this expertise can do so by writing: General Motors Corporation, Educational Relations, General Motors Building, 3044 West Grand Blvd., Detroit, Michigan 48202.

### General Electric Company

The General Electric Company has been actively involved in career education–related activities for almost twenty years. It continues to be a prime example for other large industries concerned about helping youth understand and capitalize on relationships between education and work.

In 1959, GE initiated its Summer Guidance Program designed to help high school counselors learn more about the world of work and, as a result, provide better career guidance to students. This program, designed as a six-week summer experience is conducted under arrangements with various universities under which counselors receive graduate credit for successful participation. It differs from the NAB guidance institutes described earlier primarily in that, under the GE plan, counselors study various occupations within a given GE plant in depth, including relationships among them, rather than getting an overview of a wider number of occupations in a variety of industrial settings. In recent years, as with the NAB effort, teams — consisting of a counselor, a teacher, and an administrator from a single high school — have been selected for institute attendance (rather than limiting attendance to counselors alone). This change has resulted in increased attention to implications for the teaching-learning process in the classroom as well as in the career guidance process — thus making it truly a "career education" rather than simply a "career guidance" experience. These institutes include "shadow experiences" in GE plants where individual institute members are assigned to a GE worker. By including labor union members as well as management officials, GE feels great benefits have resulted.

A recent expansion of GE effort is found in its Educators in Industry program which, like the institutes, involves teachers and school administrators as well as counselors. This fifteen-week program takes place after school hours during the school year and involves in-depth visitation to local GE plants where educators learn about various occupations in GE.

The General Electric Company also operates, through many of its local plants, the Program to Increase Minority Engineering Graduates — a systematic effort to acquaint minority high school youth with opportunities in engineering. It has resulted in a fourfold increase in just three years in the numbers of minority persons enrolling in colleges of engineering.

GE is heavily involved in a communications program that produces career guidance material directly for high school–age youth. In addition to a series of very attractive and well-done booklets carrying such titles as "Planning Your Career" and "So You Want to Go to Work," they also include a series of posters, appearing as ads in student publications, designed to help youth relate their hobbies and interests to various possible career choices. Typical of these are posters carrying messages such as: "Jim Bennette is often lost in space. What kind of job do you think that'll get him?" and "If there's one thing Elaine Griffin knows, it's how to spend money. What kind of job do you think that'll get her?" Each is accompanied by a short list of suggestions of possible occupations such youth may want to explore. These have been very popular.

Finally, GE has produced a "hands-on" career exploration display, transported in a van, for students with interests in engineering, entitled "Expo-Tech." Entirely self-contained, the seventeen sections of "Expo-Tech" provide many youth each year with opportunity to learn basic principles of engineering through actually handling equipment of various kinds. Designed primarily for junior high school students, this traveling van has found wide acceptance in inner-city schools. Like other GE materials, it is accmpanied by an "Educator's Guide" containing suggestions for teachers and counselors on ways to prepare students for "Expo-Tech" and following up on this experience.

Each of these GE programs holds great potential for those interested in the implementation of career education. Those persons wishing to learn more about GE's involvement should write to: General Electric Company, Corporate Education Relations, 3135 Easton Turnpike, Fairfield, Connecticut 06431.

## On the Horizon: Emerging Community Resources

These major national community resources for career education and their local counterparts are only a small portion of those that will soon become available in communities throughout the nation. These — and many more — should soon have active local collaborative involvement in the total community career education effort.

(1) *National Council of Churches:* With its local counterparts everywhere, the National Council of Churches represents one such emerging effort. In 1975, this group began exploring the topic "Career Education and the Churches" — with particular interest in personal values questions posed by career education and its humanistic definition of the word "work." One outgrowth of this has been the establishment of a National Center on Christian Studies in Education and Work. Activities have initially been limited to obtaining consultant help from recognized national lenders in career guidance and counseling. Current efforts are under

way to locate 80 to 100 local churches prepared to launch pilot sites throughout the country to promote career education. If this study effort becomes a national action program, it holds great significance as a vital community resource for career education in both rural and urban America.

(2) *American Legion:* This organization adopted a major policy endorsing career education in 1976. Plans are now under way to convert this policy into a set of action suggestions for local Legion posts, including the Legion Auxiliary.

(3) *The Comprehensive Employment and Training Act of 1973:* This act established local programs under the direction of governors, majors, and county officials to help disadvantaged persons prepare for and find employment. Helping disadvantaged senior high school youth in their career preparation is not beyond the bounds of the legislation. Prime sponsors of CETA must, of necessity, maintain close relationships with both educational officials and with the local business-labor-industry community. The local CETA advisory councils are similar in composition to those envisioned for community career education action councils. Local educators interested in implementing career education have already used CETA as a valuable resource in such communities as Prince Georges County, Maryland, and in Dade County, Florida. Nationwide, however, much remains to be done in building close and effective working relationships between CETA and school-based career education efforts at the local level.

(4) *Rotary International:* In the spring of 1976 Rotary International devoted a special issue of its magazine to problems of education-work relationships. Local service clubs, such as Rotary, exist in almost every community in the nation. Several are already active in assisting local school systems in the implementation of career education. Yet we have barely scratched the surface in terms of the great potential such local service clubs have for participating in community career education

implementation efforts. Members of such clubs — Kiwanis and Lions International as well as Rotary cover collectively most of the business-industry community, including many small businesses whose active participation will be essential to the success of career education. They are a valuable potential community resource.

(5) *Organized labor:* Also involved in career education is organized labor, but not to the extent required. Career education policy statements have already been adopted by the United Autoworkers and the United Rubber, Plastic, and Linoleum Workers of America. Their examples could and should be followed by other national organizations that should also encourage their local unions to get involved. If organized labor is to become the kind of valuable career education resource it should, it must be involved as representatives in the early stages of organization and operation of community career education action councils. Organized labor has a real interest and stake in the goals of career education, but it rightfully resists the notion of being brought into the picture "after the fact."

(6) *The all-volunteer armed forces:* Yet another powerful potential community resource for the implementation of career education is the armed forces. Each branch now employs a number of professionals who relate to educators with respect to educational and occupational opportunities in the military. Since both education and work are found in the all-volunteer armed forces, this segment of society should surely be given careful consideration by youth trying to solve problems of education-work relationships. The education specialists of the all-volunteer armed forces could very well become career education resource persons serving educators in local communities.

(7) *New York Life Insurance Company:* Recently, the New York Life Insurance Company has launched a new national effort aimed at producing both films and printed materials for use in helping high school and

college students in the career decision-making process. This is but one of many possible examples of large national organizations which could combine a national career education campaign with strong urging of their local representatives to become involved at the community level.

## Examples of Use of Local Community Resources for Career Education

It is the local counterparts of these national efforts which are of interest to the high school career educator. Since local communities vary widely in terms of career education resources, the pattern of operations must also vary greatly from community to community. A few examples of local actions should be helpful in illustrating what can be done by local communities.

### Educational Resources Association

Dr. John Reynard has been loaned by the DuPont Corporation (with DuPont paying his salary) to join with one teacher and one secretary paid for by the local school system to form the Educational Resources Association in New Castle County, Delaware. It operates as a nonprofit organization charged with finding and using both personnel and facilities in the business-labor-industry community for use in career education. In a one-year period, 175 business organizations signed up to participate under a "controlled use frequency" arrangement guaranteeing each that it will not be asked to participate to any greater extent than it indicates is desirable and possible.

The association has developed evaluation sheets for use by business-industry personnel in evaluating both classroom and field trip experiences in which they are involved. A similar set of evaluation sheets has been developed for use by educators. In arranging for the use of business-labor-industry personnel as resource persons in the classroom, the association has developed a system under which the business representative meets with the teacher two weeks prior to the actual visit to make plans. A resource catalog has been prepared for teacher use, listing the persons and the physical facilities available as community career education resources. In addition, two booklets have been developed — one titled "Tips for Teachers on Using Community Resources," and the other, "Tips for Community Speakers in the Classroom."

Under this system, the teacher makes contact with the community through the Educational Resources Association. In this way, indiscriminate school requests are avoided. The directory is coded so that the teacher does not know the name of the person or industry being requested. Instead, if the teacher can specify the kind of help needed, the association can locate an appropriate person or facility for meeting that need and is available at the desired time. The prime career education activities involved are: (1) use of resource persons in the classroom, and (2) field trips for students and educators into the community.

### Frisby Manufacturing Company

Tim Frisby operates with about 150 employees and, as one employer, has been actively engaged for some time in stimulating the implementation of career education in his community of Elk Grove, Illinois. Initial efforts were thwarted by an expressed lack of interest on the part of school officials. This did not stop Frisby. He eventually helped implement Project EVE, a hands-on career exploration program for teachers. This project operated as a graduate-level course in after-school hours and allowed teachers, with the help of twenty local firms, to visit plants, observe workers on the job, and then share their experiences in the classroom.

In addition, partly through Frisby's efforts, an economics teacher project has been initiated in which local teachers are taught a twenty-week course in economics by personnel from the local business-industry community. It was a helpful way of increasing teacher knowledge of their own business-industry community. On another occasion, Frisby was able to secure a number of industrial resource people to speak at local PTA meetings, informing parents of the community and the opportunities for youth career choices. In one elementary school,

Frisby helped get a "Popcorn Factory" project under way which in one day exposed elementary school pupils, in a hands-on experience, to an awareness of more than forty different occupations.

The essence of this example is the concerned person from the business-industry community volunteering his time to get some career education activities initiated in the local school system. The initial resistance confronted among school administrators is not unusual, but it is becoming much less frequent as the career education movement gains momentum. The fact that, despite such initial resistance, positive initial career education steps were taken is an excellent example of what can happen when only *one* person from a given community becomes interested and involved in career education.

### Institute of Public Affairs Relations

Several years ago, a group of concerned business-labor-industry leaders in Portland, Oregon, became concerned about what they regarded as a lack of understanding by high school students of the democratic form of government and the free enterprise system. As a result, they formed the Institute for Public Affairs Relations aimed at finding ways in which key persons from the business-labor-industry community could go into high schools and interact with high school students. Paid for by contributions from the local business-labor-industry community, the institute employed an executive director and began operations as a nonprofit agency.

When the career education concept emerged, the institute converted its activities into a comprehensive community career education effort. It now operates a central clearinghouse of community resources for career education available to teachers and counselors in the Greater Portland area. Its activities include the identification and utilization of community resource persons, field trips for students, and even a job placement operation. School officials are represented on the institutes advisory board, but this was not something started by the schools. Institute members today want their acronyn "IPAR" to stand for "I participate" — and indeed they do! It is today a very well organized and effective organization for use of comminity resources in career education — one from which many other communities could learn much.

## Jacksonville, Florida

An opposite way of involving community resources for career education can be found in Jacksonville, Florida, where the career education effort was initially launched by school personnel. The interest and willingness to help on the part of the business-labor-industry community was quickly discovered and has been widely used throughout the Greater Jacksonville area. In the spring of 1976, they held their first "Community Career Education Appreciation Night" in the auditorium of the First National Bank in Jacksonville. There, before a crowd of several hundred persons from the schools and the business-labor-industry community, they engaged in an "Emmy Award" procedure under which, for each of the fifteen USOE occupational clusters, three "nominees" from the local business-labor-industry community were named and one selected to receive a plaque for outstanding contributions to the Jacksonville career education effort. Such a procedure could be initiated in any community.

## McCormick Spice Company

In 1969, the McCormick Spice Company, Baltimore, Maryland, initiated efforts with one inner-city school located close to its plant, aimed at encouraging teachers to help pupils with problems of education-work relationships. Teachers requested that materials supplied by McCormick officials be organized for classroom presentations. As a result, the company employed three professional writers, brought them into its plant for a week to study occupations, and then asked them to write a series of learning packages for use in social studies courses. Currently, forty such learning packages exist, which can be used on a group or individualized basis, covering such topics as "how to apply for a job," "the worker and his community," "I am important," and "how to make a budget."

A second effort of the company involved arranging plant tours for secondary school students. During such tours, students are assigned to employees on a one-on-one basis, with the employee actually conducting the tour for the individual student. This procedure has helped many students establish contacts with adult employed workers who can then be used as resources for help in various kinds of decisions — including career decisions — faced by the student. The McCormick Spice Company is convinced that this procedure has helped both students and its own employees recognize and appreciate their own worth and the value of work.

## *In Retrospect*

The examples reported here serve as clear and convincing evidence that community resources for career education do exist, are being used, and are available to every high school in the land. These should serve as valuable suggestions for those interested in using community resources in career education efforts. At the same time, these examples raise a number of crucial policy and directional questions for career education.

## *Does Community Support for Career Education Exist?*

While career education has been endorsed by most of the major professional education associations, many educators seem still to be unsure whether to embark on a career education effort in their local communities. The two prime questions being asked still are: (1) will the community really support career education, and (2) is career education truly a lasting reform movement or simply another educational fad?

The examples presented here should make it clear that, outside of formal education, attempts to initiate what can only be called a career education emphasis have existed and operated for many years. A deep and serious concern for helping youth understand the free enterprise system, the current and projected nature of the world of paid employment, the personal meaningfulness work can hold in the life-style of the individual, and the changing relationships between education and work has existed outside the formal structure of education for many years. Had such groups as those alone not perceived a need for these kinds of activities, they would not have begun them. In many ways and for many years, each has tried to enlist the support and participation of educators in their efforts. One of the most common comments as they describe such attempts is the resistance found among professional educators. It is likely that this perceived resistance and lack of interest are what led many such community institutions to initiate their efforts independently of professional educators. An objective view of the community resources described here can lead to no other answer than that the community is interested in career education.

The long history of several of the national efforts described here makes it clear that community interest in career education is neither new nor temporary in nature. If the career education concept is new to the formal education system, it is not new to the broader community. If schools are wondering whether they should initiate or continue a career education emphasis, there is no doubt on the part of the broader community. Based on past history, it seems more legitimate to ask whether the education system will work with the broader community in career education than to ask whether the community is willing to work with the formal education system.

Those school systems which have sought community support for and involvement in their career education efforts have, almost without exception, reported that such interest is present and that this interest and involvement grows as career education takes place. While exceptions may be found in certain communities, it seems valid to state that in general the broader community is both ready and willing to commit resources to the career education effort.

### What Is Different about Career Education?

The examples of national and local community career education actions cited here make it legitimate to ask the question: Is career education simply an attempt on the part of the formal education system to do what the broader community has been trying to do for many years? Two important reasons justify a "no" answer.

In the first place, career education represents an attempt to secure an *internal* professional commitment to change on the part of educators themselves. The recognized need for such changes in the attitudes and actions of educators is evident when one examines the significant educator staff development activities being carried out both by the National Alliance of Businessmen and by General Electric. However, the examples reported here illustrate attempts on the part of the broader community to seek cooperation from educators, but *not* to change the basic attitudes or actions of educators themselves. Career education starts from a basic premise that it is time the rising concern for education-work relationships that has led to formation of many of these external efforts be translated into internal professional commitment to change on the part of teachers, counselors, and administrators at every level of education and throughout the system of American education. If the career education effort is successful, such internal changes in professional educators will take place.

Second, career education differs from earlier efforts in its emphasis on the need for *collaboration* in community efforts. Many of the existing community efforts have been started and continue to operate completely independently of all others. While each has been successful in many ways, none has been as successful as it could be if it joined forces with all others. Career education asks all to coordinate their efforts in ways that keep a primary focus on the individual and how that individual can best be served by all of the resources existing in the community.

### Career Education: A Concept or a Program?

Statements that certain community programs are good examples of career education in action could lead some to believe that career education advocates are trying to "take over" all such community programs. The same concern is often voiced by educators who fear that career education will "take over" the entire education system. These are impressions that must be corrected.

Within the formal system of education, career education operates as a concept to be infused into all existing programs, not as a new program to be added to all others. As a concept, career education seeks to fuse the philosophy of vocationalism with the philosophy of humanism in ways that will make "work" be perceived as a human right of all human beings, not as an unwanted societal obligation. Further, career education seeks to fuse the teaching-learning process with the career development process in ways that will make education, as preparation for work, a major goal of all who teach and all who learn. In doing so, career education does not ask for new curriculums, new buildings, or new kinds of specialists at the building level. Rather, it asks all educators — teachers, counselors, curriculum specialists, administrators, and so forth — to infuse the career education concept into their operational programs. Career education is a concept, not a program.

Similarly, within the broader community, career education does not seek to become a competing effort with such earlier programs as Junior Achievement, the Girl Scouts, or any other. Rather, it seeks to join with such efforts within the community in ways that by working together, youth can be better served. Within any given community, there should never be a career education *program*. The community career education action council, with whatever staff it may possess, should not be responsible for operating any programs. Rather, it should seek to help all existing programs grow in effectiveness by working together and by increasing the ease and effectiveness with which they work with educational personnel.

The power of career education properly lies in the power of position, prestige, or financial control. The career education concept will derive its power to help solve problems of education-work relationships through building effective action programs both within education and in the broader community that emphasize ways in which all can work together in the interest of youth. Credit can go to anyone and everyone, but *help* should go to the youth.

## Who Should Coordinate Career Education Efforts in the Community?

At several points in this discussion, the concept of a community career education action council has been referred to. The idea of such a council differs from the concept of the industry-education councils being championed by the National Association for Industry-Education Cooperation only in terms of its emphasis on collaboration and on the need for changes within professional educators themselves. There is nothing new or startling about the idea of a "coordinating council."

The community career education action council envisioned here would involve all segments of the community — the education system, business and industry, organized labor, parents, local government leaders, community volunteer groups, and youth. One would hope that it would receive funds from some combination of sources to employ the services of one or more "career education coordinators" charged with responsibility for bringing the total community — the education system included — together in a concerted career education effort. Like the career education concept itself, it would operate only with the power of persuasion. It would seek consensus in building plans, not in imposing plans devised by its own staff members.

Whether the leader of the community career education action council should be an educator, a business-industry person, a labor union official, a parent, or a local politician is viewed here as relatively unimportant. The significant thing is that this person understand and appreciate the multiple efforts of all segments of the community. Of course, it will be essential that this person be especially sensitive to the needs and problems of educators since in the long run most of these community efforts involve interaction with the education system to some degree. This does not mean that the person selected to head the effort should necessarily be an educator.

Whoever is selected, the most important point to recognize here is that *someone* should be selected and *some kind* of coordinating agency should be established. If this is not done, we will all continue on our separate ways and, once again, youth will have been served less adequately than they could be. That is the real importance of the career education concept and of community resources within it.

# 13

# The Ideal
# Approach

As an exercise in imagination—and anticipation—and hope, we offer the following "ideal" high school approach to career education. Of course, there can be no educational program which is ideal for everybody, or everyplace, and each high school and each school district will tailor the program to meet the specific needs of the specific population of the specific community. Our ideal approach has not been put into effect in any one place, any more than has the ideal high school for which it is designed, but literally every facet of our imaginary career education application is based on successful activities in hundreds of high schools from all parts of the United States.

We shall confine our discussion primarily to the broad overview of this ideal; the reader can fill in the details from her or his own knowledge and experience and from the information contained in the preceding chapters of this book. We describe career education as an "approach" rather than a "program" advisedly. "Program" connotes something that is formalized, sequential, and structured. Career education is a type of education, not a program of education. Career education is an activity, a component, an emphasis; it is not a course or a department or something in which a student accumulates credits.

Indeed, in our ideal high school, career education will be invisible at least insofar as course listings, department designations, and office titles are concerned (although there is a career education coordinator and an action council). The visitor to the school will not be able to find a course in career education or an office of career education or someone labeled as a "career education teacher." But if the visitor spends some time in the classroom — almost any classroom — or some time talking with students, then the visitor will become acutely aware that the high school has adopted career education and has put it to work. The visitor will find the community in the classroom and the classroom in the community. The visitor will be unable to escape the conclusion that career education is characterized by relevance — relevance of all education to work and to the occupational needs of students, and relevance of the students and their work to the society in which they live. This will be evident in the ways in which course material is presented, in the ways in which students deal with subject matter, in the content of displays in classrooms and hallways, in the scheduling of student activities, and in the casual conversations of both students and teachers.

## A Visit to "Ideal High School"

In order to assist the visitor to understanding Ideal High School's career education approach, it will be useful to examine at least five components of the school and the ways in which these components have changed under the influence of career education: (1) the curriculum, (2) the faculty and staff, (3) student organizations, (4) student activities, and (5) organization and administration at the district as well as the building level.

### Career Education and the Curriculum

The curriculum of Ideal High differs little from the curriculum of the average high school in the United States today. The same departmental structure exists, the same sequences are offered, and the same courses are available to students. Depending on the school district and its location, the basic approach may vary from the traditional structured approach to modular scheduling, to alternative education, or to any of the variety of other innovative educational approaches used in high schools throughout the nation. Career education is equally at home within any of those approaches. Whatever the approach, the visitor will still find students engaged in the study of mathematics, English, languages, physical education, fine and practical arts, social studies and the sciences, and all the other subjects available in the average high school. The classrooms and the laboratories will appear much the same as they always have.

But if the visitor observes carefully, he or she will notice one distinct difference: Students are more thoroughly involved in their studies, better motivated, visibly more active in the search for information. In every classroom, four basic teaching-learning strategies would be clearly evidenced: (1) an emphasis on purposefulness and meaningfulness by both students and teachers; (2) an emphasis on rewarding performance and demonstrated accomplishment — on an individualized basis where the student is his or her own criterion; (3) an emphasis on bringing *variety* to the teaching-learning process in terms of ways in which students are helped to learn; and (4) an emphasis on use of both physical and personnel resources from the community as valuable contributions to the teaching-learning process. The net result of these four emphases should be demonstrated increases in educational productivity: i.e., student achievement in the classroom. The career education concept is viewed as useful for accomplishing these objectives.

The visitor will also notice two unmistakable differences in emphasis within the curriculum. First, the vocational education program will be a strong program and fairly wide ranging. It will include specific vocational skills training for those preparing to enter the labor market directly from high school, career exploration experiences for those considering post-high school vocational-technical education, and, in addition, opportunities for college-bound students to acquire vocational skills that can contribute to earnings and productive uses of leisure time. Second, experience with work will have become a general education methodology and a pervasive component of the curriculum. School credit will be provided for work experience education of some type in many fields.

The vocational education program differs from traditional programs primarily in emphasis, not in content. For one thing, the work experience emphasis mentioned above will not be limited to the vocational education program. Considerable efforts are expended by faculty and staff to help students who wish to do so acquire vocational skills through work experience which uses the resources of the community instead of relying strictly on the facilities of the schoolbuilding. Students move in and out of the building on their way to and from the various work stations in the community, and similar migrations occur with faculty and visiting specialists as they counsel with students and with one another regarding student progress.

The vocational education program is characterized by an unusual amount of openness. A high percentage of students from all disciplines enroll in vocational courses at one time or another during their high school tenure in order to use those courses as career exploration or career preparation activities, or simply as a means of acquiring basic skills that can be used in helping them make more productive use of leisure time. For example, the school offers a one-semester course in auto mechanics which is open to college-bound girls and boys, and there is a half-semester course titled "Homemaking for the Single Person" in which boys and girls learn how to shop for, live in, and decorate a bachelor apartment.

Graduation requirements have been modified so that those students who change occupational goals are not penalized. Previously, a student who changed from one vocational field to another, or who changed from a vocational curriculum to the college preparatory curriculum (or vice versa) was required to spend an extra semester or year to meet graduation requirements. Consequently, many students dropped out or just went through the motions while they stayed in a curriculum they no longer desired. Now, there is no separation of students into rigid curriculums. Instead, each student has a program tailored to her or his individual goals. And this program is modified as the individual's goals change. If a late change means that the student will not meet occupational entry requirements, the effect is a change in post-graduate or post-secondary school education, not a delay in high school graduation.

The observer notes evidence of strong and direct relationships between the high school vocational education departments and post-secondary schools and institutions which offer vocational or technical training. The high school obviously does not attempt to compete with such institutions, and the vocational education faculty assists students in identifying those particular post-secondary offerings which might benefit them most.

Finally, stereotyping is conspicuous by its absence. No classes are segregated by sex, either intentionally or "accidentally." The student with the spark plug wrench is as likely to be a girl as a boy, and the souffle cook is as likely to be a boy as a girl. The student who has an assured honors scholarship for college works beside a so-called "slow learner" as both try to acquire skill on the metal lathe, and either one doing it for avocational use or for occupational development. Most faculty members are sincerely dedicated to providing meaningful vocational education to *all* interested students and are eager to offer special assistance to handicapped or disadvantaged students.

As mentioned above, work experience is not solely the province of vocational education students; it extends to all students and covers many interests. It is not just a special program, but an educational methodology. Students and teachers seek out work experience, some of which is paid employment, some volunteer work, and some merely observation on a regular basis. Students are encouraged to actually experience the workplace of the occupation they have tentatively selected as their own, and they are assisted in finding sources for that experience. Viable intern programs — similar to the Executive High School Internship Program — are available for some college-bound students headed toward professional training. Academic credit is awarded for many types of work experience, even if it means increasing the number of credits required for high school graduation.

In classrooms outside the vocational education department, course material, course goals and objectives, and teaching methods are changed in limited ways. A majority of teachers has infused career education practices into the teaching-learning process. They use career implications of subject matter to motivate students, and they use community resources to add both diversity of approach and comprehensiveness of effort in helping students learn more subject matter and in pointing out the relationships between what students are learning and the "real" world of adult living. In fact, career education has become so much a part of total education in Ideal High that it is automatic. Both teachers and students automatically think of the work implications — both vocational and avocational work — of the subject matter. They automatically relate what they are studying to their own interests or to the interests of others with whom they are familiar. And when the relationship is not obvious, the class may stop long enough to search it out, for no subject matter is without its practical application when practicality applies to careers and when the term "career" encompasses all of the work done in a lifetime, including home-making, voluntary activities, and avocational pursuits.

In this regard, most classes at Ideal High are likely to have "connections" with the practical world outside the school-building. This means field trips, in-class guests, and homework assignments which require person-to-person interviews almost as often as they require library research. Visiting resource persons in the English classroom may be a writer, an editor, or a language specialist, but they may also be a shop foreman, an executive secretary, or a small business entrepreneur who has come to class to explain why knowledge of English is important to his or her work and to answer questions from students about why they should study communication. The visitor to the mathematics classroom may be a consumer advocate explaining how to use mathematics in the supermarket to make wise purchases. The history class may visit museums, but it could also visit newspapers and printing plants to learn about the relationships between the development of printing technology and the growth of civilization. The teacher calls attention to the typesetters directing their computerized machines and indicates the important role those individuals play in the dissemination of knowledge and information. Students in a social studies class have an assignment to write about the life-styles of occupations in which they are interested, with special instructions to interview at least two workers in that occupation.

In other words, at one or more points in the course outlines of most classes at Ideal High there is some emphasis on the principle that one goal of education is to prepare students for work. Teachers and administrators fully understand that the term "work" applies equally to paid employment *and* to work done as part of one's productive use of leisure time. It includes volunteer work, schoolwork, the work one does in relation to one's hobby, the work involved in active citizenship, and the work of establishing and raising a family for both men and women. At Ideal High the word "work" is hardly every used in a negative or even neutral sense; it is regarded as a positive activity which contributes to the worth of the individual and to the well-being of society. At the same time, there is concern with the ways in which workplaces can be improved so that work can be made more satisfying.

This is not meant to imply that faculty and students at Ideal High School regard preparation for work as the *only* goal of education — or even the major goal of education. They understand that education has many goals, and that while work may be an important part of every individual's life, it is but one of the many life roles an individual must play. Ideal High students need to understand the cultural heritage which is theirs; they need to develop taste and self-concept; they need to acquire social skills; they need physical training and mental discipline; they need to appreciate other peoples and other cultures; they need value systems which extend beyond the values of the workplace; they need to be able to deal with the physical and biological forces of their universe; and they need many other foundations which education can provide for them. But along with these goals and as enhancement to these goals, Ideal High students need to be prepared for the world of work. And this is a function of career education. Whatever the educational goal, the curriculum must be characterized as meaningful and purposeful for both students and teachers.

The curriculum at Ideal High has one other important characteristic: It is a year-round, clock-round, age-round curriculum. It is not a lock-step curriculum. It allows wide latitude for open-entry and open-exit opportunities. Students can "stop out" without becoming "dropouts." Adults can "drop in" as fully matriculated students in the daytime curriculum or in special evening classes which parallel the daytime curriculum in many respects. Since career education is an activity which extends literally from womb to tomb, adults need a community center where they can acquire skills, seek knowledge, and prepare themselves for the inevitable changes in their own work patterns. Ideal High serves this function, not by expanding its curriculum but by extending its existing curriculum to a broader audience. Ideal High does have a course labeled "Career Education" in its evening curriculum. The course is for those adults who did not have the advantages of career education during their school years, and it concentrates specifically on work values, career exploration, and job changing skills.

## Career Education and the Faculty and Staff

The effect of career education on the faculty and staff of Ideal High School is primarily procedural rather than substantive, with one exception: The paid staff is no different from the staff of any other high school. We do notice the addition of one or two persons in the guidance and counseling office to help with the added responsibilities created when that office assumed the coordination of career education activities. (At Ideal High these responsibilities were accepted by the counseling staff, but they could have been assumed just as effectively by any other well organized staff in any other discipline, so long as they were committed to the principles of career education.) Responsibilities include organization and management of a community career education action council, the coordination of career education offerings at various levels, coordination of work experience opportunities, identification and contact with resource persons from the business-labor-industry community, liaison with representatives of elementary and junior high schools in the area to coordinate career education offerings, liaison with post-secondary institutions to coordinate student career development with available training opportunities, coordination of career education workshops for students and nonstudents, coordination of in-service training for faculty and staff, and liaison with the district career education resource center and placement service.

The Ideal High School Community Career Education Action Council includes representatives from the faculty, the staff, the student population, parents, and the business-labor-industry community. It meets regularly to set policies with regard to career education, to identify needs, and to prescribe remedies for problems and weak spots in career education activities. The group watches developments in the school and in the community as they relate to career education, and it seeks to react to these developments in a positive fashion. It examines such things as employment activities of recent graduates, changes in the local labor market, and student demand for programs or courses.

An active effort is made by the advisory group, by the career education coordinator, and by the entire staff to involve the business-labor-industry community in school affairs, particularly as they relate to career education. The visitor to Ideal High notices an unusual number of nonstaff personnel actively participating. They talk with students on both formal and informal bases, act as resource persons in the classrooms, and counsel with teachers regarding the practical application of various subject matter. These "volunteers" are business representatives, labor leaders, representatives of government agencies, production line workers, and professionals who donate their time in the interest of student development. They are parents of students, members of the career education advisory group, representatives of various professional and craft organizations, or just friends of the school. They come because they believe in career education — having learned about it through their own occupational associations — and because they are asked and are listened to.

Another difference at Ideal High — although less obvious — is greater liaison between the high school and its surrounding educational institutions. The staff knows exactly what kinds of career education activities are offered at area elementary schools and junior high schools. Students are not asked to repeat activities they have experienced before; they are asked to build upon those previous experiences. At the same time, most of the staff of Ideal High are aware of training opportunities in post-secondary institutions in the area. They understand the strengths and weaknesses of those institutions, and they are as likely to recommend post-secondary vocational or technical training to students as they are to recommend college or university enrollment.

Few of the faculty and staff members at Ideal High had training in career education at the colleges and universities from which they graduated. Therefore, many of these individuals are involved with in-service training programs in career education. These are offered through the school district and also at Ideal High itself through the efforts of the career education coordinator. Teachers are encouraged to participate in these in-service programs, which offer them extra compensation, released time, or certification credit through the state university. The in-service training programs take many forms, but most of them fall within three broad categories: concept instruction, methodology, and work experience. The concept instruction includes structured courses in which the principles, concepts, and goals of career education are taught. These courses range from simple introductory materials to fairly complex philosophical and theoretical treatments of career education.

The methodology training usually involves more technique sharing than formal instruction. Teachers share ideas for incorporating career education into various types of courses, and they use the case-study approach to become acquainted with the experiences of other teachers in other schools and from schools throughout the nation. The scope of subject matter is broad in order to ensure an eclectic approach and to encourage the cross fertilization of ideas among various disciplines. Ideal High teachers are offered certification credit for certain kinds of work experience outside the classroom. Teachers are encouraged to explore the world of work through paid or voluntary employment, and they are offered "sabbatical leave" in order to take advantage of work opportunities in the belief that employment outside the education field offers many of the same self-improvement benefits as post-graduate education.

In addition to traditional departmental meetings at Ideal High, there are also interdepartmental meetings where teachers from various disciplines plan together sets of activities designed to coordinate an emphasis on education-work relationships into the teaching-learning process. For example, no longer do English teachers visit only with other English teachers. The interdepartmental groupings encompass several teachers, each of whom has contact with the same students. They include both academic and vocational education teachers.

Ideal High maintains a curriculum materials center for the use of its faculty and staff. The center provides a wide variety of career education materials, including concept books, films and filmstrips, simulation materials, and books and pamphlets about job opportunities in specific occupational fields. Additional materials are available from the district career education resource center.

The school library also has a career education center where students may assess information concerning specific occupations or occupational fields. The school librarian is involved in a project with several other school librarians in the area to develop a cross-index file of career education references in the general library collection. The group has already completed the classification of the modern fiction collection into occupational categories so that a student interested in medicine can identify a number of works of fiction in which the main characters are medical personnel, or a student interested in labor unions can find several novels which revolve round the labor movement and union-oriented themes.

Finally, there is evidence at Ideal High of much interest in student placement after graduation. This is especially true in the counseling office, but most teachers are also interested in the future activities of their students and have developed an understanding of the placement process and placement resources in order that they might be able to answer student questions and direct students to the proper resource persons. The school does not conduct a placement service (that is done at the district level), but the counselors have considerable training in and understanding of placement and they are often called upon to discuss it in their frequent guest appearances in various classes.

The counseling office maintains complete records concerning the career activities of graduates, and staff members analyze these records in an effort to determine strengths and weaknesses of the career education effort at Ideal High. The records also provide employment patterns and post-secondary education patterns for use in the counseling and placement processes. Students are urged to consider decision making as a process, and to think realistically in terms of career goals and objectives after graduation. They are counseled in seeking employment or training which fits into a pattern, not that which is available by chance or accident, and they are assisted in finding meaningful employment or training through the placement service at the district career education resource center.

## Career Education and Student Organizations

The activities schedule board at Ideal High has just been enlarged to accommodate notices from the many student organizations in the school. Almost every student belongs to one or more student organizations, many of which are directly involved with career education.

Several active Explorer groups operate in close cooperation with school personnel. Membership in the Explorer groups is made up primarily of lower division students, but some seniors are still active. Explorers are encouraged to "graduate" into organizations dealing with specific occupational fields. The boys and girls who are members of each Explorer group determine their own programs with the assistance of an adviser. The goal is to look at as many occupational fields as possible with a view to learning about the kinds of careers available in the field, the life-style characteristic of the field, and the training required for entry into the field. The groups visit local businesses or invite representatives of the business-labor-industry community to meet with them. Representatives of other career education student organizations are also frequent visitors to Explorer meetings. Members are encouraged to share their own career education experiences, and thus a "life-style" paper delivered in the sociology class may also be discussed in the Explorer meeting.

The Junior Achievement organization is active at Ideal High. Students create, organize, and operate their own businesses, learning in the process about the difficulties and rewards of entrepreneurship, and learning to understand some of the factors involved in business operation. In most instances, Junior Achievement is accepted in fulfillment of the work experience requirement for graduation from Ideal High.

In the vocational education area, youth clubs have been organized in each of the vocational fields. These include chapters of the Future Farmers of America, Future Homemakers of America, Distributive Education Clubs of America, Future Business Leaders of America, and vocational-industrial clubs. Since Ideal High is located in an area where the electronics industry is of substantial size, the students in electronics courses have formed a club called the "Semiconductors." The adviser is the production manager from one of the local firms, and the primary activities of the club revolve round exploring career possibilities in electronics production. The club also actively works for additional training stations in the school's cooperative education program.

A number of preprofessional youth clubs are also organized and active at Ideal High. These include chapters of the Future Teachers of America, the Junior Engineering Technical Society, and the Junior Academy of Science. At the present time a communications club, a health occupations club, and a thespians club are active, as students with interests in those fields have banded together to make contacts with professionals and to explore career possibilities in those fields. These types of clubs tend to come and go as interest groups arise and fade within the school. Students are encouraged to organize such clubs on a year-to-year basis and to allow them to dissolve when interest wanes. In this way, these clubs can be responsive to changing labor market conditions.

Last year the students of Ideal High School decided to organize a career club steering committee. This group is made up of representatives from each of the career education youth clubs. It meets regularly to examine the programs of the various clubs, to encourage cooperation between clubs, and to provide assistance to those clubs which need advice or support.

## *Career Education and Student Activities*

No one argues that career education will drastically change the nature of students or the responses of students to the education experience. Therefore, the students at Ideal High act much the same as students at any other high school. Ideal High still has discipline problems, dropouts, and troublemakers. Students still dislike some teachers and revere others. They still "forget" to come to class on time and fabricate marvelously creative excuses for being tardy with homework assignments.

But there are subtle differences in degree. Disciplinary problems are fewer and less severe for at least two reasons. First, students at Ideal High tend to be more involved in their schoolwork because they understand it is work and because they have more appreciation for the value of work. Thus, even troublemakers tend to be a little less motivated toward making trouble and a little more motivated toward making progress. Second, peer pressure is likely to be positive because students tend to resent interferences with the work they are doing. They don't encourage disruption, and they often refuse to tolerate it.

Dropouts are a concern of all the personnel at Ideal High, but the concern is not statistical. The dropout is not a number but an individual. No student can drop out of school without being fully aware of three important factors. First, it is impossible to have attended Ideal High for even one year and not to have acquired at least some job-related skills. They may be such specific skills as how to operate a lathe and a drill press, or they may be more general skills such as where to go to apply for a job. But the dropout cannot deny the fact that he or she knows something about work and the workplace as a result of attendance at Ideal High. Second, the dropout knows he or she will not be forgotten by the high school staff. Each knows it is important to the school to keep track of former students and to know what they are doing, and that every effort will be made to determine and keep current such information. Dropouts know that this is not for the purpose of "judging" or "spying" but for the purpose of improving the school's own program. Third, dropouts know that they will be welcomed back into Ideal High at any time in the future without the slightest prejudice and without any penalty. The school's belief in open-exit/open-entry is not just a policy but a practice. Furthermore, both counseling and placement services offered through Ideal High and the school district are permanently available to dropouts as well as graduates.

As a general rule, students at Ideal High tend to regard education as a personal goal rather than as an imposed requirement. They understand the "if...then" relationship of education to life, particularly as it applies to an individual's career, but also as it applies to other aspects of life. They may not like the rigors of education any more than other students, and they are certainly not yet grasping all of the long-range implications of education, but they are more likely to perceive education as part of a continuum rather than as a transitory experience. They believe their classes contribute directly to their own worth as human beings and to their own capacity to contribute to society by way of the work function. They are struggling with their own value systems, trying to understand why those value systems are no longer "pure" and why they differ from those of their classmates, but they have some feeling for variational values and for the fact that it is not necessary or possible for everyone's values to be in agreement. They are willing to examine their own goals, based on their own values, without struggling to modify these values in a futile effort to conform.

This is not to claim that Ideal High students have in every case achieved the level of maturity implied by the preceding discussion. But they are more likely to be moving in that direction than are students who have not had the benefits of career education, benefits which include some understanding of value formation, experience in decision making, and personal confrontation with the philosophical, psychological, and economic foundations of work. Nor do we claim that career education is the only way to acquire these benefits. They can indeed be acquired in other ways, just as they have been acquired by *some* students — including all of the authors of this book and most of the readers — through traditional forms of education and through experiences which had other goals. But career education makes these benefits available to almost *all* students early and often by making them immediately relevant to all students.

And so the visitor to Ideal High notes some of these qualities in the students. It is evidenced in class discussions, in casual
conversation outside the class, and in the organizational activities of students described above.

Once again, we make no pretense that the Millennium has
arrived at Ideal High. Rather, we have stopped waiting for the
Millennium to come — when all students will be geniuses — and
we have begun to deal with the practical realities of life as it
has been, as it will continue to be, and as it can be made to be.
Work is here to stay. It is an individual need; it is a social need.
Individuals contribute to society through the work they do,
and education is directly relevant to an individual's preparation
for work. Career education simply recognizes these relationships
and does something about them.

### Career Education and the School District

Ideal High is not an isolated entity. It is part of a school
district and a state school system. In the following section we
will discuss the role of that structure in the implementation
of career education, but as an operating institution, it is impossible to separate Ideal High from its school district, and there
are certain functions which the district must perform as part
of Ideal High School's career education effort. The three
primary components of career education at the district level
are career education specialists, a career education advisory
council, and a career education resource center.

There may be some disagreement about the desirability
of installing a career education specialist at the schoolbuilding
level. We tend toward the view that a specialist is not needed
at that level, that existing personnel can assume the necessary
responsibilities without becoming specialists. We fear that the
specialist may work too hard at creating a "program" and not
hard enough at infusing career education into all programs,
or that the specialist will engender unnecessary power struggles
among faculty and staff. Career education will not be successful unless it is the responsibility of almost all members of the
faculty and staff and not the "job" of a single individual.

But there is little argument against the premise that every
school district should employ a career education specialist who

would act as coordinator of career education in the district. This individual can be a trained counselor, a vocational educator, an academician, or a business person so long as he or she is completely committed to the principles and concepts of career education, has had enough experience to be able to institute these concepts, and is energetic enough to accomplish the multiple duties of a career education coordinator. The bulk of these duties consists of coordinating the career education efforts of various schools in the district, but the duties also include such sensitive activities as organizing and managing a community career education advisory council and supervising the operation of the district career education resource center.

The community career education action council serves primarily as a resource tool for the total career education effort in the district. Of course, it provides advice and counsel regarding various aspects of career education, but it also assists the career education coordinator in making contacts within the business-labor-industry community; it applies gentle pressure upon representatives of that community to collaborate with the career education effort; and it carries the message of career education to various community groups. The community advisory council is a vital link in career education because it legitimizes the effort by helping to build better relations between the school and the community.

Through the untiring efforts of the career education coordinator, the council is an active group which involves itself in all aspects of career education. Its members support career education both formally and informally in their daily activities and through other organizations to which they belong. In the case of the district in which Ideal High School is located, the advisory council consists of six local business representatives from a variety of businesses, two labor union representatives, a member of the town council, a vocational education teacher from Ideal High, a faculty member from the college of education at the state university, and the executive director of the local chamber of commerce. The career education coordinator attends all the meetings as the representative of the district superintendent, but is not a voting member of the council.

The community career education council was instrumental in establishing the district career education resource center in a centrally located building formerly used as a grocery store. The building was equipped by contributions from the business-labor-industry community, but the center is staffed primarily by school district personnel. While the center serves both youth and adults, it concentrates on the needs of the community school population and recent graduates. Most adults are referred to the local employment security office, as are other clients who need the special services of that agency. Most of the personnel at the center are trained counselors and guidance persons, and they are primarily responsible for career guidance, counseling, and job placement for the young people who come into the center from the various area schools. The career education resource center is a combination information center, counseling center, activity center, and placement service.

The center contains an operational system of local labor market information, along with state, regional, and national systems of occupational and labor market information. In this respect it is similar to the employment security office, but the information concentrates much more on entry-level jobs and youth-oriented labor market conditions.

An equally complete and operational information system is available at the center regarding all kinds of post-secondary educational opportunities, including community colleges, proprietary schools, four-year colleges and universities, government-supported manpower training programs, apprenticeships, and the all-volunteer armed forces. Representatives from each of the institutions which conduct these programs visit the center on a regular schedule to counsel with students and center personnel.

Several rooms in the center are set aside as counseling rooms where students can talk, either individually or in groups, with teachers, counselors, representatives of the business-labor-industry community, parents, and others about career plans. All students from Ideal High visit the center at least twice during their high school tenure, and most visit much more frequently upon their own volition, or at the suggestion of teachers or school counselors, or as part of an information-gathering assignment for one or more classes.

As stated above, the center contains the most complete assortment of career education materials available in the community. Some of the materials are available to students, and some are restricted for teacher use. The center circulates a periodic bulletin describing new materials, assessing the value of various items, and suggesting uses for materials. Some of the materials are commercial products, and some have been created by teachers and by the business-labor-industry community for specific local applications.

Part of the building has been set aside as a career exploration simulation center. It contains some of the elaborate simulation equipment which is not economically feasible for every school to maintain, and it provides an opportunity for youth and adults to actually "try out" various kinds of activities in a hands-on experience. This helps them become aware of their own interests and aptitudes for particular occupations or occupational areas. This portion of the center is staffed in part by personnel "on loan" from the business-labor-industry community.

Finally, the center contains a well-equipped placement service similar to those operated by many universities. The service not only helps students and former students find part-time and full-time jobs, it also helps them identify and seek entry to post-secondary educational and training institutions in the field of their choice. The placement service is operated in close cooperation with the employment security office, and most of the time a representative of that agency is assigned to duty at the center.

Since the district career education resource center is the pioneer center in the state, it applied for and received special funds from the state office of education to conduct an outreach program. Representatives from the center visit high schools throughout the state, particularly in rural areas, to explain to students about the services offered at the center, and to invite students to visit the center when they have the opportunity or if they should ever seek employment in the Ideal High community. A substantial sample of the simulated work equipment and guidance materials is also installed in a van which periodically visits outlying junior and senior high schools in the district and occasionally travels upon request to other schools about the state.

## Implementation of Career Education

Having wandered through the halls of Ideal High, and having examined the operation of the district career education resource center, we must now return to reality. The reality is that Ideal High School doesn't exist — except in bits and pieces scattered throughout the nation. But we see no reason why Ideal High School — many ideal high schools — cannot exist in the near future. After all, thousands of high schools have already made beginnings. After all, hundreds of school districts have established career education as a priority. After all, viable career education already exists in thousands of elementary schools and junior high schools. It is time to implement career education in the nation's high schools.

We can offer here only some general guidelines concerning what must be done, for each state and school district must develop its own implementation program, complete with specific objectives and a specific timetable. However, we can look briefly at what must be done at the state level, at the district level, at the school level, and in each individual classroom.

### Implementation at the State Level

The place to begin career education is with the state legislature itself. If career education is to be available throughout the state, the legislature must clearly indicate its intent to support the program. It must provide a mandate for the state school board and for local school districts. Perhaps the best way for the legislature to indicate its support is to provide stimulus for in-service training of teachers and staff in the principles of career education. This should include not only a clear resolution of support, but the provision of adequate funding for in-service training. The legislature should provide for modest compensation of teachers who enlist in the training program, for certification credit for those teachers, and for adequate materials to conduct such a training program. The funds required for such an effort are slight indeed, particularly when compared to the potential that career education offers for increasing worker satisfaction, productivity, and employment.

Once the legislature has established its support though a resolution of intent and minimal funding, then the state school board and the state office of education must give meaning to the legislative purpose. This can be done by employing all of the regulatory and procedural powers the state board has at its disposal. Obviously, the state board can issue a position statement supporting career education and, more importantly, directing each school district to prepare specific implementation plans to meet state guidelines regarding career education. The board can also take action to make certain that career education is included in the guidelines for state accreditation visits, that textbooks oriented toward career education are included in the adoptions list, and that other steps are taken to encourage the development of career education at the local level. (At least one state has added certain aspects of career education — including work experience — to its graduation requirements.)

It is also important that the state school office conduct career education in-service training for its own staff, particularly for the subject matter specialists. The message of career education is much more effective if delivered to local districts by subject matter specialists instead of, or in addition to, the state coordinator of career education. (Every state has now appointed a career education coordinator. Unfortunately, too often the duties involved are "in addition to" instead of "in lieu of" the previous responsibilities of that individual.)

Some states have found it advantageous to appoint a state career education advisory council with heavy representation from the business-labor-industry community. That must remain an option for each state to be decided, based upon such considerations as the size of the state and the nature of the business and industry establishment in the state. A state-level council will probably be more expedient in smaller states than in large states.

### Implementation at the District Level

In the movement toward career education, the local school district is probably the key point of implementation. No matter what happens at the state or school level, career education cannot succeed without the full support of the district superintendent and the district staff. This is true for several reasons. First, the district career education coordinator is a vital operator in the overall concept. Without such a person, career education is incomplete and has little direction. Second, the district must fully support and encourage in-service training for teachers and staff. Some training can take place at the school level, but much of it must occur at the district level in order to facilitate the sharing of ideas from school to school and from department to department.

Third, the school district can more easily form a career education advisory council which is inclusive of the total area labor market. Few students will seek employment in the geographic area of their own high school; many more will seek employment within the geographic area of their local school district. Thus it is important to include areawide representation on a career education advisory council. In many cases, a multidistrict organization will be necessary. Fourth, we believe that the best use of resources is achieved by establishing a district career education resource center and by conducting the placement function at the district level.

For these and other reasons, career education depends heavily upon the active support of the district board and the district superintendent. This support is evidenced by the appointment of a full-time career education coordinator, by the adequate funding of a career education office, by the aggressive planning and management of in-service teacher training in career education, and by the official sanction of an advisory council. Once again, it should be emphasized that workshops conducted by subject matter specialists tend to be more effective with teachers in that subject area than similar workshops conducted by a career education specialist. Therefore, it is important to conduct in-service training for staff members at the district level prior to offering such programs to teachers.

### Implementation at the High School Level

The success of career education in a single high school is directly proportional to the number of teachers in that school who accept preparation for work as one of the goals of education. No school will have total acceptance by teachers; and no school should expect it. But if students are not exposed to career education regularly and frequently, they cannot reap its benefits. This means that those individuals who believe in career education must sell the idea to others.

Of course, the principal must accept it and support it. He or she must assign the responsibilities of career education coordination to an individual or individuals who have the ability to handle such duties, and that individual or individuals must be given enough released time to allow for community contacts outside the school. The principal must be willing to support improvements in the vocational education offerings, increases in the work experience program, and additions to the counseling staff.

The counseling staff itself must be prepared to change direction, to acquire a broader outlook regarding post-secondary training, and to be more concerned with student placement.

### Implementation in the Classroom

In the early days of career education, teachers were almost totally on their own in implementing the principles of career education in the classroom. There were few materials available and few examples to build upon. This condition is changing rapidly, but career education is still largely dependent upon the wisdom and creative ability of the individual teacher as she or he incorporates career education into the daily lesson material. (Suprisingly, however, more materials have appeared on the market for the lower grades than for the high school, even though the high school is the pivot point between traditional education and the world of work.)

As more and more teachers experiment with career education in their classrooms, they will begin to share their successes and their failures, and more materials will become available through reports in the literature and through commercial publication.

We said at the beginning of this book that those teachers who have tried career education in their classrooms almost universally praise it as a teaching method which motivates students and which makes school life more interesting for both teacher and students. With this kind of testimonial, what teacher can resist the temptation to experiment at least a little with career education in his or her own classroom?

## *Summary*

Career education is still an ideal, particularly at the high school level, but it is an ideal well worth striving for. It does not demand major changes in the curriculum, in staffing, or in teaching methodology. It asks only that concern for the goal of education as preparation for work be elevated to equal status with the other traditional goals of education. Since education has always and inevitably had preparation for work as one of its goals, career education is only an expression of reality. It is reality expressed in the classroom, in student services, and in the activity of the students themselves.

In return, career education offers an increase in the perceived relevance of education which will result in greater involvement of students in the educational process, higher motivation for learning, closer ties between education and the community, a higher level of overall service to society, and concomitant enhancement of *all* of the goals of education.

The ideal of career education is not likely to be reached by many high schools in the near future. But it will be achieved by some. And parts of it will be achieved soon by most. Because it works.

# Index

ability to adjust to change, 24
academies, private, 18–19
accomplishment as a basis for
    understanding, 64–66
activities. *See also* exercises
    calling for collaborative
        efforts, 395–96
    stereotyping in the class-
        room, 128–33
administrator
    analysis, 47
    execution of programs, 48
    responsibilities, 38–39
advantages of cooperative
    education programs, 319–23
advertising, distributive
    education: "The Creative
    Team," 300
advisory committee, coopera-
    tive education programs, 326
agriculture and applied biology,
    practical applications, 287–91
    brainstorming for occupa-
        tions, 292

field trips, 291–92
    "How Much Did Johnnie
        Make?" 290–91
    role-playing, 291
    "Situational Question,"
        289–90
    "What's My Job Family?"
        290
alternatives, decision making,
    193–96
American
    Legion, 413
    Personnel and Guidance
        Association (APGA),
        policy statement, 366–67
    Telephone & Telegraph
        Company, 407–08
    versus European man-
        power development
        systems, 140–41
analysis of organization of
    schools, 46–47
anthropology, example, 224
Appalachian Education

Laboratory, 330–33
application for specific subject
matter, 210–39; of learning,
cooperative education
programs, 320
appreciation
and attitudes, business
education:
"Everybody's Different,"
295,
decision making, simula-
tion, 297,
economic awareness,
budgeting, 296–97,
employability skills,
race-role confusion, 295–
96; home economics
exercise, 285–86
of others, 24
arguments for career preparation in high school, 245–49
art-related careers, example,
221–27
attitudes
and work values, 16–17
industrial arts: "Learning
to Work Together,"
305–06
of parents, 35
avocational goals, 259

baby boom, 135–36
barriers, job, 168–69
basic competencies required
by counselors, 385–87; goals
of education, 22
basis for career education,
32–33; for understanding,
64–66
beginning competency, home
economics exercise, 286–87
blacks, stereotyping, 112–14
Boy Scouts of America, 257,
394, 398–400
building a program for values
clarification, 92–103
Business and Professional
Women's Foundation, 403–04

business education, 292–97
appreciation and attitudes:
"Everybody's Different,"
295
decision making, simula-
tion, 297
economic awareness,
budgeting, 296–97
employability skills: race-
role confusion, 295–96
business-labor-industry involvement, 376; responsibilities, 376

cardinal principles of secondary
education, 19–20
career
capabilities, cooperative
education programs,
320–21
counseling, 352–65
decision making, 181–98,
356–59; change, 68;
choice, 66–70; concept of,
66–70; dilemmas, 70–78;
emphasis on, 66–70;
importance of, 68–69;
freedom of choice, 67–69;
possibility of career
choice, 69–70; reality of
choice, 67; right to
change, 68
development and the
counselor, 352–56;
practices in senior high
school, 62–70;
problems for girls and
women, 77–78
education activities calling
for collaborative efforts,
395–96; and the cur-
riculum, 426–32; and the
faculty and staff, at
Ideal High School, 432–
36; and student activi-
ties, 438–40; and student
organizations at Ideal
High School, 436–37;

and the school district,
440–43; collaboration in,
391–96; concept or pro-
gram? 421–22; examples
of use of local communi-
ty resources, 415–19;
experience-based, 330–40;
implications at Ideal
High School, 444–48; in
the high school, 43–49;
national programs, 396–
412; philosophy and
counseling theory, 352–
65; teamwork 46–49;
resource center, 383;
techniques for practic-
ing, 205–10; what is
different about it?
420–21
    exploration, distributive
education exercise: "To
Market, To Market,"
299–300; for low-income
and minority youth,
75–76; health occupa-
tions exercise: "Emer-
gency!" 309
    guidance, cooperative
education programs,
322–23
    ladder, 140–41
    maturation, 52–55
    preparation, arguments for
high school, 245–49;
criticisms, 247–49; cur-
rent status, 242–44; for
the professions, 262–65;
nonspecific, 266–68;
vocational education
phase, 249–55
    planning exercise, 154–58
    skills, general, 62–64
Career Development Inventory,
180
careers related to art,
exercise, 227–28
certainty of occupational
change, 55–57

challenge of uncertainty,
177–79
change
    at Ideal High School,
429–30
    career, instructional
materials, 154
    for high schools, 28–29
    in counselor attitudes,
387–88
    personnel and guidance,
implications for, 384–85
    reviewing and modifying
decisions, 97–98
    right to, 68
choice. See also decision
making
    alternatives, 193–96
    decision, 176; making,
66–70, 146–48
citizenship, acceptance of,
23–24
civic competence, 29
clarification of values, 24, 86–
92; building programs for,
92–103
classification of jobs, 57–59
classroom implementation,
Ideal High School, 447–48;
incorporating career education, 205–10
"clerks or consultants?"
counselor role, 381–83
collaboration
    career education, 391–96
    community affairs, 421
    counseling significance,
362–65
College Entrance Exam Board,
180
college placement services, 152–
53; preparatory school as a
type of high school, 21–22
Commission on the Reforming
of Secondary Education,
22–26; on the Reorganization
of Secondary Education, 19
communication skills, 23

community
    coordination, who should
        do it? 423–24
    laboratory instruction
        plan, cooperative educa-
        tion, 328–29
    needs, cooperative educa-
        tion programs, 325;
        relationship to, 322
    resources, collaboration,
        392–94; emerging, 412–
        15; examples of use of
        local, 415–19
    support, does it exist?
        419–20
"Comparison Trips," home
    economics exercise, 286
compensatory programs for
    disadvantaged, 124–26
competencies, basic, required
    by counselors, 385–87
complexity of life, 56–57
comportment, 162
Comprehensive Employment
    and Training Act (CETA),
    413
computation skills, 23
coordinator role in cooperative
    education programs, 323–30
"Creative Team," distributive
    education exercise, 300
criticisms of high school career
    preparation, vocational
    education, 247–49
critics of American education,
    responsibilities to, 41–43
current programs of vocational
    education, 252–54; status of
    career preparation, 242–44
curricular requirements, 120–22
curriculum
    and career education,
        426–31
    at Ideal High School,
        431–42
    development, counselor
        role, 368
concept of career decision

making, 66–70; of work,
    61–62
concepts and content of career
    education, 31–32
constraints, 342–47; on decision
    making, 183–85
consumer education, home
    economics exercise, 287
contacts outside school, job
    information, 145
content goals, 23–24
cooperative
    education, evaluation,
        329–30; programs, 264,
        266–68; role of teacher-
        coordinator, 323–30
    model, 164–65
coordination, jobs, 164–65;
    who should do it? 423–24
coordinator-teacher, role in
    cooperative education pro-
    grams, 323–30
counseling and guidance per-
    sonnel responsibilities, 38;
    theory, 352–65
counselors
    and career decision
        making, 356–59; and
        career education,
        seminar, 367–69
    as teachers, 378–80
    basic competencies, 385–87
    change of emphasis, 48; in
        attitudes, 387–88
    coordinating jobs, 164–65
    in career development
        theory, 352–56
    job placement, 166–68
    practical problems,
        facing, 377–83
    role in curriculum
    role in curriculum develop-
        ment, 368; suggested,
        365–69

decision making. See also
    choice

challenge of uncertainty,
177–79
constraints, 183–85
counselor and, 356–59
exploring oneself, 186–91
identifying, 182–85
implementing program,
196–97
industrial arts: "Exploring
Apprenticeship Pro-
grams," 304–05
information gathering,
183–91
irreversible, 184
low-income youth, 74–76
occupational, 191–92
process, 181–98
reviewing and modifying,
197–98
risk, 183–84
scope of the process,
198–99
skills, 146–48
theoretical foundations,
179–81
decision tree, 174–76
dehumanizing roles, 66
designs and sewing, 283
dilemmas of career decision
making, 70–78
disappearance of work? 104–09
disciplines, academic goals,
201–05
distributive education, 297–301
Distributive Education Clubs
of America, 256, 437
district-level implementation at
Ideal High School, 445–46;
school, career education at
Ideal High School, 440–43
distinction between occu-
pational and vocational
education, 260–61
DOT classification scheme,
57–58

economic
awareness, budgeting,

business education exer-
cise, 296–97; industrial
arts: "Where the Jobs
Are," 305
understanding, 23
economics, example, 223
educational attainment, 106–
09; reform, 40–41
Educational Policies Com-
mission, 20–21; Resources
Association, 415–16
elementary education goals,
17–18; school students, 51
"Emergency!" health occupations exercise, 305
emerging community resources,
412–15
emphasis on career decision
making, 66–70; on general
career skills, 62–64
employability skills, business
education exercise, 295–96;
home economics exercise, 286
employer attitudes about
education, 137
employment
private agencies, 151–53
public services, 150–53
ending sex and racial stereotyping, 46
English, examples, 217–20
enrollment in vocational
education, 27
entry procedures, decision
making, 195–96
environmental restraints, 52–70
European manpower development system, 140–41
evaluation
counselor role, 368
of cooperative education
programs, 329–30
"Everybody's Different," business education exercise, 295
examples of use of local community resources for career
education, 415–19
exercises (activities, models,

examples). *See also* model
  advertising, distributive
  education, 300
agriculture and applied
  biology, practical applications, 287–91
anthropology, 224
appreciation and attitude,
  business education, 295;
  home economics, 285–86
art-related careers, 221–27
attitudes, industrial arts,
  305–06
beginning competency,
  home economics, 286–87
brainstorming for occu-
  pations, agriculture, 292
budgeting, business education, 296–97
business education, practical applications, 292–97
career exploration, distributive education, 299–
  300; health occupations,
  309; planning, 154–58
careers related to art,
  227–28
consumer education, home
  economics, 287
decision making, industrial
  arts, 304–05
distributive education,
  297–301
economic awareness,
  business education, 296–
  97; industrial arts, 305
economics, 223
employability skills, business education, 295–96;
  home economics, 286
English, 217–20
field trips, agriculture,
  291–92
foods and nutrition, home
  economics, 287
foreign languages, 229–33
geography, 223
hands-on experience,

health occupations, 310
health occupations, practical applications, 306–10;
  sciences, 233–35
history, 222–23
home economics, 282–87
"How Much Did Johnnie
  Make?" agriculture,
  290–91
industrial arts, practical
  applications, 301–06
marriage and family living,
  home economics, 287
mathematics, 213–17
philosophy, 224–35
physical education, 233,
  235–37
political science, 224
psychology, 224–25
random activities, home
  economics, 287
recreation, 233, 237–38
"Road Ahead: A Research
  Paper," health occupa-
  tions, 309–10
role-playing, agriculture,
  291; distributive edu-
  cation, 300–01
science, 211–13
self-awareness, home
  economics, 285
"Situational Question,"
  agriculture, 289–90
social studies, 220–25
sociology, 224
study-discussion approach,
  227
values clarification, 93–103
visual arts, 225–29
vocational education,
  274–78
"The Volunteer," health
  occupations, 310
"What's My Job Family?"
  agriculture, 290
expanding career opportunities,
  25
experience-based career edu-

cation (EBCE), 330–40
exploration phase, vocational
    education, 244–49
Explorer Scouts, 257
"Exploring Apprenticeship
    Programs," industrial arts
    exercise, 304–05
exploring oneself, decision
    making, 186–91
extracurricular activities,
    122–23

faculty at Ideal High School,
    432–36
family
    living and marriage, home
        economics exercise, 287
    participation in career
        education, 377
    responsibilities, 38
Far West Laboratory, 333–36
finances, 47, 48
fine arts, status of, 257–60
flexibility of schedule, 47
foods and nutrition, home
    economics exercise, 287,
    283–84
Ford Foundation study, 26
foreign languages, examples,
    229–33
4-H Clubs, 257
freedom to choose, 67–69
Frisby Manufacturing
    Company, 416–17
functions of career education
    APGA policy statement,
        366–67
    USOE-sponsored seminar,
        367
Future Business Leaders of
    America, 256, 437; Farmers
    of America, 256, 437; Home-
    makers of America, 437;
    Teachers of America, 256,
    437
future of work, 103–10

general career skills, 62–64

General Aptitude Battery
    (GATB) test, 153–54; Electric
    Company, 410–12, 421;
    Motor Corporation, 409–10
geography, exercise, 223
gifted and talented, career
    decision making, 70–72
Girl Scouts of the U.S.A.,
    400–01
girls. See also women
    career development prob-
        lems, 77–78
    freedom of choice, decision
        making, 194–95
    participation rates, 138–40
goals
    alternatives to reach,
        193–96
    avocational, 259
    between career education
        and academic disciplines,
        201–05
    career, 66–69
    content, 23–24
    decision making, 184–85
    of high school education,
        17–31; of individual
        students, 39
    secondary education, 17–31
    two-exit, 246–47
graduation requirements at
    Ideal High School, 428–29
grooming, 162
guidance
    career, cooperative edu-
        cation programs, 322–23
    decision making, 188–89
    materials library, 145

handbook, occupational, 141–
    44, 192, 266
handicapped, stereotyping,
    126–27
hands-on experience, health
    occupations: "The Volun-
    teer," 310
health
    occupations, Columbus

High School, 264; practical applications, 306 10
sciences, examples, 233–35
helping teachers in career education, 371–73
help wanted sections of newspapers, 152
high school
    curriculums, 21–22; goals, 17–31; implementation at Ideal High, 446–47
    limitations of vocational education programs, 254–55
history, example, 222–23
home economics, 282–87
housekeeping, home economics, 294
Human Potential Seminars, 188

Ideal High School, 426–48
identifying decisions to be made, 182–85
implementation of career education at Ideal High School, 444–48
implementing decisions of a program, 196–97
implications for change in the personnel and guidance movement, 384–85
importance of decision naming, 68–69
improving transition, 140–48
independent service model, 165–68
individuality, 56
industrial arts, 301–06; unions, 151
information
    decision-making process, 180–98
    gathering, decision making, 185–91; occupational, 191–92
informing students about work,

59–62; on world of work, 57–62
in-school instructional plan, cooperative education programs, 326–28
Institute of Public Affairs Relations, 417–18
instructional materials on career change, 154
interdependence of forms of work, 60–61
interim objectives, 197
intermediaries, labor market, 150–52
issues and responses, collaboration, 392–94
"I Spy," home economics exercise, 285–86

Jacksonville, Florida, 418
job. See also occupation
    access and barriers, 168–69
    development, counselors, 166–68
    getting skills, 35
    information sources, 141–45
    placement, 26
    search, counselors, 166–68; techniques, 148–50
    seeking, 138–40
Job Service, 150–53, 187
Junior Academy of Sciences, 256, 437; Achievement, 257, 396–98, 437; Engineering Technical Society (JETS), 256, 265, 437
junior high school goals, 17–18

KALAMAZOO case, 18
knowledge of self, 24
Kuder Interest Inventory, 153–54

laboratory instruction plan, community, cooperative education programs, 328–29
labor market intermediaries, 150–53

leadership
  functions, APGA policy
    statement, 366
  providing professional,
    369–71
  USOE-sponsored seminar,
    368
"Learning to Work Together,"
  industrial arts exercise,
  305–06
leisure activities, values clarification exercise, 96–97
limitations of the typical high
  school vocational education
  program, 254–55
low-income youth, career
  decision making, 74–76;
  socioeconomic group, special
  concerns, 123–26

manpower planning offices,
  152; training control, cooperative education programs,
  321–22
marriage and family living,
  home economics exercise, 287
mathematics, examples, 213–17
McCormick Spice Company,
  418–19
meaning of values, 86–92; of
  work, 61, 103–10
meeting the needs of types of
  students, 53
mentally handicapped, career
  decision making, 72–74;
  retarded, stereotyping, 127
mini-courses (units), 208–10,
  339
minorities
  in the labor force, 105–06
  special concerns, 123–26
  youth, career decision
    making, 74–76
"M-m-m Good," home eco-
  nomics exercise, 286–87
model. See also exercises
  cooperative, 164–65
  independent service, 165–68

original USOE, 51–52
modifying decisions, 197–98
Morrill Act of 1862, 18

National
  Advisory Commission on
    Civil Disorders, 29–30
  Alliance of Businessmen,
    401–02, 421
  Association for Industry-
    Education Cooperation,
    166, 405, 423; of Manu-
    facturers, 404
  Council of Churches,
    412–13
  Society for the Promotion
    of Industrial Education
    (1906), 19
national programs involving
  career education, 396–412
nature of stereotyping, 112–15
New York Life Insurance
  Company, 414–15
nonspecific career preparation,
  266–68
nonwhites, stereotyping, 113–14
Northwest Regional Education
  Laboratory, 336–38
nutrition, home economics
  exercise, 287

objectives, interim, 197
occupation. See also job
  freedom of choice, 194–95
  home economics exercise,
    282–87
  information, decision
    making, 191–92
  personal inventory in
    readiness for, 186–91
  women, 194–95
occupational
  change, certainty of, 55–59
  clusters, 51–52
  competency, 23,28
  decisions, 53–54
  direction, 17
  education in the high

school, 260–62
preparation, 18; program
  for low-income and
  minority youth, 76
sources, 141–45
stereotyping in secondary
  textbooks, 118–20
*Occupational Outlook Hand-
  book*, 141–44, 192, 266
Occupational Values Inventory
  tests, 102–03
official declaration, 365–69
on the horizon: emerging
  community resources, 412–15
organization of school, analysis,
  46–47
organized labor, 414

participatory functions, APGA
  policy statement, 366–67
pathologies in transition, 140
patterns of transition, 136–48
personal inventory, 186–91;
  restraints, 52–70
personnel department as
  intermediary, 152
philosophy
  career education and
    counseling theory, 352–
    65
  example, 224–25
physically handicapped, career
  decision making, 72–74
physical education, examples,
  235–37
"Pick a Number," distributive
  education exercise, 300–01
pivot point, the high school
  as, 48–49
placement service, school,
  163–64, 166–68
policy paper, USOE, 365;
  statement, APGA, 366–67
political science, example, 224
possibility of career choice,
  69–70
post-secondary plans, 53
practical

arts, installing career
  education, 271–78; status
  of, 257–60
problems facing counselors,
  377–83
prepatory schools, 18, 19
principle of collaboration in
  career education, 591–96
prioritizing, work values exercises, 97
private academies, 18–19;
  employment agencies, 151–53
problems
  resolving, experience-based
    career education, 342–47
  world of work, 57–62
process goals, 24; of decision
  making, 181–98
professional commitment, 421;
  leadership, 369–65
proficiency in critical and
  objective thinking, 23
program
  consideration, 33–36
  implementation, requisites,
    36–39
  vocational education,
    current, 252–54
psychology, example, 224–25
public employment service,
  150–53
published material on job
  information, 144–45


race
  role confusion, business
    education exercise,
    295–96
  stereotyping, 46; in early
    readers, 114–18; in
    secondary textbooks,
    118–20
"Rank Order," values clarification exercise, 98–101
reality of choice, decision
  making, 67
recommendations of National

Commission of the Reform-
ing of Secondary Education,
25–26
recreation, examples, 237–38
relevance of curriculum and
instruction, cooperative
education programs, 319–20
requisites of program implementation, 36–37
Research for Better Schools,
Philadelphia, 338–40
respect for law and authority,
29
responses and issues, collaboration, 392–94
responsibilities
administrator, 38–39
business-labor-industry,
37–38
counseling and guidance
personnel, 38
family, 38
high school, 43–49, 63–64
school board, 38–39
staff, 46–47
teacher, 37
resolving problems, experience-
based, career education,
342–47
resource
center, career education,
383
community, emerging, 412–
15; example of use of
local, 415–19
restraints, personal and environmental, 52–70
retarded, stereotyping, 127
reviewing and modifying
decisions, 197–98
right to change, 68
"Road Ahead: A Research
Paper," health occupations
exercise, 309–10
role-playing, distributive education exercise, 300–01
roles, counselor, 365–69
Rotary International, 413–14

school
board responsibilities,
38–39
district and career edu-
cation at Ideal High
School, 440–43
placement service, 163–64,
166–68
to-work transition, 153–62
work, 136–39
science, examples, 211–13
scope of decision-making
process, 198–99.
secondary education, goals,
17–31
self-awareness, home economics
exercise, 285; versus "careers"
dilemma, 380–81
sequencing, work values exercise, 97
service model, independent,
165–68
sewing and design, 283
sex
segregated courses, 114–15
stereotyping, 46, 112, 114–
18; in early readers,
115–18; in secondary
textbooks, 118–20
tracking, 120–22
skills
communication, 23
decision making, 146–48
general career, 62–64
job getting, 35
list, 156–62
training, helping to emphasize, 260–71; vocational,
unfilled assignments,
260–71
Smith-Hughes Education Act
of 1917, 19, 27, 241
social studies, examples, 220–25
sociology, example, 224
sources of job information,
141–45
staff at Ideal High, 432–36;
responsibilities, 46–47

state-level implementation,
    Ideal High School, 444 45
status of career preparation,
    current, 242-44; of fine and
    practical arts, 257-60
steering committee at Ideal
    High School, 437
stereotyping
    at Ideal High School, 429
    decision making, 193-94
    in the classroom, 128-33
student. *See also* youth
    activities at Ideal High,
        438-40
    and academic goals, 201-05
    as part of the work force,
        135-36
    counselor role toward,
        368-69, 373-75
    involvement at Ideal High
        School, 427-28
    needs, cooperative educa-
        tion programs, 323-25
    organizations at Ideal
        High, 436-37
study-discussion, example, 227
subject matter, application,
    210-39
survey of superintendents,
    principals, teachers, others,
    24-25

teacher
    coordinator, role in cooper-
        ative education pro-
        grams, 323-30
    counselor as, 378-80
    helping in career educa-
        tion, 371-73
    in career education, 367
    responsibilities, 37
teaching
    function possible for
        counselors, 367
    moments, 206-08
    work values in the high
        school, 85-86
teamwork to make career

education work, 46-49
techniques
    for practicing career
        education, 205-10; for
        teaching industrial arts,
        303-04
    job search, 148-50
tenet of career education, 65
test
    GATB, 153-54
    Kuder Interest Inventory,
        153-54
    of knowledge of world of
        work, 278-80
theoretical foundations, deci-
    sion making, 179-81
"To Market, To Market,"
    distributive education exer-
    cise, 299-300
toward a work ethic, 84-85;
    meaningful work 109-10
tracking, vocational education,
    246-47
training, cooperative education
    programs, 321. *See also* skills
    training
transition
    improving, 140-48
    pathologies in, 140
    patterns, 136-48
    school-to-work, 153-62
tree, decision, 174-76
"Twenty Things You Have to
    Do," values clarification
    exercise, 95-97
two-exit goal, 246-47

uncertainty, challenge of,
    177-79
unemployment of youth, 73,
    74-75
unions, industrial, 151
U.S. Chamber of Commerce,
    406-07
USOE policy paper, 365

values
    academic goals, 201-05

clarification, exercise, 124
formation, 106–07
information gathering for
  decision making, 185–91
meaning and clarification,
  85–92
work, 85–86
"Values Voting," values clarification exercise, 97–98
variables in decision making,
  179–81
visual arts, examples, 225–29
vocational
    education amendments,
      165–67; and "prep"
      phase of career educa-
      tion, 249–55; as general
      education for work, 268–
      71; current programs,
      252–54; distinction,
      occupational education,
      260–61; exercises, 274–
      78; industrial clubs at
      Ideal High, 437; limita-
      tions of high school pro-
      gram, 254–55; problems
      in relationship to career
      education, 272–74; pro-
      grams at Ideal High,
      428, 429–30; skills train-
      ing, 375–77; unfilled
      assignments, 260–71
    school as type of high
      school, 21–22
Vocational
    Education Act of 1963,
      26–27, amendments,
      26–27
    Industrial Clubs of
      America, 256
"The Volunteer," health occu-
pations exercise, 310

weaknesses of work experience
  programs, 341–42
what
    does career education offer
      high school? 43–49

is different about career
  education? 420–21
to do about stereotyping in
  the classroom, 128–33
"Where the Jobs Are," indus-
rial arts exercise, 305
who should coordinate career
education efforts in the
community, 423–24
women
    career development prob-
      lems, 77–78
    in the labor force, 105–06
    occupational freedom,
      194–95
    sex stereotyping, 112–20
work
    and leisure activities,
      values clarification
      exercise, 96–97
    at Ideal High School, 431
    attitudes, 16–17
    concept, 64–65; counseling
      significance, 359–61
    disappearance of? 104–09
    emphasis on, 66
    ethic, 84–85
    experience needs, 145–46
    future and meaning of,
      103–10
    past experiences, 81–83
    study programs, 317
    values, 16–17, 47, 61; in the
      high school, 85–86
working with students, 373–75;
  with teachers, 367
world of work
    exploring, 315–16
    informing students about,
      57–62
    test of knowledge, 278–80

youth
    clubs, 265; in career
      education, 255–57
    in the labor force, 104–09
    stereotyping, 113–14
    unemployment, 27–28